Springer Series on PSYCHIATRY

Carl Eisdorfer, Ph.D., M.D., Series Editor

Stress and Human Health

Analysis and Implications of Research

A Study by the Institute of Medicine/
National Academy of Sciences

Glen R. Elliott, Ph.D., M.D.
Carl Eisdorfer, Ph.D., M.D.
Editors

Springer Publishing Company
New York

The project that is the subject of this report was approved by the Governing Board of the National Research Council, whose members are drawn from the Councils of the National Academy of Sciences, the National Academy of Engineering, and the Institute of Medicine. Members of the committee responsible for the report were chosen for their special competencies and with regard for appropriate balance. This report has been reviewed by a group other than the authors according to procedures approved by a Report Review Committee consisting of members of the National Academy of Sciences, the National Academy of Engineering, and the Institute of Medicine.

This Study was supported by the Office of Science Technology and Policy, Executive Office of the President; the Office of Prevention, National Institute of Mental Health; the National Science Foundation; and the Institute on Aging under contract Nos. ST-9B-90 (OSTP) and 79-02700 (NSF).

The Institute of Medicine was chartered in 1970 by the National Academy of Sciences to enlist distinguished members of the appropriate professions in the examination of policy matters pertaining to the health of the public. In this, the Institute acts under both the Academy's 1863 Congressional charter responsibility to be an advisor to the Federal Government and its own initiative in identifying issues of medical care, research, and education.

Publication IOM 81-05

Springer Publishing Company, Inc.
200 Park Avenue South
New York, New York 10003

ISBN 0-8261-4110-2
Library of Congress Catalog Card No.: 82-50101
Printed in the United States of America

Contents

Foreword

An Outlook on
Stress Research and Health

During my term of office as President of the Institute of Medicine, National Academy of Sciences, 1975-
1980, no aspect of health and disease elicited more
interest among leaders of the United States government
than the subject dealt with in this report. Senators,
congressmen, cabinet officers, and other leaders
repeatedly expressed concern to me about the possible
effects of very difficult life experiences on health.

In part, this interest reflected dramatic events:
the hostages in Iran, the radiation accident at Three
Mile Island, the experiences of Vietnam War veterans,
the reactions of the Love Canal area residents to the
threat of chemical wastes, the effects of a devastating
earthquake, the threat of assassination of political
leaders. But much of this interest, not only among our
leaders but by all of us, stems from personal experience
and observation of those whose lives cross ours. Indeed,
throughout our lives we encounter loss and bereavement,
drastic changes of location and responsibilities, the
threat of serious illness or lasting disability--
emotionally charged events of many kinds and deep
personal significance. So it should not be surprising
that there is widespread public interest in the topics
covered in this volume. Hardly a week passes without a
new course, book, article, or movie on ways of dealing
with stress in industry, education, government, or
marriage--as well as in medical settings.

Yet, there has been a discrepancy between the high
level of public interest and the low priority of scientific commitment to this subject. There are many
reasons. One is that the topic is inherently complex
and the problems difficult. Another is that only a
small cadre of investigators with the necessary scientific training have addressed these questions explicitly.
Also, the problems are interdisciplinary by nature, and
we have much to learn about the conduct of interdisciplinary efforts in most of science. And, there has been

a certain inertia to overcome in the directions of attention in the health science community.

Therefore, we in the Institute of Medicine welcomed enthusiastically a request in 1979 from the Office of Science and Technology Policy (OSTP) for a critical assessment of the state of the sciences pertinent to stress, health, and disease. It was especially appropriate that this broadly integrative inquiry should be sponsored in the first instance by the scientific advisory apparatus of the President of the United States. This office has broad responsibilty for science in the nation, cutting across all ordinary jurisdictional lines. It was also most appropriate that three other agencies supported the inquiry: the National Science Foundation, which has earned world-wide respect as the principal bastion for support of basic science; the National Institute of Mental Health, which has long fostered interaction between biomedical and behavioral sciences; and the National Institute on Aging, which has shown ingenuity in promoting interdisciplinary research on complex health problems.

The subject of this inquiry is intrinsically fascinating, when given open-minded reflection, because it deals with the nature of human adaptability. It rests upon integrative biology--pulling together observations at all levels of organization from molecular to behavioral characteristics of living organisms. In the essence of our adaptability over the long course of our history as a species, we human beings have had to deal with very difficult circumstances. Can it be that contemporary circumstances are somehow more difficult than those of our ancestors? From a material standpoint that is surely not the case. It is very hard to compare today's life experiences with those of a century ago, let alone a millenium ago. Doubtless, we are in many ways better off than ever before. Yet, there are some challenging novelties in our experience today--especially in the dramatic transformations since the Industrial Revolution. We have created in some measure a new way of life for ourselves, and we now try to adapt to it.

But, is it true that difficult experiences, old or new, can make us sick? There are widespread impressions that this is so--impressions that many physicians and nurses share with the general public. Indeed, there have long been some carefully documented clinical observations strongly suggesting that, for some people at least, very difficult circumstances can trigger the onset of illness or a flare-up of an existing disease.

Yet there are many gaps and paradoxes. For example, in a society as mobile as ours, a recently married couple commonly will move to a city where both are strangers--a circumstance inherently somewhat stressful. But, the meaning of the experience may be quite different for the two. He may be immersed in fascinating new work with respectful co-workers; she may be largely isolated with a new baby. Or conversely, he may be under harsh competitive pressures in a nonsupportive work environment, while she is welcomed into a friendly, respectful neighborhood group. Many other circumstances might differentiate their experiences. The general point is that the same experience--painted in broad brush strokes--can have very different meanings for different people, even people as close as husband and wife. And the different meanings can elicit very different emotional responses and hence very different physiological responses. To make matters still more complicated, different people may in many ways have different susceptibility to virtually identical experiences. For a given kind of stress, some are more vulnerable than others, and the sources of such variability are manifold.

All well and good. But are there any general tendencies in the relation of stress and illness? Do certain kinds of experiences tend to increase the likelihood of illness, at least for certain kinds of people? On the average, for large populations, does bereavement, for example, make people more vulnerable? Are some more vulnerable than others? How can we find out? For that matter, how could stressful experience make someone ill? What processes or mechanisms could link human emotional experience and tissue damage? What are the biological effects of difficult experiences? In what ways could they precipitate illness--or perhaps even promote health? Finally, how can we protect ourselves from those stressful experiences that are not helpful, but harmful? Can science identify individual coping strategies that tend to be protective? What is the role of social support networks, mutual aid relationships and self-help groups? Can we discover biological mechanisms that would lead to specific preventive or therapeutic interventions or to self-help for people who are at high risk? These are all fascinating subjects for scientific inquiry, not only for the satisfaction of long-standing human curiosity, but also for the future relief of much human suffering.

Most species that have ever existed are now extinct. What is there about human structure, function, and behavior that has permitted this peculiar species to survive--so far at least? We and our ancestors over a

very long time have overcome many vicissitudes in the
course of our survival--from tropical jungles to ice
ages; infections, parasites, drought, famine, flood, geographical barriers, fire, murder and mass murder. To say
that we somehow have survived is not sufficient. A spark
of wonder, of fascination, must be struck by the realization that our species has survived so long in the face of
so many difficulties. How has this been possible? What
mechanisms have facilitated our adaptation? How can we
make useful approaches to their scientific study?

Biological research has clarified a good deal about
the ways in which our species has in fact adapted--though
very much more remains in doubt. Adaptation occurs on
all levels of organization. For example, when we are
exposed to a very cold environment, changes occur at the
molecular level within the cell, at the level of whole
cells, at the level of organs, at the level of functional
systems, and at the level of the whole organism--what is
usually called behavior. Biological sciences typically
have concentrated on the lower levels, the smaller units,
the component parts of the organism; behavioral sciences
have studied mainly whole organisms or aggregates of
them. An adequate understanding of human adaptation will
require both biological and behavioral perspectives--a
broad and coherent view of the life sciences.

In biological research, behavior is viewed in a
framework of adaptation. How does behavior meet adaptive
tasks, i.e., requirements for survival and reproduction?
Sometimes this is easy, routine, habitual, unremarkable.
Sometimes it is difficult, risky, troublesome, alarming.
These latter occasions are the ones we call stressful.
But what makes them so difficult? Essentially they are
appraised by the individual as jeopardizing opportunities
for survival, reproduction, or both--however these may
be defined in a particular group.

Fundamental motivations, then, incline us to do what
needs doing to insure survival and reproduction. In most
societies throughout history, these survival criteria
have been extended in various ways into a set of basic
values that constitute the grounds for being viewed as a
person of worth in a given society. If these basic
values are threatened, an experience becomes stressful.

Coping with life-threatening experiences is a distinctive and difficult feature of medical and nursing
care. Poignant human experiences in this sphere are
especially accessible to the health professions; yet they

have not been the object of much systematic research in medicine. To the extent that they have been studied, the emphasis has been on impact, distress, and incapacity. Much less attention has been given to effective ways of responding, meeting stern challenges, even learning from difficult experiences. In other words, the clinical literature on life-threatening situations is long on stress and short on coping. Some recent work seeks to redress this imbalance.

One crucial linkage of the biomedical and behavioral sciences occurs in a final common pathway through which the brain controls the endocrine and autonomic nervous systems. Over the past three decades, much has been learned about these systems and their roles in mediating human responses to changing circumstances. The adaptations involved in stressful circumstances refer to the flow of changes in environmental conditions that affect the organism at all levels of biological organization. If those changes are drastic, they tend to be experienced as difficult and distressing. That is what we usually mean by stressful conditions. There is a broad biology of stress that is being revived in a new context, with new techniques that were virtually unimaginable when the term stress came into common use several decades ago.

As described in this report, these compelling issues were tackled by a broadly composed group of distinguished scientists bringing an extraordinary diversity of strengths to the task. The study steering committee contained scientists from a wide range of basic and clinical disciplines, including many who have made important contributions in stress research and some whose work has not been tied closely to stress. They were critical and tough-minded as they sought the best paths to future clarification. Let us now consider briefly some of the highlights of their inquiry that I found to be particularly salient.

Major advances are emerging in biochemical, anatomical, physiological, pharmacological, pathological, and behavioral aspects of the nervous system. For example, less than 30 years ago, many students of the brain believed that communication among nerve cells in the brain had to be electrical; only in the 1950s did the overwhelming importance of chemical communication become clear. Ten years ago, less than a dozen chemicals had been identified as probable neuroregulators in the brain. In the past few years, that number has risen sharply, precise maps of brain distributions are available for

several neuroregulators, and good progress has been made
in clarifying the role of some of them in normal and
abnormal behavior. Many of these neuroregulatory systems
are involved in stress reactions. The catecholamines--
compounds of the adrenalin family (epinephrine, norepinephrine) that are found both in the adrenal gland and
in several parts of the brain--have long been associated
with stress; and studies of the catecholamines continue
to be a vigorous part of stress research in which knowledge has grown dramatically. Another clearly relevant
group of compounds are the endorphins, recently discovered, morphine-like peptides. Found in the brain,
the pituitary gland, and adrenals, they are involved in
the perception of and response to pain. Pain and other
stress responses are closely related.

With respect to promising directions of research
into the biological mechanisms through which stress may
affect health and disease, much of the relevant scientific investigation has not been done formally as stress
research. In fact, many of the exciting leads have come
from basic efforts to learn more about biological systems, with little emphasis on possible relations to
stress or disease. The study group prepared thorough
background papers on endocrinology, neurochemistry,
genetics, pain, immunology, physiological sociology, and
cardiovascular physiology. For each, the main thrust
was to identify recent advances that might be relevant
to stress problems, promising directions for further
research in stress, and difficulties that investigators
might face in addressing these problems.

In the past few years, neuroscientists have discovered and are beginning to study dozens of neuroactive
substances whose presence was previously unsuspected.
Much of this research is possible because of newly
developed techniques: fluorimetric, mass-spectrometric,
gas-chromatographic, enzymatic, and radioimmunological
assays that can detect and quantitate these compounds,
their precursors, and their metabolic products. Also,
investigators are beginning to find ways to investigate
in living animals and humans the basic regulatory mechanisms that control neuroregulator function, including
synthesis, storage, release, receptor interaction, and
metabolism.

Advances in sample collection now permit investigators to monitor and obtain samples from essentially
all parts of the body, including the brain, while the
organism moves about freely or undergoes controlled

exposure to stressors or other behavioral circumstances. Thus, scientists have associated blood concentrations of the catecholamines with stress responses for decades, but only in the last few years have they been able to take small blood samples from freely moving human subjects and measure how these substances change during exposure to a stressor. In combination, animal and human studies should provide a wealth of new information about the effects of stress.

When a change occurs in personal circumstances--as necessarily happens hour-by-hour, day-by-day, sometimes drastic, sometimes not--a personal appraisal occurs, mostly automatically but sometimes with conscious deliberation. Such appraisals may be freely translated into a set of questions whose relevance to adaptation is apparent. What is it? What does it mean for me? How can I respond? Will action be required? If so, what action would be effective in meeting the challenge? Such questions, even if vaguely formulated, are answered in ways that produce a coordinated set of metabolic and cardiovascular changes that prepare the organism for action. The course of action is guided by the brain as reappraisal proceeds in light of on-going feedback. Recent research has done much to clarify the complex brain circuits that mediate these crucial integrative processes that have long been important in the adaptability and indeed the survival of our species.

Early in the history of stress research, the primary interest in biological components of stress were adrenal hormones--catecholamines made by the adrenal medulla and corticosteroids made by the adrenal cortex. Since then, many other hormones have been found to be responsive to stress. Among these are prolactin, insulin, growth hormone, testosterone, and luteinizing hormone. A growing body of evidence indicates that hormonal responses to stress are quite variable from person to person and from circumstance to circumstance. They can be affected by a variety of biological and psychosocial mediators.

Although stressors activate both the adrenal cortex and the adrenal medulla, the two parts work in different ways. For both, the major control related to the response to stress is through the brain; indeed the brain controls all of the hormonal responses to stress. For the adrenal cortex, messages from areas of the brain are sent to the pituitary gland, sometimes referred to as the master gland; the pituitary secretes a polypeptide messenger, adrenocorticotroin factor (ACTH), which goes

through the blood to the adrenal cortex, where it stimulates corticosteroid synthesis. For the adrenal medulla,
a message is sent directly from the brain via nerve
cells; those impulses stimulate the release of the
adrenal medullar hormones, particularly epinephrine.
Curiosity about stress responses, stimulated over decades
by such great scientists as the physiologist Walter
Cannon, has done much to clarify the structure and
function of brain-adrenal relations and the effects of
adrenal secretions on most cells and tissues of the body.

What circumstances activate these systems? In
general, situations that elicit an appraisal of threat,
a sense of alarm, or a feeling of distress. But, it is
interesting to note that adrenal activation is not
limited to such circumstances. Unpredictability has
been shown in both animal and human experiments to be a
fairly potent stimulus for this system. When a strange
situation is encountered--or when established and predictable events are altered so that expectations are no
longer met--adrenal activation is likely to occur. Then,
the physiological and biochemical effects of the several
adrenal hormones may have significant ramifications
throughout the body.
In recent years, new assay techniques have enabled
investigators to measure many hormones in human blood
under a variety of natural and experimental conditions.
These techniques will permit a new wave of interesting
and informative studies. For example, one research group
quite recently compared the effects on plasma catecholamines of public speaking and moderate exercise. Both
raised plasma epinephrine and norepinephrine; however,
norepinephrine increased more than twice as much during
exercise as during speaking, and epinephrine increased
about three times more for speaking than for exercise.
Thus, the prospect is emerging of specific and differentiated analysis of relationships among stress, hormones,
and behavior.

During the last three decades, significant progress
has been made regarding the role of the central nervous
system in controlling normal cardiovascular function.
This knowledge has enhanced our appreciation of the ways
in which environmental or behavioral factors can contribute to disease. A wealth of information suggests that
common cardiovascular diseases are multifactorial in origin. Thus, the effects of stress on the pathogenesis of
cardiovascular disorders must be viewed in the context
of other metabolic or circulatory abnormalities that
contribute to the disease process. Repeated, sustained
stressful experiences may well affect the cardiovascular

system in such ways that predisposed people--especially genetically predisposed--are likely to develop high blood pressure. In this context, it is important to note that the circulatory alterations associated with alarm reactions to severe stressors resemble those that accompany the development of experimental and human hypertension. This suggests, but does not prove, that the stimulus which brings about the onset of hypertension has an effect on brain mechanisms that regulate cardiovascular function. Animal experiments and human clinical research increasingly point toward involvement of brain and behavior in a sizeable fraction of cardiovascular diseases. These diseases constitute the nation's largest burden of illness, so this line of inquiry is of great interest.

Everyone is exposed to stressful experiences; yet for any noxious agent (biological or psychosocial), there is marked individuality in response. Both genetic and environmental factors pertinent to such individuality of responses are beginning to be clarified, and studies of such factors will deserve attention in the years ahead, especially in view of the truly dramatic advances that are occurring in genetics. The applicability of these advances to human problems is increasing sharply.

Studies of the influence of genetic factors on elements of response to stressful experience are now of great interest. Such work requires identification of the genes involved in susceptibilty and resistance to particular diseases. Studies of how such genes interact with specific environmental factors may point the way to sharply focused preventive interventions. Linkages of genetics, biochemistry, psychology, and clinical medicine will be important in sorting out these interactions.

An understanding of stress genetics requires investigation of the genetic basis of differences in the endocrine and behavioral reactions to and consequences of stress. These range from differences in the perception of external and internal stimuli as stressors to differences in the responses of body tissues and brain function to the hormones released during stress. The main substances that have been studied in this context are the corticosteroids and catecholamines produced by the adrenal gland. Equally important, however, are the neuroregulators within the brain and in the peripheral nervous system that modulate stress responses.

What is needed is the identification of the genes that are responsible for such differences. The effects on the stress response for each identified gene then must

xvii

be investigated to establish which are regulatory and
which structural. Genetic mapping of these variants is
needed to identify regulatory sites. Particularly from
the perspective of studying acute stressors, dynamic processes such as the induction of enzymes or the modulation
of receptor molecules also must be examined. The systems
should be studied in both developing and mature animals,
because stress susceptibility changes considerably during
development. Research into major pathological mutations
affecting the stress response systems of experimental
animals deserves high priority; such studies can provide
useful animal models of specific human diseases.

There is a great need for genetic studies to be
integrated with studies of environmentally caused variation in responses to stress. Different individuals
clearly can respond to the same environmental variable
quite differently, and the patterns of immediate and
delayed responses to stressors also may differ markedly.
Such interactions between genetic and environmental
influences can help to reveal differences that previously
were hidden.

Another set of factors that affect vulnerability to
stressful life experiences lies in the social environment. From numerous epidemiological studies of varying
design--using different populations, health outcome measures, and stress indicators--there has come considerable
convergence of evidence indicating that many disorders
are precipitated by environmental stressors such as
moving, unemployment, or bereavement. The extent of
community disintegration, a lack of social supports, and
the number of stressful events in the life of an individual have been found to affect illness, productivity,
and indeed life expectancy.

A recent body of research is of unusual interest in
this context. Relationships between human attachments,
illness, and mortality have been studied both intensively
and extensively. The evidence is steadily growing that
people whose human attachments are weak also are more
prone to illness and early death. Although the mechanisms of such vulnerability remain to be established
firmly, this work and related research suggest that
natural support systems can be effective in buffering
stressful experiences. Such networks also can influence
the use of health services and adherence to medical
regimens. This is pertinent to the requirements for
behavior change in smoking cessation, weight control, or
long-term adherence to antihypertensive medication.

Social support systems facilitate the development of coping strategies that help people contain distress within tolerable limits, maintain self-esteem, preserve interpersonal relationships, meet the requirements of new situations, and prepare for the future. An interesting area for future research will be the experimental construction of social support networks such as self-help groups where natural ones are lacking.

In my view, one of the most important conclusions of this stress study is that individuals who experience any of a wide range of stressful events or situations are at increased risk of developing a physical or mental disorder. That conclusion is based on accumulated evidence from much careful, systematic research--clinical and epidemiological. Studies of the health effects of natural or man-made disasters suggest that about half of the physically unharmed survivors experience an acute emotional, physical, or psychosomatic consequence; many of these victims suffer long-term changes in health. More common events such as bereavement, physical injury, buying a house, or retirement also are associated with an increased risk of becoming ill. Similarly, illness rates are disproportionately high among workers in high-stress jobs that involve high levels of workload, responsiblity, and interpersonal or role conflicts. A difference between work skills and work requirements also is a risk factor, whether the worker perceives the job demand to be too high or too low.

Research has shown that life stressors are associated with a wide array of physical and mental disorders. Almost any major organ system may be involved. Physical disorders in which stressors have been implicated as risk factors include bronchial asthma, hypertension, peptic ulcers, hyperthyroidism, and sudden cardiac death. Impressive evidence also suggests that stressors are risk factors for the precipitation of mental disorders such as depression, schizophrenia, alcoholism, and drug abuse. This does not mean that stressful experience is the sole or even the primary cause of these disorders. Historically, simple cause-effect concepts of stress and disease have been prominent in stress research. As this study points out, such formulations fail to recognize important interactions among stressors, reactions, mediators, and consequences. Thus, both genetic and environmental mediators shape the biological reactions and clinical consequences of stressful experience. The relations are surely complex and difficult to disentangle. But there is no longer reasonable doubt that the game is worth the

xix

candle. The problems are too important and the prospects, too promising to justify neglect.

Studies of coping behavior in difficult, distressing
circumstances fall mainly into three types: (1) life-
threatening situations, (2) major psychosocial transitions, and (3) major psychobiological transitions in the
life cycle. One striking observation, repeated in many
studies, is that different individuals exhibit a great
diversity of responses under a given set of environmental
conditions, however difficult. The extent to which a
particular set of environmental conditions is perceived
as threatening depends on cognitive processes of
appraisal, through which the events take on personal
meaning in relation to an individual's priority of
motivations. Among these fundamental motivations are
those concerned with individual survival, self-esteem,
close attachment with significant others, and a sense of
belonging in a valued group.

The stressed individual needs to accomplish the
following tasks: (1) contain the distress within limits
that are personally tolerable, (2) maintain self-esteem,
(3) preserve interpersonal relationships, and (4) meet
the conditions of the new circumstances. For each of
these tasks, multiple strategies may be employed at
various levels of awareness. These strategies reflect
not only the person's developmental history but also the
different circumstances surrounding each major transitional situation and cultural influences that define
preferred strategies. Some strategies are drawn readily
from cultural prescriptions or institutional arrangements. Others require considerable improvising by the
individual. Recent research has examined both individual
strategies and social support systems in mediating human
responses to stressful experiences.

Behavior under stress tends toward converting the
unfamiliar to a familiar conditon, thus making the environment predictable. The more nearly predictable the
situation and subsequent response, the more feasible it
is to take adaptive measures. Thus, preparation for
major, stressful transitions may offer promise for
prevention of considerable human suffering. Moreover,
observations suggest a certain durability in those new
patterns that prove effective, implying a cumulative
quality to the progression of coping sequences through
different stresses over time. Within a moderate range
of severity, successful resolution of earlier stresses
often augments coping with later transitions.

On the whole, how individuals attempt to cope with stress has been a neglected area of great potential importance. In years to come, a deeper understanding of human coping behavior can be useful in devising reasonable therapeutic and preventive interventions. The promise of such interventions is clearest with respect to mental health; but they also have direct relevance to general health, because health-damaging coping efforts such as smoking, alcohol use, and risky driving weigh heavily in the burden of illness.

The present study, and related Institute of Medicine efforts such as the recent study of scientific opportunities in alcohol-related problems, are fostering collaboration among behavioral and biomedical scientists in addressing problems that have great significance for health. These inquiries attempt to stimulate new lines of investigation and new applications of existing knowledge by exposing basic scientists to important clinical and public health problems and health professionals to relevant advances in basic research. Such efforts may well yield some near-term dividends; but they are also investments in the future, challenging some of the best minds in the life sciences to envision domains of inquiry in behavioral and biomedical research that are likely to be productive over the next decade--and that tend to be neglected. Not all of those lines of investigation will yield useful applications. Nevertheless, such research needs to be fostered in its own right for its intrinsic worth, as well as for its potential relevance to a wide range of practical problems. Surely, a deeper understanding of the nature, sources, and limits of human adaptability is a worthy quest. It is close to the heart of the human condition.

As we learn more about the current burden of illness within our society, the important effects of behavioral factors of health become increasingly apparent. In addition, an awareness of how the major components of that burden have changed over the years emphasizes that the sciences needed to lessen it also must change. Similarly, as new scientific opportunities arise, those who are responsible for the health of the nation must judge their relevance to combatting disease. New gardens of science must be cultivated. Not long ago, the emerging discipline of biochemistry was depreciated as weak chemistry by chemists and as weak biology by biologists. Yet today, this hybrid is the core of biomedical research. Not many years ago, few leaders in medicine thought that the field of genetics would have any practi-

cal significance for health in the twentieth century.
Today, it is one of the most dynamic areas in medicine.
Similar observations can be made about the neurosciences
and about large-scale prevention programs. Such lessons
should be borne in mind in the years ahead as the health
sciences adapt to new problems and seek to capitalize on
new opportunities.

It is an exciting and demanding time for the biomedical and behavioral sciences. As illustrated in this
volume, the opportunities for progress in basic and
applied knowledge are unprecedented; the potential
rewards, measured in terms either of decreased mortality
and morbidity or of improved quality of life are profoundly encouraging. The tasks are surely complex and
difficult. And progress often has been exasperatingly
slow. Yet, we should make no mistake: in the life
sciences, broadly conceived, and in their significance
for health in the future, we stand today on the threshold
of a new era of awesome potentiality.

David A. Hamburg, M.D.
Director
Division of Health Policy
Research and Education
Harvard University

National Academy of Sciences
Institute of Medicine

Study Steering Committee

<u>Chair</u>

Carl EISDORFER, Ph.D., M.D., President, Montefiore Hospital, New York, NY

<u>Members</u>

Julius AXELROD, Ph.D., Chief, Section of Pharmacology, Laboratory of Clinical Sciences, National Institute of Mental Health, Bethesda, MD

John C. BECK, M.D., Director, Multicampus Division of Geriatric Medicine, University of California, Los Angeles, CA

William E. BUNNEY, Jr., M.D., Deputy Director, Division of Clinical and Behavioral Research, National Institute of Mental Health, Bethesda, MD

Roland D. CIARANELLO, M.D., Assistant Professor, Department of Psychiatry and Behavioral Sciences, Stanford School of Medicine, Stanford, CA

John A. CLAUSEN, Ph.D., Professor of Sociology, Institute of Human Development, University of California, Berkeley, CA

Frances COHEN, Ph.D., Assistant Professor of Medical Psychology, Graduate Group in Psychology, University of California, San Francisco, CA

Bruce P. DOHRENWEND, Ph.D., Professor of Social Science, Department of Psychiatry, Columbia University, New York, NY

Marianne FRANKENHAEUSER, Ph.D., Professor and Head, Department of Psychology, Karolinska Institute, Stockholm, Sweden

Roger GUILLEMIN, M.D., Ph.D., Director, Department of Neuroendocrinology, The Salk Institute, San Diego, CA

Beatrix A. HAMBURG, M.D., Associate Professor of Psychiatry, Children's Hospital Medical Center, Harvard Medical School, Boston, MA

Robert L. KAHN, Ph.D., Professor of Psychology, Survey Research Center, University of Michigan, Ann Arbor, MI

Irwin J. KOPIN, M.D., Chief, Section of Medicine, Laboratory of Clinical Sciences, National Institute of Mental Health, Bethesda, MD

Richard S. LAZARUS, Ph.D., Professor, Department of Psychology, University of California, Berkeley, CA

Lennart LEVI, M.D., Ph.D., Professor and Chairman, Laboratory for Clinical Stress Research, Stockholm, Sweden

Morris A. LIPTON, Ph.D., M.D., Sarah Graham Kenan Distinguished Professor of Psychiatry, University of North Carolina, Chapel Hill, NC

Alan A. McLEAN, M.D., Medical Director, Eastern Region, IBM, New York, NY

Leonard PEARLIN, Ph.D., Research Sociologist, Laboratory of Socio-Environmental Study, National Institute of Mental Health, Bethesda, MD

Chester M. PIERCE, M.D., Professor of Education and Psychiatry, Harvard University, Cambridge, MA

Richard H. RAHE, M.D., Director, Clinical Services, Navy Regional Medical Group, Long Beach, CA

Matilda W. RILEY, D.Sc., Associate Director for Social and Behavioral Research, National Institute on Aging, Bethesda, MD

Robert M. ROSE, M.D., Professor and Chairman, Department of Psychiatry and Behavioral Sciences, University of Texas Medical Branch, Galveston, TX

Alvin P. SHAPIRO, M.D., Professor, Department of Internal Medicine, University of Pittsburgh School of Medicine, Pittsburgh, PA

Marvin STEIN, M.D., Professor and Chairman, Department of Psychiatry, Mt. Sinai School of Medicine, New York, NY

National Academy of Sciences
Institute of Medicine

Frederick C. Robbins, M.D., President

Study Staff

Division of Mental Health and Behavioral Medicine

  Glen R. Elliott, Ph.D., M.D., Study Director

  Fredric Solomon, M.D., Division Director

  Delores L. Parron, Ph.D., Associate Division Director

  Caren Carney, Research Assistant

  Jane Takeuchi, Research Assistant

  DeAnn Gradington, Secretary

Acknowledgments

The committee thanks the many individuals who contributed
to this report. Those who prepared background material
for the committee are listed in Appendix C. In addition,
many others informally offered insights into research
needs in the stress field. The committee also is grate-
ful to the scientists who reviewed portions of the draft
report for their helpful comments and suggestions.

PART I

PERSPECTIVES AND CONCLUSIONS

CHAPTER 1

Introduction

This National Academy of Sciences' Institute of Medicine study of "Research on Stress in Health and Disease" developed from a July 1979 request from the Office of Science and Technology Policy (OSTP), Executive Office of the President. In its charge, the OSTP requested a "definition of research issues, delineation of desirable and adverse aspects of stress in its various forms, and biomedical, behavioral, and sociological approaches to the description and alleviation of excessive stresses." Several other agencies joined the OSTP in supporting this project: the National Science Foundation (NSF), the Office of Prevention of the National Institute of Mental Health (NIMH), and the National Institute on Aging (NIA).

The principal audiences for this report include scientists and administrators who are engaged in stress research or in research that relates to it and scholars who wish to examine some of the promise and problems of investigating the interrelationships between stress and health and disease. Although it also may be of interest to some members of the public and to clinicians, this report does not attempt a comprehensive review of the many issues relating stress and health that do not have an empirical base at this time. Instead, it concentrates on research trends, methodologies, and concepts that are especially representative of useful directions for future stress research. A brief summary of general attitudes that the public and scientists hold about the role of stress in health and disease may help to explain both the broad interest in this topic and the type of examination undertaken by the study committee.

Public Interest

Since shortly before World War II, the suspected adverse effects of stress have been a popular topic for the information media. Typical features include stories about someone for whom a major traumatic event was followed closely by a serious physical or mental disorder, reports of strong associations between "stressful" life styles and increased vulnerability to disease, and suggestions that certain types of employment or work settings are stressful and thereby induce illness. In the aggregate, such media coverage has conveyed an impression that stress is a major disrupting feature of contemporary life and that it has predictably negative consequences on adaptation and health.

One measure of the perceived importance of stress to many members of the public is the money and attention given to combatting its effects. The committee made no effort even to estimate how much is spent each year to prevent or alleviate stress-related problems, but the amount must be substantial. For example, a thriving industry of executive management courses and many other self-help programs respond to people's desires to learn how to cope with stress; and a wide range of best-selling books assert that people can avoid developing hypertension, heart attacks, depression, anxiety, and many other disorders by changing their lifestyles in ways that reduce stress. In addition, stress-related medical complaints have helped to make antianxiety medications such as diazepam (Valium) and chlordiazepoxide (Librium) the most widely prescribed drugs in the United States. Furthermore, recent legal actions have attracted attention to occupational stress as contributing to employee dysfunction, suggesting that "excessive" stress may increasingly enter into disability claims for which employees may receive compensation.

Scientific Interest

Modern scientific interest in the relevance of stress to health and disease also developed earlier in this century. As investigators began to discover mechanisms by which the brain monitors and controls what is

4

happening in the rest of the body, they started to question how such systems might influence disease processes. Investigators such as Walter Cannon, Hans Selye, and John Mason found that animals exposed to severe physical or psychological conditions exhibited a number of hormonal and physiological responses, some of which could lead to physical impairment or even death. Clinicians such as Stewart Wolf, Franz Alexander, and Arthur Mirsky found many examples of associations between persistent disruptive conditions and disease.

Notwithstanding its promising beginnings, stress research has been filled with controversy, inconsistency, and uncertainty. Many of the early studies of stress and disease had major methodological flaws. Also, as discussed in the next chapter, different and conflicting definitions of stress arose as investigators emphasized various aspects of the process. Starting from a set of reasonably well-defined concerns about the effects of certain types of stimuli on the body, the stress concept has broadened markedly as different investigators have invoked it to explain their data. It now encompasses a wide array of empirical studies and a descriptive literature of uneven quality that is scattered throughout almost the entire range of the behavioral, biological, psychological, and medical sciences.

Controversies continue to plague the field. Some scientists believe that the stress concept has become so overgeneralized and the available research of such uncertain quality that it lacks heuristic value; they suggest that needed research relating to stress should be performed in different contexts. Other investigators acknowledge that the field has serious problems but counter that the concept of stress provides an invaluable unifying terminology for a particular type of important research; they believe that the current difficulties can be resolved and that continued efforts to promote attention to stress research are warranted.

Support for stress research in many ways reflects the turmoil in the field. As discussed in Patterns of Financial Support of Health-Related Stress Research (Appendix A), the committee tried to estimate the magnitude and distribution of funding in the field in the United States. Many different federal agencies support some aspects of stress research, but there is no centralized compilation of what is being done. Even using broad criteria that include work only marginally related

5

to stress, total support for stress research in the
United States for calendar year 1979 probably did not
exceed $35 million, almost all from federal sources.

Study Organization

The steering committee for this study contained
individuals from a wide range of basic and clinical
disciplines and included investigators who are known in
stress research as well as scientists whose work has not
been tied closely to stress. In its early deliberations,
the committee concluded that confusion, commercialism,
and rhetoric around the stress concept have obscured a
number of basic considerations. If research suggests
that exposure to stress is associated with changes in an
individual's susceptibility to or recovery from disease,
it should not be discounted because of public exuberance
or because of methodological problems in some reports.
If essential facts are not available, it is important to
identify strengths and weaknesses of past research
efforts and highlight useful research strategies. The
committee hoped particularly to alert the scientific
community to promising areas for health-related research
in the stress field.

Faced with a huge, complicated literature and limited
time, the steering committee narrowed the scope of the
study in several ways. First, it restricted its attention to the formal research literature. Second, the
group acknowledged the existence of a number of excellent
reviews and summaries of stress research and decided not
to replicate such work. It considered primarily those
parts of the stress literature that highlight the
strengths and weaknesses of existing data and suggest
useful lines of investigation for future research.
Third, the committee concluded that identification and
evaluation of the growing number of prevention and
treatment regimens for stress was beyond the scope of
this study. However, in keeping with its emphasis on
research, the group did consider promising approaches to
studying the effects of intervention in the stress response and the potential relevance of progress in other
areas of stress research to prevention and treatment
strategies. The committee concurred that questions about
the efficacy and appropriateness of existing prevention
and treatment approaches to stress-related problems merit
study in their own right.

Recognizing that the stress field encompasses a wide
range of research topics, the steering committee formed

6

panels to examine major areas in detail. The work of these panels constitutes the bulk of this report. Three groups, collectively called the Stress and Environment Panel, considered specific aspects of the environment that have been identified as stressful: the chapter on Stress and Life Events examines the extensive literature on associations between disruptive personal experiences and adverse changes in health that may follow; the chapter on Stress in Organizational Settings evaluates research on the ways in which individuals may be stressed in particular settings such as the workplace or school; and the chapter on Work Stress Related to Social Structures and Processes describes research, primarily done in Scandinavian countries, that has attempted to modify such settings to minimize adverse effects from stress. The chapter by the Panel on Psychosocial Assets and Modifiers of Stress surveys literature about psychological and social factors that may alter the effects of stress on health. The chapter by the Panel on Biological Substrates of Stress explores research issues in the spectrum of basic biological disciplines that may help to elucidate mechanisms through which stress can affect health. Finally, the Stress and Illness chapter describes the current state of knowledge about the role of stress in certain, major, physical and mental disorders.

Largely working independently of one another, the panels provided a way to look at specific needs for future research in various disciplines that relate to the stress field. Each panel was encouraged to examine all aspects of stress research that related to its area, even though this resulted in some overlap among panels. Thus, each panel report can stand independently as an analysis of research needs and potential in the stress field in its particular area.

All of the panel chairs also served on the steering committee, as did many of the panel members. This permitted the committee to draw on analyses of the complex and often confusing stress literature from a variety of perspectives, helping to highlight different aspects of the existing knowledge and of potential avenues for furthering an understanding of how stress affects health. The committee served as a meeting ground for exploring common issues as they emerged from the panel work. The next two chapters reflect the important consequences of the discussions among committee members. The chapter on Conceptual Issues in Stress Research briefly discusses past efforts to define stress and outlines a framework that the committee developed to organize and systematize the diverse studies that constitute stress research. The

chapter on Major Conclusions and Research Needs describes
how existing work within the stress field fits into that
framework and where additional information is needed,
drawing from the individual panel reports to provide
illustrations of each point.

Summary

The committee was charged to evaluate the evidence
that stress can affect health and disease and to identify
research needed to gain a better understanding of such
effects. The members were impressed both with the array
of evidence for relationships between stressors and
changes in health and with the wide range of promising
research directions in the stress field.

A growing body of well-controlled studies document
that disruptive life events are associated with an
increased risk of a number of mild and severe physical
and mental disorders. For example, such life events as
job loss, bereavement, moving to a new location, or
marriage have been associated with increased likelihood
of developing minor infections, sudden cardiac death,
cancer, and depression. At the same time, basic scientists are measuring with increasing sensitivity the
effects that severe stressors can have on hormonal
responses, on brain function, and on the cardiovascular,
immune, and endocrine systems. Investigators also have
demonstrated the importance of psychosocial factors as
mediators of responses to stressors and are developing
better methods for measuring such effects. Factors such
as the interpretation of an event or the availability of
adequate social supports may influence greatly how an
individual responds to a disruptive life event. Taken
together, the evidence strongly supports the conclusion
that stress can affect physical and mental processes in
ways that might alter an individual's susceptibility to
disease.

The many definitions of stress that exist in the
field appear to meet specific needs for different types
of research; it seems unlikely that any single definition
can meet all of those needs at this time. The committee
did construct a conceptual framework into which all of
the definitions seem to fit. This framework divides the
stress response into its elements--stressors (x), reactions (y), consequences (z), and mediators. Stressors
are events or conditions that elicit physical or psychosocial reactions. To avoid the tautology inherent in
such a definition, the committee recommended that events

8

or conditions be identified as potential stressors, based on the probability that they will be stressors in a particular individual under a given circumstance. Reactions are biological and psychosocial responses of an individual to a stressor. Consequences are physical or psychosocial results of such reactions. And mediators are filters and modifiers that define the context in which the stressor-reaction-consequence (x-y-z) sequence occurs.

The committee discovered that ongoing research on various aspects of this conceptual framework is advancing at quite different rates. As with many other areas of research, subspecialization has been an important trend within the stress field for many years. Much basic research has focused on the biological and physiological reactions to stressors (x-y). Other research has concentrated on associations between stressors and consequences (x-z). Such subspecialization has fostered development of advanced technologies and of a more detailed understanding of specific components of the stress response. However, it also has left important gaps. Thus, almost no research is being done to determine which patterns of reactions to stressors lead to specific disease consequences (y-z). In addition, the role of mediators often has been ignored, particularly in biological research on stress. There is a pressing need for more multidisciplinary collaboration that combines perspectives and technical skills of several specialties. For example, efforts to establish the mechanisms that link disruptive life events with a physiological disorder such as heart disease or cancer may require cooperation among such diverse disciplines as epidemiology, sociology, psychology, neurochemistry, and cardiovascular physiology.

The conceptual framework also highlighted a strong source of bias in stress research. For many years, stress researchers have emphasized mainly adverse consequences of stress, and many people think of stressors as being "bad." Yet, such an evaluative judgment can be applied only to consequences. Stressors and reactions may produce a wide range of consequences, only some of which may be undesirable. Much more attention should be given to positive consequences that may be associated with stressors. Perhaps stressors have a conditioning effect, just as physical exercise can improve muscle strength and endurance.

One of the goals of stress research is to find ways to treat or prevent adverse consequences from exposure to stressors. Often, interventions will involve changing

9

the way an individual perceives or reacts to a stressor or blocking an undesirable consequence from such a reaction. For example, if stomach ulcers were shown in some cases to result from increased hyperacidity in reaction to a stressor, it might be possible stop the reaction by blocking acid formation or secretion in the stomach. At other times, it may be desirable to consider ways in which to alter the condition that results in exposure to the stressor. Research on sources of stress in the work place suggests that, in some instances, the environment can be changed in ways that improve health without unduly affecting other social goals. Such research on the role of the environment in the stress response is a valuable complement to other aspects of stress research.

The data suggest that investigators should move beyond questions about whether stress can affect health and explore more fully the mechanisms through which stressors might produce such consequences. The individual panel reports document the range of promising research directions available for the many disciplines within the stress field. Often, advances those specialties have made in other contexts have yet to be applied to the particular question of how stress can alter physical and mental health. At other times, progress will require new combinations of collaborative efforts among investigators with quite different skills. Such multidisciplinary studies will be challenging but offer great potential for providing vital new insights into the stress response. The opportunity to advance basic knowledge is great, as is the potential for applying that knowledge to the alleviation of major health problems.

CHAPTER 2

Conceptual Issues in Stress Research

At its first meeting, the study steering committee addressed the difficulty of defining stress. The discussion illustrated a source of continuing controversy and confusion in the stress-research field: after thirty-five years, no one has formulated a definition of stress that satisfies even a majority of stress researchers. Several committee members cited definitions that they found useful. One suggested that stress is any demand or change that provokes an attempt to adapt or respond. Another defined it as the reaction of individuals to an upset of the equilibrium. Depending on the context, "stress" may mean a stimulus, the reaction to that stimulus, or the result of that reaction. Some definitions are so broad that they include essentially anything that might happen to someone. Others rely on physiological or psychological manifestations of stress, making assumptions about its effects that may not be valid. Still others carry such assumptions even further, defining as stressful only events that result in a deterioration of performance or health.

Although the limitations of existing definitions of stress are readily apparent, viable alternatives to them are not. Early in the study, the steering committee agreed that it would not be fruitful to try either to select a definition of stress from among those already in use or to formulate its own definition. Instead, the group chose to maintain a broad perspective, seeking information about typical definitions in different areas of stress research, the similarities and differences

among them, and the advantages and limitations of each.
In the course of the study, two things became clear:
first, the stress field encompasses an important body of
research that spans many disciplines and that can be
imprecisely characterized as studies that examine how
people react to significant events or conditions; second,
much of the relevant work being done is not identified
specifically as stress research. The group found that
all of this work could be classified under a conceptual
framework which identifies the elements that characterize
interactions between an individual and the environment.
That framework also provided a way to categorize different types of stress definitions and to highlight some of
their interrelationships. The following material first
reviews briefly the evolution of stress definitions and
then describes the framework that the committee used to
systematize the relevant research.

Evolution of Stress Definitions

Other sections of this report describe in some detail
the major health-related themes in the stress literature.
In addition, several good reviews of stress definitions
are available elsewhere (cf. Appley and Trumbull, 1967;
Mason, 1975a,b; Selye, 1975; Buell and Eliot, 1979;
Burchfield, 1979). The following discussion is limited
to a brief examination of how definitions of stress have
evolved over the past few decades, with particular attention to the origins of the present confusion within the
field.

Systematic consideration of the possible effects of
stress on the body can be traced to the work of Walter
Cannon in the early 1900s. In his work on blood hormones, Cannon (1935) frequently studied the effects of
physical or emotional "stress," by which he meant
stimuli that disrupted an individual's normal internal
environment. He thought that a stress which exceeded a
critical threshold could strain people beyond their
adaptive limits. This formulation is analogous to the
definition of stress in physics as a force that, in
sufficient magnitude, produces strain in an object to
which it is applied.

Most stress researchers readily acknowledge the role
that Hans Selye played in popularizing stress research.
Selye has recounted the origins of his interest in stress
often (cf. Selye, 1956). While attempting to discover a
new sex hormone, he found that rats receiving multiple

12

doses of a crude ovarian extract developed adrenal enlargement, involution of the thymus and lymph glands, and gastric ulcers. Crude extracts of other organs produced identical results, as did administration of a wide variety of other stimuli such as extreme cold or heat, epinephrine, pain, and infectious agents. He suggested that individuals exposed to a noxious stimulus respond with what he called the General Adaptation Syndrome. Selye (1975) identified three stages to this syndrome: "(1) an alarm reaction, in which adaptation has not yet been acquired; (2) the stage of resistance, in which adaptation is optimal; and (3) the stage of exhaustion, in which the acquired adaptation is lost again." He postulated that this response was nonspecific, so that any noxious stimulus would produce the same stages of response.

In a review of stress research, Mason (1975a) noted that Selye's initial work in the 1930's appeared to use "stress" in the conventional manner as a synonym for "stimulus." Only later did Selye propose that "stress" should refer, instead, to the nonspecific response of an individual to such stimuli, which he called "stressors" (Selye, 1950). One attractive feature of this change was its increased emphasis on the importance of the individual. Thus, a stimulus was a stressor only if it produced a stress response, which consisted of specific, objective, physiological changes. Selye's forceful exposition of his stress concept has profoundly influenced research in neurobiology and medicine; much has been learned about endocrine and other physiological responses to stressful situations. Also, his hypothesis that either physical or emotional stressors might produce stress reactions provided strong impetus to psychosomatic research. Yet, despite these significant achievements, many issues about Selye's stress concept remain unsettled. Mason (1975a) concluded that scientific opinion has changed little since the 1950s: "There are still some workers who accept Selye's views on stress, some who use modifications of them, some who regard them yet as unproven working hypotheses, and some who simply reject or ignore them."

Because Selye heavily emphasized the physiological responses to stressors, such responses would seem to be a natural focus for stress research. As described in Chapter 8, Biological Substrates of Stress, there have been substantial advances in understanding both brain mechanisms and systems that connect the brain with other parts of the body. However, many of the most exciting

developments have come from inquiries that were unrelated
to stress, and application of this new knowledge to
elucidating how stress affects health and disease is
lagging far behind. Naturally, there are many possible
explanations for such unequal progress. Thus, it is
much easier to establish the physiological effects of
specific stimuli than it is to show how those effects
lead to a permanent change in a person's health. Still,
at least part of the difficulty may have been excessive
emphasis on responses, without adequate attention to the
stressors.

Table 2.1 lists some typical stressors used in animal
research. As discussed in Chapter 8, scientists in basic
research often have used such stimuli as tools with which
to manipulate a physiological system. Typically, they
choose stimuli that are severely stressful to decrease
variability in responses among test subjects. In accord
with Selye's belief that all stressors produce the same,
nonspecific stress response, researchers often select a
stressor on the basis of convenience or familiarity,
with little attention to whether stressors really are
interchangeable. Although such studies provide valuable
information about stress effects, they yield little
insight into what makes a particular stimulus stressful.
In addition, the results obtained from using such severe
stressors may relate only tangentially to the effects of
less extreme stimuli.

Selye's emphasis on nonspecific physiological responses to stressors has been questioned. For example,
Mason (1971) suggested that the profound physiological

TABLE 2.1

TYPICAL STRESSORS USED IN ANIMAL RESEARCH

Cardiac catheterization	Immobilization
Cold Exposure	Maternal deprivation
Competitive social interaction	Novel environments
Electric shock	Prolonged forced swimming
Food deprivation	Sensory deprivation
Handling	Sleep deprivation
Heat Exposure	Social crowding
Immersion in ice water	Social isolation

effects of such physical stressors as exercise, cold, heat, and fasting are strongly mediated by psychological factors. He found that if physical stressors are not viewed as noxious or alarming, they produce smaller or even opposite physiological responses. Thus, monkeys exposed to a rapid rise in the environmental temperature show a brisk rise in adrenal corticosteroid secretion, a classical stress response; yet, if the temperature is raised just as high but at a much slower rate to avoid the perception of it as novel, steroid secretion is suppressed, rather than elevated. Furthermore, it now is possible to measure simultaneously a number of hormones that are responsive to stressors, including corticosteroids, catecholamines, growth hormone, insulin, and testosterone. Some evidence suggests that particular stressors may produce rather specific patterns of hormonal responses (Mason, 1974). Thus, both public speaking and moderate physical exercise raise plasma concentrations of the catecholamines epinephrine and norepinephrine; yet, norepinephrine is more than twice as high during exercise than during speaking, and epinephrine is about three times higher during speaking than during exercise (Dimsdale and Moss, 1980). Such findings raise serious concerns about the appropriateness of defining stress entirely on the basis of physiological responses.

Human studies rarely involve life-threatening or other uniformly stressful situations, and they often do not lend themselves to extensive physiological or biochemical measures. As a result, the development of stress definitions has followed a different course in clinical research than it has in basic animal research. Table 2.2 lists some typical stressors in human studies. Such stressors are discussed further in Chapter 4, Stress and Life Events, and Chapter 7, Psychosocial Assets and Modifiers. The key feature of these stressors is that they are likely to produce such strong psychological responses as feelings of fear or anger (Appley and Trumbull, 1967; Glass, 1977). Several years ago, Lazarus (1966) began to elaborate the viewpoint that an event can be stressful only if the individual perceives it to be so. A recent expression of this position is illustrated by Burchfield (1979), who defined stress as "anything that causes an alteration of psychological homeostatic processes." These definitions again call the response stress, with the stimulus being the stressor. Lazarus (1971) has gone even further, suggesting that "stress" really should refer to the entire phenomenon of stimulus, response, and intervening variables.

TABLE 2.2

TYPICAL STRESSORS USED IN HUMAN RESEARCH

Experimental Stimuli

Acute Stressors	Chronic Stressors
Threatening, unpleasant films	Sleep deprivation
Understimulation/Demand underload	
Overstimulation/Demand overload	
Noise, unexpected or uncontrollable	
Prestige or status loss	
Electric shock	
Approach-avoidance conflicts	
Uncontrollable situations	

Natural Events

Acute Stressors

Physical illness (including surgery, hospitalization)
Threats to self esteem
Traumatic experiences

Stress-event sequences

Bereavement
Losses of any type (physical, psychological, or social)
Migration
Retirement
Status change (e.g., job change, salary change, marriage)

Chronic and chronic intermittent stressors

Daily "hassles"
Demand overload or underload
Role strains
Social isolation

Adding a psychological component to stress has had
important practical and theoretical implications. For
clinical studies, it has legitimized the inclusion of
events such as job loss or marriage, which most people

16

would agree can be stressful, even if the events are not accompanied by the physiological changes identified by Selye. On the other hand, it raises the possibility of definitional conflicts and further complicates attempts to define a stressor on the basis of responses it induces. Suppose, for example, that three people hear an unexpected, loud noise. The first reports being startled and feeling upset but shows no physiological response; the second denies being startled and yet shows clear physiological changes; and the third has both psychological and physiological responses. For whom was the noise a stressor? Does it matter if failure to report stressful feelings is a result of failure to hear the noise or from denial of its importance? Are these three individuals equally likely to suffer from any adverse health effects that may be associated with exposure to such a stressor?

Historically, interest in stress stemmed from its potential role in causing illness, and most definitions equate stressors with adverse events and stress with negative outcomes. Such definitions arbitrarily exclude the possibility that stressors have positive effects. This emphasis on the negative aspects of stress, along with the emphasis on physiological outcomes, recognizes only some of the consequences that can result from interactions between the environment and the individual and encourages the identification of stressors as being "bad." As discussed by several of the panels, stressors also may have desirable effects associated with successfully meeting physical or psychosocial demands. Among such changes might be increased physical stamina, more effective coping styles, or stronger social ties.

In summary, research on stress has resulted in the proliferation of a wide array of definitions. Efforts to formulate more precise definitions have uniformly failed to distinguish all stressful events from all nonstressful ones, emphasizing the critical importance of intervening variables in a given individual and in the surrounding environment. Yet despite these difficulties, the concept of stress continues to be compelling for the general public and investigators alike. Common experience and good research evidence suggest that certain events or conditions are stressful, and that these somehow are associated with changes in health in some people. It was the task of this committee to examine the most compelling evidence available about the nature of that association.

A Behavioral Science Framework for Stress Research

The multiple ways in which the term "stress" is used has helped to blur critical, distinct steps in the process that leads from a stressor to a disease. Stress research has grown over the past decades from a few studies of the physiological effects of some known stressors to a large body of work sharing as its theme the tenet that a wide variety of circumstances can contribute to adverse health effects. "Stress" and "stress-induced disease" have become convenient catchwords, subsuming a large but ill-defined number of biological, psychological, and social processes. A rift in research endeavors also seems to have developed. In the biological sciences, investigators have tended to use stressors primarily as experimental tools, with most of the major discoveries of potential biological substrates for stress effects coming from scientists who do not identify themselves as stress researchers. In contrast, investigators in the psychological and social sciences have demonstrated strong associations between certain psychosocial events and physical and mental illness. However, they often have used "stress" as a causal explanation for such correlations, without trying to elucidate the physiological and psychological mechanisms through which such stressors might act.

Components of the Framework

Faced with an impressive array of research, the committee sought a way to examine the available information systematically. The group wanted to classify relevant studies, whether or not they were labeled as stress-related, so that it could more easily identify areas of strength as well as important gaps in the research literature. The committee members were able to reach agreement on many aspects of the field by looking at stress research and other relevant work within a broader framework that focuses on how the environment can affect the individual.

An analysis of the effects of the environment on an individual reveals three primary elements. First, something in the environment becomes an activator; second, the individual reacts to that activator; and third, that reaction leads to a consequence. For convenience, this activator-reaction-consequence series can be referred to as the x-y-z sequence (Figure 2.1). Sometimes, specific elements of an x-y-z sequence are readily identifiable. For example, injection of an antigenic substance (activa-

FIGURE 2.1

A FRAMEWORK FOR INTERACTIONS BETWEEN THE INDIVIDUAL AND THE ENVIRONMENT

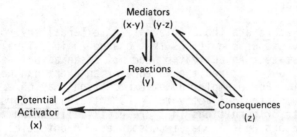

Descriptors:

    Organizational Level
    Intensity
    Quantity
    Temporal Pattern
    Evaluative Quality (for Consequences only)

tor) under the skin of a healthy individual results in an immediate immunologic response (reaction) that neutralizes the antigen and produces local swelling, redness, and tenderness (consequences). Other times, only part of the sequence may be known. Thus, forced immobilization of rats reliably produces gastric ulceration (x-z), but the reactions that produce that consequence still are incompletely understood. Similarly, chronic administration of amphetamine to humans will produce a psychotic state, with hallucinations, delusions, and feelings of persecution (x-z); again, the intervening steps of the sequence remain to be established.

As noted earlier, basic scientists typically select stressful activators that consistently produce a desired reaction or consequence. Except for experimental settings, few situations provide such simple interrelationships. Usually, reactions to an environmental event or condition vary from one individual to another and, for the same individual, from one setting to another.

Also, the reaction to an activator is seldom simply present or absent; it may vary in intensity, effectiveness, or appropriateness. In addition, a single activator may produce many reactions, only a few of which, alone or in combination with other reactions, lead to significant consequences. Therefore, in analyzing a specific x-y-z sequence, one must identify the characteristics, or descriptors, of each potential activator, reaction, and consequence.

Activators are those internal and external environmental events or conditions that change an individual's present state. An activator need not be an actual stimulus, because even the absence of an event can be important. For example, unmet expectations may be a potent psychological activator. Potential activators are events or conditions that are empirically known to be activators under some circumstances. A potential activator can be defined independently of its actual effects; it must have only the potential to produce a change. Even so, potential activators must be defined with respect to an individual. A falling tree per se is not an activator. However, if that tree very nearly hits someone, it may produce the potential activator of fear; if it actually strikes the individual, the potential activators of injury and pain may be added. Activators may act at any level of organizational complexity, from a single enzyme through organ systems to psychological states. Other descriptors are intensity, quantity, and temporal pattern. For example, a single light tap might have far different effects than would a rapid series of sharp blows, which might also differ from single blows that occur sporadically but unpredictably.

When defined this broadly, the concept of potential activators is not very useful. Essentially everything becomes a potential activator, even though most have little or no impact on the individual. However, a subset of activators is sufficiently intense or frequent to qualify as stressors, or activators that can produce significant physical or psychosocial reactions. This use of the term "stressor" is analogous to that described earlier, but application of the concept of potential activators adds a new dimension. It should be possible to identify and characterize potential stressors for specific settings or individuals, by defining them in terms of their probability of being stressors. Such an approach would circumvent many of the problems of post hoc definitions of stressors and should promote more systematic attention to the conditions that make a potential stressor stressful.

20

Reactions are the biological or psychosocial responses of an individual to an activator. Like activators, reactions can occur at many different levels of complexity. Thus, drug ingestion may result in the induction of a metabolic enzyme in the liver and in changes in psychological perceptions. Other descriptors for reactions are intensity, quantity, and temporal pattern. Moving from lying to standing leads to an increase in the activity of the sympathetic nervous system, which helps to maintain blood pressure; this same system reacts far more vigorously to physical exercise or to a perceived threat. Over time, reactions to a single activator may change. Thus, the initial reaction to a honking horn may be fear of being hit by a car, followed shortly by anger that someone is following too closely for safety. Many reactions are transient and produce no notable consequences, but some are intense enough or accumulate sufficiently to produce important consequences.

Consequences are the sequellae to reactions. Distinctions between reactions and consequences are not always easy to make. The terms are used to differentiate between transient responses to specific activators (reactions) and more prolonged or cumulative effects of those reactions (consequences). Sometimes, consequences can occur after a substantial time lag. For purposes of this study, the consequences of primary interest are changes in health; but they could be any other result of the individual's reactions. Consequences can be biological, as occurs with the destruction of liver tissue as a result of carbon tetrachloride ingestion; psychological, as happens with some people who become depressed after bereavement; or sociological, as frequently occurs with paranoid schizophrenics, whose feelings of persecution make it impossible to maintain social ties. Again, consequences can occur at all levels of structural complexity from molecular and physiological through psychological and social. They also can differ from one another in intensity, quantity, and temporal pattern.

A consequence also has an evaluative component: is it desirable or undesirable relative to some social or personal standard? Many people consider ill health to be a potentially negative consequence of stressors; however, some stressors may produce positive consequences such as socially desirable personality traits or increased work productivity. If a specific activator is associated with a negative consequence, the activator is often labeled as "bad." And yet, for other individuals, that same stressor may produce reactions that yield neutral or even positive consequences. For that reason, evaluative assessments must be limited to consequences, rather than to either the responsible stressor or the intervening reaction.

The x-y-z sequence of activator to reaction to consequence can be straightforward and predictable under some circumstances. Usually, however, such simplicity occurs only under extreme conditions, like an experimental setting. Ordinarily, sequences are much more confusing. Seemingly identical potential activators may produce no reaction at all in one person, only a transient reaction in another, and an extreme reaction with marked consequences in a third. Also, they may produce different reactions for the same person as a result of changes during the life course. Basic scientists generally have tried to minimize these unpredictable variations in responses either by using only extreme stimuli that produce the desired reaction every time or by using large sample sizes so that differences between individuals cancel one another. However, the individual differences also can contain important information that can and should be studied.

Mediators are the filters and modifiers that act on each stage in the sequence to produce individual variations in the x-y-z sequence. Activators are filtered through many processes in the x-y step to reactions. Biological and psychological mediators may greatly alter the significance of a specific potential activator. Thus, a genetic defect in a metabolic enzyme may permit accumulation of a drug that normally is cleared rapidly, or strong denial may blunt the effects of an otherwise overwhelming event such as bereavement or physical injury. Physical setting also can be a mediator. Thus, the sound of footsteps approaching from behind has a much different meaning during the day in a crowd than it does at night on a lonely street. Social setting provides an additional type of mediator. The effect of a failing grade in school may be much different for a student whose family expects him not to graduate from high school than for one who plans to go to college. A grief reaction over a loss may be self-limiting in most individuals but progress to a profound depression if there is a biological or psychological predisposition.

Mediators help to explain why many people seem to experience many potential stressors without having any apparent consequences, while others react markedly and have many consequences. Appropriate methodologies for

22

animal, epidemiological, and clinical research should
make it possible to discover what mediators are important and to explore objectively how they influence the
conversion of activator to reaction or reaction to
consequence. The x-y and y-z steps probably entail
different types of mediators and may have to be studied
separately. For example, certain personality characteristics or social settings may increase the likelihood
that frustration or competition will produce marked
increases in the activity of the sympathetic nervous
system; those same mediators probably have no effect on
the consequences resulting from repeated activation of
the sympathetic system.

Of necessity, each component of the x-y-z sequence
has been discussed in static isolation. And yet interactions among these components are a crucial feature of
the model. Usually, an individual is exposed continuously to large numbers of potential activators, and the
resulting reactions interact with one another to produce
change. Each element in the sequence also continually
modifies and is modified by the other components.
Mediators help to pattern each x-y-z sequence for a
specific individual and are themselves modified by the
cumulative effects of past reactions and consequences.
Suppose, for example, that a series of reactions has
resulted in damage to the heart. That damaged heart
then becomes an important mediator that might enable the
potential stressor of intense anger to lead to a cardiac
arrhythmia and death. Such an ever-changing, inter-
linking system is not only difficult to describe but
also impossible to study in its entirety. For this
reason, investigators inevitably try to simplify the
system as much as possible by studying one small portion
at a time. It is vital to remember that such studies are
only partial approximations of what actually occurs.

References

Appley, M. H., and Trumbull, R. On the concept of psychological stress. IN: Psychological Stress: Issues in Research (Appley, M. H., and Trumbull, R., eds.) New York: Appleton-Century-Crofts, 1967, pp. 1-13.

Buell, J. C., and Eliot, R. S. Stress and cardiovascular disease. Mod. Con. Cardiovasc. Dis. 48:19-24, 1979.

Burchfield, S. R. The stress response: a new perspective. Psychosom. Med. 41:661-672, 1979.

Cannon, W. B. Stresses and strains of homeostasis. Amer. J. Med. Sci. 189:1-14, 1935.

Dimsdale, J. E., and Moss, J. Plasma catecholamines in stress and exercise. J. Amer. Med. Assoc. 243:340-342, 1980.

Glass, D. C. Behavior Patterns, Stress, and Coronary Disease New York: Wiley, 1977.

Lazarus, R. S. Psychological Stress and the Coping Process New York: McGraw Hill, 1966.

Lazarus, R. S. The concepts of stress and disease. IN: Society, Stress, and Disease: The Psychosocial Environment and Psychosomatic Diseases, Vol. I. (Levi, L., ed.) London: Oxford University Press, 1971, pp. 53-58.

Mason, J. W. A reevaluation of the concept of non-specificity in stress theory. J. Psychiatr. Res. 8:323-333, 1971.

Mason, J. W. Specificity in the organization of neuroendocrine response profiles. IN: Frontiers in Neurology and Neuroscience Research (Seeman, P., and Brown, G., eds.) Toronto: University of Toronto, 1974, pp. 68-80.

Mason, J. W. A historical view of the stress field. Part I. J. Hum. Stress 1:6-12, 1975a.

Mason, J. W. A historical view of the stress field. Part II. J. Hum. Stress 1:22-36, 1975b.

Selye, H. The Physiology and Pathology of Exposure to Stress Montreal: Acta, 1950.

Selye, H. Stress and distress. Comp. Ther. 1:9-13, 1975.

Selye, H. Forty years of stress research: principal remaining problems and misconceptions. Can. Med. Assoc. J. 115:53-56, 1976.

CHAPTER 3

Major Conclusions and Research Needs

Each panel was asked to identify specific research needs in its area of inquiry. Those detailed assessments are presented in the respective chapters. In addition, the steering committee identified several conclusions and research needs that cut across topical boundaries. These are presented below. Following some general observations, we discuss research needs for the stressor, reaction, consequence, and mediator components of the framework of stress effects and then describe promising lines of investigation into the interactions among those components. Finally, we examine several specific research strategies that may be useful in furthering stress research. We have drawn on material from the panel reports to support and illustrate those points.

General Observations about Stress and Health

Stress can have important effects on health. One of the strongest themes running through all of the panel reports is that individuals who experience a variety of disruptive events or situations are at increased risk of developing a physical or mental disorder. Such events typically are sudden and adverse, demanding a change in attitude or behavior; in many instances, there is laboratory evidence that they can be associated with at least transient physiological changes. The Stress and Environment chapters in Part II examine how such events and situations have been identified and measured for use in clinical studies of stress.

25

Part of the stress literature involves studies of people for whom the occurrence of important life events such as marriage, birth of a child, bereavement, loss of a job, or a promotion is associated with the development of a physical or mental illness at some later time. Because of the importance of this life-events approach to stress research, Chapter 4, Stress and Life Events, explores in detail the strengths and weaknesses of the method and identifies research directions that might promote a better understanding of the underlying causes for the observed associations between life events and changes in health. A complementary approach is to examine environmental settings in which individuals are likely to experience stress. As discussed in Chapter 5, Stress in Organizational Settings, and Chapter 6, Work Stress Related to Social Structures and Processes, most relevant research has entailed studies of the work place. These chapters focus both on important features of the work environment that may be stressful and on characteristics of individuals that may increase susceptibility to the adverse effects of such environments.

The Stress and Environment chapters and Chapter 9, Stress and Illness, document an association between stressors and an array of physical and mental disorders. The few available studies of the health effects of natural or man-made disasters suggest that from 50 to 90 percent of the physically unharmed survivors experience some form of acute emotional, physical, or psychosomatic consequence, and many may suffer long-term changes in health. More common events such as physical injury or bereavement or an accumulation of events, including buying a house, job loss, or retirement, also have been found to increase a person's risk for becoming ill. In addition, jobs that involve high levels of workload, responsibility, and interpersonal or role conflicts that the individual perceives to be stressful can increase the risk of becoming ill. A mismatch between an individual's skills and job demand also is a risk factor, whether the demand is too high or too low.

The range of physical and mental disorders that have been found to be associated with increased levels of life events is impressive. As detailed in Chapter 9, almost every major organ system is involved. Physical disorders for which associations with stress have been reported include colds, minor infections, bronchial asthma, peptic ulcers, hypertension, hyperthyroidism, sudden cardiac death, and cancer. Similarly, evidence suggests that stress can be a risk factor for mental disorders such as depression, schizophrenia, and alcoholism and drug abuse.

The stress response is a complex and interactive process. Simplistic concepts of stress causing disease have dominated stress research in the past. All of the panels agreed that an essential part of efforts to develop a better understanding of the influence of stress on health must be the explicit recognition of interactions among stressors, reactions, mediators, and consequences. Not only do mediators modify the reactions and consequences that follow a stressor; but those reactions and consequences change the individual, altering the mediators in ways that can affect reactions and consequences resulting from exposure to new stressors.

Studies of reactions to stressors illustrate some of the complexities of the stress response. Chapter 8, Biological Substrates of Stress, reviews several physiological systems in which reactions to a single exposure to a stressor differ markedly from those to multiple exposures to the same stressor. For example, plasma steroid levels rise dramatically when an animal is exposed to a novel stressor; this reaction decreases rapidly on repeated exposure to the same situation. However, a brisk response is again seen when a new stressor is introduced. As discussed in Chapter 7, Psychosocial Assets and Modifiers of Stress, anticipation and interpretation of events also can alter psychological reactions to them. For example, hospitalization and surgery have different meanings for different people. Although many people consider hospitalization to be stressful, those who view their usual social setting as frustrating and full of unwanted responsibilities may find it a welcome relief. Similarly, for soldiers seriously wounded in battle, surgery can mean release from the battlefield and a probable return home.

Stress in Organizational Settings (Chapter 5) emphasizes the importance of both subjective and objective evaluations of a job demand in affecting health consequences. The two interact to determine what potential stressors will occur and how the individual will respond to them. Neither in isolation can supply a complete description of the factors that contribute to associations between stressors and health changes.

Another potentially important example of the interactive aspects of the stress response is discussed in Stress and Illness (Chapter 9). Several years ago, investigators began to characterize some hypertensives as being withdrawn, uncommunicative, and anxious to avoid even appropriate confrontations. These observations led to the hypothesis that hypertension results

27

from anger directed inward, caused by an inability to express anger properly to others. More recently, however, additional data have led researchers to suggest that such behaviors might be beneficial for the hypertensive, acting as mediators to minimize reactions that would elevate blood pressure. An understanding of how such behaviors influence and are influenced by the development of hypertension might be tremendously useful in designing psychosocial preventive and treatment strategies for the disorder.

Reactions and consequences are determined by the interaction of potential stressors with mediators imposed by the individual and the setting. A frequent criticism of the stress literature is the observation that most experiences, even disturbing ones, are not associated with adverse health consequences. For a given individual, the probability that any illness will follow a single stressor is relatively low, and there seem to be few strong associations between a particular category of stressor and a specific disease consequence. Of course, similar observations could be made about cigarette smoking, which is associated with lung cancer in only a relatively small minority of those who smoke and which also is a risk factor for several other types of cancers and for heart disease. And yet smoking clearly is a risk factor for those disorders, even though the mechanisms through which it acts remain to be fully understood. The type and magnitude of reactions to stressors depend on mediators such as genetic traits, physiological condition, prior experience, current expectations, type and quality of social supports, and social context; in the same way, reactions are filtered and shaped by mediators to produce consequences.

As discussed in Biological Substrates of Stress (Chapter 8), genetic factors in stress responses have not been studied adequately, even though they can potentially influence the process at every step from the perception of external and internal stimuli as stressors to the resulting pattern of physiological reactions and the spectrum of ensuing consequences. Of special interest are interactions between genetic and environmental influences. For example, researchers have identified two strains of mice that have similar plasma steroid responses to several types of acute stressors; however, when these strains are exposed to alcohol, one shows a steroid elevation and the other shows a decline.

The importance of at least some mediators also has been shown in clinical studies, as discussed in Chapter 9. Thus, stressors usually are associated with sudden cardiac death only if there is some sort of preexisting heart pathology, typically ischemic heart disease. There also are suggestions that the association between stress and peptic ulcers is much higher among individuals who have high serum concentrations of pepsinogen, a substance secreted in the stomach. Similarly, there is little evidence that acutely stressful life events can cause schizophrenia, but such events appear to be risk factors for the occurrence of an acute episode in some people who already have a predisposition for the disorder.

Particular reactions and consequences to stressors often may be understood best when viewed in the context of the life course of individuals. Life-course processes can markedly influence the occurrence of specific potential stressors, reactions, mediators, and health consequences. Often, recognition of the importance of the life course is implicit in research designs. For example, studies of the effects of potential stressors associated with teenage pregnancy acknowledge the special physiological, psychological, and social vulnerabilities that young mothers may have. However, few investigators have begun to directly examine this potentially rich area of research.

One interesting, though controversial, finding that may reflect the importance of the life course is discussed both in Stress and Illness (Chapter 9) and in Stress and Life Events (Chapter 4). Some investigators have suggested that, if a parent dies when children are less than 11 years old, they are much more likely to suffer from depression as adults. Some reports, discussed in Psychosocial Assets and Modifiers (Chapter 7), suggest that stressors may be associated with much more serious consequences if they occur at unexpected times during the life course than if they happen at more customary times. Thus, bereavement may be associated with a greater incidence of physical and mental distress among women who are widowed in their thirties than among those who become widows in their sixties.

Stressors, reactions, and mediators are neither "good" nor "bad"; only consequences can appropriately be qualified as being desirable or undesirable. Common

29

emotional reactions that people have during stress include fear, anger, and unhappiness; it is not surprising, therefore, that many people attach negative descriptors to the stressors themselves. Furthermore, much of stress research explicitly seeks connections between stressful events and such undesirable consequences as illness. In fact, many investigators define stressors as those events or situations that are associated with increased incidences of illness. However, as discussed in Biological Substrates of Stress (Chapter 8), animal studies illustrate the limitations of such an approach. In mice, social isolation decreases resistance to some types of viral infections but increases resistance to others. It seems difficult to argue that social isolation is a stressor in the former case but not in the latter. Similarly, animals respond very differently to identical amounts of shock, depending on whether they have the ability to escape it. Those who cannot escape become passive and fail to attempt to escape when subsequently reexposed to shock--a phenomenon called "learned helplessness." Again, it does not seem reasonable to define only the inescapable shock as a stressor.

Reactions to stressors also receive inappropriate evaluative labels. The body permits a wide range of transient reactions in response to a stressor; but changes in blood pressure, hormone levels, immune function, emotional states, and behavior do not necessarily produce undesirable consequences. No compelling evidence exists to suggest, for example, that transient changes in blood pressure as a reaction to stress contribute to the development of hypertension. Even if such a relationship were found for some individuals, it is still the consequence of hypertension that is undesirable, not the initial reaction of elevated blood pressure. For many years, certain types of psychological reactions such as denial and hostility were thought to be maladaptive. Although they may contribute to adverse consequences under some circumstances, they may be associated with positive outcomes under other conditions. Thus, some evidence suggests that people who are strong deniers are more likely to survive the acute phase of a heart attack and that cancer patients who manifest high levels of hostility may live longer than those expressing less hostility.

Perhaps one of the best-known mediators in the stress field is Type A behavior, which refers to a cluster of traits including high levels of aggressiveness and competitiveness and a constant sense of time urgency. A

number of studies of men have shown that, compared with
Type B people, in whom these traits are much less apparent, Type A individuals are at significantly greater
risk of having a heart attack at an early age. These
traits are thought to alter the way Type A people react
to stressors. But, this cluster of mediators has not
been shown to be associated with hypertension, and its
relationship to other negative health consequences
remains to be determined. Type A behavior is likely to
be identified with a number of socially desirable consequences, including success in the workplace. Thus, this
cluster of mediators is neither good nor bad. Rather, it
is a useful predictor of certain types of consequences
that may be more or less desirable.

Research Needs on Components of the Stress Response

Stress research will greatly benefit from clear distinctions among stressors, reactions, consequences, and
mediators. Most investigators agree that certain extreme
events are uniformly disruptive. But efforts to define
"stress" and "stressor" under more usual circumstances
continue to foster controversies, because reactions can
vary greatly for different individuals and settings. The
committee was struck by the pervasiveness of definitional
problems throughout the stress field. Particularly apparent are the differences between the types of stressors
that are used in basic animal research and those that
are usually studied in people.

As discussed in Chapter 8, Biological Substrates of
Stress, many biological scientists are interested primarily in the physiological system being studied and use
stressors as tools to manipulate that system. Electric
shock, food deprivation, loud noises, and novel situations are among the many stressors that investigators
apply in the laboratory setting in efforts to learn how
the body and brain work. In such a setting, mediators
are seldom of concern, because the stressors are chosen
to ensure that as many test subjects as possible will
react. Also, potential consequences are of only minor
interest. The primary emphasis is on mechanisms that
produce acute reactions of the system to stressors (x-y).

In contrast to biological investigators, many psychological and social scientists have focused on natural
settings in which the stressors being studied are life
events. As discussed in Conceptual Issues of Stress
Research (Chapter 2) and in Psychosocial Assets and

31

Modifers (Chapter 7), such stressors may be discrete and time-limited, like parachute jumping or awaiting surgery; sequences of events such as the series of life changes that follow a divorce or job loss; intermittently recurrent, as in the case of sexual difficulties or conflict-filled visits to relatives; or chronic, as with permanent physical disabilities or chronic job stress. Attention has usually focused on associations between stressors and consequences (x-z) or on psychosocial reactions to stressors (x-y).

Different parts of the stress field are using the term "stress" to refer to distinctly different events and situations. Most areas of research have developed implicit or explicit conventions about what constitutes stress, but these appear to vary markedly across disciplines. Lack of clarity about what is being studied has contributed greatly to confusion in the field. At present, researchers should, as completely as possible, describe the stressors being studied, differentiate stressors from ensuing reactions and consequences, and identify mediators that may affect stressor-to-reaction (x-y) and reaction-to-consequence (y-z) sequences.

Many events, conditions, and settings are potential stressors (x); much more must be learned about the critical determinants that actually make them stressful. As discussed in Conceptual Issues of Stress Research (Chapter 2), early concepts of stress suggested that the characteristics of the stressor were not important because the resulting physiological response seemed to be nonspecific. Many basic scientists have selected stressors on the basis of familiarity and convenience, with little attention to whether the stimuli are interchangeable. However, some work suggests that many of the physiological effects that severe stressors produce are strongly mediated by the psychological perception of them as noxious or alarming. When those emotional responses are absent, the same stressors produce smaller, or even opposite effects.

Critics of the field charge that stress research is tautological: stressors are those events that are bad because they are associated with unwanted consequences. Presently, it usually is true that stressors cannot be defined independently of the individual or context. However, a complete understanding of the potential stressors and of relevant mediators would lead to accurate predictions concerning reactions and conse-

32

quences. Studies of a range of stressors could produce
needed information about what descriptors help to make
an event or situation stressful. Such data should permit
the compilation of lists of potential stressors that have
a reasonable probability of being stressors in specific
settings. Such a probabilistic approach could promote a
better understanding of important characteristics of
potential stressors and open new avenues of research as
investigators explore what reactions and what desirable
and undesirable consequences are associated with those
potential stressors under particular conditions.

Basic research in the neurosciences, psychology, and
sociology has identified many mechanisms through which
stressors might act to produce reactions. Specific
research is needed on the effects of stressors on those
mechanisms. From its inception, the stress research has
depended heavily on the investigative tools of many disciplines. Often, the complexities of the interactions
between stress and health have surpassed the limits of
available techniques for measuring physiological, psychological, and social changes. A number of recent
developments in basic research provide a rich new
resource of techniques that have yet to be applied to
problems in stress.

Much of the literature reviewed in Chapter 8, Biological Substrates of Stress, is not formally identified
as stress research. In the past few years, scientists
have made impressive strides both in elucidating
important regulatory mechanisms for a large number of
physiological systems and in improving techniques for
studying those systems in animals and humans. Until
recently neuroscientists had identified only a few dozen
substances that seemed to be involved in transferring
information between nerve cells. Now, the number of
possible neuroregulators has risen to several hundred,
many of which may be involved in reactions to stress.
One of the most clearly relevant group of compounds are
the endorphins, endogenous peptides that appear to be
involved in brain regulation of pain perception and
response. Also of interest is recent evidence that the
immune system may be influenced directly by brain
activity. Mechanisms for such an effect remain to be
established, but they suggest new ways in which stressors
might alter health.

Techniques for quantification of biological and physiological changes are improving rapidly. In the early

33

days of stress research, researchers often looked for a reaction by weighing a gland such as the adrenal or thymus or looking for pathological changes such as stomach ulcers. Newly developed biological, fluorimetric, chromatographic, mass spectrometric, enzymatic, and radioimmunologic assays now enable investigators to assay minute amounts of neuroregulators and their metabolites. In addition, it now is possible to study in living animals and humans many basic regulatory mechanisms that affect physiological reactions. For example, in animals, a tiny needle can be implanted in precise areas of the brain, through which small samples of brain neuroregulators can be removed for assay; or, using the same implant, compounds can be administered locally to interfere with neuroregulator function at that site. In humans, investigators can constantly monitor the function of the heart or electrical activity of the brain or repeatedly remove small samples of blood for study without interfering with normal behavior.

Important advances also have been made in the psychological and social sciences. Stress and Life Events (Chapter 4) documents the careful scrutiny that investigators are giving one of the basic approaches to clinical research in stress. There is an increased awareness that for many illnesses, life events may be the result of the disease process, rather than its cause. For example, someone who is becoming depressed may have difficulties that could lead to a divorce or to the loss of a job, even before the depression becomes clinically evident. The development of reliable methods for disentangling stressors that are followed by health changes from stressors that result from such changes is crucial for continued progress in stress research.

Stress in Organizational Settings (Chapter 5) and Psychosocial Assets and Modifiers (Chapter 7) also discuss important areas of study in the psychological and social sciences that may be useful for stress researchers. For example, there is a need for a conceptual language to describe stress-relevant aspects of organizations. Such a conceptual framework must accommodate at least three levels of abstraction--the organization itself, its functional parts, and the specific positions or roles that individuals encounter. Also important are continuing efforts to evaluate stressors that are not included in most life events scales. Existing research methods typically exclude both chronic stress situations and acute stressors that do not involve major life changes. Some studies already indicate that chronic conditions such as sex role conflicts, unequal status between spouses, and inappropriate work load are risk factors for adverse health consequences.

Many major and minor disease consequences have been associated with stressors. Efforts to identify health changes that are associated with exposure to stressors should continue, particularly with respect to positive or neutral health consequences. The important step made in establishing the existence of associations between stress and disease must be extended to other types of potential relationships. The initial belief that stressors cause disease has resulted almost exclusively in studies that test that assumption. Other important consequences also should be studied. The problems of determining which outcomes to measure are discussed in Work Stress Related to Social Structures and Processes (Chapter 6) and Psychosocial Assets and Modifiers (Chapter 7).

The way an individual deals with stress may differentially affect physical health, psychological well-being, and social functioning. Most studies have considered only the matter of physical or mental health. For example, although Type A behavior correlates with an increased risk for heart disease, it may also be associated with a sense of personal satisfaction and community respect. Thus, increased risk might be found only in the physiological domain, and positive consequences may predominate for other types of consequences. Shift work requires employees to work during the day part of the week or month and during the evening or nights during the rest of the time. Shift work is a risk factor for a variety of adverse health consequences; yet, from the perspective of society, it has the desirable consequence of increased productivity. Also, individual workers may vary in their adaptation to the change in the usual work cycle. Identification of patterns of consequences associated with a single stressor or group of stressors might offer a better understanding of the cumulative effects of stressors and facilitate efforts to make informed decisions about how to balance those that are wanted with those that are not.

Mediators play a crucial role in determining how individuals react to stressors and what health consequences those reactions produce. Investigators need to study various types of mediators and to identify which systems they affect. Research on mediators may suggest

35

ways to identify individuals who are most likely to have
a particular reaction or consequence to a specific stressor. Such information could be of great diagnostic and
therapeutic value. This area of study is particularly
intertwined with advances in related basic sciences; it
depends on a detailed understanding of the regulation of
physiological and psychosocial mechanisms through which
stressors produce reactions and consequences.

Several research areas described in Biological Substrates of Stress (Chapter 8) may help to identify
mediators of the stress response. Genetic factors may
be important mediators of the stressor-to-reaction (x-y)
step in some instances. For example, in inbred strains
of mice, excretion of catecholamines and corticosteroids
in response to stress appears to be under strong genetic
control; other physiological reactions may be under
similar control. Genetic studies should be integrated
with studies of other mediators. For example, a low-fat
diet unmasked marked differences in steroid breakdown
between two strains of mice that did not differ on a
high-fat diet.

A few investigators have begun to examine the effects
of social mediators on physiological reactions to stressors. For example, when members of a group work on a
collective task, they evolve patterns of interaction
that reflect differences in the distribution of power
and prestige among them, so that objectively measurable
differences in status emerge during the interaction.
Experimental studies of such small-group interactions
suggest that this status ranking may affect physiological
responses of the participants to the stressful situation.
There is no relationship between acquired status and
catecholamine concentrations in urinary samples taken
before the interactions, but test subjects with higher
acquired status have higher epinephrine and lower norepinephrine in samples taken at the end of the test. Thus,
something in the test situation, possibly relating to
the social interactions, alters the perception of or
reaction to the stressors involved. The relevance of
such results to normal social situations remains to be
established.

Studies of mediators will demand sophisticated
methods for detecting and quantitating important
psychological and social factors. Limitations of
existing methodologies are discussed in Psychosocial
Assets and Modifiers (Chapter 7). For example, more
precise measures are needed of social networks and

supports. Some studies suggest that individuals who
have strong social supports are at decreased risk for
having some negative health consequences, including
heart disease. As mentioned earlier, the Type A behavior
pattern has received considerable attention. Probably,
only some of the cluster of personality characteristics
used to define Type A behavior account for the increased
risk for certain adverse health consequences. For
example, some investigators have suggested that hostile
competition may play a key role. It should be possible
to refine analyses of those mediators and determine
which are important and which are incidental.

Research Needs on Connections Between Stress Components

Better estimates are needed of the magnitude by which
stressors increase the risk of such adverse health consequences as physical illnesses and mental disorders.
Many people are skeptical about reports of associations
between stressors and changes in health. Often, they are
unable to understand how a psychological phenomenon like
stress could cause physiological malfunction. However,
a link between a stressor and an illness need not imply
that the stressor causes the illness. The medical profession has become increasingly aware of the value of
identifying individuals who may be likely to develop a
particular disease. The evidence may suggest a course
of preventive action even if the exact mechanisms for
the association are poorly understood. For example,
antismoking efforts were a direct response to finding an
association between cigarette smoking and a number of
adverse health consequences. The utility of a risk-
factor approach in the stress field is discussed in
Stress and Illness (Chapter 9).

Simultaneous consideration of several risk factors
may help to improve the predictive power and specificity
of this approach. For example, studies of military
inductees found that a subgroup who had high pepsinogen
secretion and psychological profiles indicating major,
unresolved conflicts over dependency and oral gratification were especially at risk for developing peptic ulcers
during training. The coexistence of these physiological
and psychological characteristics was a much stronger
risk factor than was either of the measures alone.

Existing research on physiological and psychosocial
reactions to extreme stressors provides a good foundation

37

for exploring the stressor-to-reaction sequence. Further studies are needed to examine how stressor characteristics and specific mediators influence reactions under less extreme conditions. This research is a logical extension of studies of the individual components. As the relevant features of stressors, reactions, and mediators are better understood, it should be possible to explore the precise ways in which they interact. For example, as described in Biological Substrates of Stress (Chapter 8), animal studies have shown that psychological state can markedly affect reactions and consequences to a physical stressor such as electric shock. Animals receiving unsignaled shocks have a much higher incidence of stomach ulcers, decreased body weight, and increased plasma steroids than do animals receiving the same number of signaled shocks. In fact, animals sometimes have chosen signaled shock that is four to nine times longer and two to three times more intense than unsignaled shock. Studies of people confirm that subjects given a choice will choose predictable over unpredictable shock, even when no escape from shock is possible.

Studies reviewed in Stress in Organizational Settings (Chapter 5) also suggest that the x-y transition from stressor to reaction can be understood best in the context of relevant mediators. Thus, reports of symptoms in reaction to role conflict in the work setting are more common among individuals who are flexible and extroverted than among those who are rigid, introverted, and emotionally sensitive. In addition, jobs that require frequent communication appear to exacerbate reactions to role conflict, producing greater intensity of experienced conflict, decreased job satisfaction, heightened sense of role ambiguity, increased sense of futility in the work role, and deterioration in interpersonal relations.

Research on the reaction-to-consequence step has lagged far behind other aspects of stress research. Research techniques are needed for investigating this crucial step in stress-related illnesses. The committee was unable to identify an instance in which the reaction-to-consequence (y-z) step of an illness was established. A typical example of this gap is seen in studies of the effects of stress on the immune system. As reviewed in Stress and Illness (Chapter 9), several studies suggest that stressors are risk factors for many types of infections, for rheumatoid arthritis, and for some forms of cancer. As described in Biological Substrates of Stress

38

(Chapter 8), stressors can induce changes in immune function. However, these two types of research usually are done independently, even when they involve studies of the same stressor. For example, some investigators have reported that bereavement is a risk factor for increased mortality from a number of causes. Bereavement also has been found to suppress the function of several components of the immune system. Yet, no one has shown that these two sets of observations are related. Studies of this y-z step are vital, because they can help to identify those reactions that are relevant to health consequences. If the mechanism through which such reactions act can be determined, it may be possible to design preventive or treatment strategies to selectively block the undesirable consequences with minimal side effects.

Mediators also can have important effects on the transition from reaction to consequence. Often, mediators may be facilitators that increase the likelihood of the occurrence of a possible reaction or consequence. Mediators also may be an essential part of the response. In Stress and Illness (Chapter 9), stressors that predispose to a disorder are distinguished from those that may precipitate or perpetuate it. Thus, acute stressors such as those measured in life event scales do not seem to predispose to schizophrenia; however, they can exacerbate or precipitate a new psychotic episode in vulnerable individuals. This suggests that a mediating factor sensitizes schizophrenics to particular stress reactions.

There is a need for interdisciplinary studies of the entire sequence from stressor through reaction to consequence. Subspecialization has fostered advances in many disciplines; but, as a result, few scientists now possess the range of expertise needed to study connections between stress and health. Stress researchers usually minimize the complex interdependence among components of the stress response by studying individual components of the interaction. More complete studies of the interconnections among these components are needed.

Pain research provides a good illustration of the wide range of disciplines that may be needed to explore relationships between stress and health consequences. Pain pervades many aspects of stress. It is a common reaction to a wide variety of stressors and is an important element in many major disorders. Some of the questions that confront investigators who are trying to uncover the biological concomitants of pain are explored

39

in Biological Substrates of Stress (Chapter 8). Advances
already made in understanding pain mechanisms have
involved contributions from neurophysiology, neurology,
neurochemistry, anesthesiology, and many other fields.
In addition, personality and other psychosocial factors
play a major role in the perception of and reaction to
pain, as discussed in Psychosocial Assets and Modifiers
(Chapter 7). The meaning of the pain for the patient
may greatly alter the magnitude and type of response.
In addition, social background can markedly influence
the amount of pain that an individual will report.

Some Research Strategies for Stress Research

Some studies of associations between stressors and
physical or mental disorders will require prospective,
longitudinal designs. The Department of Health and Human
Services should create an interdisciplinary over-sight
group to foster, fund, and coordinate such projects.
Much of the literature that establishes stress as a risk
factor for disease has been retrospective. Such studies
have severe methodological limitations, including potential biases about which subjects are studied, incomplete
information, psychological factors resulting from the
disease process, and possible selectivity in patient
recall of past events. For example, many people with
phobias will state that they became fearful as a result
of a stressful encounter; however, careful study often
fails to document such reported encounters. Similarly, a
depressed patient may describe vividly an incident that
precipitated the depression, even though others who were
present do not remember it as being particularly
significant at the time.

The need for prospective, longitudinal studies to
settle important questions in the stress field is
mentioned repeatedly in Stress and Illness (Chapter 9).
Longitudinal studies are of particular interest to researchers studying stress and mental disorders. The
Stress and Illness panel concluded that significant
advances in diagnostic precision and in accurate and
reliable measures of outcome provide the necessary
clinical tools for such a project and that an improved
understanding of genetic, biochemical, psychological,
and social factors for disorders such as schizophrenia,
depression, phobias, and drug and alcohol abuse provides
clues about possible risk factors. Such studies could
yield a wealth of data with both basic and therapeutic
potential. Initial data collection would provide useful

cross-sectional information about the level of exposure
individuals experience for a number of environmental
factors that might affect mental health; subsequent
collections would generate data about who gets ill, how
such illnesses correlate with what has happened to them
in the past, and how physical and mental illness
interact with one another.

Although they can be valuable, longitudinal studies
are expensive. For that reason, the steering committee
believes that a centralized group of scientists and
clinicians should be established to monitor them. Such
an oversight group could help to maximize the yield of
each study by combining related questions, where possible; by encouraging uniformity across studies; by
requiring use of appropriate past, current, and future
cohort controls; and by stimulating more extensive use
of existing study populations.

Research on the influence of the life course on reactions to and consequences of exposure to stressors should
be encouraged. Scientists have begun to appreciate the
potential effects on the stress response of the many physiological, psychological, and social changes that occur
throughout the life course. Loss of a parent through
death or the experience of a major economic depression
may evoke quite different reactions and consequences from
a child than from an adult. Furthermore, vulnerability
to adverse consequences can be exacerbated by changes
that accompany aging, including accumulation of chronic
diseases and disabilities. Mediators such as available
coping strategies, physiological resilience, and parental
or spouse support also vary over the life course. Yet,
with rare exceptions, stress research has not been viewed
from a life-course perspective. Analyses of changes in
the effects of stressors over the life course may uncover
important biological and psychosocial mechanisms and
highlight key mediators of the x-y and y-z steps.

As described in Stress in Organizational Settings
(Chapter 5), school and work may offer valuable natural
laboratories for some types of studies of the life
course. Child and adolescent development include moving
from dependence on family members to independent living;
learning to function as a useful member of society; and
completing a series of physical, psychological, and
social developmental stages. For most children in the
United States, the arena in which much of these changes
occur is school. It should be possible to learn how

41

schools prepare pupils for their role in adult organizational settings such as the work place and how they affect reactions to stressors in other organizational settings later in life.

Physical and psychological changes that occur with aging may increase vulnerability to adverse consequences to stressors. As discussed in Stress and Illness (Chapter 9), the elderly face many adverse life events, including changes in income and employment, loss of loved ones, and increased dependence on others. The cognitive losses associated with even the early stages of dementia also may greatly limit available coping strategies, thereby exacerbating the effects of stressors on the individual. Some chronic conditions may be tolerated well until these added stressors or the aging process deplete resources so severely that the individual can no longer cope with them. Far more must be learned about how events earlier in the life course affect abilities to cope with stressors in later life and about ways in which environmental factors and longstanding patterns of adaptation are mediators of the stress response.

Consideration should be given to forming one or more interdisciplinary teams trained to investigate rapidly and systematically the consequences of severe, natural or man-made stressors. Most of the panels called for studies of the health consequences that people experience after they have been exposed to transient but severe stressors such as natural or man-made disasters. Such events provide unique opportunities to examine the consequences of acute stressors that are far more severe than those that can be administered in the laboratory. Typically, efforts to study the secondary health effects of disasters have been too late or too poorly designed to yield useful data. Prepared research teams could organize in advance for studies in such extreme situations, so that they could react immediately to a variety of possible disasters. They could collect invaluable data on entire populations about short- and long-term reactions to and consequences of floods, nuclear accidents, earthquakes, and other extreme conditions and also could provide a mechanism for testing new preventive and therapeutic intervention strategies.

The steering committee was aware that past efforts to maintain groups to study disasters have failed or been discontinued. A complete exploration of the reasons for those failures was beyond the scope of this project. A

42

thorough analysis of previous attempts to foster studies
of major disasters might identify the elements necessary
for success of a new initiative.

As research suggests useful treatment and prevention
strategies, these should be tested rigorously. The
steering committee did not attempt to review the many
strategies being used to prevent or treat stress-related
disease consequences. However, the group did ask each
panel to consider how research in its area might relate
to intervention methods. The panels and the steering
committee concurred that, ideally, specific intervention
strategies would be designed on the basis of an understanding of the connection between stress reactions and
disease consequences (y-z). Without that information,
it is impossible to state with certainty which reactions
should be altered and what the side effects might be.
However, successful prevention programs in other areas
have been based on associational (x-z) data such as the
link between cigarette smoking and lung cancer or between
high blood pressure and heart disease. Carefully designed intervention trials in those and other areas not
only have identified useful preventive measures but also
have helped to uncover leads for establishing the x-y and
y-z steps involved. A comparable study within stress
research is the current effort to examine the effects on
heart disease of modifying certain aspects of the Type A
behavior pattern.

It should be possible to identify subpopulations that
seem to be particularly vulnerable to the effects of
specific stressors. Several examples of potentially
relevant mediators have already been mentioned. Thus,
high pepsinogen secretion may identify a subgroup of
individuals who are at increased risk of developing peptic ulcers following exposure to stressors. Associations
between stressors and suicide also may involve individual
vulnerability. As a group, those who attempt suicide
have a higher incidence of personality disorders, with
character traits such as impulsivity and chronic anger;
some evidence suggests that suicide victims are characterized by feelings of guilt and inferiority, anxiety,
depressed mood, and suicidal ideation. Studies of the
mechanisms through which such mediators act might suggest
approaches for developing selective interventions.

Intervention studies that utilize knowledge about
both stressor-to-reaction and reaction-to-consequence
steps should be an integral part of stress research.

43

However, until the results of such research are available, caution should be used in sponsoring untested methods intended to avoid adverse consequences associated with exposure to stressors. This is particularly true because so much remains to be learned about concomitant positive effects and underlying mechanisms.

Further studies are needed of the impact that changes in social settings such as the workplace or schools can have on exposure to or consequences of stressors on individuals. Generally, investigators in the stress field have focused on the individual. However, as discussed in Stress in Organizational Settings (Chapter 5) and in Work Stress Related to Social Structures and Processes (Chapter 6), the social context in which stressors occur also may be directly relevant. Research suggests that such work-related stressors as monotony, automation, shift work, inappropriate work load, and inadequate support systems are associated with adverse health consequences for a large number of individuals exposed to them.

Evidence suggests that it may be possible to improve the ways in which people adapt their work environments to their abilities and needs. Most hypotheses about useful changes in work conditions have yet to be tested adequately even on a small scale, particularly with the interdisciplinary evaluations needed to determine the positive and negative consequences that may ensue in terms both of individual health and of social demands. Among those interventions that appear to merit further research are: increasing a worker's control of the work arrangements; providing mechanisms for worker participation in decision making on the organization of work; avoiding monotonous, machine-paced, and short but frequent work actions; optimizing automation; helping workers to see their specific tasks in relation to the total product; avoiding quantitative work overload or underload; and fostering good communication and support systems among workmates and others. More information about these and other interventions should make it possible to explore difficult but critical issues about the balance between social needs for productivity and individual requirements for good physical and mental health. Evidence already suggests that in some instances adequate understanding of the stressful aspects of a work setting may permit improvements in both.

More systematic efforts are needed to identify and characterize stress-related research. As discussed in

44

Appendix A, Patterns of Financial Support of Health-
Related Stress Research, investigators have no readily
available way to learn what kinds of stress research are
receiving support, especially for topics that cross
disciplinary lines. In the United States, most stress
research is federally funded through the member institutes of the Alcohol, Drug Abuse, and Mental Health
Administration (ADAMHA) and the National Institutes of
Health (NIH), with lesser sums coming from other parts of
the Public Health Service, from the Department of Defense
(DOD), and from the National Science Foundation (NSF).

The committee used three data bases to obtain information about funding of stress research. The Smithsonian
Science Information Exchange is a voluntary service that
includes information from both governmental and nongovernmental sources; the NIH Information for Management,
Planning Analysis, and Coordination system contains
information primarily for NIH and ADAMHA; and the Department of Defense Technical Information Service lists only
studies that are supported by DOD. Each of these systems
categorizes stress under different terms and uses different criteria for identifying stress-relateld studies.
Use of a single scheme for classifying stress research
by all federal agencies and development of a centralized
compilation of current research would provide a valuable
resource for the field. Such a system should include
studies that were not funded as stress research but are
relevant to the field.

PART II

PANEL REPORTS

INTRODUCTION TO THE
PANEL REPORTS

A growing literature, beginning with the classic studies by Holmes and Rahe, leaves little doubt that people who experience a number of life events--usually sudden, mostly adverse, and demanding some change in attitude or behavior--are at increased risk of physical or mental illness. Not everyone becomes ill following a succession even of major losses such as deaths of several loved ones within a brief period of time; and no guidelines yet exist for distinguishing between those who will and will not develop an illness. Much work is needed to clarify how the usually transient changes in endocrine, neurophysiological, autonomic, or immunological functions associated with exposure to stressful stimuli sometimes produce more enduring alterations that lead to disease. Still, the evidence is compelling that a significant number of those who experience a major stressful event will have negative health consequences within a few months.

The following chapters were prepared for the steering committee by panels, each of which was co-chaired by two members of the committee. The panels were created to examine in detail the accomplishments and promise of major areas of stress research. The areas were chosen, in part, to reflect different approaches to the study of stress, including biological, psychological, sociological, and medical. But, members of each panel were selected to bring a variety of relevant disciplines to bear on the issues. Each panel was encouraged to cover all topics that were germane to its area. As a result, some topics in stress research are discussed by several groups. In such instances, the disciplinary perspective of each panel highlighted somewhat different aspects of the field and helped to ensure the identification of a full range of promising directions for future studies.

The three Stress and Environment panel reports (Chapters 4-6) critically examine some of the underpinnings of the research on associations between stressors with changes in health. Much of the clinical work in stress research has emphasized acute life changes. Chapter 4, Stress and Life Events, points out that the occurrence of such events often is not random. Factors such as age and socioeconomic status can alter the probability that certain events will occur. Much of the existing research confounds event and outcome. The origins and significance of life events such as getting a divorce, being fired, or having sexual difficulties may differ markedly from those for events that are totally outside the individual's control, such as death of a spouse or retirement. Chapter 5, Stress in Organizational Settings, explores some of the research potential of the work and school settings. For many, work or school is the epitome of a chronically stressful condition, and one in which they spend most of their waking hours. They could provide laboratories for studying what does and does not happen to health as a result of such conditions. Chapter 6, Work Stress Related to Social Structures and Processes, describes studies of the workplace being conducted in Scandinavia. Such factors as shift work, piece work, automation, and inappropriate task load not only appear to be physiologically arousing but also are associated with greater subjective distress and even risk for illness. Furthermore, the data suggest that deliberate interventions may help to increase job satisfaction and health without markedly decreasing job performance.

Chapter 7, Psychosocial Assets and Modifiers, begins the transition from asking whether stressful events can affect health to examining the factors that influence such effects. Both psychological and social conditions appear to be important mediators in determining what an individual will perceive as stressful and how intense and prolonged the reactions to a stressor will be. An adequate understanding of how these factors affect the stress response could explain much about individual variability in the reactions to and consequences of stressors. Such information could form the basis for greatly improved treatment and prevention efforts in reducing adverse effects from stress.

Biological Substrates of Stress, Chapter 8, continues to explore how stressors can alter health. In the past few years, scientists have gained a much better understanding of brain function and have begun to elucidate the ways in which it can monitor and affect other organ systems in the body, including the heart, lungs, endocrine system, pain system, and immune system. There are many opportunities for research to discover how a stressful event produces changes in bodily function that can result in a disease consequence.

Finally, Chapter 9, Stress and Illness, assesses research literature relating stress to specific major physical and mental disorders. The data suggest that stressors can be risk factors for such disorders as heart disease, peptic ulcer disease, cancer, bronchial asthma, depression, and schizophrenia. Depending on the disorder, stressors may be predisposing factors, may precipitate the disease in people who already are at risk, or may perpetuate it once the disease is present. The evidence suggests that there is little specificity between certain stressors and particular disease outcomes. Furthermore, almost nothing is known about the intervening chain of biological and psychosocial events that convert reactions to stressors into disease consequences.

PANEL REPORTS ON STRESS AND ENVIRONMENT

Panel Chairs:
Robert Kahn, Ph.D.
Robert Rose, M.D.

CHAPTER 4

Report on
Stress and
Life Events

Panel Members:
Bruce Dohrenwend, Ph.D., Co-chair
Leonard Pearlin, Ph.D., Co-chair
Paula Clayton, M.D.   Matilda Riley, D.Sc.
Betty Hamburg, M.D.   Robert M. Rose, M.D.
    Barbara Dohrenwend, Ph.D., Advisor

There is abundant evidence that stressful events are related to adverse changes in health. Indirect evidence comes from laboratory experiments in which healthy animals are exposed to such noxious stimuli as electric shock, frigid temperature, or social overcrowding. As described in Chapter 8, Biological Substrates of Stress, such animals regularly evidence physiological and psychological pathology. For example, inescapable shock is associated with consequences like passive acceptance of avoidable punishment, stomach ulcers, and sudden death.

More direct evidence for an association between stressors and adverse health consequences comes from research on the effects of natural and man-made disasters. Thus, when Fritz and Marks (1954) interviewed a sample of the population in a rural section of Arkansas that had been hit by a severe tornado, 90 percent of those questioned reported that they had experienced acute emotional, physical, or psychosomatic consequences. More recently, Terr (1979) studied a group of normal children who had been kidnapped and terrorized for 36 hours before escaping. Although no one was physically harmed, ten of the 26 children suffered severe post-traumatic symptomatology (cf. Chapter 9, Stress and Illness). Five months after the incident, 19 had undergone a major personality change, 14 continued to reenact the kidnapping, and 8 had declining school performance.

Fortunately, most people never experience such severe stressors as natural disasters. However, there is evidence that more common events such as the death of a loved one, birth of a first child, divorce, or loss of a job also are associated with adverse changes in health. Furthermore, their effects are additive, so that the occurrence of several such events in a short time period increases the risk of becoming ill. Major life events have been shown to be related to somatic disorders, including heart disease (Hinkle, 1974; Theorell, 1974) and childhood leukemia (Holmes and Masuda, 1974); to psychological performance deficits (Holmes and Masuda, 1974); and to mental disorders, including acute schizophrenia (Brown and Birley, 1968), depression (Brown and Harris, 1978; Paykel, 1974), and suicide attempts (Paykel, 1974). Many more examples of such associations are cited throughout this report.

The literature shows clearly that not everyone who is exposed to a stressor or series of stressors will have adverse health effects. As discussed in Chapter 9, Stress and Illness, this has led to the conceptualization of stressors as risk factors for illness. To date, few efforts have been made to determine precisely how much stressful life events increase the risk for a specific illness. One recent study examined exposure to chronically stressful conditions as a risk factor for heart disease. In a retrospective study, Orth-Gomer and Ahlbom (1980) examined a group of male Swedish workers. They compared patients who recently had had a heart attack or developed angina with normal controls and with subjects who had no known heart disease but were matched with the test subjects for such risk factors as hypertension, high cholesterol, and smoking. Study participants were questioned about chronically stressful events during the previous five years. The test subjects were significantly more likely than either of the control groups to have experienced one or more periods of great stress lasting at least six months. When the group matched for other risk factors was used as a control, the occurrence of such a stressful period increased the risk for heart attack or angina threefold; with the normal control group, there was a sixfold increase in risk.

This panel took as its charge an exploration of the theoretical underpinnings for relating stressful life events to health consequences. Panel members agreed that the accumulated evidence for such associations now is so strong that simple application of old methods to new settings no longer is warranted. The group selected four issues that seemed to merit particular attention in life events research at this time:

56

- Sources of life events. What social and economic factors influence the occurrence and distribution of life events?

- Mediators of life events. Why do even severe stressors leave some people relatively untouched, when much milder events can affect other people adversely?

- Hypotheses about the life stress process. What conceptual models can help to organize information about this process?

- Strategic alternatives for life events research. What are the relative strengths and weaknesses of and appropriate uses for available research designs?

The remainder of this chapter explores each of these topics, with special emphasis on identifying important areas that have been relatively neglected. Some of the issues chosen overlap with material discussed in other panels. This is hardly surprising, since life events constitute a major focus of most clinical stress research. The group did not undertake an extensive review of the life-events literature, because many of those studies were considered in depth by other panels. We focused, instead, on the methodological issues of how life-events research has been and should be done.

Life Events and Their Contexts

People's lives are organized around roles such as those of spouse, parent, and worker, each of which provides some continuity of circumstances and experience. One important source of stressors can be persistent problems that arise within such roles as marriage or work. Research aspects of work stress are discussed in the next two chapters. This group looked at what happens when life events diverge from the familiar and comfortable. Although few individuals anticipate the occurrence of a life event in their own lives, such events are neither anomalous nor rare in the context of an entire population. In fact, many events such as bereavement or retirement result from usual changes during the life course and, therefore, eventually are experienced by nearly everyone. Other experiences are a translation to the individual of events that take place

57

in the larger society, for example, a job loss as a
result of a widespread downturn in the economy.

Combinations of recent stressful life events such
as death of a loved one, birth of a first child, loss of
a job, or divorce increase the risk of having physical
and mental illness (Dohrenwend and Dohrenwend, 1974;
Gunderson and Rahe, 1974; Rabkin and Struening, 1976;
Rahe and Arthur, 1978). However, important conceptual
and methodological problems must be solved if these
relationships are to be understood better. The key
problem is to define life events in ways that permit
quantitative measurement of their effects independent of
a concomitant physical or mental disorder. Furthermore,
large individual differences in reactions to stressors
suggest that powerful mediating factors must influence
the intervening steps between exposure to stressors and
development of specific health consequences. Therefore,
efforts to learn more about associations between life
events and changes in health status will involve identifying and characterizing such mediators.

Relationships between life stressors and illness
can be described in a variety of ways, as illustrated by
the bewildering array of diagrams that have appeared in
the literature (Brown and Harris, 1978; Cobb, 1974;
Dohrenwend and Dohrenwend, 1980; Jenkins, 1979; Levi,
1974; Rahe, 1974; and Warheit, 1979). All of these
schemata necessarily oversimplify reality. Depending on
the aspects that they emphasize, some may be more useful
in particular research settings than are others. As
described in Chapter 2, Conceptual Issues in Stress
Research, the steering committee adopted a general framework with which to identify important components of the
stress response. Yet even within this study, different
panels had different needs. Thus, the Stress and Illness
panel focused on associations between stressors and
disease consequences; our group was concerned more with
mediating variables in the process, particularly for
recent life events.

Figure 4.1 highlights our panel's focus on the personal and social conditions that give rise to life events
and may mediate their impact. As shown, the context in
which life events occur can be divided into internal factors of personal dispositions and external factors of the
social conditions in which the events are experienced.
Personal dispositions include biological assets and
liabilities as well as learned coping abilities. The
paradigm does not exclude the possibility that remote

58

FIGURE 4.1

GENERAL PARADIGM OF THE STRESS PROCESS EXTENDED TO INCLUDE ANTECEDENTS OF STRESSFUL LIFE EVENTS

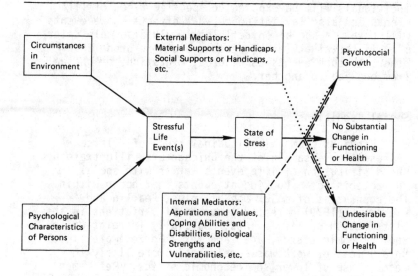

From Dohrenwend, B. S., et al., J. Health Social Behav. 19:205-229, 1978 (Figure 1). Used with permission of the American Sociological Association, Washington, D.C.

events such as death of a parent during childhood are important; such events undoubtedly influence personal dispositions later in life. Finally, the paradigm represents the process just prior to and closely following the occurrence of the stressful event; were it to be observed longer, there would be feedback loops showing how effects might come to act as antecedents.

Sources of Life Events

Most of the life events included in inventories used in research are distributed unequally in the population. Some people have experienced many of them, sometimes simultaneously; others have experienced few. What is the basis for such large differences? Much more needs to be learned about the sources of events in either the environmental setting or the psychological characteristics of persons. Gaining that information will require a social epidemiology of the occurrence of different types of life events according to such important variables as sex, age, social class, and ethnic background. Such factors contribute greatly to the likelihood that individuals will be exposed to specific types of life events and also may influence what effects those events will have. A social epidemiology would also help determine if certain types of persons are more prone than others to such events as divorce, migration, or change from one job to another.

Social Conditions

Findings from a longitudinal study of a large representative sample of the Chicago area illustrate how the distribution of life events varies with social characteristics. Looking at events that occur within the boundaries of major social roles, Pearlin and Lieberman (1979) detected a number of variations in the distribution of life events, especially in relation to socioeconomic status, age, and sex. For example, involuntary loss of work was considerably more likely to beset those of lower socioeconomic status. Retirement from work and leaving outside employment to work as a homemaker are other events that occur disproportionately among lower-placed workers. Some other occupational events, however, have the opposite association with socioeconomic status. Promotions and voluntary changes in place of employment, both of which are indicative of the process of becoming established in career lines, are somewhat more apt to be found among those of higher socioeconomic status.

In the marital and parental roles, as in the occupational realm, the occurrence of key events varies with socioeconomic status. There is a tendency, for example, for marital disruption to take place more frequently among the disadvantaged. Even the death of a child is an event more often experienced by the socioeconomically disadvantaged than by more advantaged social classes.

There are similar inequalities in the distribution of events among women and men. Compared with their male counterparts, women in the labor force experience considerably more voluntary and involuntary events involving

60

job instability. Also, women are disproportionately likely to survive a spouse; but, when their marriages are broken for any reason, they are less likely than are men to remarry. In addition, because they are more often single heads of households, they are more exposed to the events that accompany parenting.

Age is a social characteristic of special significance in the study of life events, for it provides some indication of how the events people experience change as they move through the stages of life. Life events are organized around the multiple roles people play at any given time of their lives; however, the precise structure of this organization changes as roles and statuses change throughout life. Research instruments that differentiate between expected and unexpected changes may greatly enhance their sensitivity to major life stressors.

Personal Dispositions

There is a substantial literature on situations imposed by natural and man-made disasters (Beebe, 1975; Dohrenwend and Dohrenwend, 1969; Dohrenwend, 1979) and of bereavement (Clayton, in press). For investigators, such events have the advantage of being largely independent of the personal dispositions of those who experience them. Research questions become more complicated when personal dispositions may profoundly affect the occurrence of events, as is true for divorce (Bloom et al., 1978) and unemployment (Kasl, 1979). It then becomes essential to determine whether personality traits increase the chances of an event and what effects such traits may have on disease consequences that are associated with it.

The Key Methodological Problem

Conceptualization and measurement of the stressfulness of recent life events continues to be a central methodological problem in the stress field. Investigators have attempted to identify events or conditions that are uniformly stressful to a large number of people and that are not the result of physical or mental disorders with which they may be associated. The complexities of this effort can be illustrated by referring to an early list of events developed by Holmes and Rahe (1967) in the most widely used approach to measuring stressful life events (Table 4.1). Many variations of this list have been developed, but the essential features are

TABLE 4.1

HOLMES AND RAHE SOCIAL READJUSTMENT RATING SCALE

Life Events	Mean Magnitude (Percent)	Life Events	Mean magnitude (Percent)
Death of spouse	100	• Trouble with in-laws	29
- Divorce	73	Outstanding personal	
- Marital separation	65	achievement	28
- Jail term	63	Wife begin or stop work	26
Death of close		Begin or end school	26
family member	63	Change in living	
Personal injury		conditions	25
or illness	53	• Revision of	
Marriage	50	personal habits	24
- Fired at work	47	Trouble with boss	23
Marital reconciliation	45	Change in working	
Retirement	45	hours or conditions	20
Change in health		Change in residence	20
of family member	44	Change in schools	20
Pregnancy	40	Change in recreation	19
• Sex difficulties	39	Change in church	
Gain of new		activities	19
family member	39	Change in social	
Business readjustment	39	activities	18
Change of financial		Mortgage or loan less	
state	38	than $10,000	17
Death of close friend	37	• Change in sleeping	
Change to different		habits	16
line of work	36	Change in number of	
• Change in number of		family get-togethers	15
arguments with spouse	35	• Change in	
Mortgage over $10,000	31	eating habits	15
- Foreclosure of		Vacations	13
mortgage or loan	30	Christmas	12
Change in responsi-		- Minor violations	
bilities at work	29	of the law	11
Son or daughter			
leaving home	29		

• = subjective event
- = negative objective event that may be confounded with
    psychopathology

Adapted from Holmes and Rahe (1967). The mean magnitude represents the stressfulness of different events relative to the death of a spouse, based on answers obtained from test populations.

---

unchanged. Events or conditions are identified empirically as being potentially stressful. Typically, subjects are asked to indicate which life events they experienced during a selected time period and whether

they subsequently developed physical or mental disorders
of interest. Many investigators treat all life events as
being equally important. Others attempt to acknowledge
differences in the intensity of a stressor by using
empirically developed scales such as that in Table 4.1.
The value of such weighting for improving the predictive
power of the scales continues to be controversial.

One of the problems with life events scales is that
they often fail to distinguish between objective and subjective events (Thurlow, 1971). Subjective events, which
must be reported by the subject, may be manifestations
of or responses to an underlying disorder, rather than
risk factors for it. Examples of such events, which
include "sexual difficulties," "major changes in sleeping
habits," and "major change in number of arguments with
spouse" are marked with an "o" in Table 4.1. Even some
objective events such as "divorce" or "being fired from
work" ("-", Table 4.1) may be strongly influenced by
occult disease processes. Hudgens (1974) has suggested
that 29 of the 43 events on the initial list constructed
by Holmes and Rahe (1967) and 32 of the 51 events on the
list developed by Paykel et al. (1971) are frequently
symptoms or consequences of illness.

This type of survey of life events severely limits
the inferences that can be drawn from a correlation
between the number or magnitude of events experienced
and illness (Brown, 1974; B. P. Dohrenwend, 1974). Limitations on causal inferences are especially severe in
investigations of disorders that have an insidious onset
and are likely to be most serious in studies of mental
disorders. Investigators must be able to identify the
onset of an event in relation to the onset of the pathology and learn something about whether the occurrence
of the event was within or outside the control of the
subject. Only then can they make relatively unambiguous
inferences about the etiological role of such events.
One approach is to characterize the environmental circumstances or psychological traits of the individual
that led to the event. For events such as being in
combat during wartime, originating forces are readily
apparent. For other events, including divorce, the
sources of the events are far more variable, and the
relative contributions of conditions and characteristics
are much more difficult to ascertain.

Most life-event scales also include major physical
illnesses or injuries, understandably enough because
these negative events can entail serious disruption of
usual activities. However, it is a basic proposition of

63

psychosomatic medicine that physical disorders are
accompanied by some emotional disturbance and that
emotional discord usually creates some degree of somatic
disturbance. Panel members knew of no instance in which
studies of physical illness and emotional disturbance
have failed to report a strong correlation between the
two (Lipowski, 1975). And, as Hinkle (1974, p. 39)
remarked with reference to various types of physical
illness, "the presence of one disease may imply the
presence of others and beget yet other diseases." This
observation accounted, in part, for his finding that
risk of disease is not randomly distributed in groups of
similar people who share similar experiences over long
periods of time.

Internal and External Mediating Factors

As discussed in Chapter 2, Conceptual Issues of
Stress Research, the transition from stressor through
reaction to consequence can be influenced by a number of
mediators. Within the life-events literature, mediators
of particular interest are personal dispositions and
social conditions. (See also Psychosocial Assets and
Modifiers, Chapter 7.)

Personal Dispositions

In the past two decades, clinical observations,
studies in natural settings, and laboratory experiments
have greatly enhanced information about effective psychological defense and coping responses to stressful events
(cf. Hamburg and Adams, 1967; Horowitz, 1967; Lazarus,
1966; Pearlin and Schooler, 1978). For example, Friedman
and Rosenman (1974) found that a group of traits that
they called Type A behavior is a risk factor for heart
disease. This behavior pattern is characterized by
highly competitive achievement, strong striving for
excellence, a constant sense of time urgency, and a
tendency to respond hostilely when frustrated. They and
others have suggested that this behavior is elicited by
events which might lower the esteem others have for the
Type A individual. Further analyses have shown that
there is no simple dichotomy between Type A and Type B
behavior patterns. Several behavioral traits appear to
contribute independently to Type A pattern, and appropriate stimuli are needed to elicit the characteristic
behaviors (Zyzanski and Jenkins, 1970). One critical
factor may entail a need to maintain control over the

environment (Matthews et al., 1977). Thus, Glass (1977) found that, when persons prone to Type A behavior face threatening events, they exert themselves strongly to achieve control; if they fail to achieve control, they are likely to react with extreme helplessness.

In some ways, the reaction of Type A individuals to overwhelming events resembles that postulated by Schmale (1972), who proposed a multistage model of stress-induced illness. According to his model, some individuals with a particular constitution or personality react to stress-ful life events involving loss by becoming helpless and hopeless. This response is part of a giving up/given up complex that, in the presence of environmental pathogens or constitutional vulnerability, becomes the final common pathway to illness. The helpless/hopeless response to stressors predicts general vulnerability to illness, rather than a specific vulnerability to cardiovascular disease.

Another hypothesis related to helplessness as a basis for vulnerability to stress-induced illness in-volves the concept of locus of control. Rotter (1966) suggested that individuals have a generalized expectancy about the extent to which they control rewards, punish-ments, and other events in their lives and that this expectancy ranges from internal to external. Those with an extreme internal locus of control dimension expect to be in control of their life events to a high degree, and those at the other extreme expect to have little influ-ence over what happens to them. Although there is some controversy about how an external locus of control expectancy might increase vulnerability, such individuals have been reported to be more susceptible to illness, particularly mental illness, than are those with an internal locus of control expectancy (Lefcourt, 1976). In fact, in some studies, internal locus of control ex-pectancy has been equated to competency, coping ability, and relative invulnerability to debilitating effects of stressful events (Campbell et al., 1976). People with an external locus of control expectancy strongly resemble Schmale's helpless/hopeless individuals.

Laboratory research on physiological and psychologi-cal responses to stressful stimuli has supported the idea that individuals differ in the extent to which they repress awareness of or attend to potential stressors (Epstein and Fenz, 1967; Lazarus, 1966). Studies of these response styles in relation to recovery from ill-ness suggest that repression leads to a better recovery

65

(Brown and Rawlinson, 1976; Cohen and Lazarus, 1973).
But, in the face of a threat against which the individual
must act to escape or avoid harm, repression would be
dysfunctional. Some of the work on Type A and B behavior
patterns suggests that Type A may involve repression of
responses to threatening stimuli (Glass, 1977).

A search for common themes among these constructs
suggests that it is possible that researchers with
varied theoretical and empirical backgrounds may be
converging on a central concept of factors in the
individual that are related to stress-induced illness.
For example, faced with circumstances outside their
control, people with the Type A behavior pattern may
begin to respond to loss with helplessness, have an
external locus of control expectancy, and repress
threatening stimuli and events. Unification of these
seemingly divergent concepts of personal dispositions
would greatly simplify the task of understanding how
personality functions in the life-stress process. To
date, however, these constructs have been developed
largely by separate disciplines, so that their relations
to each other have not been examined adequately.

Empirical studies of the role of various dispositions must consider the differences between a "state"
and a "trait." The discussion of the possible role of
personality in the life-stress process has emphasized
traits, which are stable tendencies to respond in particular ways to a variety of specific situations. For
example, an individual was assumed to have a particular
locus-of-control expectancy regardless of the immediate
situation. Close observation of individuals in diverse
situations has shown, however, that some dispositions
are states. States are transient, and their intensity
is influenced by the immediate situation (Kendall et
al., 1976; Lefcourt, 1976; Spielberger et al., 1979).
Thus, a person characterized as being Type A normally may
exhibit an internal locus-of-control expectancy to life
events and yet exhibit a realistic external expectancy
in relation to uncontrollable events.

The possibility of changes in state over time
suggests that studies of life stress and illness should
measure personal dispositions in relation to specific
life events. For example, in studying the effects of
personal control, Dohrenwend (1977) probed the extent to
which subjects anticipated and controlled the occurrence
of reported life events. Perceptions of control seem to

66

be influenced as much by characteristics of the particular event as by the individual's personality (Dohrenwend and Martin, 1979). More work will be necessary to determine the extent and stability of the effects of personality differences on the life stress process.

Some life events may produce long-term changes in personal dispositions that affect the way stress is handled later in life. For example, children who lose the family structure because parents divorce or separate are at increased risk for developing antisocial behavior later in life (Rutter, 1974). Others have suggested that children who lose one or both parents during childhood are at risk of being depressed as adults (Granville-Grossman, 1968). Presently, the literature on this issue is inconclusive, possibly as a result of insufficient attention to whether bereavement took place early or late in childhood. At least three studies suggest that children who lose one or both parents before age 11 have an increased vulnerability to depression (Brown and Harris, 1978) and severe psychological distress (Langner and Michael, 1963; Dohrenwend and deFigueiredo, in press) as young adults (cf. Chapter 9, Stress and Illness). There is much less information about the appealing possibility that certain types of early life experiences can decrease vulnerability to later stressful events (Bornstein et al., 1973).

Social Conditions

Recently, there also have been efforts to identify social factors in the individual's environment that may alter associations between stressors and health consequences. One of the most influential hypotheses states that social support mitigates the effects of stressful events (Gore, 1978; Hamburg and Killilea, 1978). Secondary analysis of data gathered for other reasons suggests that highly stressful events combined with low social support are much greater risk factors than are highly stressful events combined with high social support or less stressful events with high or low social support (Cobb, 1974; Gore, 1978). In a prospective study, Theorell (1974) also found that stressful life events were followed by illness only for persons in a state of discord and dissatisfaction. However, measures of social environmental conditions probably correlate with levels of personal competence, which may account for part of the effect.

Social support measures that confound environmental supports with personal competence probably will correlate more strongly with health indicators than do social support measures that are independent of such effects. For etiological investigations, the independent factors are greatly preferred to those relating to personal competence, because the former enable a more accurate assessment of the strength of the effect of social support as an element in the life-stress process. This issue is analogous to that of differentiating between objective life events and illness symptoms. Despite measurement problems, available studies indicate that social networks can markedly influence the occurrence and effects of stressful life events. A full understanding of individual variations in responses to life events will require a detailed examination of the social situations in which these events are experienced. Several questions should be asked in studies of the effects of stressful life events.

First, what is the structure of the available social network? Good measures of such networks remain to be developed, but there are promising efforts (Kahn, 1979). Many attempts to conceptualize social supports have focused on formal helping agencies such as mental health centers (Bloom, 1977; Caplan and Killilea, 1976). Still, a few have looked at somes types of informal support systems, particularly family, neighborhood, and friendship networks (Caplan, 1976; Fischer et al., 1977; Litwak and Szelenyi, 1969).

Second, how do social networks modify responses to and consequences of exposure to stressors? Most studies of social networks have emphasized the importance of emotional support. Exploratory work suggests that the availability of instrumental support such as adequate financial support also can be an important protective factor during many life events (Carveth and Gottlieb, 1979; Kaplan et al., 1977). Instrumental supports may be useful only for particular life events (Carveth and Gottlieb, 1979). For example, For a serious illness, resources for obtaining adequate medical care may be crucial. Different social supports may serve distinct functions (Litwak and Szelenyi, 1969). Thus, friends and acquaintances may be able to do more than family about helping a person find a new job, but family may be a better source of help with problems in personal relationships. Some promising methods for making a reasonably complete description of potentially supportive structures are being developed (Phillips and Fischer, in press).

Third, how much support actually is being provided? The fact that a particular type of structure can provide support does not mean that it does so in every case. Conflicts, critical attitudes, or strong emotional reactions within the family may aggravate rather than alleviate life stress (Croog, 1970; Leff and Vaughn, 1980). Life events associated with an illness that carries a social stigma, including mental illness, may lead to rejection rather than support from neighbors and the surrounding community. A full picture of the potential support available to an individual must, therefore, include an assessment of normal behaviors and expectations that are applied to that individual by people in the social networks.

Finally, to what extent are potential supports utilized or avoided? Studies suggest that the mere presence of sympathetic persons does not mitigate the effects of a stressor (Epley, 1974). It is important to determine what kinds of action in what circumstances can help to convert a potentially supportive system into one that actually is supportive.

Hypotheses about the Life Stress Process

Most studies of life stress and illness have been concerned with one or another of three types of constructs: stressful life events, personal dispositions, or social conditions. In the past few years, a number of investigators have attempted to develop theoretical and empirical formulations that would integrate these three constructs into a single concept of how stress can affect health. As shown in Figure 4.2, at least six different types of hypotheses have emerged.

Hypothesis A proposes that the occurrence of several severely stressful life events over a relatively brief time period causes adverse health changes. This model was developed empirically in studies of extreme situations such as combat and concentration camps. It has been generalized to civilian life in terms of a pathogenic triad of concomitant events that involve physical exhaustion (severe physical illness or injury), loss of social support (geographical relocation), and negative events other than physical illness or injury over which the individual has no control (death of a loved one) (Dohrenwend and Dohrenwend, 1978; Dohrenwend, 1979). The model underlies and was supported by the early work of Holmes and Rahe and their coworkers (Holmes and

69

Masuda, 1974). It could be called the victimization hypothesis.

Hypothesis B suggests that psychophysiological strain mediates the impact of life events. The model is exemplified by the work of Garrity et al. (1977). They tested the model in a college student population using a symptom scale to measure psychophysiological strain and a number of general illness indicators. They found that the scale accounted for much of the observed association between life-event scores and illness indicators. This model also describes the general form of the Friedman and Rosenman (1974) theory, which postulates that certain esteem-threatening life events elicit from predisposed individuals the Type A response pattern and of Schmale's (1972) formulation of a helplessness/hopelessness response to frustration.

Hypothesis C indicates that associations between stressful life events and adverse health changes are moderated by preexisting personal dispositions and social conditions that make an individual vulnerable. For example, a recent review of research on widowhood concluded that poor prior physical and mental health is the best predictor of poor outcome (Clayton, in press). A version of this hypothesis was developed by Rahe (1974). It also underlies the literature on vulnerability involving concepts about coping ability (Hamburg and Adams, 1967) and social support (Caplan and Killilea, 1976; Cobb, 1974; Gore, 1978). Zubin and Spring (1977) used such a model in exploring the etiology of schizophrenia, as did Brown and Harris (1978) for depression. This model is probably the major form for what could be called the vulnerability hypothesis, of which B is a variation. Its most general form, including positive and negative outcomes, is illustrated in Figure 4.1.

Hypothesis D also emphasizes the importance of personal dispositions and social conditions. The model differs from C in that dispositions and conditions augment the impact of stressful life events, rather than moderate their effects. This hypothesis gained empirical support in a study of psychological symptoms by Andrews et al. (1978). Tennant and Bebbington (1978) have suggested that it is a better fit than C for the data presented by Brown and Harris (1978) in their study of social factors in the etiology of depression. It could be characterized as the cumulative burden hypothesis.

Hypothesis E proposes that adverse health changes are caused by stable personal dispositions and social

70

FIGURE 4.2

HYPOTHESES ABOUT RECENT STRESSFUL LIFE EVENTS AND ILLNESS OUTCOMES

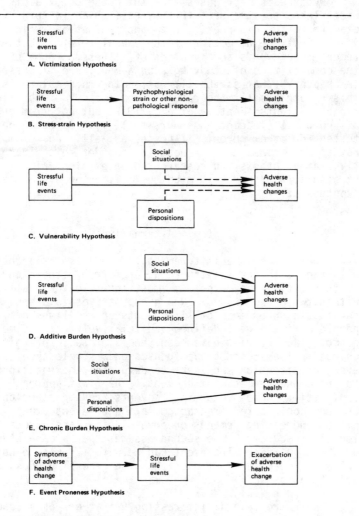

From Dohrenwend, B. S., and Dohrenwend, B. P., (Eds.)
Stressful Life Events and Their Contexts New York:
Neale Watson Academic Publ., Inc., in press. Used with
permission of Neale Watson Academic Publ., Inc., New
York.

conditions, rather than by transient stressful life events. It too is a modification of Model C. Model E was presented by Gersten et al. (1977) as an explanation of changes in children's psychological symptom patterns. It could be called the chronic burden hypothesis.

Hypothesis F proposes that the presence of a disorder leads to stressful life events, which in turn exacerbate the disorder. This model raises a crucial issue about the direction of the causal relation between recent life events and symptoms of illness. (Some of the complexities of studying such a model are discussed in Chapter 9, Stress and Illness.) In empirical tests, this hypothesis fit the results from a study of chronic mental patients (Fontana et al., 1972) but not from one of neurotics (Tennant and Andrews, 1978). It could be tested for other chronic illnesses as well. For example, Fox (1978) emphasized the need to consider this alternative, among others, in research on an etiological role of stressors in cancer. It might be called the proneness hypothesis.

Strategic Alternatives

There is no unanimity among life-events researchers with regard to the substance and preferred methodology of this field. Nevertheless, most investigators fall within two broad groups. One group strives to assess the total convergence of life events on the lives of people during a well-defined and relatively brief time period; such studies have been the major topic of this chapter. The second group focuses on a single type of event or situation and seeks to determine the reactions to and consequences of the event. The first approach implicitly assumes that single events are important only as they contribute to an accumulation of events that places increasing demands on physiological and psychological resources. The second assumes that a case study of a single major life event can help to illuminate not only the impact of that event but the general process of adjustment as well.

There are several interesting variations of a case-study approach. One type centers on certain groups that uniquely embody certain life-event experiences. Thus, people who have recently lost a spouse are ideal subjects for the study of the bereavement process (Clayton, in press). There is literature as well on a broad range of other life events such as divorce, job loss, retirement,

marriage, and childbirth. A second type of case study
utilizes natural or man-made disasters. Such events are
so overwhelming that they affect the lives of people who
possess a wide range of personal dispositions and social
networks, enabling comparisons across quite different
groups. The report on the Three Mile Island nuclear
accident is an example of this type of work (Dohrenwend
and Martin, 1979). There also may be special occupational groups whose jobs are so stressful that it becomes
vital to understand factors that make the job bearable
or unbearable (cf. Chapter 5, Stress in Organizational
Settings). A study of air traffic controllers is possibly the most comprehensive attempt to date to understand
how life events may contribute to the stressors faced by
high-pressure job holders (Rose et al., 1978). The
tensions normally experienced in the work life of this
group provide a background against which the effects of
life events take on some special meaning.

Specific Research Needs

The overwhelming majority of studies of life stress
and illness have asked if life events are associated
with changes in health. The answer to that question is
clearly affirmative for aggregate populations. The next
logical question is how life events can affect health in
individuals. Techniques used for answering the first
question may not be suitable for investigating the
second. First, some of the events used in the past are
not life events; they are, instead, subjectively experienced, insidious alterations in encompassing conditions
of life. Second, some events actually have an ambiguous
relationship to their presumed effects, because they can
be either a risk factor for or a result of the consequence being studied. Third, some events, particularly
those representing changes in health, become confounded
with the indicators of stress; high correlations in these
circumstances may simply reflect the use of different
indicators of the same phenomenon. Specific instruments
are needed with which to assess whether a stressful event
is independent of health changes under investigation.

Future research also must consider the social and
economic contexts in which life events occur. These contexts may both give rise to the events and mediate their
effects. Measures of the roles and statuses that people
occupy in the society and the networks and support systems of which they are a part need to be incorporated
into research on life events. One aspect of such con-

siderations must be the influence of changes that occur throughout the life course. Greater attention should be given to the specificity of the effects of life events. Are some classes of events, for example, selectively associated with changes in physical health and others with mental disorders? Similarly, do events differ with regard to the timing of their effects, with some having consequences that are quickly discernible and others having a long delay?

Summary

The panel concluded that substantial changes in future studies of life events and health are needed. Linkages between life events and health are influenced by many mediators: social characteristics, position along the life course, personality traits and coping repertoires, and the supportiveness of social networks. To provide a clearer view of the many elements that affect the stress process, studies should be as inclusive as possible. Thus, a study of associations between life events and disease consequences could be improved if it also considered the effects of social supports; it would be better yet if the study also included information about potentially relevant personality characteristics. Placing as much data as manageable under the umbrella of single investigations will encourage multivariate, longitudinal studies. These should be extremely useful in efforts to identify important reactions induced by life events. However, such studies are expensive and time-consuming, so efforts also should continue in further developing the methodological sophistication and efficiency of longitudinal research.

References

Andrews, G., Tennant, C., Hewson, D. M., and Vaillant, G. E. Life event stress social support, coping style, and risk of psychological impairment. J. Nerv. Ment. Dis. 166:307-317, 1978.

Beebe, G. W. Follow-up studies of World War II and Korean War prisoners. Amer. J. Epidemiol. 101:400-422, 1975.

Bornstein, P. E., Clayton, P. J., Halikas, J. A., Maurice, W. L., and Robins, E. The depression of widowhood after thirteen months. Brit. J. Psychiatry 122:561-566, 1973.

Bloom, B. L. Community Mental Health: A General Introduction Monterey: Brooks/Cole Publ. Co., 1977.

Bloom, B. L., Asher, S. J., and White S. W. Marital disruption as a stressor: review and analysis. Psychol. Bull. 85:867-894, 1978.

Brown, G. W. Meaning, measurement, and stress of life events. IN: Stressful Life Events: Their Nature and Effects (Dohrenwend, B. S. and Dohrenwend, B. P., eds.) New York: Wiley, 1974, pp. 217- 243.

Brown, G. W., and Birley, J. L. T. Crises and life changes and the onset of schizophrenia. J. Health Social Behav. 9:203-214, 1968.

Brown, G. W., and Harris, T. Social Origins of Depression: A Study of Psychiatric Disorder in Women New York: Free Press, 1978.

Brown, J., and Rawlinson, M. The morale of patients following open-heart surgery. J. Health Social Behav. 17:135-145, 1976.

Campbell, A., Converse, P. E., and Rodgers, W. L. The Quality of American Life New York: Russell Sage Foundation, 1976.

Caplan, G. The family as a support system. IN: Support Systems and Mutual Help: Multidisciplinary Explorations (Caplan, G., and Killilea, M., eds.) New York: Grune & Stratton, 1976, pp. 19-36.

Caplan, G., and Killilea, M. (Eds.) Support Systems and Mutual Help: Multidisciplinary Explorations New York: Grune & Stratton, 1976.

Carveth, W. B., and Gottlieb, B. H. The measurement of social support and its relation to stress. Can. J. Behav. Sci. 11:179-188, 1979.

Clayton, P. J. Bereavement and its management. IN: Handbook of Affective Disorders (Paykel, E. S., ed.) Edinburgh: Churchhill Livingstone, in press

Cobb, S. A model for life events and their consequences. IN: Stressful Life Events: Their Nature and Effects

(Dohrenwend, B. S., and Dohrenwend, B. P., eds.) New York: Wiley, 1974, pp. 151-156.

Cohen, F., and Lazarus, R. S. Active coping processes, coping dispositions, and recovery from surgery, Psychosom. Med. 35:375-389, 1973.

Croog, S. H. The family as a source of stress. IN: Social Stress (Levine, S., and Scotch, N., eds.) Chicago: Aldine Publ. Co., 1970, pp. 19-53.

Dohrenwend, B. P. Problems in defining and sampling the relevant population of stressful life events. IN: Stressful Life Events: Their Nature and Effects (Dohrenwend, B. S., and Dohrenwend, B. P., eds.) New York: Wiley, 1974, pp. 275-310.

Dohrenwend, B. P. Stressful life events and psychopathology: some issues of theory and method. IN: Stress and Mental Disorder (Barrett, J. W., Rose, R. M., and Klerman, G. L., eds.) New York: Raven Press, 1979, pp. 1-15.

Dohrenwend, B. P., and deFigueiredo, J. M. Remote and recent life events and psychopathology. IN: Origins of Psychopathology: Research and Public Policy (Ricks, D. L., and Dohrenwend, B. S., eds.) New York: Cambridge University Press, in press.

Dohrenwend, B. P., and Dohrenwend, B. S. Social Status and Psychological Disorder: A Causal Inquiry New York: Wiley, 1969.

Dohrenwend, B. P., and Dohrenwend, B. S. Psychiatric disorders and susceptibility to stress. IN: The Social Consequences of Psychiatric Illness (Robins, L. N., Clayton, P. J., and Wing J. K., eds.) New York: Bruner/Mazel, 1980, pp. 183-197.

Dohrenwend, B. S. Anticipation and control of stressful life events: an exploratory analysis. IN: The Origins and Course of Psychopathology (Strauss, J. W., Babigian, H. M., and Roff, M., eds.) New York: Plenum Press, 1977, pp. 135-186.

Dohrenwend, B. S., and Dohrenwend, B. P. (eds.) Stressful Life Events: Their Nature and Effects New York: Wiley, 1974.

Dohrenwend, B. S., and Dohrenwend, B. P. Some issues in research on stressful life events. J. Nerv. Ment. Dis. 166:7-15, 1978.

Dohrenwend, B. S., and Dohrenwend, B. P. Life stress and illness: formulation of the issues. IN: Stressful Life Events and Their Contexts (Dohrenwend, B. S., and Dohrenwend, B. P., eds.) New York: Neale Watson Academic Publ., Inc., in press.

Dohrenwend, B. S., Krasnoff, L., Askenasy, A. R., and Dohrenwend, B. P. Exemplification of a method for scaling life events: the PERI life events scale. J. Health Social Behav. 19:205-229, 1978.

Dohrenwend, B. S., and Martin, J. L. Personal versus
    situational determination of anticipation and control
    of the occurrence of stressful life events. Amer. J.
    Commun. Psychol. 7:453-468, 1979.
Epley, S. W. Reduction of the behavioral effects of
    aversive stimulation by the presence of companions.
    Psychol. Bull. 81:271-283, 1974.
Epstein, S., and Fenz, W. D. The detection of areas of
    emotional stress through variations in perceptual
    threshold and physiological arousal. J. Exp. Res.
    Personal. 2:191-199, 1967.
Fischer, C. S., Jackson, R. M., Stueve, C. A., Gerson,
    K., Jones, M., and Baldassarce, M. Networks and
    Places: Social Relations in the Urban Setting New
    York: The Free Press, 1977.
Fontana, A. F., Marcus, J. L., Noel, B., and Rakusin, J.
    M. Prehospitalization coping styles of psychiatric
    patients: the goal-directedness of life events. J.
    Nerv. Ment. Dis. 155:311-321, 1972.
Fox, B. H. Premorbid psychological factors as related to
    cancer incidence. J. Behav. Med. 1:45-133, 1978.
Friedman, M., and Rosenman, R. H. Type A Behavior and
    Your Heart New York: Knopf, 1974.
Fritz, C. E., and Marks, E. S. The NORC studies of human
    behavior in disaster, J. Social Issues 10:26-41, 1954.
Garrity, T. F., Somes, G. W., and Marx, M. B. The
    relationship of personality, life change, psycho-
    physiological strain and health status in a college
    population. Soc. Sci. Med. 11:257-263, 1977.
Gersten, J. C., Langner, T. S., Eisenberg, J. G., and
    Simcha-Fagan, O. An evaluation of the etiologic role
    of stressful life-change events in psychological dis-
    orders. J. Health Soc. Behav. 18, 228-244, 1977.
Glass, D. C. Behavior Patterns, Stress and Coronary
    Disease Hillsdale: Lawrence Erlbaum Assoc., 1977.
Gore, S. The effect of social support in moderating the
    health consequences of unemployment. J. Health Soc.
    Behav. 19:157-165, 1978.
Granville-Grossman, K. L. The early environment in
    effective disorder. Brit. J. Psychiatry, Special
    Publ. 2:65-79, 1968.
Gunderson, E. K. E., and Rahe, R. H. (Eds.) Life Stress
    and Illness Springfield: Thomas, 1974.
Hamburg, B. A., and Killilea, M. Relation of social
    support, stress, illness and use of health services.
    IN: Report to Surgeon General on Health Promotion
    and Disease Prevention (Institute of Medicine) Wash-
    ington, D.C.: National Academy of Sciences, 1978.
Hamburg, D., and Adams, J. A perspective on coping
    behavior: seeking and utilizing information in major
    transitions. Arch. Gen. Psychiatry 17:277-284, 1967.

Hinkle, L. E., Jr. The effect of exposure to culture change, social change, and changes in interpersonal relationships on health. IN: Stressful Life Events: Their Nature and Effects (Dohrenwend, B. S., and Dohrenwend, B. P., eds.) New York: Wiley, 1974, pp. 9-44.

Holmes, T. H., and Masuda, M. Life change and illness susceptibility. IN: Stressful Life Events: Their Nature and Effects (Dohrenwend, B. S., and Dohrenwend, B. P., eds.) New York: Wiley, 1974, pp. 45-72.

Holmes, T. H., and Rahe, R. H. The social readjustment rating scale. J. Psychosom. Res. 11:213-218, 1967.

Horowitz, M. J. Stress Response Syndromes New York: Jason Aronson, Inc., 1976.

Hudgens, R.W. Personal catastrophe and depression: a consideration of the subject with respect to medically ill adolescents, and a requiem for retrospective life-event studies. IN: Stressful Life Events: Their Nature and Effects (Dohrenwend, B. S., and Dohrenwend, B. P., eds.) New York: Wiley, 1974.

Jenkins, C. D. Psychosocial modifiers of response to stress. IN: Stress and Mental Disorder (Barrett, J. E., Rose, R. M., and Klerman, G. L., eds.) New York: Raven Press, 1979, pp. 265-278.

Kahn, R. L. Aging and social support. IN: Aging From Birth to Death: Interdisciplinary Perspectives (Riley, M. W., ed.) Boulder: Westview Press, 1979, pp. 79-91.

Kaplan, B. H., Cassel, J. C., and Gore, S. Social support and health. Med. Care 15:47-58, 1977.

Kasl, S. V. Changes in mental health status associated with job loss and retirement. IN: Stress and Mental Disorder (Barrett, J. E., Rose, R. M., and Klerman, G. L., eds.) New York: Raven Press, 1979, pp. 179-200.

Kendall, P. C., Finch, A. J., Jr., Auerbach, S. M., Hooke, J. F., and Mikulka, P. J. The State-Trait Anxiety Inventory: a systematic evaluation. J. Counsel. Clin. Psychol. 44:406-412, 1976.

Langner, T. S., and Michael, S. T. Life Stress and Mental Heath. Vol. II: The Midtown Manhattan Study New York: The Free Press, 1963.

Lazarus, R. S. Psychological Stress and the Coping Process New York: McGraw Hill, 1966.

Lefcourt, H. M. Locus of Control: Current Trends in Theory and Research New York: Lawrence Erlbaum Assoc., 1976.

Leff, J. P. and Vaughn, C. The interaction of life events and relatives' expressed emotion in schizophrenia and depressive neurosis. Brit. J. Psychiatry 136:146-153, 1980.

Levi, L. Psychosocial stress and disease: a conceptual model. IN: Life Stress and Illness (Gunderson, E. K. E., and Rahe, R. H., eds.) Springfield: Thomas, 1974, pp. 8-33.

Lipowsky, Z. J. Psychiatry of somatic diseases: epidemiology, pathogenesis, classification. Comp. Psychiatry 16:105-124, 1975.

Litwak, E., and Szelenyi, I. Primary group structures and their functions: kin, neighbors and friends. Amer. Sociol. Rev. 34:465-481, 1969.

Matthews, K. A., Glass, D. C., Rosenman, R. H., and Bortner, R. W. Competitive drive, pattern A, and coronary heart disease: a further analysis of some data from the Western Collaborative Group Study. J. Chron. Dis. 30:489-498, 1977.

Orth-Gomer, K., and Ahlbom, A. Impact of psychological stress on idiopathic heart disease when controlling for conventional risk indicators. J. Hum. Stress 6: 7-15, 1980.

Paykel, E. S. Life stress and psychiatric disorder: application of the clinical approach. IN: Stressful Life Events: Their Nature and Effects (Dohrenwend, B. S., and Dohrenwend, B. P., eds.) New York: Wiley, 1974, pp. 135-149.

Paykel, E. S., Prusoff, B. A., and Uhlenhuth, E. H. Scaling of life events. Arch. Gen. Psychiatry 25: 340-347, 1971.

Pearlin, L. I., and Lieberman, M. A. Social sources of emotional distress. IN: Research in Community and Mental Health (Simmons, R., ed.) Greenwich: JAI Press, 1979, pp. 217-248.

Pearlin, L. I., and Schooler, C. The structure of coping. J. Health Social Behav. 19:2-21, 1978.

Phillips, S. L., and Fischer, C. S. Measuring social support networks in general populations. IN: Stressful Life Events and Their Contexts (Dohrenwend, B. S., and Dohrenwend, B. P., eds.) New York: Neale Watson Academic Publ., in press.

Rabkin, J., and Struening, E. Life events, stress and illness. Science 194:1013-1020, 1976.

Rahe, R. H. The pathway between subjects' recent life changes and their near-future illness reports: representative results and methodological issues. IN: Stressful Life Events: Their Nature and Effects (Dohrenwend, B. S., and Dohrenwend, B. P., eds.) New York: Wiley, 1974, pp. 73-86.

Rahe, R. H., and Arthur, R. H. Life change and illness studies. J. Hum. Stress 4:3 15, 1978.

Rose, R. M, Jenkins, C. D., and Hurst, M. W. Air Traffic Controller Health Change Study Boston: Boston University School of Medicine, 1978.

Rotter, J. B. Generalized expectancies for internal versus external control of reinforcement. Psychol. Mono. 80:1-28, 1966.

Rutter, M. The Qualities of Mothering: Maternal Deprivation Reassessed New York: Jason Aronson, 1974.

Schmale, A. H. Giving up as a final common pathway to changes in health. Adv. Psychosom. Med. 8:20-40, 1972.

Spielberger, C. D., Gorsuch, R. C., and Lushene, R. E. Manual for the State-Anxiety Inventory Palo Alto: Consulting Psychologists Press, 1979.

Tennant, C., and Andrews, G. The cause of life events in neurosis. J. Psychosom. Res. 22:41-45, 1978.

Tennant, C., and Bebbington, P. The social causation of depression: a critique of the work of Brown and his colleagues. Psychosom. Med. 8:565-575, 1978.

Terr, L. C. Children of Chowchilla. A study of psychic trauma. Pschoanal. Study Child 34:547-623, 1979.

Theorell, T. Life events before and after the onset of a premature myocardial infarction. IN: Stressful Life Events: Their Nature and Effects (Dohrenwend, B. S., and Dohrenwend, B. P., eds.) New York: Wiley, 1974, pp. 101-117.

Thurlow, H. J. Illness in relation to life situation and sick-role tendency. J. Psychosom. Res. 15:73-88, 1971.

Warheit, G. J. Life events, coping, stress, and depressive symptomatology. Amer. J. Psychiatry 136:502-507, 1979.

Zubin, J , and Spring, B. Vulnerability--a new view of schizophrenia. J. Abnorm. Psychol. 86:103-126, 1977.

Zyzanski, S. J., and Jenkins, C. D. Basic dimensions within the coronary-prone behavior pattern. J. Chron. Dis. 22:781-795, 1970.

CHAPTER 5

Report on
Stress in
Organizational Settings

Panel Members:
Robert Kahn, Ph.D., Chair
Karen Hein, M.D.
James House, Ph.D.
Stanislav Kasl, Ph.D.
Alan McLean, M.D.

Most people in industrialized societies spend from one-third to one-half of their waking hours in organizational settings, principally at work or in schools. The proportion increases as retirement options are liberalized, as more women enter the labor force, and as children enter schools and day care centers at earlier ages. Thus, solely on the basis of exposure, stress associated with organizational settings constitutes a major part of the total stress experienced in people's lives. Organizational settings also are likely sources of stress, because they provide the main context in which society makes demands on people to perform and to relate to a broad range of others in specified ways. Some of the same organizational characteristics that generate stress, however, may be important for its alleviation. Because organizations are ready-made mechanisms of social influences, power, and communication, they can and should be utilized in any large-scale effort to reduce stress or improve health. For all these reasons, organizational settings of work and school are important both in efforts to understand psychosocial stressors and for attempts to reduce their adverse health consequences.

A growing body of theory and research on organizations, especially work organizations, shows that major stressors in organizational settings are associated with adverse physical and mental health consequences. But, there are substantive and methodological weaknesses and gaps in the literature (House, 1974a,b, 1980a; Kahn, in press; Kasl, 1978). These problems have inhibited efforts to draw clear conclusions about the effects of organizational stress on health.

The panel on Stress in Organizational Settings has attempted to highlight what is known about the role of organizations in generating and alleviating stress and disease and to identify important directions for future research in this area. The theoretical model that the group used to organize its deliberations is described below, followed by a brief summary of research findings that already are available about stress in organizational settings. In addition, the panel explored in detail four major issues that have been neglected in existing theory and research on organizationally generated stress:

- Conceptualization and measurement of potentially stressful properties of organizations. Stressors have a subjective component. How do such perceptions relate to objective organizational environments and their effects on people? Within this area, the panel considered the school setting as a source of stress similar to work organizations but at a different point in the life course. Viewing the school setting in such terms has not been done before in literature on organizational stress.

- Consideration of the effects of external conditions or events on organizational stress. To what extent is the exclusion of people from organized work or school settings, for example, unemployment, retirement, full-time homemaking, school expulsion, or dropping out, a source of stress? How does life outside of school or work affect the stress process within these organizational settings, and vice versa? Some of these issues, such as unemployment and retirement, have been addressed in the existing literature; others have yet to be studied.

- Identification of the major individual and social factors that condition the relationships among objective and psychological environments, responses, and disease. These issues are just beginning to receive the attention from investigators that they deserve.

- Exploration of ways to represent more accurately the temporal processes embodied in the translation of environmental signals into responses and disease consequences. Such investigations will require carefully designed prospective or longitudinal and field experimental research.

82

Definitions of Stress

A general theoretical model for stress research
helps identify the foci of existing work and to suggest
priorities for the future. The schema shown in Figure
5.1 is the "ISR Model" elaborated by Kahn (1970). Its
essential features resemble those for models proposed by
other stress researchers (House, 1974a; Levi, 1972;
McGrath, 1970) and is in accord with the framework
discussed in Chapter 2 on Conceptual Issues of Stress
Research. This model does not view stress as a well-
defined concept or phenomenon but as a generic label for
a set of phenomena and processes involving six classes
of causally linked variables. Objective organizational
environments (1) or situations give rise to psychological
perceptions of those environments (2), including perceptions of stress--feelings that environmental demands are
excessive relative to the person's abilities or that
environmental opportunities are inadequate to justify
the person's needs (French, 1974). These perceptions
give rise to short-term affective, physiological, or
behavioral responses (3), including responses that may

FIGURE 5.1

ISR MODEL OF STRESS

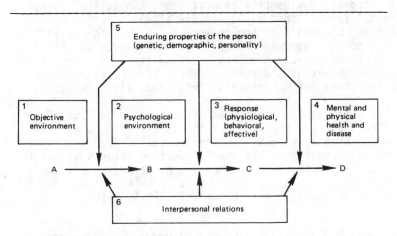

From Kahn, R. L., Work and Health New York: Wiley
Interscience, 1981 (Figure 4.2). Reproduced by permission of John Wiley & Sons, Inc., New York, New York.

alter the objective environment or the person's perceptions of it (termed respectively coping and defense or,
more generally, adaptation). Finally, depending on their
nature, intensity, and duration, these responses may lead
to more sustained changes in mental and physical health
(4). Each of these relationships or effects (Figure 5.1,
arrows A-D) can be conceived of as a process occurring
and recurring over time, with the nature of the relationship or effect being conditional on an individual's
enduring characteristics (5) and interpersonal situation
or environment (6) (Figure 5.1, vertical arrows). For
example, more competent people appear to be less likely
to perceive given objective conditions as stressful
(Pearlin and Johnson, 1977), and people with trustful or
supportive interpersonal relations are less likely to
experience adverse health outcomes following exposure to
stressors (Cassell, 1976; Cobb, 1976).

This model suggests two alternative, but complementary, scientific strategies. One is to identify health
or disease outcomes first, and then try to trace back
along the sequence to their causes. This strategy char-
acterizes much of traditional epidemiology and has met
with considerable success--for example, in finding the
cause of Legionnaire's disease or identifying vinyl
chloride as a cause of angiosarcoma. The identification
of Type A behavior pattern provides an example of this
approach in the psychosocial area (cf. Chapter 7, Psychosocial Assets and Modifiers of Stress). The other
strategy is to identify objective and subjective environmental factors that may adversely affect a range of
health outcomes and then to work forward in the causal
sequence to determine their effects. Studies of the
effects of radiation on health exemplify this approach,
as do studies of the health effects of life events or
transitions (cf. Chapter 4, Stress and Life Events).

This chapter usually emphasizes the second strategy,
without denying the value of the first. The panel believes that as stress-inducing aspects of organizational
settings are identified, their specific effects on health
can be established. The emphasis on stress-generating
properties is also a useful basis for efforts to reduce
stress and improve health (Cassell, 1974, 1976).

Health Effects of Stress in Organizational Settings

Several good reviews of the impact of stress in
occupational roles on health are available (Cassell,

1976; House, 1974a,b, 1980b; Jenkins, 1976). The following summarizes the data only briefly as background for consideration of research needs.

On the broadest level, large differences in morbidity and mortality among occupations suggest that they can have an effect on health. One compelling type of evidence derives from comparisons of workers in high- and low-stress jobs, as determined both by external observers and by self-reports of the workers. High-stress jobs involve high levels of workload, responsibility, and interpersonal or role conflicts or inadequate opportunity for doing interesting and valued work. Workers in high-stress jobs have a higher prevalence and incidence of a wide range of diseases, and the greater the stress the greater the disease. For example, air traffic controllers, especially those in high-traffic airports, have a greater incidence of a variety of illnesses, including hypertension, peptic ulcers, and diabetes mellitus, than do other workers (Cobb and Rose, 1973; Rose et al., 1978). Similarly, Frankenhaeuser and Gardell (1976) showed that workers in stressful blue-collar occupations such as machine-paced jobs with short work cycles exhibit more adverse psychological and physiological responses conducive to disease than do workers in less stressful jobs, even in the same plants (cf. Chapter 6, Work Stress Related to Social Structures and Processes).

As Kasl (1978) has observed, most research on occupational stress and health has been cross-sectional, rather than longitudinal or experimental. At least in theory, results such as those just cited might reflect a tendency of individuals who are already ill or are highly disease-prone to selectively enter more stressful occupations. Moreover, research has primarily considered the relationship of perceived stress to immediate responses, usually in the form of self-reported symptoms of physical and mental distress (Figure 5.1, boxes 2 and 3). Despite such methodological flaws, results from a number of studies have shown considerable agreement. But, Kasl correctly argues that these kinds of studies provide only a weak basis for inferences about the causal impact of stress on health. They fail to consider crucial issues in the larger paradigm outlined in Figure 5.1--for example, the relationship of objective organizational factors (Box 1) to perceived stress (Box 2) and health (Box 4).

There have been a few prospective studies in the work place in which persons free of disease are followed until they develop disease. These studies also strongly suggest an etiological role for organizational stress in chronic disease morbidity and mortality. The best studied psychosocial correlate and predictor of coronary disease is the Type A Behavior Pattern identified by Friedman and Rosenman (1971) (cf. Psychosocial Assets and Modifers, Chapter 7). At least two prospective studies, the Western Collaborative Group Study and the Framingham Heart Study, have found that, compared with Type B people, Type A individuals have about twice the risk of heart disease, at least in white-collar popula-tions. This relative risk is independent of other risk factors such as smoking, blood pressure, and cholesterol; and its magnitude is comparable to the increased risk associated with these other factors.

There is some reason to believe that the Type A variable may be relevant to organizational and occupa-tional stress. Jenkins (1976) identified competitive drive and time urgency or impatience as key attributes of the Type A syndrome, emphasizing that it seemed to be a style with which some people habitually respond to disruptive or stressful circumstances. As discussed later, this means that Type A may be an enduring trait which conditions perceptions of and responses to occupa-tional or other social stressors. In addition, Type A behavior may promote both more exposure to objectively stressful conditions of work and greater subjective per-ception of occupational stressors. For example, Friedman and Rosenman (1971) characterized Type A individuals as having high levels of job involvement and occupational pressure and suggested that the behavior is a new pheno-menon which has arisen in response to the organizational and other pressures of modern industrialized societies.

Data from the Framingham study implicate occu-pational stress more directly as a risk factor for cardiovascular disease. The Framingham Type A scale is composed half of items indicating general traits of competitiveness and time urgency and half of items indicating perceived occupational stress (Haynes et al., 1978). The overall measure predicted both prevalence and incidence of heart disease among working men and women, especially those in white-collar jobs (Haynes and Feinleib, 1980; Haynes et al., 1980). Job-related items and the general traits were equally predictive of heart disease. Among working women, clerical workers were especially susceptible; within that group, low rates of job mobility and lack of support from worker supervisors were strong risk factors. These results relate only to cardiovascular disease, but they suggest that it should

86

be possible to design studies that document and explore
the way in which occupational stress can affect health.

Conceptualization of Organizational Settings

Organizational Theory and Organizational Stress

All strategies for linking indicators of health and
illness to organizational settings have one requirement
in common: they need a conceptual language to describe
the stress-relevant aspects of organizations and organizational roles. No vocabulary yet exists that is fully
adequate for that purpose. The difficulty lies partly
with the wide range of stressors that may occur in
organizational settings--punitive supervisory behaviors,
exposure to chemicals, sustained demands for vigilance,
and a long list of other seemingly unrelated characteristics. A further difficulty arises from that seeming
unrelatedness: no single theory of human organizations
has yet emerged as dominant in the social and behavioral
sciences. Finally, the conceptual language needed must
encompass at least three major levels of abstraction:
the organization itself, its major functional parts, and
the organizational position or role as the individual
encounters it. It needs to consider not only what makes
a role stressful but also why some organizations generate
stressful roles and others do not. The answer to that
question may well involve a fourth conceptual level,
that of the environment or context (cultural, political,
economic) in which organizations exist.

Students of stress in organizational settings have
an interest in the development of organizational theory
and concepts. Presently, they can choose from an array
of concepts and measures that come from various theories
at the organizational level and at the role level. They
also can use pragmatic terms of classification that
describe organizations and organizational roles without
reference to a general theory. Industry and occupation
are such terms. Classification of occupational titles
and of industries has been developed in great detail,
mainly by the United States Department of Labor and the
Bureau of the Census. Such terms locate stressors in
organizational space and thus lead to the next task of
explaining occupational and industrial differences after
they have been discovered.

Most occupation-based research on stress has begun
with hypotheses about kinds of work that might be stress-

ful and then tried to show unusual prevalence of symptoms
or diseases that already are recognized as stress-related
(McLean, 1979). Air traffic controllers, physicians,
assembly-line workers, policemen, supervisors, and other
occupations have been studied, with results that range
from major to minuscule. The problem in summarizing and
interpreting this body of research is conceptual: there
are no objective criteria for comparing those occupations
to other jobs in terms of inherent psychological job
stress factors and health consequences. Smith et al.
(1978) undertook an occupational analysis of some 22,000
health records of persons with disorders judged to be
stress-related, to determine whether certain occupations
were overrepresented. Of some 130 occupations studied,
incidence of stress-related diseases was greater than
expected for general and construction laborers, secre-
taries, inspectors, clinical laboratory technicians,
office managers, managers and administrators, foremen,
waitresses and waiters, machine operatives (including
assembly-line workers), farm workers, and painters.
These findings both focus and intensify the search for
explanation. Why are certain occupations apparently
characterized by higher levels of stress? What are the
common threads across occupations and organizations?
Answers to those questions will require the development
of a more comprehensive way of describing organizational
settings, particularly with respect to properties of
organizations and positions (roles) that generate stress.

Properties of Organizations

There is reasonable agreement among social scientists that an organization can be viewed as a system
engaged in continuous exchange with its environment and
in the creation of some distinctive product or service.
Among others, Katz and Kahn (1978), March and Simon
(1958), Miller (1965, 1978), Parsons (1956a,b), and
Thompson (1967) share this orientation. Even here, there
is some disagreement. For example, Hage (1980) recently
offered a differentiated description of organizational
theories. Characterizing the March and Simon (1958)
theory as thesis, he identified three successive anti-
theses: structural/functional, political and conflict/
critical, and cybernetic/adaptive (open-system). If
organizations are regarded as a subset of open systems,
it follows that they share certain defining characteristics with other open systems and also possess certain
additional characteristics distinctive to their subset.
Both sets of characteristics imply certain continuing

88

tasks or problems for the human organization--things that must be done if the organizaton is to survive. Those tasks can be performed in many ways, with varying degrees of success and demands on organization members.

The implications of all this for stress research are clear in general but difficult to work out in specific terms. What identifying properties of entire organizations tend to make life within them either stressful or relatively stress free? How do stressors change with different approaches to basic problems of organizational maintenance and survival? How does stressfulness vary among different positions in the organizational structure? Are pivotal roles for maintaining the defining properties of the organization itself especially stressful? For example, one of the defining characteristics of any open system is its patterned, cyclical character: the product exported into the environment, directly or by exchange, taps the sources of energy for repeating the cycle of activities that create that product. This patterned, repetitive quality, which is automatic or instinctive in biological organisms, is a persistent problem for human organizations. The organization somehow must induce its individual human parts to remain within it and to enact dependably those behaviors that define the organization and are required for its survival. Every organization, therefore, must by some means reduce the spontaneous variability of individual human behavior.

Stress researchers who are reminded of these organizational characteristics immediately become interested in how different organizations attain this reduction in individual variability, by whom the necessary power or influence is exercised, to whom the influence attempts are addressed, and to what extent individual behavior is constrained. These questions imply comparative studies of stress in which the comparisons are among alternative bases and methods of exercising power and varying degrees of autonomy or dependence on the instructions of others. Comparative studies of the control structure of organizations have been done (Tannenbaum et al., 1978), but they have not been used to predict stress-related disorders.

Katz and Kahn (1978) list ten properties that human organizations have in common with all other open systems (Table 5.1). They propose an additional set of properties that differentiate human organizations from other open systems. These properties include the contrived nature of organizations; the resulting problems of

89

TABLE 5.1

OPEN-SYSTEM PROPERTIES OF HUMAN ORGANIZATIONS

Importation of energy from the external environment

Throughput--transformation of energy in some way, work

Output--exporting of some product to the environment

Creation of cycles of events--patterned repetitive
    exchange

Attainment of negative entropy--imports exceeding exports

Negative feedback--continuing information and correction

Maintenance of a steady state--dynamic homeostasis

Tendency toward differentiation--growth and elaboration

Coordination--integration of parts for unified
    functioning

Equifinality--different paths to the same end state.

From Katz, D., and Kahn, R. L. The Social Psychology of
Organizations, 2nd Ed. New York: Wiley, 1978. Reproduced by permission of John Wiley & Sons, Inc., New York.

inducing members to remain in the organization and perform the required activities; the reliance on roles,
norms, and values as the means of keeping the organization together; and the use of rules, backed by rewards
and penalties, to ensure the required role behavior.
Organizations differ in their modes of solving these
problems, and each difference is a potential source of
hypotheses for stress research, in much the same way as
we have illustrated above for the contrived nature of
organizations. The explicit development of such hypotheses and systematic tests of them have yet to be done.

Subsystems of Organization

    Just as no single theory of organizations dominates
the field, so too there is no consensus on how the com-

ponents or subsystems of organizations should be defined. Some categories have come into general use--staff and line, direct and indirect, hourly and exempt (salaried), management and worker--but none is comprehensive. Like occupation and industry, such categories are surrogate variables for the research worker, invented for pragmatic purposes and unrelated to any theory of organizations. Of the organizational subdivisions proposed for study by social scientists, that of Parsons (1956a,b) has been most influential. Katz and Kahn (1978) describe five basic subsystems of organizations: (1) the productive subsystem, concerned with the organization throughput or essential work that gets done in the organization; (2) the boundary or production-supportive subsystem, carrying on transactions between the organization and its environment (procurement, sales or other forms of disposal, and institutional relations); (3) the maintenance subsystem, responsible for keeping people tied into their organizational roles (personnel, training, wage and salary administration); (4) the adaptive subsystem, designed to sense relevant changes in the outside world and translate their meaning for the organization; and (5) the managerial subsystem, cutting across the other four and concerned with controlling, coordinating, and directing their activities.

This concept of organizational subsystems should be a useful source of hypotheses about organizational stress. Each subsystem has its distinctive dynamic and is likely to generate stressful demands of a particular kind. Moreover, the different functions of the several subsystems suggest plausible hypotheses about their interactions, which are also sources of potential stressors. For example, the dynamic of the production subsystem is proficiency, and in the name of proficiency this subsystem typically moves toward specializing and fractionating the elements of the work process. Potential stressors might involve workload (overload) or monotony and repetition in the performance of small tasks. The proficiency dynamic is likely to be expressed as opposition to product variety and change, which may be stressful under some conditions. In contrast, the adaptive subsystem dynamic is toward change. The adaptive subsystem, in identifying and interpreting changes outside the organization, is also a proposer of change within the organization. Members of this subsystem may be more likely to encounter stressful role conflicts as they try to reconcile externally generated change demands with the almost inevitable resistance to change within certain parts of the organization.

91

Some research on stress in organizational settings can be understood in terms of subsystem differences. Examples include studies of routine jobs in the lumber industry (Frankenhaeuser and Gardell, 1976), of organizational boundary roles (Adams, 1976), and of the effects of administrative responsibility (Caplan, 1972). Stress research would benefit, however, from a comprehensive attempt to predict and measure subsystem differences in the kinds of potential stressors characteristically generated, in the people who find them to be stressors, and in the nature and incidence of stress-related disorders.

Differences Among Organizations

Most research on stress in organizations has focused on individual positions or roles and the differences among them. Such research should be augmented by efforts to identify sources of stress at levels above that of the job. Differences among organizational subsystems exemplify this, and similar points can be made with respect to differences among organizations. Organizations differ in type, that is, in the basic function that they perform in society; in their stage of development, from birth to death; and in the environment within which they function. Each of these areas of difference among organizations is relevant for research on organization stress, and none of them has yet been studied in depth by stress researchers.

Organizational Types. A rough typology of organizations is implied by such colloquial terms for their designation as factory, school, hospital, store, or political party. Cross-cutting dichotomies distinguish for-profit from nonprofit organizations or privately owned from public enterprises. For research purposes, however, it would be preferable to have a logically complete typology that differentiates organizations in terms of some overall theoretical schema and offers some explanatory power in the study of stress. No such schema have been develped fully, but many authors have categorized organizations along some dimensions or in terms of some syndrome that was relevant to their own theoretical purposes. For example, McGregor (1960) suggested a dichotomy of "Theory X and Theory Y," classifying organizations according to managerial philosophy or, more precisely, the assumptions about human nature manifested in their operations. Likert (1961) used a combination of managerial style and decision-making structure in his "System 1 through System 4." Parsons

(1956a,b, 1960) used genotypic function--the core
activity in which different organizations are engaged as
subsystems of the larger society--as a basis for classification. Building on this proposal, Katz and Kahn
(1978) identified four basic types of organizations:
productive, maintenance, adaptative, and managerial.
These categories refer to the main contributions of the
organization to the surrounding social structure.
Moreover, they are parallel to the categories used to
identify substructures within the organization itself.

Productive or economic organizations are concerned
with creation of wealth, manufacture of goods, and provision of services. These organizations can be divided
further into the primary activities of agriculture and
mining, the secondary activities of manufacturing and
processing, and the tertiary activities of service and
communication. Maintenance organizations are engaged in
the socialization of people for their roles in other
organizations and in the society at large. Schools and
churches are major examples. Adapative organizations
create knowledge, develop and test theories, and attempt
to show the relevance of new information for existing
problems. Research and development organizations, universities (in their research aspects), and corporate
research units are examples. Managerial organizations,
starting with the state itself, perform essentially political societal functions--adjudication; coordination; and
control of resources, people, and other organizations.

Organizations of different genotypic classes may
differ in their tendency to impose stressors of various
kinds on their members. To our knowledge, no research
has yet attempted to link stressors and organizational
type systematically. A partial exception to this state-
ment is the use of Census industrial categories such as
agriculture, mining, construction, and manufacturing as
a first step in identifying probability of exposure to
toxic substances or unusual hazards. It seems unlikely,
however, that these industrial categories will be sufficient for the study of all types of stressors.

A genotypic typology is only one possibility for
stress research, and at least two others should be
considered--categorizing organizations by the nature of
their throughput and categorizing them by the primary
basis for their maintenance. With respect to the former,
a stress-relevant distinction might be made between
organizations primarily engaged in the transformation of
objects and organizations that act directly on people.

93

Parsons (1960) and Goffman (1961) have emphasized the importance of this distinction, but its effects on organizational stress remain to be explored.

Hasenfeld and English (1974) also distinguish between people-processing organizations like employment agencies and people-changing organizations such as mental hospitals. The phenomenon of "burnout" among professionals in people-changing organizations has been much discussed in recent years and has been explained as a response to the unique stresses of such organizations--chronic overload, inadequate power and resources for the presenting problems, and persistent conflict between bureaucratic organizational demands and the unique and intimate needs of those who come for service. Some research evidence for such problems and the responses of staff members to them has been developed (Maslach, 1978), but the relevant comparisons between people-changing organizations and other types have yet to be made.

In addition to creating a product or service, social systems have the continuous task of self-maintenance. Some motivational base is necessary to attract members, hold them, and persuade them to invest their energies in fulfilling their organizational roles. Many rewards and penalties are used for these purposes, and their patterns suggest another promising approach for predicting organizational stressors (cf. Chapter 6, Work Stress Related to Social Structures and Processes). Classifying organizations by their primary basis of self-maintenance might begin with a distinction between expressive and instrumental behavior--that is between activities that are intrinsically rewarding and those that are undertaken only because they are a condition for obtaining some extrinsic reward.

Developmental Stages. Loosely speaking, organizations are born and eventually die; but the metaphor of the biological life course goes little further. How long an organization will endure, how rapidly it will grow, what size it will attain, and what forms it will assume are not questions to which answers can be predicted with certainty. No genetic material programs organizational growth. Still, it seems likely that well-conceptualized measures of developmental stage and growth rate would be among the predictors of organizational stress.

No general theory of organizational development is available for stress researchers, but some areas of progress may be relevant. These involve organizational

94

size; level of maturation; and, for those that are growing, forms of growth. Kahn et al. (1964) found that reports of job-related tension increased with organizational size, although the relationship was curvilinear; increases in size became irrelevant among organizations numbering thousands of members. Size and changes in size, both positive and negative, deserve investigation as predictors of organizational stress. Rates of change in size should also be studied over an extended period, to enable consideration of the effects of size stability or lability. Each of these aspects of size may have different effects on stress levels.

Organizational growth may take various forms; choices among them can be regarded as deliberate at some level in the organization. Four forms of growth can be distinguished: increasing the size of existing subunits of an organization, increasing the number of subunits doing identical work, differentiating or increasing the number of specialized subunits performing different functions, and merging with other organizations. The implications of these growth forms to stress research, and interactions with rate of overall growth, remain to be determined.

Research on organizational growth still is primarily at a descriptive level, doing the useful work of replacing folklore with empirical data. For example, generalizations such as Parkinson's law are replaced by Blau's (1970) finding that organizational growth involves opposing principles of increased needs for coordination and administrative economics of scale. The consequences for stress have yet to be explored. However, at least four of the problems that arise with increasing organizational size seem to be stress-relevant: loss of the primary group in motivating people to achieve organizational goals, omissions and errors in communication, weaknesses in utilizing the skill and knowledge of members, and sheer social traffic and congestion.

Organization Environments. Some excellent work has been done on organizational environments (Emery and Trist, 1965; Lawrence and Lorsch, 1967), but not in connection with stress. It seems reasonable that the environmental constraints and opportunities for an organization affect the stressors that are imposed on its members. Four properties of an organization's environment may be good predictors of internal stressors: stability/turbulence, clustering/randomness, scarcity/munificence, and uniformity/diversity. Stability/

turbulence affects the predictability of organizational
life and the magnitude of change demands within the
organization. Clustering/randomness refers to the
degrees of organization of the environment itself.
Scarcity/munificence defines the availability of those
inputs that mean organizational life or death. And
uniformity/diversity speaks to the variety of external
demands that an organization must meet.

Stress probably increases under conditions of
environmental turbulence, scarcity, diversity, and
randomness. Such effects undoubtedly are modified by
organizational task, technology, and internal structure.
The prediction of stress on the basis of environmental
characteristics, therefore, probably should take the
form of a contingency theory. The contingency approach
has had some success in the prediction of organizational
effectiveness under different environmental characteristics, the conclusion being that an effective organization
is one that parallels in its own departments the characteristics of the most relevant sector of its environment
(Burns and Stalker, 1961; Lawrence and Lorsch, 1967).

Properties of Organizational Roles. Most research
on psychosocial stress in organizational settings has
been conducted at the level of the individual and has
sought to identify stressful demands in the specific job
or organizational role. These studies, some in the
laboratory and some in the field, have been attempts to
disaggregate the concept of occupation. McGrath (1976)
has summarized the results of such studies:

- Task content: riskiness of decisions, difficulty
  of task, time pressure for task completion, dull-
  ness and repetitiveness of task.

- Social-psychological conditions: threat of evaluation, task failure, interpersonal disagreement, role
  disadvantages (conflict, ambiguity, low status),
  and vicarious exposure to these and other stressful
  experiences (films, staged incidents).

- Physical conditions: electric shock, injection or
  puncture, sleep deprivation, auditory or visual
  distraction, environmental restriction (sensory
  deprivation, limitation of movement or space),
  drugs, and visual or vicarious exposure to any of
  these stimuli.

96

Field studies have identified as stressful such properties as role ambiguity; role conflict; work overload;
and excessive responsibility, especially for persons
rather than things. For reviews, see Cooper and Payne
(1978), House (1974b), Katz and Kahn (1978), and McLean
(1979). Reported consequences of such stressors are
diverse, ranging from self-reported discomfort and dissatisfaction through changes in physiological indicators
to specific diseases, including hypertension, myocardial
infarction, and peptic ulcers.

Most field studies of stress have dealt with problems of excessive demands or inputs to the person. But,
some Swedish workers have focused on jobs that underuti-
lize the skills and abilities of workers or place heavy
demands on only a few skills (Frankenhaeuser and Gardell,
1976). In the lumber industry, jobs characterized by
extremely short operating cycles, high dependence on
machines for determining work pace, limited opportunity
for movement, and sustained requirement for vigilance
were associated both with a number of stress-related
reactions such as elevated blood pressure and increased
blood concentrations of catecholamines and with adverse
health consequences like headache, peptic ulcers, and
back ailments. Additional studies are needed that employ
a uniform set of occupational (role) descriptors and
measures, use them to develop profiles or patterns of
stressors in different organizational roles, and examine
the consequences in both physiological and psychological
terms (cf. Chapter 6, Work Stress Related to Social
Structures and Processes).

School and Work Settings

Childhood and adolescent development includes moving
from dependence on family members to independent living,
learning to function as a useful member of society, and
completing a series of physical and psychological developmental stages. For most children in the United States,
the arena in which these developments occur is school.
When children or adolescents are not at home or engaged
in leisure activities, they are expected to be at school.
Those not in school are categorized as a nonstudent
subpopulation (truant, deviant, institutionalized, or
transitional).

Success or failure of schools as organizational
settings has been measured in a variety of ways. Of

particular interest have been factors that correlate with academic achievement. Reviews of school influences on children's behavior and development portray the different emphases that researchers have used in assessing the factors that have bearing on health or development. Coleman et al. (1966) and Jencks (1972) concluded that schools contribute little to cognitive inequality. These studies have three limitations: measurements of attainment usually relied on verbal abilities alone; the qualities of the schools as social institutions were not assessed; and, the goals of the studies were to reduce inequalities in attainment, rather than to maximize individual achievement.

Two recent studies have looked at schools as "people processing institutions" or organizational settings for youth. The Safe School Study (National Institute of Education, 1978) surveyed public schools about the incidence of illegal and disruptive activities and the ways in which the schools attempted to cope with crime and disruption. The characteristics of the schools, communities, and pupils were analyzed in relation to criminal behaviors; several organizational factors that contributed to a climate of order and learning were delineated. In a study of the effects of English secondary schools on the learning and behavior of pupils, Rutter (1980) concluded that financial resources, school and class size, organizational structure, and punishment had limited effects on pupil outcome. Features that fostered pupil success included availability of rewards and praise, chances for students to assume responsibilities, emphasis on academic progress, positive models provided by teachers, and style of group management in the classroom.

These studies underscore the role of schools as social organizations. Schools constitute a major area of influence on children's well-being, so the relation of schools to determining and alleviating stressors is crucial to the students' health or disease. Table 5.2 compares schools and the work place as organizational settings. It is offered as a guide in constructing the kinds of studies in school settings that have already been applied to adults in the work place. Analogies in the school setting emphasize the need to include schools in studies of the effects of organizational settings for youth in relation to stress, health and disease.

Further research is needed that uses the model of the school as a people-processing institution to deter-

mine the place of the school in preparing youngsters for
their roles in adult organizational settings such as the
work place. Studies that elucidate particular health
risks for youngsters in schools are also relevant.
Examples include a study of the specific benefits of
establishing independent health behaviors in students
(Lewis et al., 1977) and a report highlighting injuries
in sports programs (American Academy of Pediatrics,
1980). Also of interest are longitudinal studies that
consider how experiences in school mold subsequent
responses to stresses in other organizational settings.

Work and Nonwork

Appropriately, most research on stress in organizational settings has concentrated on work settings and
the work role. However, life consists of many different
roles and activities at any given time, and these change
throughout the life course. Beyond work and school are
the family, community, and other public and private
organizations with which people interact. Outside events
may be important mediators of the effects of organizational stress and changes in health. It would be
impossible to identify and monitor potential influences
in all of these domains, but it should be possible to
focus on several key issues.

Out of Work and Out of School

Although organizational settings create a great deal
of objective and perceived stress, escape from these
settings may not be the way to reduce stress. A segment
of the population spends little or no time at work or
school, because they are considered ineligible by these
organizations (preschool children, retirees, handicapped
persons), choose not to work outside the home (housewives
or househusbands), or are unable to find appropriate work
or school roles (school drop-outs, unemployed workers).
Recent evidence indicates that these roles may be equally
or even more stressful than work or school roles.

The loss or lack of socially expected and valued
work and school rules is associated with both stress and
disease. Brenner (1973, 1976) has presented data that
suggest that increases in unemployment lead directly to
higher rates of mortality and hospitalization for mental
disorders. Aggregate relationships between annual unemployment rates and annual rates of mortality or mental

99

TABLE 5.2

SCHOOLS AND THE WORK PLACE:
A COMPARISON OF POTENTIAL ORGANIZATIONAL STRESSORS

Variable	School Setting	Work Setting
PHYSICAL STRUCTURE		
Environmental Risks	Exposures to contagions, toxins, pollutants	Similar
Physical Risks	High rate of athletic injuries (1 million during football season alone)	Accidents (more regulation of high risk situations)
Monitoring Mechanism	None	Occupational Safety and Health Assoc.
SOCIAL STRUCTURE		
Composition	Sorting and assignment by developmental assessment	Assignment by other kinds of criteria
	Demographic characteristics may influence nature of learning experience and/or age gradation	Can affect work conditions
Social Relations	Power relations, authority relations, and affinity relations contribute to wellbeing	Same
Organizational Model	Period of redefinition of labor/management roles (from family model toward industrial model)	Stable
SOCIAL FUNCTION		
Instruction	Primary goal of school (amount of time, quality, extent of individualization and special assistance are areas of concern)	Instruction limited to initial phase of employment

100

TABLE 5.2
(continued)

Variable	School Setting	Work Setting
Custody/Control	Principle of in loco parentis dictates nature and extent of rules (rule clarity, statement of rights, rule enforcement, surveillance, and areas of potential conflict), programs, discipline measures	Workers above age of majority
Socialization	First non-familial socialization experience (student-staff and student-student interactions)	Patterns of socialization well established
Evaluation/ Certification	"Product" supposed to be individual advancement of pupil (modified by teacher expectation, promotion policies)	Individual productivity measured as it pertains to group productivity
Selection	"Mainstreaming" (extent and characteristics of tracking, criteria for recruitment and establishment of special programs now undergoing major revision)	Variable, depending on occupation

SOCIAL CLIMATE

Variable	School Setting	Work Setting
Strain	Measured by pressure to deviate as a function of a means/end disjunction	Similar
Identification	Feelings of attachment to school and personnel	Similar
Commitment	Individual's sense of commitment to goals of school	Similar
Involvement	Individuals's involvement in school activities	Similar

TABLE 5.2
(continued)

Variable	School Setting	Work Setting
Belief	Faith in moral validity of rules and goals	Similar
Fate Control	Sense of personal power	Similar

ROLE OF THE INDIVIDUAL

Normative Data

Biological	Objective measurements available by age, pubertal development for physiological and chemical determinations	Less variation in adulthood
Socio-behavioral	Scales of psychological, cognitive, moral, life stress must use developmental approach	Similar (need for correlation with life stage)
Health Habits	Being established in childhood/adolescence	Already established
Control	Control often assumed by adult authority	Control resides within worker
Intervention	More likely to affect health behavior if intervention tried at early age	More difficult for established health habits

Disease states

Predisposing Factors	Antecedents not well substantiated in childhood/adolescence	Some well established, e.g., Type A behavior
Clinical Manifestations	Assume different forms in childhood, e.g. abdominal pain, headaches	Ulcers, hypertension, myocardial infarction

TABLE 5.2
(continued)

Variable	School Setting	Work Setting
Effects of Labeling	May alter subsequent personal advancement and health	Similar

OUTCOME CRITERIA

Achievement	Standardized achievement tests, percent of students promoted, academic grades	Production, profit, promotion
Failure to Achieve	Truancy, disruptive behavior, promotion lag	Absenteeism; production, profit, or promotion lag

COMMUNITY CONTEXT

Social Control	Conflicting views of importance of in loco parentis. Competing responsibilities with parents, families, other social institutions	Social control resides within adult workers and management
Social Expectations	Schools often viewed as source and solution of many social ills (as expressed in recent concern over vandalism, riots and disruptive behavior)	More limited expectations from adult workers as to benefits, rewards of work
Predictive Value of Experience	School performance as predictor of income earning potential and productivity (usefulness of trans-situational comparisons)	Use of schooling, school performance, as basis of selection of workers

hospital admission are open to a variety of alternative explanations. However, in a quasi-experimental study of men who lost their jobs due to plant shutdowns, Cobb and Kasl (1977) found that more unemployed men suffered psychological and physical illnesses over the course of the study than did stably employed workers in similar plants and communities. A range of diseases and disease indicators, including suicide, stomach upset, joint swelling, high cholesterol, hypertension, and rapid hair loss, were higher among men who lost their jobs than among controls. Negative affective states such as anxiety and depression also occurred more frequently among unemployed men, but only if the men experienced the combination of lower than average social support from friends and greater than average time until reemployment.

Current evidence indicates that, among persons who normally expect or are expected to work, unemployment is a risk factor for illness. Similar results may apply for school drop-outs, and relevant data should be collected. In contrast, many people expect and are expected neither to work nor to go to school. Preschool children, retirees, the disabled or handicapped, and housewives occupy enduring social roles that lie outside formal organizations. Current data show that such roles are stressful in their own ways. For example, Gove and Geerken (1977) found that married women who do not work manifest as many psychiatric symptoms as do working married women, and Haynes et al. (1980) found that housewives had about the same incidence of cardiovascular disease as did working women. Even a nonworking role such as retirement appears to be neither more nor less stressful or healthful than the work role.

Organizational Aspects Outside School or Work Settings

Studies of mental health and the quality of life consistently find that most people believe marriage and family are more important than work to their overall well-being, and research is accumulating about which nonwork aspects of life are good measures of well-being (Andrews and Withey, 1976; Bradburn, 1969; and Campbell et al., 1976). Until recently, traditional sex roles and an intact nuclear family were the dominant pattern of family organization to which schools and work organizations related in predictable ways. The past two decades have produced major changes in that pattern that are important in themselves and that also affect work and school roles. Schools increasingly must deal with pupils

104

who are in single-parent families or with two working parents. Increasingly, work organizations are populated with both men and women and with workers who also have parental responsibilities. Conversely, work and school organizations impose major structural constraints on personal and family development (Kanter, 1977).

Few data are available about these concerns. Studies of shift work find that it not only disrupts individuals' diurnal rhythms with significant health consequences, but creates strains in marital and family roles that also tend to be deleterious for health (Mott et al., 1965). Evidence is just beginning to accumulate on the impact on an individual of trying to meet all of the demands of the roles of worker, spouse, and parent. Haynes et al. (1980) found that rates of cardiovascular disease were higher among women who had ever married, especially among those who raised three or more children. Gove and Geerken (1977) found that the levels of psychiatric symptoms among employed wives without children were identical to those for men and lower than those for nonworking married women without children; working or nonworking women with children had twice the rate of major psychiatric symptoms as men.

Work and school still remain the frame around which to organize much basic and applied research on stress and health most effectively. Organizational populations can be contacted and followed over time more easily than can general population samples. As discussed in the next chapter, organizational settings also provide a potential laboratory in which to alter objective social environments and study changes in perceived stress and health.

Moderators and Conditioners

The path from a stressor in the objective organizational environment to a health consequence is complex. Modifiers may influence any of the steps through the perceived environment; immediate emotional, physiological, and behavioral reactions; and eventual consequences. In the model (Figure 5.1), two main categories of conditioning variables are considered: relatively enduring properties of the individual, which can be thought of as characteristic vulnerability or resistance to any specific stressor, and properties of the context or situation in which that stressor is imposed. That context may be supportive and stress-buffering or threatening and stress-intensifying.

Individual Vulnerability

Individual vulnerability to specific, job-related stressors varies widely (McLean, 1979); genetic and developmental factors can be strongly influential. To call these characteristics enduring does not deny the possibility of change; it only emphasizes the slower pace or greater difficulty of change. For instance, vulnerability to many stressors alters with age. Grinker (1974) has noted that inadequate reactions may reflect difficulties in a specific phase of the life course. In general, each phase seems to be characterized by its own patterns of organization, its own vulnerabilities, and its own methods of coping.

Vulnerability to different stressors also varies with personality. For example, reported symptoms in reaction to role conflict were greater among persons who were flexible and extroverted than among those who were rigid, introverted, and scored high in emotional sensitivity (Kahn et al., 1964). Higher diastolic blood pressure was associated with executive responsibility for the futures of other people, but only among executives who scored high on one or more of Type A characteristics (Cobb, 1973; Friedman and Rosenman, 1974; Sales, 1969). Other personal characteristics also may moderate relationships between stress and adverse consequences. For instance, how prepared is the individual for the event? How much previous experience has been gained from similar types of change earlier? What personal and cultural values and aspirations might influence the interpretation of and efforts to cope with life changes? (cf. Chapter 7, Psychosocial Assets and Modifiers of Stress)

Individual vulnerability to stress can be thought of as varying for each person as well as between persons. Individuals may have characteristic vulnerabilities to a certain stressor; but there would presumably be detectable variations, depending on moods, daily events, and other current experiences. These less enduring personal properties would then act to moderate or exaggerate responses to stress, much as do more stable characteristics. The accumulation of stressful events also can be thought of in terms of individual vulnerability. Several studies (McLean, 1979) have demonstrated that stressful job changes may be associated with a mental disorder if the indiviudal already has experienced another stressful event off the job. In such cases, was the stressor really the combination of two events, or did the first event increase the vulnerability and the second result in the observed consequence? The greater

the time lapse between the relevant events, the more
appropriate is the latter conceptualization.

Context

The context in which a person encounters a stressor
also can alter reactions and consequences markedly.
Contextual factors can be supportive and buffering, or
they can heighten the stress effect. Relevant social,
physical, or economic contexts may be as broad as the
economy or as narrow as the family unit. Contextual
variables on the job may be industry-wide or limited to
a single organization or one of its subsystems. In the
work setting, context also is set by management policy
and by union activity.

During a recession, with fewer employment opportunities, an individual's reactions to job-related stressors
may be subjectively more significant than they would be
when economic security is not threatened. The closing
of a factory or other enterprise almost always involves
disruption and change (Cobb and Kasl, 1977), but the
events are more threatening and the effects more serious
when the state of the economy is bad. As noted earlier,
Brenner (1973, 1976) found associations between economic
factors and disease consequences. One interpretation of
these data would be that the interactive effects of adverse economic conditions with other life events augment
the association of the latter with negative effects on
health.

An example of contextual influence in the immediate
work situation is provided by the research of Kahn et al.
(1964) on the stressor of role conflict and ambiguity.
Frequency of communication, functional dependence, and
power affected responses for a number of stressors.
Thus, with frequent communication, a given degree of
objective role conflict led to greater intensity of experienced conflict, heightened sense of role ambiguity,
decreased job satisfaction, increased sense of futility
in the work role, and deterioration in interpersonal
relations. Power and functional dependence had similar
contextual effects; they heightened the effect of role
conflict.

As discussed in Psychosocial Assets and Modifiers
of Stress (Chapter 7), one moderating variable of stress
reactions that has been studied in depth is social support, a term that has been variously defined to include
relationships characterized by liking, respect, exchange

of confidences, and mutual obligation. Several kinds of organizational stress are less marked for people with supportive relationships than for those who lack such supports. These results have held, with significant but imperfect consistency, in a variety of settings and experimental designs including studies of unemployment (Cobb and Kasl, 1977), overload and administrative responsibility (French, 1973), and monotonous work in the rubber and chemical industry (House and Wells, 1978). The buffering effect also was apparent in a sample of 2,000 men in 23 varied occupations (Caplan et al., 1975; LaRocoo et al., 1980). In all these studies, social support had apparent main effects in stress reduction, as well as the buffering effects just described.

Goodness of Fit

The introduction of moderating or conditioning variables, especially enduring properties of the person, explicitly relates stressfulness of a potential stressor to vulnerability or resistance of the individual. What is too much for one person may be optimal for another. French et al. (1974) have developed a model in which stress is defined on any given stimulus dimension as lack of fit between the needs or abilities of an individual and the supplies or demands of the environment. Measurement of goodness of fit for someone in a given situation requires that each relevant property of the person and of the situation be measured in the same terms--for example, the demand of a job for sustained vigilance and the capacity of the person for such vigilance.

This model has been tested, first with a population of some 200 men in government employment (French, 1973) and subsequently in a purposeful sample of 2,000 men in 23 occupations (Caplan et al., 1975). In both studies, the power of psychosocial stressors to predict various criteria of strain was enhanced when goodness-of-fit with the needs of the individuals was taken into account. However, the effects were not uniform; they were not always strong; and they were sometimes linear, rather than curvilinear, as if too much of a good thing or too little of a bad one were not stressful. This model both merits and needs additional work.

Specific Research Needs

The traditional paradigm in occupational epidemiology is a useful starting point for a discussion of

108

strategies in stress research. The basic paradigm is simple: establish differences in morbidity and mortality by occupation and place of work and then search in the work place for environmental agents that might explain these differences. Sometimes, the usefulness of this approach is undermined by complicating factors such as self-selection or company selection into particular occupations, health-related reasons for job mobility or retirement, inadequate measures of exposure, incomplete personnel and medical records, loss to follow-up.

Unfortunately, application of this paradigm to the study of work stress and health consequences has had limited success. Representative of such studies is one dealing with job stress and psychiatric illness in the Navy. The approach failed on two grounds: (1) jobs with high rates of psychiatric consultations had little in common, and diverse assessments of working conditions failed to identify any clearly related hazards in the work setting; and (2) individuals in high-risk jobs were older, less educated, from a lower social class of origin, and more likely to be divorced or separated. Thus, they had many of the characteristics traditionally associated with higher rates of distress and mental illness, and these self-selection characteristics in no way directly implicated the work environment.

In response to the complexity of studying work stressors, many researchers have increased the richness of data collection by studying also subjective perceptions, evaluations, and reactions of individuals in different work settings. Most conceptualizations of stress emphasize the importance of subjective assessments of demands, resources, and consequences. These subjective formulations of stress, however, have led to methodological problems. For example, it can be quite difficult to establish firm links between objective dimensions of the work setting and subjective appraisals and reactions that presumably reflect them. In the absence of such links, the work both of the basic scientist wishing to clarify intervening processes in a causal chain and of the applied scientist wanting to alter some aspect of the work setting becomes much more difficult and tenuous. It is not yet clear to what extent improvements in the assessment of objective and subjective dimensions of work will reveal stronger links, as opposed to demonstrating that the links are truly weak. However, much remains to be done to identify and operationalize the relevant, stressful dimensions and to develop truly commensurate objective and subjective pairs of dimensions.

109

Another problem associated with the subjective formulation of stress is the large methodological and conceptual overlap between the independent variable-- the subjectively appraised stressor--and dependent variables such as distress or impaired functioning. Basically, the appraisal of one's situation as stressful and of oneself as being distressed or affected by it must be viewed as nearly one and the same process, and any correlations relating the two are only marginally illuminating. For example, a correlation between high qualitative overload and low occupational self-esteem may simply reflect similar ways of negatively evaluating one's traits and abilities in relation to the demands of a particular setting.

For all these reasons, studies need to include the full range of the stress response, beginning with objective or independently measured elements in the organizational setting and ending with measures of health or illness that go beyond self-report. Efforts to establish links between differential disease rates and objective work conditions or job categories are especially valuable, as are studies of factors that con- tribute to variations in the impact of the work setting.

Many of the studies needed must be prospective and longitudinal, to avoid biases that cloud retrospective research. However, recognition of the limitations of the cross-sectional, retrospective approach sometimes has led to simplistic endorsement of repeated data collection, as if simply resampling the same population at two or more points in time negates the limitations of the cross- sectional design. For studies of organizational stress, the design must be prospective, as much as possible, with respect to the exposure or risk factors of interest to avoid problems of self-selection and prior exposure to other risk factors.

It is possible to escalate demands for well-designed studies of organizational stress beyond feasible or fund- able bounds. Still, selective use of special research opportunities can increase considerably the ability to conduct necessary research. Particularly useful may be "natural" experiments involving socially signficant events. Planned or predictable changes like automating or closing a plant or revising a retirement policy can have health implications and may reveal something about adaptation to stressful conditions. These events can be studied in their natural settings, frequently with a good deal of scientific rigor. This is particularly true when the exposure to such events takes place with a minimum of self-selection and when adequate comparison groups not exposed to such events can be found.

Discussions of prospective studies also highlight broader concerns about the temporal dimension of research in this area. Two such concerns are mentioned here as illustrations. The first, reflecting the life-course perspective, is the possibility that the consequences of organizational stress vary according to the age of the individuals being studied. For example, when would one study mental health consequences of a dull and monotonous blue-collar job? A 10-year, longitudinal study of men and women who are 35 years or older and have 10 years of seniority may miss the phenomenon completely: casualties of inadequate adaptation may have disappeared from obser- vation; the remainder have adapted, but the costs of such adaptation can no longer be identified. Similarly, in studying the impact of job loss on blue collar workers, it may be necessary to avoid or study separately older workers, who can convert the role of the unemployed into a retirement or sick role, and younger workers, who can rethink their career plans and resume the student role.

Another concern with the temporal dimension involves stress itself and the time dimension of stress effects and adaptation. Occupational stress can vary from inter- mittent or self-limiting to chronic, and reactions can range from quick habituation through active adaptation to failure to adapt. It follows that occupational environ- ments which are characterized by chronic stressors to which adaptation is difficult should be early targets of stress studies. Unfortunately, the existing literature of occupational stress only provides a few hints about what to look for. For example, studies of air traffic controllers suggest that situations demanding constant vigilance and carrying a high level of responsibility for the lives and safety of other people may be a prototypi- cal stress situation. Other recent work suggests that some demanding jobs that have severe limits on discretion or latitude of job performance and adaptive behaviors may also have particularly adverse health effects.

Even the most chronic work stressor is self-limiting in the sense that the vast majority of individuals give up the work role each day, at least temporarily, and take on other roles outside the work place. This suggests that a more complete understanding of the health impact of work stress will require studies of interrelationships among the different life roles. For example, perhaps family and recreational activities of the air traffic controller, rather than on-the-job coping and adaptation,

111

are the significant determinants of whether the daily impact of the demanding job situation is defused daily or accumulates and becomes health-threatening.

Summary

To provide greater insights into the health impact of occupational stress, future research should have the following characteristics:

- Balanced inclusion of biological and psychosocial risk factors and descriptors. The impact of stressors should be assessed as factors that add to or interact with the established risk factors for particular disease outcomes.

- Exploitation of research opportunities presented by "natural" experiments. Such settings offer the possibility of prospective longitudinal designs with high comparability to control groups and minimal problems of self-selection.

- Focus on the most important variables in the work environment, studied in susceptible workers. This calls for a purposive study of chronic stressors for which adaptation is difficult in people who have not yet passed through the critical stages of feeling the impact of such work environment and coping with it.

- Careful assessment of work environment and dimensions (demands and resources) and of characteristics of the individual (needs and abilities). Such analyses will enable study of important components of fit between personal and environmental characteristics, permitting a richer, interactive formulation of ways in which occupational stressors can affect health.

The conduct and design of such studies in turn requires agreement among research workers that this type of investigation is important, the willingness of funding agencies to consider longer and more costly research designs when scientific requirements are clear, and the accessibility of appropriate populations in organizational settings. None of these conditions is met easily, but all seem attainable and worthy of the effort.

References

Adams, J. S. The structure and dynamics of behavior in organizational boundary roles. IN: Handbook of Industrial and Organizational Psychology (Dunnette, M. D., ed.) Chicago: Rand-McNally, 1976, pp. 1175-1199.

American Academy of Pediatrics Committee on Pediatric Effect of Physical Fitness, Recreation, and Sports. Injuries in Sports. Pediatrics 65:A53-A54, 1980.

Andrews, F. M., and Withey, S. B. Social Indicators of Well-Being: Americans' Perceptions of Life Quality New York: Plenum, 1976.

Blau, P. M. A formal theory of differentiation in organizations. Amer. Sociol. Rev. 35:201-218, 1970.

Bradburn, N. M. The Structure of Psychological Well-Being Chicago: Aldine, 1969.

Brenner, M. H. Mental Illness and the Economy Cambridge: Harvard University Press, 1973.

Brenner, M. H. Estimating the Social Costs of National Economic Policy: Implications for Mental and Physical Health and Criminal Aggression Washington, D.C.: U.S. Government Printing Office, 1976.

Burns, T., and Stalker, G. M. The Management of Innovations London: Tavistock, 1961.

Campbell, A., Converse, P. E., and Rodgers, W. L. The Quality of American Life: Perceptions, Evaluations and Satisfactions New York: Russell Sage Foundation, 1976.

Caplan, R. D. Organizational Stress and Individual Strain: A Sociopsychological Study of Risk Factors in Coronary Heart Disease among Administrators, Engineers, and Scientists Unpublished doctoral dissertation, University of Michigan, 1972.

Caplan, R. D. Cobb, S., French, J. R. P., Jr., Harrison, R. D., and Pinneau, S. R., Jr. Job Demands and Worker Health: Main Effects and Occupational Differences Washington, D.C.: U.S. Government Printing Office, 1975.

Cassell, J. C. An epidemiological perspective of psychosocial factors in disease etiology. Amer. J. Pub. Health 64:1040-1043, 1974.

Cassell, J. The contribution of the social environment to host resistance. Amer. J. Epidemiol. 104:107-123, 1976.

Cobb, S. Workload and coronary heart disease. Proceedings, Social Statistics Section, American Statistical Association, December 30, 1973, pp. 170-173.

Cobb, S. Social support as a moderator of life stress. Psychosom. Med. 38:300-314, 1976.

Cobb, S., and Kasl, S. V. Termination: The Consequences of Job Loss Washington, D.C.: U.S. Government Printing Office, 1977, DHEW (NIOSH), Publ. No. 77-224.

113

Cobb, S., and Rose, R. M. Hypertension, peptic ulcer, and diabetes in air traffic controllers. J. Amer. Med. Soc. 224:489-492, 1973.

Coleman, J. E., et al. Equality of Educational Opportunity Washington, D.C.: U.S. Government Printing Office, 1966, DHEW, Office of Education, Publ. No. OE-38001.

Cooper, C. L., and Payne, R. (Eds.) Stress at Work New York: Wiley, 1978.

Emery, F. E., and Trist, E. L. The causal texture of organizational environments. Hum. Relations 18:21-32, 1965.

Frankenhaeuser, M., and Gardell, B. Underload and overload in working life: outline of a multidisciplinary approach. J. Hum. Stress 2: 35-46, 1976.

French, J. R. P., Jr. Organizational stress and individual strain. IN: The Failure of Success (Marrow, A. J., ed.) New York: American Management Association, 1973.

French, J. R. P., Jr. Person-role fit. IN: Occupational Stress (McLean, A. A., ed.) Springfield: Thomas, 1974, pp. 70-79.

French, J. R. P., Jr., Rodgers, W., and Cobb, S. Adjustments as person-environment fit. IN: Coping and Adaptation (Coelho, G. V., Hamburg, D. A., and Adams, J. E., eds.) New York: Basic Books, 1974, pp. 316-333.

Friedman, M., and Rosenman, R. H. Type A behavior pattern: its association with coronary heart disease. Ann. Clin. Res. 3:300-312, 1971.

Friedman, M., and Rosenman, R. H. Type A: Your Behavior and Your Heart New York: Knopf, 1974.

Goffman, E. Asylums Garden City: Doubleday, 1961.

Gove, W. R., and Geerken, M. R. The effect of children and employment on the mental health of married men and women. Social Forces 56:66-76, 1977.

Grinker, R. R., Sr. Foreword. IN: Coping and Adaptation (Coelho, G. V., Hamburg, D. A., and Adams, J. E., eds.) New York: Basic Books, 1974, pp. xi-xiii.

Hage, J. Theories of Organizations New York: Wiley, 1980.

Hasenfeld, Y., and English, R. A. Human Service Organizations: A Book of Readings Ann Arbor: University of Michigan Press, 1974.

Haynes, S., Levine, S., Scotch, N., Feinleib, M., and Kannell, W. B. The relationship of psychosocial factors to coronary heart disease in the Framingham study. I. Methods and risk factors. Amer. J. Epidemiol. 107:362-383, 1978.

Haynes, S. G., and Feinleib, M. Women, work and coronary
heart disease: prospective findings from the Framing-
ingham heart study. Amer. J. Pub. Health 70:133-141,
1980.
Haynes, S. G., Feinleib, M., and Kannell, W. B. The
relationships of psychosocial factors to coronary
heart disease in the Framingham study. III. Eight-
year incidence of coronary heart disease. Amer. J.
Epidemiol. 111:37-58, 1980.
House, J. S. Occupational stress and coronary heart
disease: a review and theoretical integration. J.
Health Soc. Behav. 15:12-27, 1974a.
House, J. S. The effects of occupational stress on
physical health. IN: Work and Quality of Life--
Resource Papers for Work in America (O'Toole, J.,
ed.) Cambridge: MIT Press, 1974b, pp. 145-170.
House, J. Work Stress and Social Support Reading:
Addison-Wesley, 1980a.
House, J. Occupational Stress and the Mental and Physi-
cal Health of Factory Workers Ann Arbor: Institute
for Social Research, 1980b.
House, J. S., and Wells, J. A. Occupational stress,
social support, and health. IN: Reducing Occupa-
tional Stress: Proceedings of a Conference (McLean,
A., Black, G., and Colligan, M., eds.) Washington,
D.C.: U.S. Government Printing Office, 1978, DHEW
(NIOSH) Publ. No. 78-140, pp. 8-29.
Jencks, C., et al. Inequality: A Reassessment of the
Effect of Family and Schooling in America New York:
Basic Books, 1972.
Jenkins, C. D. Psychologic and social precursors of
coronary disease. New Engl. J. Med. 294:987-994,
1976.
Kahn, R. L., Wolfe, D. M., Quinn, R. P., and Snoek, J. D.
Organizational Stress: Studies in Role Conflict and
Ambiguity New York: Wiley, 1964.
Kahn, R. L. Some propositions toward a researchable
conceptualization of stress. IN: Social and Psycho-
logical Factors in Stress (McGrath, J. E., ed.) New
York: Holt, Rinehart, & Winston, 1970, pp. 97-103.
Kahn, R. L. Work and Health New York: Wiley Inter-
science, 1981.
Kanter, R. M. Work and Family in the United States: A
Critical Review and Agenda for Research and Policy
New York: Russell Sage Foundation, 1977.
Kasl, S. V. Epidemiological contributions to the study
of work stress. IN: Stress at Work (Cooper, C. L.,
and Payne, R., eds.) New York: Wiley, 1978, pp.
3-48.

Katz, D., and Kahn, R. L. The Social Psychology of Organizations, 2nd Ed. New York: Wiley, 1978.

LaRocco, J. M., House, J. S., and French, J. R. P., Jr. Social support occupational stress and health. J. Health Soc. Behav. 21:202-218, 1980.

Lawrence, P. R., and Lorsch, J. W. Organization and Environment Boston: Harvard Business School, 1967.

Levi, L. Stress and Distress in Response to Psycho-Social Stimuli Oxford: Pergamon Press, 1972.

Lewis, C. E., Lewis, M. A., Lorimer, A., and Palmer, B. B. Child-initiated care: the use of school nursing services by children in an "adult-free" system. Pediatrics 60:499-507, 1977.

Likert, R. New Patterns of Management New York: McGraw-Hill, 1961.

March, J. G., and Simon, H. A. Organizations New York: Wiley, 1958.

Maslach, C. Job burnout: how people cope. Pub. Welfare 36:56-58, 1978.

McGrath, J. E. (Ed.) Social and Psychological Factors in Stress New York: Holt, Rinehart & Winston, 1970.

McGrath, J. E. Stress and behavior in organizations. IN: Handbook of Industrial Organizational Psychology (Dunnett, M. D., ed.) Chicago: Rand McNally, 1976.

McGregor, D. The Human Side of Enterprise New York: McGraw-Hill, 1960.

McLean, A. A. Work Stress Reading: Addison-Wesley, 1979.

Miller, J. G. Living Systems: Basic Concepts. Behav. Sci. 10:193-237, 1965.

Miller, J. G. Living Systems New York: McGraw-Hill, 1978.

Mott, P. E., Mann, F. C., McLaughlin, Q., and Warwich, D. P. Shift Work Ann Arbor: University of Michigan Press, 1965.

National Institute of Education. The Safe Schools Study Washington, D.C.: U.S. Government Printing Office, 1978.

Parsons, T. Suggestions for a sociological approach to the theory of organizations, I. Admin. Sci. Q. 1:63-85, 1956a.

Parsons, T. Suggestions for a sociological approach to the theory of organizations, II. Admin. Sci. Q. 1: 225-239, 1956b.

Parsons, T. Structure and Process in Modern Societies Glencoe: Free Press, 1960.

Pearlin, L., and Johnson, J. S. Marital status, life strains, and depression. Amer. Sociol. Rev. 42: 704-715, 1977.

Rose, R. M., Jenkins, C. D., and Hurst, M. W. Air Traffic Controller Health Change Study Boston: Boston
University, 1978.

Rutter, M. Changing Youth in a Changing Society: Patterns of Adolescent Development and Disorder Cambridge: Harvard University Press, 1980.

Sales, S. M. Differences Among Individuals in Effective,
Behavioral, Biochemical and Physiological Responses to
Variations in Workload Unpublished doctoral disserta-
tion, University of Michigan, 1969.

Smith, M. J., Collisan, M. J., and Hurrell, J. A review
of NIOSH psychological stress research. IN: Occupational Stress (Department of Health, Education, and
Welfare) Washington, D.C.: U.S. Government Printing
Office, 1978, DHEW (NIOSH) Publ. No. 78-156.

Tannenbaum, A. S., and Cooke, R. A. Organizational control: a review of research employing the control
graph method. IN: Organizations Alike and Unlike
(Lammers, C. J., and Hickson, D. J., eds.) London:
Routledge and Kegan Paul, 1978.

Thompson, J. D. Organizations in Action New York:
McGraw-Hill, 1967.

117

CHAPTER 6

Report on
Work Stress Related to
Social Structures and Processes

Panel Members:
Lennart Levi, M.D., Chair
Marianne Frankenhaeuser, Ph.D.
Bertil Gardell, Ph.D.

In the United States, as in most other industrialized countries, rapid, fundamental changes are taking
place in such basic social structures as the way children
are reared, the types of environments in which people
work, and the mechanisms for taking care of the old and
sick. These changes are influenced by and influence
phenomena such as urbanization, mechanization and automation, environmental pollution, uneven distribution of
resources, and shortages of work and housing. At the
same time, increases in communication, education, and
advertising have resulted in greater expectations.

Singly and together, these phenomena have obvious
signficance to stress and disease. These structural
problems have not been dealt with adequately in the context and scope of modern stress research, environmental
planning, and health care. This chapter is complementary
to the preceding one, Stress in Organizational Settings.
That report discussed ways in which to assess what in
the social surroundings is stressful and what health
changes are associated with such stressors. Our group
has attempted to highlight a few studies that have
addressed these issues, suggesting lines of research
that might improve the state of existing knowledge and
possible directions for prevention of health-related
problems associated with stress-promoting social structures. Both chapters give particular attention to the
work setting, because of its pervasive importance to
most people and because most of the available research
in this area has taken place in such settings.

Stressful Social Structures

In 1976, at a meeting sponsored by the World Health Organization (WHO), senior public health authorities of ten countries concluded that important stressful psychosocial situations fall into four general categories (World Health Organization, 1976):

- Uprooting, in the sense of depriving individuals and groups of experiences and material means that provide emotional support, sense of belonging, and purpose in life. Migration and resettlement, rural proverty, urban slums, and cultural displacement of old people or adolescents are all components of uprooting.

- Dehumanization of societal institutions, in the sense that needed services are provided impersonally and mechanically--ignoring the total being, treating people only as passive recipients of care, and not considering individual differences. Over-reliance on technology or absence of individual and community participation in planning and providing health care also can lead to dehumanization.

- Psychosocial side-effects of the spread of innovations, in the sense that a given technology or product of technology may change the behavior of people in an unexpected and sometimes hazardous manner--for example, the trends in industry toward increasing mechanization and automation; increasing proportions of large enterprises; increasing anonymity, division of labor, and heterogeneity of life; and increasing distances in relationships between worker and worker, worker and union official, worker and management, and producer and consumer.

- Psychosocial factors as constraints on environmental and health programs and activities, in the sense that important health measures meet obstacles arising out of cultural and behavioral characteristics of the population. Included, for instance, are clashes of values among planners, care givers, administrators, and care receivers and communication difficulties arising from differing priorities and cultural and linguistic diversity.

There is little direct evidence of a relationship between such social structures and processes and their

resulting changes and the incidence and prevalence of ill
health, lack of well-being, and low quality of life.
But, a substantial body of indirect evidence strongly
suggests that such associations exist and emphasizes the
need to better understand their role in the etiology of
some major social and health problems. For example, the
President's Commission on Mental Health (1978) recently
examined mental health needs of people in the United
States. It found that 5 to 15 percent of children 3 to
15 years old suffer from persistent, handicapping mental
health problems. These conditions include emotional disorders, the so-called conduct disorders, and impairments
or delays in psychological development. Alcohol abuse
is a major social, physical, and mental health problem
with an estimated annual cost of over $40 billion.
About ten million Americans have alcohol-related problems. Nearly 15 percent of the population needs some
form of mental health services at any one time. As many
as 25 percent suffer from mild to moderate depression,
anxiety, and other indicators of emotional disorder.
Also important, although unquantifiable, is the damage
to mental health that is associated with unrelenting
poverty, unemployment, and the institutionalized discrimination that occurs on the basis of race, sex, class,
age, and mental and psychological distress. These too
are due, in part, to social structures and processes.

These problems exist in spite of considerable
improvements in the United States, as in other industrialized countries in terms of wealth, level of education,
nutrition, sanitation, and investment in health care.
Halfdan Mahler (1977), Director-General of WHO, recently
noted that "cardiovascular diseases are rampant; drugs,
alcohol, cigarettes and traffic accidents nowadays kill
more people than did all the epidemics together in earlier centuries; the aged are overwhelmed with diagnostic
tools and abstruse technology, but their psychosocial
and mental well-being is left largely unattended and
uncared for." Common denominators in the etiology of
stress-related ill health appear to flow from a discrepancy between human needs and environmental possibilities
for their satisfaction, human capacity and environmental
demands, or human expectations and the perceived situation (Kagan and Levi, 1974; Levi and Andersson, 1975).

Stressful Components of Working Life

As illustrated in the previous chapter, discussions
of work stress usually emphasize psychosocial stressors
(cf. Levi, 1980) and often ignore physical environmental

factors, even though such factors can influence the
worker both physiologically, as when an organic solvent
affects brain function, and psychosocially. An example
of the latter effect might be distress resulting from
odors, glare, noise, or extremes with regard to air,
temperature, or humidity. Secondary distress also can
arise from the worker's awareness, suspicion, or fear of
being exposed to life-threatening chemical hazards or to
accident risks. Real-life conditions usually involve a
combination of many exposures. Such combinations may
lead to complex interactions that are hard to predict in
advance. Thus, a seemingly trivial environmental factor,
added to a considerable preexisting environmental load,
may trigger major physiological or psychosocial reactions
that can lead to severe health consequences. Unfortunately, very little is known about the net effects of
such combined exposures.

With regard to psychosocial stresssors in the work
environment, existing evidence supports the assumption
that a number of properties of system design and job
content are critical with regard both to job satisfaction
and to health (Frankenhaeuser, 1976, 1981; Frankenhaeuser
and Gardell, 1976; Frankenhaeuser and Johansson, 1976;
Gardell, 1980; Johansson et al., 1978; Levi, 1972, 1981):

● Quantitative overload: too much to do, excessive
time pressure, or repetitive work-flow in combination with one-sided job demands and superficial
attention. This is, to a great extent, typical of
mass-production technology and routine office work.

● Qualitative underload: too narrow and one-sided job
content, lack of stimulus variation, no demands on
creativity or problem-solving, or low opportunities
for social interaction. These jobs seem to become
more common with automation and increased use of
computers in both offices and manufacturing.

● Lack of control: especially in relation to pace of
work and working methods.

● Lack of social support: inadequate social networks
at home and with fellow workers.

Thus, work stress appears to be associated with two
types of adverse consequences: first, there may be a
direct association between certain objective conditions

at work--physiological and psychological stressors--and
ill health; second, certain stress conditions may create
fatigue or passivity in individuals and thus make it
more difficult for them to involve themselves actively
in efforts to change those working conditions, including
physical and chemical risk factors, that may be detri-
mental to health. This latter aspect is especially
relevant when interest is focused on ill-health prevention on the systems level.

Often, several of these characteristics appear
together and jointly affect health and well-being.
For example, in a study of the male Swedish labor force,
workers having jobs characterized by heavy loads together
with low control over the work situation were found to
have disproportionately high frequencies of symptoms of
depression, excessive fatigue, cardiovascular disease,
and mortality; the least probability for illness and
death was found among groups with moderate loads who also
had high control over the work situation (Ahlbom et al.,
1977; Karasek, 1979, 1981).

As pointed out by Gardell (1976), Wilensky (1981)
and others, ill effects of mass-production technology
include alienation of the worker not only during working
hours but with a spillover to leisure time as well. An
increase in apathy may grow out of this disaffection,
leading to a decreased willingness of the worker to take
part in activities outside work. It seems reasonable
that the speed with which a person "unwinds" after work
could influence the magnitude of the physiological and
psychosocial effects. Hence, the speed of unwinding also
is likely to affect the extent to which stress at work is
carried over into leisure time (Frankenhaeuser, 1977a,b).

Temporal patterns of psychological and physiological
reactions to stressors differ greatly among individuals.
As discussed in Biological Substrates of Stress (Chapter
8), one frequent physiological reaction to a stressor is
an elevation in blood concentrations of the catecholamines norepinephrine (noradrenaline) and epinephrine
(adrenaline). Until recently, changes in catecholamine
concentrations could be monitored in humans only by
measuring how much was excreted in urine. There is evidence that, after exposure to a stressor is over, some
people rapidly decrease their excretion of epinephrine
and others show a slower decline (Johansson and Frankenhaeuser, 1973). Studies indicate that "rapid decreasers"
are better balanced psychologically and more efficient
in achievement situations than are "slow decreasers."

Also, an individual's state of general well-being may be a mediator of this phenomenon. Thus, in a group of industrial workers, the proportion of rapid epinephrine decreasers was significantly higher after a vacation period that had improved the workers' physical and psychological well-being (Johansson, 1976). In contrast, when female clerks had to work overtime, catecholamine excretion was elevated throughout the overtime period, both during the day and in the evening (Rissler, 1977), and there was a pronounced increase in epinephrine output in the evening, when the clerks were home, away from the work setting (Frankenhaeuser, 1979, 1981). This biochemical change was accompanied by a markedly elevated heart rate and feelings of fatigue and irritability.

Stressful Aspects of Mass-Production Technology

During the last century, many jobs have changed from requiring the completion of a well-defined activity with a clearly recognized end product to involving narrow and highly specified subunits of endeavor bearing little apparent relation to the end product. The growing size of factory units has resulted in a long chain of command between the individual worker and management, giving rise to feelings of remoteness between the two groups. The worker also is remote from the consumer, for requirements of marketing, distribution, and selling interpose many steps between producer and consumer (Maule et al., 1973).

Mass production typically involves not only a marked fragmentation of the work process but also a decrease in worker control of it, partly because work organization, content, and pace are determined by machines and partly because of the detailed preplanning that is necessary in such systems. Such constrictions usually result in monotony, social isolation, lack of freedom, and increased time pressure--all of which might have long-term effects on health and well-being. With its pronounced fragmentation of the work process, mass production also favors the introduction of piece wages; and heavy investment in machinery, alone or combined with shorter hours of work, has increased the proportion of people working in shifts. Another effect of mass production, and of automation, is that large industrial concerns have grown at the expense of medium-sized and small enterprises.

Work on the assembly line is characterized by the machine system's rigorous control over the worker. The job is understimulating in the sense that the individual operations often are extremely simple, there are no options for variety in either pace or content, and opportunities for social interaction are minimal. Simultaneously, the work contains elements of overload, such as rapid pacing, coercion, and demands for sustained attention. Workers have no control over the pace, and body posture and mobility are restricted. In a classical study, Walker and Guest (1952) found that assembly-line work was accompanied by feelings of worker discontent, stress, and alienation. Others have reported similar results (Blauner, 1964; Zdravomyslov and Yadov, 1966). Studies that focus on task structure and its variations within similar technologies emphasize that the amount of flexibility workers have for exercising skill and control of their work affects not only alienation but also mental health (Kornhauser, 1965; Gardell, 1971). By integrating concepts and methods from psychophysiology and social psychology, it is possible to link both job dissatisfaction and physiological stress reactions to specific job characteristics (Frankenhaeuser, 1980a, 1981).

In a study of sawmill workers, Frankenhaeuser and Gardell (1976) compared catecholamine excretion patterns of a "high-risk" group of workers whose jobs were extremely constricted to those of a "low-risk" control group of workers from the same mill, whose job was not as constricted physically or mentally. Catecholamine excretion during work was significantly higher in the high-risk group than in controls. Furthermore, the time course was strikingly different in the two groups: catecholamine excretion decreased toward the end of the workday in the control group but increased in the high-risk group. Interview data showed that inability to relax after work was a frequent complaint in the latter group; moreover, absenteeism and psychosomatic symptoms were very prevalent in this group.

These relationships were examined further by comparing subgroups of workers who differed with regard to specific job characteristics (Johansson et al., 1978). Catecholamine excretion was greatest when the job was highly repetitious, when the worker had to maintain the same posture throughout working hours, and when the work pace was controlled by the machine system. Thus, lack of control again was the common factor. The influence of controllability on catecholamine excretion also has been demonstrated in laboratory studies of human subjects (Frankenhaeuser and Rissler, 1970; Frankenhaeuser et al., 1980; Glass et al., in press; Lundberg and Frankenhaeuser, 1978, 1980).

Similar issues are addressed in studies of reactions and consequences associated with a remuneration system involving piece wages (cf. Gardell, 1979; Levi, 1972). Piece-work systems have in common the payment of a price or rate per piece or unit of work; the price may be uniform at all levels of output or vary as production rises. Several different, though related, systems are included under this term. Systems in which earnings increase more than output permit workers to benefit from the reduction of overhead costs that is achieved as output rises. With a high piece-rate system, earnings and output are not linearly related, as they are under straight piece-work; instead, a greater increment is paid for each increase in output. For example, an increment of 1.33 percent may be awarded to the workers' time-rate for each 1 percent increase in output. Accelerating premium systems are based on the principle that earning increments are small for low and average levels of output, but become increasingly larger as output exceeds the average. At low output, the differences are small and scarcely apparent to the workers; but at high output, they provide a powerful stimulus to increase output more and more.

It is generally agreed that piece-wages strengthen motivation at work and constitute an important incentive for boosting productivity (Levi, 1972). Many claim that piece-wages are necessary for good performance, yielding higher earnings for workers and lower costs for management. In spite of its widespread use, little is known about the psychological and physiological effects of this remuneration system. For example, could excessively strong, prolonged motivation lead to undue strain that might be harmful to health and well-being? At least for a time, the desire--or need--to earn more can induce individuals to work harder, despite mental and physical "warnings" such as tiredness, nervousness, and functional disturbances. Another possible effect is that employees who are bent on raising their output and earnings may violate safety regulations, thereby increasing the risk of occupational disease and of accidents to themselves and others (Levi, 1976). In addition, handicapped or elderly employees working in groups with collective piece rates are likely to come under social pressure from their coworkers, and employees with individual piece rates might be less disposed to help each other. None of these potential problems have been studied adequately.

Efforts to study noneconomic effects of piece wages and experiments with wage payment methods must be done in relatively natural settings, making it difficult to

126

isolate the effects of piecework from other factors that affect an individual's feelings and behavior at the same time. For example, work content and remuneration system are intimately interlinked. Thus, almost by definition, piece-rated jobs must consist of operations that can be measured. As a rule, this also means a rather narrow and repetitive job.

In a large state-owned mining company, the introduction of fixed salaries was evaluated by an independent research team at one year (Kronlund, 1974) and by the company itself at three years (Kjellgren, 1975). Both studies showed a large decline in severe accidents, a smaller decline in moderately severe ones, and a rise in minor accidents. Both concluded that a system of fixed wages was associated with less stress and risk-taking. In the independent study, the rise in minor accidents was explained by the opportunity for workers under fixed wages to seek care for minor accidents without loss of income. The company study found an overall loss in productivity of ten percent in the mining operation and no decline in productivity in the more automated dressing plants. Similarly, for Swedish forest industries, one-year follow-up studies of the introduction of fixed wages in logging showed a decline in severe accidents. In one case, the total number of accidents decreased by 10 percent, but days lost through accidents were reduced by 50 percent (Swedish Forest Service, 1975). The Forest industries had productivity losses of 10 to 15 percent, but product quality increased (SCA-tidningen, 1975).

The above observations from epidemiological studies are supported further by data from experimental investigations (Levi, 1964, 1972). Healthy female office clerks were studied under conditions very similar to those involved in their everyday work. The introduction of highly progressive piece wages on the first and third day of the study resulted in significant increases in productivity but also in feelings of rush, fatigue, and physical discomfort and in increases of urinary epinephrine and norepinephrine excretion and in urine flow.

These and related findings point to piece-rate as a factor with several negative aspects from the point of view of health, well-being, and safety. Above all, piece-rates seem to induce such potentially stressful changes as intensified working rhythm, greater risk-taking, and competition between individuals or teams (Poyhonen, 1975). Thus, although piece-rates may lead to increased productivity, that effect may be at a cost carried by the worker and the larger society.

Stressful Aspects of Highly Automated Work Processes

In many industries, repetitive, manual elements now are performed by machines, and workers are left with mainly supervisory controlling functions. This kind of work usually is rather skilled, it is not regulated in detail, and the worker is free to move about (Blauner, 1964; Gardell, 1971). Accordingly, the introduction of automation is generally considered to be a positive step toward diminishing stress on the worker and improving occupational health and well-being. This may be true for those stages of automation where the operator is assisted by the computer but maintains some control over its services. However, if the computer obviates the need for operator skills and knowledge, a new impoverishment of the work may result, with reintroduction of monotony, social isolation, and lack of control.

Work conditions of control-room operators in large-scale plants offer a useful system in which to examine potential effects of extensive automation (Bainbridge, 1978; Frankenhaeuser, 1981; Johansson and Gardell, 1978). Such monitoring demands attention to detail and readiness to act throughout a monotonous period of duty. Yet, the brain needs a moderately varied flow of stimuli in order to maintain optimal alertness, and the ability to detect critical signals in a monotonous environment declines rapidly within the first half hour (Broadbent, 1971). Also, because process operators work in shifts, they may have to perform an attention-demanding task when they are out of phase with their biological rhythm, for example, when epinephrine secretion is low and ability to concentrate reduced (Froberg et al., 1975a,b; Levi, 1972). To this must be added the stress inherent in knowing that temporary inattention or an intrinsically slight error can have extensive economic and other disastrous consequences (Frankenhaeuser, 1977c, 1981; Levi, 1980). The pressing reality of such concerns is readily apparent, for example, for a process operator in the control room of a nuclear power plant (Frankenhaeuser, 1980b).

Other critical aspects of process control are associated with special demands on mental skill. Operators are concerned with abstract signals on arrays of instrument and are not in touch with the actual product of their work. How does this affect their perception of the importance of their task? Furthermore, high technical skill is required to enable them to carry out their work; yet, they spend most of their time in monotonous monitoring. Over time, how will these highly skilled operators cope with work conditions that permit them to use their training during only a fraction of their work hours? Research is needed to analyze the psychological and performance implications of such requirements.

Questions similar to those for industrial automation arise in connection with highly computerized administrative work. Office workers may spend nearly all of their day at a computer terminal. As long as the computer system functions adequately, the work runs smoothly. But when the computer breaks down, the worker is helpless and forced to remain in a state of passive expectation for an unpredictable period of time, holding up the flow of work (Frankenhaeuser, 1981). These machinery breakdowns occur irregularly and unpredictably and constitute a source of stressors that produce both psychological and physiological reactions (Johansson, 1979; Johansson and Aronsson, 1980). As in the case of highly automated industrial production systems, stress research is needed to provide knowledge that can aid in guiding technological developments to suit human needs and abilities. Information is needed to determine how automation can be introduced in ways that retain critical components for the worker, including meaningful work content and adequate demands on needed skills. Thus defined, optimal automation is not likely to be the same as maximal, readily available automation.

Stressful Aspects of Shift Work

Cyclical changes are an important property of all organic life. A special example of this rhythmicity is circadian rhythms, or those that occur in a twenty-four hour cycle. Many physiological and psychological functions have been shown to exhibit circadian rhythms. The peaks and valleys of such rhythms usually correspond with potential demand. Thus, systems that are responsive to the environment are most active during waking hours. At least until recently, these circadian rhythms have been well adapted to environmental demands, favoring a variety of life- and species-preserving activities during the day and sleep during the night (Akerstedt and Levi, 1978; Levi, 1980). But, increasing demands for services and introduction of extremely expensive and complex modern technology have created social structures that require greater human occuptional activity throughout the day.

Such circumstances have led to creation of work shifts in which people work at times other than during

129

the day, usually during late afternoon and evening or throughout the night. As a result, some individuals must work when they are out of synchrony with the usual circadian rhythms. In such cases, the rhythmical biological changes may no longer coincide with environmental demands. Activation may occur during the day, when these workers need to sleep, and deactivation may occur during the night, when they are expected to work and be alert. Further complications may result from social conflicts that arise in a social environment that is not designed for the needs of shift workers. These difficulties may be compounded greatly if employees are compelled to rotate shifts, so that they work during the days part of the time and during evenings or nights at other times.

Evidence suggests that use of two shifts during the day creates relatively few problems. However, even that arrangement can produce some strains on the worker. For example, employees on the morning shift may have problems with access to breakfast and public transportation. Difficulties that can be associated with the afternoon shift include decreased interactions with preschool and school children, relatives, and friends, as well as limited chances to participate in cultural, political, and other social activities (Magnusson and Nilsson, 1979). When there are three shifts to cover the entire twenty-four hour period, major disturbances appear to be unavoidable. Of particular importance are the social obstacles that those working on the night shift face in trying to secure a relatively long continuous period of free time in which to make up for a sleep deficit. Work schedules that appear to have the most negative consequences are rotating shifts, as occur, for example, in health and transportation services. In such situations, adaptational demands become part of ordinary life, with little predictability.

Temporal demands made on the shift workers by the work schedules are well known. Much less is known about the ability of individuals to meet those demands and of the psychobiological costs of such adaptation. Some of these problems have been the focus of a series of interdisciplinary investigations utilizing experimental and epidemiological approaches (Akerstedt, 1976; Akerstedt and Froberg, 1976).

Laboratory Experiments

One interesting series of studies looked for properties of the endogenous temporal variation of some important physiological and psychological functions by studying biological circadian rhythms in the absence of the normal time cues. More than 100 healthy volunteers of both sexes were exposed to three days and three nights of continuous work (Levi, 1972). Despite strict standardization and equalization of environmental stimuli, most circadian rhythms persisted throughout the vigil. During the night, there were pronounced decreases in epinephrine excretion, body temperature, and performance and increases in fatigue ratings and melatonin excretion (Akerstedt and Froberg, 1977; Froberg et al., 1975 a,b; Froberg, 1977; Levi, 1972).

Interdisciplinary, Observational Studies

A logical second step to studying the potential health effects of shift work was to look for persisting circadian rhythms in a real-life situation of environmental demands that were in conflict with such rhythms. Physiological, psychological, chronobiological, and social reactions were investigated in response to the introduction of three weeks of night work in habitual daytime workers (Akerstedt and Theorell, 1976; Theorell and Akerstedt, 1976). During the test period, the endocrine system started to adapt to the environmental demands by shifting its circadian cycle. However, one week of night work, which is typical for many rotating shifts, was not enough time for complete adaptation. In fact, even after three weeks of night work, the original circadian rhythms had either flattened or persisted for most subjects. These disturbed biological circadian rhythms were associated with difficulties in sleeping and possible indigestion. In addition, a switch from habitual day work to three weeks of night work was accompanied by increases in a number of indices of physiological stress and in social problems in the workers and in their families.

Real-Life Experiments

Observations on possible adverse effects of shift work were confirmed in an epidemiological study of the well-being of a large group of shift workers (Akerstedt and Torsvall, 1977a,b). A region was chosen in which no other jobs were available near to where the workers lived, thus minimizing the chances of self-selection to or away from shift work. Health questionnaires showed higher frequencies of sleep, mood, digestive, and social disturbances among shift workers than among day workers.

131

Complaints about lack of well-being were most common during the night shift. In a natural experiment within this setting, two experimental groups were switched to two-shift work or to day work only. A two-year follow-up demonstrated that the change to work schedules without night shift were accompanied by improved physical, mental, and social well-being (Akerstedt and Torsvall, 1978). In contrast, a comparable control group who remained on its habitual three-shift work schedule showed no such improvements.

Very recently, a study was conducted on police officers in Stockholm, who traditionally have worked on a schedule of rapidly rotating shifts, with each shift being earlier than the previous one (a counterclockwise rotation) (Orth-Gomer and Olivegard Landen, 1981). Based on other research, some work schedules were altered so that shifts rotated clockwise, as a possible improvement. Interdisciplinary cross-over evaluation showed that, compared with controls who remained on the old schedule, officers on the new rotation had an increased sense of well-being and a decrease in serum triglycerides, uric acid, and glucose.

These studies illustrate that shift work can be associated with a sense of reduced well-being, possibly as a result of a lack of fit between the work demands and the physiological, psychological, and social circadian patterns of the individual. Such research has both theoretical and practical significance. For example, the study cited earlier, in which subjects shifted to three weeks of night work, did not prove that night work was harmful for everyone (Akerstedt and Theorell, 1976). However, it did provide sufficient evidence of risk and dissatisfaction to persuade both management and workers that shift work was undesirable in that setting. Because the risk was deemed not to be worth any modest advantages that might be gained by having a night shift, the National Swedish Railway Company agreed to eliminate night work for the specific group of railway workers that was studied.

In summary, these studies and a critical review of the scientific literature justify several conclusions (Akerstedt 1979; Akerstedt et al., 1978). First, physical, mental, and social problems and complaints increase with the introduction of night shifts and decrease if night shifts are eliminated. Major concerns are sleep and digestion problems. Social problems and problems of health and well-being tend to coincide in the same individuals. When workers are rotating through three shifts, complaints are usually most pronounced for those on the night shift. Second, increased absenteeism is found in elderly shift workers, even though there is no overall increase in absenteeism in shift workers in comparison to day workers. This suggests that adverse consequences of shift work may be cumulative or more pronounced in older workers. Third, workers on permanent night shift exhibit a better biological adaptation than do those on rotating shifts: compared to day workers, their circadian rhythms are reversed, indicating that they are prepared for high levels of activity during the night. Such adaptation does not appear to occur for individuals who are on rotating shifts, regardless of the length of exposure. These insights into the effects of shift work are intriguing and emphasize the need for more research to learn who is at risk for adverse effects and what biological and psychosocial reactions contribute to undesirable reactions.

Relationships between Work and Other Social Structures and Processes

Social structures in the society outside work may be intimately intertwined with health and well-being in the work setting. For example, inadequate housing certainly is not the only factor that hinders shift workers from sleeping during their time off from work, but improved housing may enhance their ability to fall asleep and stay asleep during the day. In general, this interaction between social structure and the health effects of the work setting has not been studied adequately.

One social structure whose effects on work may be of great interest is that of commuting to work. Many workers must travel long distances between the work place and area of residence. In urban areas, they may rely on public transportation that often is unreliable, overcrowded, and otherwise unpleasant. Exposure to such conditions has been demonstrated to result in increased epinephrine excretion (Lundberg, 1976; Singer et al., 1978). It seems reasonable that commuting may influence effects of the work setting on health consequences in a number of important ways.

Insufficient or inadequate day care for preschool children may add considerably to the stress experienced by working parents and their children. The importance of the quality of care was shown in a cross-over study in which an increase in the number of nurses per child was introduced into the psychosocial environment (Kagan et al., 1978). A longitudinal and interdisciplinary evaluation of the effects of this intervention showed that both epinephrine excretion and behavioral deviations among the children decreased, that absenteeism among the nurses declined sharply, and that there may have been secondary effects on the situation and health of the children's parents.

Effects of other social structures also should be studied. For example, how does the design of industrial and office buildings affect the work-related stressors experienced by disabled workers? For immigrant workers, what additional effects can cultural shock have on normal occupational stressors? For example, in what ways does insufficient knowledge of the language used at work alter a worker's ability to handle job demands without adverse health consequences? All of these types of research contain within them the question of what sorts of interventions might ameliorate any undesirable effects on health that such social structures or processes may foster in the work setting. In fact, as illustrated in the examples above, well-designed studies of carefully chosen interventions often are a valuable means of investigating these types of complex interactions.

Occupational stressors also can affect a worker's existence outside work. Studies have shown that narrow and socially isolated jobs foster passivity or social helplessness. Some workers never participate in planning or decision making, rarely cooperate with or talk to other people during the workday, and perform the same routine day in and day out. They may learn to act basically the same way in situations outside work. Such individuals have been called the "politically poor," because they have few affiliations with political and trade-union groups that are best equipped to help them to deal with problems at work. One set of studies found that a person's ability to develop active relations during spare time diminished when temporal, spatial, or technical restrictions built into the work process curtailed the exercise of discretion in work (Gardell, 1976; Meissner, 1971; Westlander, 1976). People whose jobs seriously constrain autonomy and social interaction at work take far less part in organized and goal-oriented activities that require planning and cooperation with others outside work.

A representative survey of the Swedish male labor force carried out in 1968 found that workers doing

134

psychologically unrewarding work took much less part in various organized leisure activities than did those who did not have such jobs (Karasek, 1981). This finding was true especially for cultural, political, and trade-union activities that required active participation and communication with others. For workers in unrewarding jobs, leisure activities centered around the nuclear family, sports, outdoor life, and television. A six-year follow-up showed that those whose primary employment had changed in the direction of a richer job content and greater control showed increased participation outside the job in voluntary associations, study work, trade unions, and political activities. In contrast, those whose jobs had become more narrow and confined through computers or other forms of automation were less engaged in such activities outside the job in 1974 than they had been in 1968.

Different Motives for Stress Research

Research into the stress-related aspects of social structure and processes can be approached with reference to one or more of the following four value concerns (Gardell, 1980): a humanistic/idealistic desire for the good society and the good working life; a drive for health and well-being; a belief in citizen participation, influence, and control at the level of the individual; and economic interest in competitiveness and profits of business organization and of the economic system. To a large extent, the impact of stress research depends on the political priorities given to these four value areas. Thus, knowledge about working life usually has been applied to problems that relate to economic goals and effectiveness of organizations. Less attention has been given to research on working life that is oriented toward promoting health, well-being, and personal development as values in their own right. Furthermore, the effort typically is to help workers adapt to existing conditions, rather than to approach such conditions as man-made and adaptable to man's abilities and needs.

In recent years, high priority has been given in the Scandinavian countries to studies aimed at providing knowledge that can serve as a basis for legislation; for trade union and management policies; for training of technical experts; and, through these collective means, for adapting structures and processes to human abilities and needs. In discussing these approaches, people often argue that every human being is unique and that job conditions and environments must be tailored individually to the capacities and needs of each worker. Such an approach is unlikely to be practicable except, perhaps, in relatively isolated cases such as handicapped workers. It also may be unnecessary. As more information is gathered, it may be possible to identify specific aspects of work settings that are associated with negative consequences for nearly everyone exposed to them.

Strategies for Social Change

A variety of mechanisms can be envisioned for changing conditions in the work place that are associated with negative health consequences for the workers. One method used in Scandinavian countries involves efforts to increase, organize, and vitalize people's own resources. Thus, the workers themselves constitute a key resource in identifying hazards at the work place on their own or with the aid of trained scientists working on their behalf. Often, effective systems may require legislation that permits such actions on the workers' behalf and promotes the types of research needed.

Effective interventions to alter adverse interactions between individuals and their social environments must occur at the level both of the individual and of the system (cf. Gardell, 1980; Levi, 1980). Interventions with the individual tie easily into traditional medical models. They include efforts to discourage high-risk behaviors such as smoking, excessive drinking, and overeating and to encourage desirable behaviors such as physical exercise, appropriate relaxation, and adequate rest. Analogous nonmedical interventions might include retraining or placement into other types of jobs.

Prevention at the systems level is much more difficult and controversial. Experience indicates a need for public intervention, creation of public resources, and development of strategies at the enterprise level. Effectiveness of government intervention depends, in part, on national institutional traditions. Legislation can provide statutory authority to employees to act on certain problems with an array of acceptable approaches. For example, rules and regulations related to the work environment may be designed to facilitate identification of important problems and potential remedies to be applied by the workers. Such an approach is evident in the Swedish and the Norwegian Work Environment Acts, especially in the latter. Government intervention may also mean that money and knowledge is available to companies to foster environmental changes for research purposes, as well as for information and training activities.

At the enterprise level, the main issue appears to be how to increase, organize, and vitalize worker resources. Most developed countries rely on trade unions and bureaucratic and negotiating machinery to deal with health hazards in the work place. Through such mechanisms, worker representatives can be given certain rights and means, regulated by laws, in order to act effectively on behalf of their colleagues. The European countries have adopted a variety of organizational approaches to the problems just discussed, conferring widely different amounts of discretionary authority to the workers. In some countries, for instance, employees may have the right to influence decisions about such factors as organizational and technological design, equipment, work methods, the use of certain types of material and products, and personnel policies. In others, they also may have the right to stop dangerous work or to call in experts to help make assessments or to conduct research of potentially hazardous conditions on their behalf.

Organization of worker resources is necessary but not sufficient. It is also very important, though perhaps more difficult, to try to find ways to stimulate individuals to take care of their own problems. As indicated earlier, narrow and system-paced jobs for workers who have little influence on management decisions eventually may foster passive and alienated attitudes that mitigate against such employees protesting even exposure to serious occupational health hazards. If so, awareness must be increased in and competence and power extended to the workers themselves to help them identify and change unhealthy work conditions. This has been the goal of recent Scandinavian legislation. In Sweden, the Work Environment Act (1977) emphasizes the importance of personal control over the work situation, whereas the Co-determination Act (1976) focuses on the influence of workers as a group. On the basis of these two acts, fundamental changes in working life might be accomplished. These aims are shared by the Norwegian Work Environment Act, which expresses the following provisions:

- General requirements: Technology, work organization, work time (shift plans), and payment systems are to be designed so that negative physiological or psychological effects for employees are avoided, as are negative influences on the alertness necessary

137

for observance of safety. Employees are to be given possibilities for personal development and for the maintenance and development of skills.

- Design of jobs: Jobs should be designed to include opportunities for employee self-determination and skill maintenance. Monotonous, repetitive work and work that is paced by machine or assembly line in such a way that no room is left for variation in work rhythm should be avoided. Jobs should be designed to include task variation, contact with others, an understanding of the interdependence between elements that constitute a job, and information and feedback to employees about production requirements and results.

- Systems for planning and control: Employees or their elected representatives are to be kept informed about systems used for planning and control, for example automatic data processing systems, and about any changes in such systems. They are to be given training necessary to understand the systems and the right to influence their design.

- Mode of remuneration and risk to safety. Piece-rate payment and related forms of compensation are not to be used if salaried systems can increase the safety level.

The Swedish legislative approach is two-fold. A new Work Environment Act has been in effect since July 1, 1978. It is an open-frame law with general statements such as "working conditions shall be adapted to man's mental and physical capacities," and "jobs shall be designed so that the employees themselves may influence their work situation." This framework is complemented by specifications from two sources, the National Board of Occupational Safety and Health (1980) and, perhaps more importantly for mental health purposes, the Co-determination Act (1976). The latter act requires that employee union representatives receive information about working conditions on all matters and at all levels. It entitles local unions to negotiate on any matter that may influence their job situation. The parties themselves, the managers and the employees at the local plants, must agree on the job specifications that they consider suitable. In order to guide local action, the Swedish Confederation of Trade Unions has endorsed a special action program on psychosocial aspects of the work environment (LO, 1980).

138

Whether these laws and related recommendations will produce the desired results remains to be seen. They contain many laudable sentiments, but they are not very specific. The general intent of the law is given, but offences are not specified. Much will depend on how they are used and what costs are attached to effective remedies. Even more questions must be raised about the relevance of results in Scandanavian countries to other nations. Certainly, there are many differences in the political and work organizations in the United States. And yet, it seems possible that some lessons may be drawn from this compelling natural experiment.

Specific Research Needs

The basic assumption for research on stress and occupational health is that psychosocial factors can precipitate or counteract ill health, influence well-being, and modify the outcome of health measures. It follows that the major goals are to identify high-risk situations such as shift work, piece wages, or sensory overload; high-risk groups such as working mothers or migrant workers; and high-risk reactions such as endocrine or immunological dysfunction. Delineation of such situations, groups, and reactions should facilitate efforts to design and selectively introduce therapeutic or preventive interventions for evaluation (Kagan and Levi, 1974; Levi, 1979, 1980). Research strategies should combine basic research on key hypotheses with applied research on health measures and collection of information on the interrelationship of various parts of the man-environment interactions (Kagan and Levi, 1974).

Research projects should be carried out in three logically consecutive steps: problem identification with survey techniques and morbidity data; longitudinal, multidisciplinary studies of the intersection of high-risk situations and high-risk groups as compared with controls; and controlled intervention, including both laboratory experiments and appropriate therapeutic or preventive interventions.

The data discussed in this chapter have highlighted a few of the ideas that already exist for improving the ways in which people adapt their total environment to their abilities and needs. Most of these suggestions have yet to be tested adequately even on a small scale, particularly in ways that incorporate the interdisciplinary evaluation needed to determine the positive and negative consequences that may follow in terms both of

individual health and of social demands. Among those
interventions for which preliminary evidence suggest the
value of additional research are:

- Increasing a worker's control of work arrangements

- Providing mechanisms for worker participation in
  decision making on the organization of work

- Avoiding monotonous, machine-paced, and short but
  frequent work actions

- Optimizing automation

- Helping workers see their specific task in relation
  to the total product

- Avoiding quantitative work overload or underload

- Facilitating communication and support systems
  among work mates and others.

As more information about these and other interventions
become available, it should be possible to begin to
explore difficult but critical issues about the balance
between social needs for productivity and individual
requirements for good physical and mental health. Available evidence already suggests that, in some instances,
adequate understanding of the stressful aspects of a work
setting may make it possible actually to improve both.

Some might regard the goals underlying the above
proposals as clearly utopian, and no doubt they are in
many parts of the world. Still, although they certainly
cannot be obtained overnight, these goals indicate the
desirable direction for future studies in this critical
and often neglected aspect of stress research.

References

Ahlbom, A., Karasek, R., and Theorell, T. Psychosocial
occupational demands and risk for cardiovascular death
(Swedish). Lakartidningen 77:4243-4245, 1977.

Akerstedt, T. Interindividual differences in adjustment
to shift work. IN: Proceedings from the 6th Congress
of the International Ergonomics Association, 1976.

Akerstedt, T. Altered sleep/wake patterns and circadian
rhythms. Laboratory and field studies of sympathoadrenomedullary and related variables. Acta Physiol.
Scand., Suppl. 469, 1979.

Akerstedt, T., and Froberg, J. E. Shift work and
health--interdisciplinary aspects. IN: Shift Work
and Health, A Symposium (Rentos, P. G., and Shaphard,
R. D., eds.) Washington, D.C.: U.S. Government
Printing Office DHEW (NIOSH) Publ. No. 76-203, 1976.

Akerstedt, T., and Froberg, J. E. Psychophysiological
circadian rhythms in females during 75 hours of sleep
deprivation with continuous activity. Waking and
Sleeping 4:387-394, 1977.

Akerstedt, T., Forberg, J. E., Levi, L., Torsvall, L.,
and Zamore, K. Shift work and wellbeing (Swedish)
Stockholm: Arbetarskyddsnamnden, 1978.

Akerstedt, T., and Levi, L. Circadian rhythms in the
secretion of cortisol, adrenaline and noradrenaline.
Eur. J. Clin. Invest. 8: 57-58, 1978.

Akerstedt, T., and Theorell, T. Exposure to night work:
relations between serum gastrin reactions, psychosomatic complaints and personality variables. J. Psychosom. Res. 20:479-484, 1976.

Akerstedt, T., and Torsvall, L. Experimental changes in
shift schedules--their effects on well-being. IN:
Proceedings of the IVth Symposium on Night and Shift
Work (Rutenfranz, J., Colquhoun, P., Kauth, P., and
Folkards, S., eds.) Dortmund: 1977a.

Akerstedt, T., and Torsvall, L. Medical, psychological
and social aspects of shift work at the Special Steel
Mills in Soderfors (Swedish). Reports from the Laboratory for Clinical Stress Research, No. 64, University of Stockholm, 1977b.

Akerstedt, T., and Torsvall, L. Experimental changes in
shift schedules--their effects on well-being. Ergonomics 21:849-856, 1978.

Bainbridge, L. The process controller. IN: The Study
of Real Skill (Singleton, W. T., ed.) London: MTP
Press, 1978.

Blauner, R. Alienation and Freedom--The Factory Worker
and His Industry Chicago: University of Chicago
Press, 1964.

141

Broadbent, D. E. Decision and Stress New York: Academic Press, 1971
Co-determination Act. The Swedish Code of Statutes, No. 580, 1976.
Frankenhaeuser, M. The role of peripheral catecholamines in adaptation to understimulation and overstimulation. IN: Psychopathology of Human Adaptation (Serban, G., ed.) New York: Plenum Press, 1976, pp. 173-191.
Frankenhaeuser, M. Quality of life: criteria for behavioral adjustment. Int. J. Psychol. 12:99-110, 1977a.
Frankenhaeuser, M. Job demands, health and wellbeing. J. Psychosom. Res. 21, 313-321, 1977b.
Frankenhaeuser, M. Living in technified society: stress tolerance and cost of adaptation (Swedish). Reports of the Psychological Institute, No. 15 University of Stockholm, 1977c.
Frankenhaeuser, M. Psychoneuroendocrine approaches to the study of emotion as related to stress and coping. IN: Nebraska Symposium on Motivation (Howe, H. E., and Dienstbier, R. A., eds.) Lincoln: University of Nebraska Press, 1979, pp. 123-161.
Frankenhaeuser, M. Psychobiological aspects of life stress. IN: Coping and Health (Levine, S., and Ursin, H., eds.) New York: Plenum Press, 1980a, pp. 203-223.
Frankenhaeuser, M. The human factor--an obstacle to safe nuclear power. Stockholm, 1980b, Mimeograph.
Frankenhaeuser, M. Coping with job stress--a psychobiological approach. IN: Working Life: A Social Science Contribution to Work Reform (Gardell, B., and Johansson, G., eds.) London: Wiley, 1981.
Frankenhaeuser, M., and Gardell, B. Underload and overload in working life: outline of a multidisciplinary approach. J. Hum. Stress 2: 35-46, 1976.
Frankenhaeuser, M., and Johansson, G. Task demand as reflected in catecholamine excretion and heart rate. J. Hum. Stress 2:15-23, 1976.
Frankenhaeuser, M., Lundberg, U., and Forsman, L. Dissociation between sympathetic-adrenal and pituitary-adrenal responses to an achievement situation characterized by high controllability: comparison between Type A and Type B males and females. Biol. Psychol. 10: 79-91, 1980.
Frankenhaeuser, M., and Rissler, A. Effects of punishment on catecholamine release and efficiency of performance. Psychopharmacologia 17:378-390, 1970.
Froberg, J. E. Twenty-four hour patterns in human performance, subjective and physiological variables and differences between morning and evening active subjects. Biol. Psychol. 5:119-134, 1977.

Froberg, J. E., Karlsson, C. G., Levi, L., and Lidberg,
  L. Circadian rhythms of catecholamine excretion,
  shooting range performance and self-ratings of fatigue
  during sleep deprivation. Biol. Psychol. 2: 175-188,
  1975a.
Froberg, J. E., Karlsson, C. G., Levi, L., and Lidberg,
  L. Psychobiological circadian rhythms during a 72-
  hour vigil. Forsvarsmedicin 11:192-201, 1975b.
Gardell, B. Technology, Alienation and Mental Health.
  A Sociopsychological Study of Industrial Work
  (Swedish) Stockholm: PA-Council, 1971.
Gardell, B. Job Content and Quality of Life (Swedish)
  Stockholm: Prisma, 1976.
Gardell, B. Work environment of white collar workers:
  psychosocial work environment and health (Swedish).
  Working Paper. Department of Psychology, University
  of Stockholm, 1979.
Gardell, B. Psychosocial aspects of industrial pro-
  duction methods. Reports from the Department of
  Psychology Suppl. 47, University of Stockholm, 1979.
Gardell, B. Scandinavian research on stress in working
  life. Paper presented at the IRRA-Symposium on
  Stress in Working Life, Denver, Colorado, September
  5-7, 1980.
Glass, D. C., Krakoff, L. R., Contrada, R., Hilton, W.
  F., Kehoe, K., Mannucci, E. G., Collins, C., Snow,
  B., and Elting, E. Effect of harassment and competi-
  tion upon cardiovascular and plasma catecholamine
  responses in Type A and Type B individuals. Psycho-
  physiology 17:453-463, 1980.
Johansson, G. Subjective wellbeing and temporal patterns
  of sympathetic adrenal medullary activity. Biol.
  Psychol. 4:157-172, 1976.
Johansson, G. Psychoneuroendocrine reactions to mech-
  anized and computerized work routines. IN: Response
  to Stress: Occupational Aspects (Mackay, C., and
  Cox, T., eds.) London: IPC Science and Technology
  Press, 1979, pp. 142-149.
Johansson, G., and Aronsson, G. Stress reactions in
  computerized administrative work. Reports from the
  Department of Psychology, Suppl. 50, University of
  Stockholm, 1980.
Johansson, G., Aronsson, G., and Lindstrom, B. O. Social
  psychological and neuroendocrine stress reactions in
  highly mechanized work. Ergonomics 21:583-599, 1978.
Johansson, G., and Frankenhaeuser, M. Temporal factors
  in sympathoadrenomedullary activity following acute
  behavioral activation. Biol. Psychol. 1:63-73, 1973.
Johansson, G., and Gardell, B. Psychosocial aspects of
  process control (Swedish). Reports of the Psychological Institute, No. 15 University of Stockholm, 1978.

143

Kagan, A. R., Cederblad, M., Hook, B., and Levi, L.
Evaluation of the effect of increasing the number of
nurses on health and behaviour of 3-year old children
in day care, satisfaction of their parents and health
and satisfaction of their nurses. Reports from the
Laboratory for Clinical Stress Research, No. 89
University of Stockholm, 1978.

Kagan, A. R., and Levi, L. Health and environment--
psychosocial stimuli. A review. Social Sci. Med. 8:
225-241, 1974.

Karasek, R. A., Jr. Job demands, job decision latitude,
and mental strain: implications for job redesign.
Admin. Sci. Quart. 24:285-308, 1979.

Karasek, R. Job socialization and job strain. The implications of two related psychosocial mechanisms for
job design. IN: Working Life: A Social Science Contribution to Work Reform (Gardell, B., and Johansson,
G., eds.) London: Wiley, 1981.

Kjellgren, O. Wage Administrative Study (Swedish)
Stockholm: LKAB, 1975.

Kornhauser, A. Mental Health of the Industrial Worker
New York: Wiley, 1965.

Kronlund, J. Democracy Without Power (Swedish) Stockholm: Prisma, 1974.

Levi, L. The stress of everyday work as reflected in
productiveness, subjective feelings, and urinary output of adrenaline and noradrenaline under salaried and
piece-work conditions. J. Psychosom. Res. 8:199-202,
1964.

Levi, L. Stress and distress in response to psychosocial
stimuli. Acta Med. Scand. 191, Suppl. 528, 1972.

Levi, L. Psychosocial conditions in the work environment: effects on health and wellbeing (Swedish).
Arbetsmiljoutredningens betankande, Bilaga 2:87-118,
1976.

Levi, L. Psychosocial factors in preventive medicine.
IN: Healthy People. The Surgeon General's Report on
Health Promotion and Disease Prevention. Background
papers (Hamburg, D. A., Nightingale, E. O., and
Kalmar, V., eds.) Washington, D.C.: U.S. Government
Printing Office, 1979.

Levi, L. Preventing Work Stress Reading: Addison-
Wesley, 1980.

Levi, L. (Ed.) Society, Stress and Disease: Working
Life., Vol. IV New York: Oxford University Press,
1981.

Levi, L., and Andersson, L. Psychosocial Stress: Population, Environment and Quality of Life New York:
Spectrum Publications, 1975.

LO (Swedish Trade Union Confederation). Mental and Social Hazards to Health in the Working Environment. Programme of Action Stockholm: LO, 1980.

Lundberg, U. Urban commuting: crowdedness and catecholamine excretion. J. Hum. Stress 2:26-32, 1976.

Lundberg, U., and Frankenhaeuser, M. Psychophysiological reactions to noise as modified by personal control over noise intensity. Biol. Psychol. 6:51-59, 1978.

Lundberg, U., and Frankenhaeuser, M. Pituitary-adrenal and sympathetic-adrenal correlates of distress and effort. J. Psychosom. Res. 24: 125-130, 1980.

Magnusson, M., and Nilsson, C. To Work at Inconvenient Hours (Swedish) Lund: Prisma, 1979.

Mahler, H. Tomorrow's medicine and tomorrow's doctors. WHO Chronicle 31:60-62, 1977.

Maule, H. G., Levi, L., McLean, A., Pardon, N., and Savicevic, M. Occupational Mental Health Geneva: World Health Organization, 1973.

Meissner, M. The long arm of the job: a study of work and leisure. Indust. Rel. 10:238-260, 1971.

National Board of Occupational Safety and Health. Mental and Social Aspects of the Work Environment (Swedish) Stockholm: Arbetarskyddsstryrelsens forfattningssamling, AFS 1980: 14.

Orth-Gomer, K., and Olivegard Landen, R. Intervention on risk factors for coronary heart disease by changing working conditions of Swedish police officers. Reports from the Laboratory for Clinical Stress Research, No. 126, University of Stockholm, 1981.

President's Commission on Mental Health. Report to the President, Vol. I Washington, D.C.: U.S. Government Printing Office, 1978.

Poyhonen, M. Piece-Rates and Stress (Swedish) Helsingfors: Institute for Work Hygiene, Report No. 115, 1975.

Rissler, A. Stress reactions at work and after work during a period of quantitative overload. Ergonomics 20:13-16, 1977.

SCA-tidningen. Monthly Salaries in Logging (Swedish) Sweden: Sundsvall, No. 10, 1975.

Singer, J. E., Lundberg, U., and Frankenhaeuser, M. Stress on the train: a study of urban commuting. IN: Advances in Environmental Psychology. Vol. 1: The Urban Environment (Baum, A., Singer, J. E., and Valins, S., eds.) Hillsdale: Lawrence Erlbaum Associates, 1978, pp. 41-56.

Swedish Forest Service. One-year Report on Experiment with Monthly Salaries in Logging (Swedish) Stockholm: Domanverket, November 13, 1975, Mimeograph.

145

Theorell, T., and Akerstedt, T. Day and night work:
  changes in cholesterol, uric acid, glucose, and
  potassium in serum and in circadian patterns of
  urinary catecholamine excretion: a longitudinal
  cross-over study of railway workers. Acta Med.
  Scand. 200:47-53, 1976.
Walker, C. R., and Guest, R. H. The Man on the Assembly
  Line Cambridge: Harvard University Press, 1952.
Westlander, G. Working Conditions and the Content of
  Leisure (Swedish) Stockholm: Swedish Council for
  Personal Administration, 1976.
Work Environment Act. The Swedish Code of Statutes, No.
  1160, 1977.
World Health Organization. Report of the First WHO
  Interdisciplinary Workshop on Psychosocial Factors
  and Health Geneva: World Health Organization, 1976.
Wilensky, H. L. Family life cycle, work, and the qual-
  ity of life. Reflections on the roots of happiness,
  despair, and indifference in modern society. IN:
  Working Life: A Social Science Contribution to Work
  Reform (Gardell, B., and Johansson, G., eds.) Lon-
  don: Wiley, 1981.
Zdravomyslov, A. G., and Yadov, V. A. Effect of voca-
  tional distinctions on the attitude to work. IN:
  Industry and Labour in the USSR (Osipov, G. V., ed.)
  London: Tavistock Publ., 1966, pp. 99-125.

CHAPTER 7

Panel Report on Psychosocial Assets and Modifiers of Stress

Panel Members:
Frances Cohen, Ph.D., Chair
Mardi J. Horowitz, M.D.
Richard S. Lazarus, Ph.D.
Rudolf H. Moos, Ph.D.

Lee N. Robins, M.D.
Robert M. Rose, M.D.
Michael Rutter M.D.

The link between stress and disease is not straight-forward. The context in which the stress occurs, the way individuals appraise it, how they cope, and the social and personal resources available to them can be important mediating influences. The task of this panel was to identify those psychological and social factors that might modify the relationship between stress and disease and to discuss where future research might best be directed. To set the stage for this discussion, we briefly comment on some issues involved in defining stress and then note the types of variables that might modify a stress-disease relationship. The bulk of this chapter reviews what is known about psychosocial assets and modifiers, discusses the methodological problems involved in studying their relationships to stress, and pinpoints research strategies that will further our understanding in this area.

Definitions of Stress

The dilemmas posed by efforts to define stress are discussed in Chapter 2, Conceptual Issues of Stress Research. Many biological investigators define stress on the basis of a physiological reaction, such as an increase in corticosteroid secretion (Selye, 1956). However, evidence suggests that psychological processes can affect the meaning given to the noxious stimulus and may have a powerful influence on such physiological responses (Mason, 1968, 1974). Thus, individuals might have quite different physiological reactions to the same stressful event. For investigators interested in such psychosocial factors, physiological definitions are of limited usefulness, because they eliminate from study those people who show no physiological response in a potentially stressful stituation. Such individuals are precisely the ones in whom it may be possible to study the factors that moderate the relationship between stress and adaptational outcomes. The group preferred a broader

149

definition of stress that considers both physiological and psychological reactions to stressful events. In accord with the framework described in Conceptual Issues of Stress Research (Chapter 2), the members found it useful to distinguish stressful events, or stressors, from psychological states such as feelings of threat, harm, or loss that may accompany stress (Lazarus and Launier, 1978) and from psychological, physiological, or behavioral reactions to the stressors.

Types of Stressors

Stressors include specific events and environmental conditions. Our panel gave primary attention to events that constitute a change from a person's customary life activities. However, we also included under the rubric of stress those situations such as monotony that do not involve change but may produce psychological and physiological stress reactions (Frankenhaeuser, 1976) and those conditions in which there is a major discrepancy between expectation and reality, as when a possible promotion does not materialize or a life course change does not occur at the usual time (Gersten et al., 1974).

Stress events are not homogeneous; they differ greatly in quality. The manner in which an event is appraised and the coping strategies used in response are affected by a number of factors. For example, how long does the event last, and how frequently does it occur in the population or subgroup? Is it anticipated or unexpected, controllable or uncontrollable? Does it occur in the customary part of the life course, or is it "off time," as happens when a wife becomes a widow in her early thirties? Is it happening out of the usual order with respect to related events, for example having a child before getting married? What are its expected consequences, either desirable or undesirable?

The panel identified four broad types of stressors, differing primarily in their duration:

1. Acute, time-limited stressors such as going parachute jumping, awaiting surgery, or encountering a rattlesnake

2. Stressor sequences, or series of events that occur over an extended period of time as the result of an initiating event such as job loss, divorce, or bereavement

150

3. Chronic <u>intermittent stressors</u> such as conflict-filled visits to in-laws or sexual difficulties, which may occur once a day, once a week, once a month

4. <u>Chronic stressors</u> such as permanent disabilities, parental discord, or chronic job stress, which may or may not be initiated by a discrete event and which persist continuously for a long time.

With stressor sequences and chronic stressors, psychological and physiological reactions may occur over an extended time. This raises serious questions about the validity of measuring people's responses at only one time interval during the sequence (Lazarus, 1981).

Much remains to be learned about the specific psychosocial and physiological effects of each of these different types of stressors. Are different strategies needed for dealing with acute as opposed to chronic stressors? Do individuals exposed to chronic stressors reach an equilibrium in which constant coping efforts are not required? As discussed in Chapter 8, Biological Substrates of Stress, most biological stress research has been on acute stressors; this is particularly true for research on humans. The information gained from such studies is valuable, but it may offer few insights into reactions to stressor sequences or chronic stressors. Do intermittent stressors produce greater physiological reactions than do chronic stress conditions? Are physiological reactions to a time-limited stressor identical to reactions to chronic stressors? If there are differences, how do they affect the resulting consequences to health? Is the chronicity of the stress response an important predictor of changes in health?

Positive Versus Negative Life Events. Some life events such as getting married or getting a raise are pleasant; others such as having a major physical illness or getting a divorce are not. Stress researchers typically have been interested in negative life events as risk factors for symptoms and disease. Some of the early life-events research seemed to imply that both positive and negative life events could be associated with undesirable consequences (Holmes and Masuda, 1974; Rahe et al., 1964). However, evidence is accumulating that the two types of events may have different psychological and physiological consequences. For example, blood concentrations of such substances as catecholamines, cortisol, thyroxine, and growth hormone all

151

increase if an individual is exposed to negative stress events; only catecholamine concentrations rise after pleasurable events (Rose, 1980). Furthermore, negative life events are stronger predictors of disease outcomes than are positive life events (Vinokur and Selzer, 1975). Thus, in studying associations between depression and the addition or loss of new members to a subject's social setting, Paykel (1974) found that social exits were more common among depressive patients than among controls but social entrances occurred with equal frequencies in the two groups.

Problems of Measurement. Life events are assessed by scales such as the Schedule for Recent Experiences (SRE) (Holmes and Rahe, 1967). As discussed in Chapter 4, Stress and Life Events, such scales have come under considerable attack on both methodological and conceptual grounds (cf. Cleary, 1974; Dohrenwend and Dohrenwend, 1974; Jenkins et al., 1979; Rabkin and Struening, 1976). The reliability of reporting of life events is adequate only for events in the six-month period before test administration (Jenkins et al., 1979). For some commonly used events such as divorce or sex difficulties, it is impossible to determine whether their occurrence is independent of the disease process. In some instances, the events may be a result of disease-induced changes that arise before the disease is diagnosed. Inclusion of such events in research can inflate associations between life events and illness (Hudgens, 1974). Revised versions of the scale have been developed, including some that offer individual weighting of items according to when they occurred relative to the onset of disease (Horowitz et al., 1977; Sarason et al., 1978).

Life-events scales identify as stressful a specific set of life changes that require individuals to make readjustments. They typically exclude other types of life stressors that also may influence health. Chronic conditions such as sex role conflicts (Pearlin, 1975a), work overload or underload (Frankenhaeuser and Gardell, 1976), and status incongruity between spouses (Pearlin, 1975b) have important associations with changes in health and morale. Some investigators have emphasized that seemingly minor stressors of daily life also can have adaptational significance; in fact, they have suggested that such daily hassles may be even more powerful pre-dictors of health outcomes than are the events identified on life-events scales (Pearlin and Schooler, 1978; Kanner et al., 1981). Much more research is needed to determine the adequacy of existing measures of stress, to identify the types of potential stressors that can have adaptational significance, and to develop reliable and sensitive research tools with which to detect and quantitate those stressors.

Stress as Growth-Enhancing

For many years, researchers have emphasized the deleterious effects of stress. However, there is increasing interest in the possibility that stress may enhance personal growth and development under some circumstances. Perhaps exposure to stressors at one time period fosters the later development of needed competencies. Individuals who have faced severe life stressors also may find that they have increased self-esteem, are able to perform better in similar situations at a later time, learn empathy, or can take advantage of new opportunities. Certain stressors are inevitable throughout the life course, yet most people do not appear to suffer adverse effects. For example, children must learn to separate from their parents and to cope with such major life events as changes in environment, loss of friends, and the experience of failure. By using their ego resources and drawing on social supports, children master threatening events and achieve personal growth (Murphy, 1962). Protecting children from such experiences would leave them ill-equipped for dealing with life (Block, 1971).

Questions about the growth-enhancing qualities of stress are analogous to those asked many years ago about the relationship between stress and performance, as are the answers: sometimes stressors facilitate performance, sometimes they impair it, and sometimes they increase variability among individuals (Lazarus et al., 1952). Characteristics of the stressor, the person's resources, the task required, and the nature of the surrounding environment all affect this relationship. Whether a stressful event leads to growth, temporary difficulty, or trauma is probably a function of: (1) the pervasiveness and persistence of the stressors, (2) the timing of the event within the life course, (3) the personal resources available for reacting to the stressor, (4) the opportunities available to act on the environment, and (5) the meaning given to the experience (Benner et al., 1980).

Many people welcome exposure to stressors, at least in controlled amounts. The popularity of carnival rides, hang-gliding, and car racing suggests that some people seek out highly stressful environments to enhance personal pleasure (Klausner, 1968; Zuckerman, 1979). Such risk-taking may be a way to test competence, build a feeling of mastery, relieve boredom, or reach altered states of consciousness. People may be willing to tolerate a certain level of tension as a means of building resources, coping with other stresses, or achieving peak experiences. It is unclear whether individuals who seek such potential stressors feel stressed by them and whether exposure to those stressors increases their risk for adverse health consequences that are unrelated to direct injuries that may occur.

Many interesting questions about growth-enhancing aspects of stress remain to be explored. How do children cope with the expected stressors of life? Do the coping strategies used in dealing with expected life stressors determine the strategies employed later in unexpected serious life crises? Under what conditions are stressful experiences growth-enhancing, and for whom? Do people with many personal resources benefit more from stress than those with few resources? How important is the amount and type of stress or the developmental period in which it occurs? Research directed at these questions will help to disentangle the positive and negative effects of stressful life experiences. A better understanding of the positive effects of stressful life experiences will make it easier to determine whether particular interventions are beneficial or interfere with needed growth and the acquistion of new coping skills.

Criterion Measures

Research on how stress affects health requires measures not only of the stressors but also of the health consequences associated with exposure to those stressors. In considering measures of health and illness outcomes, the following issues must be addressed: (1) the adequacy of the measures, (2) the range of health or illness consequences that are measured, (3) the levels of impairment that can be assessed, and (4) the ability of the measures to detect and distinguish between short-term and long-lasting effects.

Adequacy of the Measures

Studies of the role of stress in the development of physical disease have used the following types of ill-

ness indicators: number of visits to a physician,
self-reports of physical symptoms or illness, medical
confirmation of physical illness in a patient population,
and illness confirmed by medical examination in a population sample (Cohen, 1979). Some researchers believe
that the first three indicators reflect illness behavior
rather than illness (Cohen, 1979; Mechanic, 1962, 1968).
Use of physician visits as an indicator permits biases
from patient self-selection and from inclusion of a
subgroup of subjects who do not have organic disease--
those Garfield (1970) has called the "worried well."
Similarly, self-reports of illness are influenced by the
sophistication and knowledge of the subjects; some
disorders undoubtedly are underreported and others are
overreported. Patients whose illness is diagnosed
because they have elected to seek treatment may not be
representative of all people with that illness. Medical
examination of a representative sample of the population
is the most expensive of the four indicators, because
investigators must select, contact, and obtain the participation of a large number of subjects, many of whom
are not ill and may have no interest in the research.
However, it also is the only one of the indicators that
definitely provides a reliable measure of the development
of illness, rather than of illness behavior or self-
report. This indicator also enables investigators to
distinguish concomitants of the physical illness being
studied from more general psychological problems of
living. Stress researchers are becoming increasingly
sensitive to the need for this type of direct examination of population samples (Rahe and Arthur, 1978;
Weiner, 1977).

Range of Health and Illness Consequences Measured

        As discussed in Conceptual Issues of Stress Research
(Chapter 2), reactions to stressors can produce an array
of physiological, psychological, and social consequences.
Most stress research has focused on only one or two
possible consequences, such as the onset of a disease.
Such unidimensional studies may present a distorted
picture of exactly how stress can affect individuals
(Cohen and Lazarus, 1979). For example, as discussed in
Stress and Illness, the Type A behavior pattern is a risk
factor for the undesirable health consequence of coronary
heart disease. However, it also may be associated with
such desirable consequences as high self-esteem and positive regard by peers. As another example, many people
prefer to be physically active when facing stressful

situations. Being active may reduce the psychological
experience of distress at the cost of increasing physiological responses (Gal and Lazarus, 1975; Singer, 1974).
Thus, studies are needed which look at a much fuller
range of possible changes in physical health, psychological wellbeing, and social functioning.

Much past research has used physiological variables
as outcome measures, both because of the initial emphasis
on the physiological aspects of the stress response and
because such measures are objective. Further work is
needed to develop adequate measures of psychological outcome. For example, it may be useful to measure intrusive
and repetitive thoughts as a reaction to stress or to
study the ways in which stressors alter the perception
of and responses to ideas and emotions (Horowitz, 1975;
Horowitz and Wilner, 1976; Horowitz et al., 1979).

Outcome measures also should monitor potentially
desirable consequences. Past stress definitions have
emphasized negative outcomes, precluding studies of
health-enhancing consequences and of the positive ways
in which people cope with stressors (Antonovsky, 1979).
Evaluating both positive and negative effects of stress
may help to explain why stressors are associated with
disease for some people and with growth for others.

Development of methods for evaluating a full range
of consequences that may be associated with exposure to
stressors will require collaboration. Investigators from
different disciplines will be needed to determine what
shoud be measured and to make feasible research designs.
Such collaborations should begin before expensive longitudinal studies are undertaken, to ensure that the data
gathered can be used to answer all of the questions
being asked. Continued support of multidisciplinary
research centers within and among universities might be
one method of fostering such collaborative efforts.

Level of Impairment Assessed

Most clinical stress research has focused appropriately on the association of stress with major physical
and mental disorders. But health and illness measures
should not be restricted to assessments of major dys-
functions. Careful study of less severe consequences
and of reactions to common life situations may be a
necessary part of efforts to gain a better understanding
of why there are individual differences in pathological

processes. For example, some have suggested that the higher incidence of depression in women may reflect the way girls learn to respond to failure (Rutter, 1980a). Adolescent girls appear to consider failure to be an indication of an unchangeable personal trait such as low intelligence, whereas boys interpret failure as evidence that they did not try hard enough (Dweck and Bush, 1976; Dweck et al., 1978).

Short-Term and Longlasting Effects

Whenever possible, outcomes should be evaluated for both immediate and delayed effects. For example, denial defenses may be adaptive for parents caring for a child with leukemia, enabling them to perform their necessary duties and to provide emotional support for the child (Wolff et al., 1964); however, if the child dies, those same defenses can lead to devastating consequences both for the marriage and for the parents as individuals (Chodoff et al., 1964). Similarly, denial is associated both with reduced mortality in the coronary care unit (Hackett et al., 1968) and with a tendency to resist medical advice about work, rest, and smoking one year after the myocardial infarction (Croog et al., 1971). Unless both long- and short-term results are considered, important consequences will be overlooked. At present, even appropriate time intervals and necessary duration for such studies of stress effects are unclear. Resolution of these uncertainties will require longitudinal studies over an extended time span with repeated assessments of transient and lasting consequences at varying intervals.

Potential Mediators

Recently, there has been increasing interest in the role of psychosocial variables in the precipitation or prevention of disease (Lipowski, 1977; Weiner, 1977; Cohen, 1979). Although many stress researchers believe that stress is a major factor in disease etiology, others emphasize that there is no simple relationship between stress and pathological outcomes. Many people experience negative life events without becoming ill (Hinkle, 1974; Wershow and Reinhart, 1974).

Some important modifers of the stress response were mentioned earlier. One potentially important variable is whether a stressor occurs at an expected time in the life course. Studies suggest that reactions to stressors

that occur at the customary time (on time) can be quite
different than those associated with stressors that
occur at an unexpected point in the life course (off
time) (Neugarten, 1970). Other important mediating
factors include perception of the situation, personal
resources available, coping strategies used, and age.
Aspects of the surrounding environment, including the
amount of social support received from others and the
institutionalized means available for dealing with
change, also may be influential.

Modifiers also may affect the health consequences
associated with exposure to stressors. For example, age,
sex, social networks, available coping modes, the social
environment, and family history have all been linked to
increased prevalence of different types of illness (cf.
Chapter 9, Stress and Illness). This list closely resembles that cited for mediators of reactions to stressors.
Undoubtedly, many factors can influence either or both
of these relationships; but, some modifiers may be quite
specific. For example, the availability of strong social
supports may have little effect on acute physiological
reactions to a stressor but may moderate certain undesirable health consequences such as heart disease. Most
of these mediators also can influence each other. Thus,
personal resources affect the coping strategies used; and
age affects such mediators as appraisals of stressors,
available resources, and coping styles.

Table 7.1 provides a partial list of potential mediators of stress and suggests one scheme for organizing
them. Mediators such as temperament, personality, and
sociodemographic status usually are considered to be
stable characteristics of the individual or environment,
changing only slowly over time, if at all; others,
including cognitive appraisal and coping strategies are
the result of interactions of the individual with the
environment and may last only during a specific interaction. Many modifiers undergo considerable change during
the life course. It will be important to discover the
mechanisms that produce such changes over time and to
determine the effects of those changes on associations
between stressors and disease consequences (Brim and
Kagan, 1980).

Most of the research on stress and disease has involved measures of the strength of associations between
the stressor and a disease consequence. Much less attention has been given to identifying potentially important
psychosocial factors. This is an unfortunate gap in research, because an understanding of stress modifiers may

yield valuable insights into ways in which undesirable
consequences can be prevented or treated. Descriptions
of research being done on a few of the psychosocial
mediators listed in Table 7.1 may help to illustrate the
potential value of these types of studies.

Person Factors

Personality. Stress researchers have been studying
the role of personality factors in the development of
physical illness for at least the last sixty years. Some
studies have looked for associations between personality
factors and specific disease; others have tried to
determine if some personality factors are nonspecific
risk factors for a number of diseases (Weiner, 1977).
For example, Alexander (1950) studied the relationship
between unconscious psychological conflicts and the
development of such specific psychosomatic disorders as
bronchial asthma or ulcerative colitis. Other investigators hypothesized that patients suffering from a
number of different psychosomatic diseases shared a
common personality organization (Grinker, 1953; Ruesch,
1948; Sifneos, 1973). More recently, investigators have
begun to explore the effects of stress on physical
diseases not traditionally classified as psychosomatic
(Cohen, 1979). The current status of such work for a
number of major physical and mental disorders is discussed in Stress and Illness (Chapter 9).

The methodological problems of studying associations between personality factors and changes in health
are considerable (Cohen, 1979; Fox, 1978). Carefully
designed prospective studies using appropriate control
groups, free of observer bias, and employing reliable
and valid measurement instruments are a necesssary step
in gaining a clearer understanding of those personality
factors related to specific physical diseases. To date,
the most methodologically sound work may be that linking
Type A behavior to increased risk of coronary heart
disease (Jenkins, 1976; Rosenman et al., 1975).

Only a few studies have looked for personality
factors that may protect people from a wide variety of
physical disease. Based on observations of people who
were experiencing considerable life change, Hinkle
(1974) suggested that, compared to subjects who were more
likely to become ill, those who remained healthy were
emotionally insulated and showed a lack of concern for
others and little involvement in life affairs. Kobasa

TABLE 7.1

POTENTIAL MEDIATORS OF THE RELATIONSHIP
BETWEEN STRESS AND ILLNESS

Person Factors

Personality (personality traits, coping dispositions)

Personal resources (intelligence, special skills, motivation; some personality variables)

Temperament (beliefs, attitudes)

Past history (past experiences, repertoire of skills, previous psychiatric history)

Sociodemographic variables (age, sex, race, socioeconomic status)

Genetic variables (biological predispositions to illness)

Biological variables not genetically transmitted (physical condition, diseased organs)

Process Factors

Cognitive appraisal (meaning of an event, significance for well-being)

Coping (strategies used to react to or negate the effects of an event)

Environmental Factors

Interpersonal Factors (social networks, social supports)

Other External Factors

Physical setting (geographic and architectural characteristics)

Organizational factors (institution size and structure)

Human aggregate (characteristics of the persons inhabiting a particular environment)

Social climate (social prejudices, social expectations)

Cultural factors (cultural belief systems, insitutionalized means for dealing with change)

Other environmental stressors (war, economic upheaval)

(1979) concluded that people who experienced many stressful life events and did not become ill had a strong sense of meaningfulness and commitment to self, a vigorous attitude to life, and an internal locus of control--a constellation she termed "hardiness." These results exemplify the ways in which personality factors might modify the relationship between stress and disease. More work is needed, using validated personality measures.

There is considerably less systematic work relating personality factors to psychopathological disease. A current evaluation of the factors related to the development of depressive disorders is available (Depue, 1979). Some researchers have found that certain styles of perceiving and thinking about the environment may precede the development of particular forms of psychopathology (Gardner et al., 1959; Shapiro, 1965; Witkin, 1965). A continuing problem with such research is the inability to distinguish personality traits from early symptoms of some mental disorders. Progress for this type of research may have to await advances in other areas. For example, biological markers of severe mental disorders such as depression or schizophrenia might enable investigators to disentangle predisposing personality traits from symptoms of the mental disorder.

Stressful life events may have different impacts on different types of people. Horowitz (1976) analyzed in detail the influence of various personality types on the interpretation of information about major life events. For example, people with hysterical personality disorders showed high levels of inhibition while recalling stressful life experiences. Obsessional patients were much less able to inhibit memories of past life events; instead, they switched back and forth among various alternative meanings associated with the stressful event. Narcissistic personalities tended to alter the significance of an event by exaggerating or minimizing its implications. Thus, some types of stress research might benefit from the development of quantitative measures of general personality factors. People who have relatively immature self concepts and views of relationships between themselves and others may respond to serious life events or use social supports in ways that are distinct from those used by people who have more mature or differentiated and stable self concepts.

One of the central questions in stress research is why some people are especially vulnerable to certain kinds of stress. For example, why do some individuals

develop pathological grief reactions after the death of
a loved one and others cope adequately? Epidemiological
studies suggest that several factors can contribute to
such susceptibilities. For example, Brown et al. (1977)
found an increased incidence of depression among women
who were under the age of eleven when one or both parents
died, who had a strained marriage or limited social relationships, and who had no stable work situation outside
the home. Correlations for these factors individually
all were much lower than the correlation for the three
taken together, suggesting at least an additive effect.

Some of the observed effects of personality types on
reactions to stressors may reflect problems in personality development. Thus, a recent study found that
different types of pathological grief reactions to the
death of a loved one depended partly on latent self
concepts (Horowitz et al., 1980). People who viewed
themselves as incomplete had more difficulty with the
frightening sadness that may occur during a bereavement.
Those whose pre-existing self-concepts involved hatred
of self or of others were more likely to have difficulty
in the normal rage reaction that may follow bereavement
and episodically lost control.

Developmental vulnerabilities may be exacerbated by
particular styles of coping and defense (Horowitz, 1979).
People who habitually use extensive inhibitions may be
prone to painful and even overwhelmingly intrusive episodes of ideas and feelings following a stressful life
event. In contrast, people who tend to distort meanings
are likely to enter long periods of dulled, apathetic,
and listless reactivity following serious life events,
unless social relationships help them counter these
tendencies to evade the implications of a loss or injury.
These impressions, gained by the clinical investigation
of people after serious events, must be supplemented by
a more rigorous, reliable, and quantitative means of
assessing such variables.

It still is unclear which personality traits are the
most useful for predicting health outcomes or modifying
associations between stress and disease. At this time,
it may be advisable for investigators to include several
personality measures in their studies to determine which
are the most relevant. The Minnesota Multiphasic Personality Inventory, 16 Personality Factor Questionnaire,
California Psychological Inventory, Internal-External
Locus of Control Scale, and the Type A interview are examples of personality scales that already have been found
to have significant correlations to health outcomes.

Personal Resources. In recent years, stress researchers have given more attention to the role of personal resources, assets, and competencies in helping people to meet life challenges and to deal effectively with significant losses (Antonovsky, 1974, 1979; Beiser et al., 1972; Rutter, 1979; White, 1974). However, factors that provide support or protect against life stressors still are poorly understood. Rutter (1979) studied English children who came from disadvantaged backgrounds. Only half of his subjects evidenced difficulties in adjustment, and one in seven showed some type of outstanding ability. Some potentially important positive influences are genetic factors, high intelligence, special talents such as music or athletics, even temperament, high self-esteem, and a large repertoire of coping skills. These factors also can modify the child's environment and experiences. For example, children who are temperamentally difficult are twice as likely to be the target of parental anger as are children who are less difficult (Rutter, 1979).

Antonovsky (1979) has suggested that a sense of coherence is the common theme that links psychological, biological, and social resources and good health. Individuals have a sense of coherence if they view the world as comprehensible, manageable, and meaningful. In many ways, coherence resembles Kobasa's concept of hardiness, which was mentioned earlier. Much information is needed about such potentially protective characteristics. Is someone who has many personal resources more likely to have this psychological perspective than are people with more limited resources? Exactly how can resources promote a sense of coherence? Are resources additive or substitutable? Are some resources more important than others? Can psychological interventions enhance a person's sense of coherence?

More comprehensive conceptual frameworks and better measurement tools are needed to promote advances in research on the ways in which personal resources influence disease or help people cope with stressful life events. Distinctions between internal and external resources continue to be imprecise. Past internal competencies can influence current external resources, making the area difficult to investigate. For example, someone with a warm and outgoing personality is likely to develop strong social supports. Further, scales that measure social competence (Phillips, 1968) or social assets (Luborsky et al., 1973; Pesznecker and McNeill, 1975) include a conglomeration of variables: abilities of the person, for example intelligence; indications of status mobility,

163

like differences between the educational background of
subjects and their parents; measures of social participation such as numbers and types of club memberships; size
of the social network; and indications of current status,
including ownership of home and television. Knowledge
of what factors build social competence and protect
against illness should greatly facilitate efforts to
design better interventions for those who are deprived.

Process Factors

  Cognitive Appraisal. Lazarus (1966) was one of the
first to emphasize that cognitive appraisal plays a key
part in determining whether an event is stressful for a
particular individual; he and several other investigators
have explored some implications of that observation in
recent years (Beck, 1971; Carr, 1974; Depue et al.,
1979; Holmes and Houston, 1974; Lazarus et al., 1970;
Neufeld, 1970, 1975). If someone has the resources to
meet a stressful situation or fails to perceive that
danger exists, reactions to the stressor may be minimal,
suggesting that the meaning of an event is a critical
determinant of outcome. For example, in a study of
refugees from the Hungarian Revolution of 1956, Hinkle et
al. (1959) found that, notwithstanding social upheaval,
separation from friends, and other changes, most refugees
reported that they had less illness following their
flight to the United States than they had had previously.
Similarly, hospitalization and surgery have different
meanings to different people. While some view hospitalization as stressful, others who exist in a social world
that they find frustrating and demanding may welcome it
as a relief from unwanted responsibilities (Johns et
al., 1973).

  Coping Strategies. Numerous studies have shown that
the way an individual copes can influence the amount of
physiological arousal a stressor will induce (cf. Rose,
1980). For example, studies of people in combat situations (Bourne et al., 1967), of parents whose leukemic
child is dying (Friedman et al., 1963), and of patients
awaiting surgery (Katz et al., 1970) all confirm that
some defense mechanisms are associated with lower excretion of adrenal corticosteroids than are others. In
threatening situations, overt motor activity increases
physiological arousal, especially of corticosteroids
(Gal and Lazarus, 1975). A consensus is growing that
the way in which one copes with stress is an important
modifier of the stress-disease relationship (Antonovsky,

1979; Jenkins, 1979; Lazarus, 1981; Rahe and Arthur, 1978). Further work is needed to determine which coping processes are effective modifiers of the stress-disease relationship and which ones are directly linked to the incidence of physical or mental illness.

The way people cope with illness or medical proced- ures may affect their recovery (Cohen and Lazarus, 1973). For example, people who refuse to be passive patients when they are ill have difficulty adjusting to a hospital environment but show better long-term rehabilitation after a serious illness than do patients who accept the sick role. Expression of emotion can exacerbate respi- ratory symptoms and hasten physical decompensation in certain diseases such as chronic obstructive lung dis- ease or attract the attention of physicians to medical problems, resulting in increased treatment efforts that may prolong survival from a disease such as cancer.

Investigators also have implicated an inability to cope as a risk factor for disease (Engel, 1968; Engel and Schmale, 1967; Schmale, 1972). They suggest that some individuals react to life stressors, especially to a loss, with a "giving-up/given-up" complex characterized by feelings of helplessness. Some evidence suggests that individuals who experience such reactions may be at in- creased risk for becoming ill. Engel (1968) hypothesized that a conservation/withdrawal reaction debilitates the body's defense systems. Although there has been much interest in the giving-up/given-up complex, serious meth- odological problems exist with the research, including the lack of truly predictive studies, absence of control groups, observer bias, and alternative explanations (Cohen, 1979).

Habitual psychological defenses have been among the most important personality concepts discussed in dynamic theories. Vaillant (1977) has suggested that people who utilize defenses which exert relatively little distortion on information processing are at less risk for developing an illness or maladaptive behavior in the face of serious life events than are those with less advanced defenses. Some researchers distinguish between adaptive qualities of coping and defense mechanisms or between conscious behavior patterns and unconscious intrapsychic patterns. Others have not found such dichotomies to be very useful in their efforts to analyze responses to stress. Many theorists, from psychoanalysts to cognitive behavior- ists, agree that the entire theory of defense should be revised. Research on psychosocial adaptation to serious

165

life events may provide an important empirical basis for such revisions in general psychological theories of mental processes.

Studies of coping are seriously hampered by inadequate measurement techniques. At present, coping is assessed either as a trait, disposition, or style or as a process or episode (Averill and Opton, 1968). Coping traits are tendencies to use a particular coping response for a variety of stressful encounters (Moos, 1974b). Measures of coping traits include repression/sensitization (Byrne, 1961, 1964); repression/isolation (Gardner et al., 1959; Levine and Spivack, 1964); avoidance/coping (Andrew, 1970; Goldstein, 1959); measures of coping, defense, and ego fragmentation (Haan, 1977); and a defense-mechanisms inventory (Gleser and Ihilevich, 1969). All of these instruments assume that coping modes are stable over time and across situations. However, there is little evidence for such consistency. Recent work suggests that coping strategies can vary during different phases of a stressful encounter and from one situation to another (Cohen and Lazarus, 1979). Furthermore, trait measures are poor predictors of coping proccesses actually used in threat situations (Austin, 1974; Cohen and Lazarus, 1973). People who are asked to report their coping habits may not know what stratagies they use (Kasl, 1978). In addition, most measures assess only one coping trait, so they cannot reflect the complexity of the varied coping processes displayed in stressful encounters.

Assessment of coping as a process or episodic variable requires that a subject's thoughts and behaviors be observed in a particular situation of threat; the mode of coping then is inferred. Process measures of coping typically show stronger relationships to outcome than do coping trait measures; however, there remain a number of problems in trying to assess coping as a process (Cohen and Lazarus, 1979; Folkman and Lazarus, 1980). More efficient methods are needed for obtaining reliable and accurate information about coping processes. Also, a simple system is needed for categorizing the rich and complex group of strategies used even in one encounter. Such a system must be able to distinguish clearly between the coping process and its outcome. Clinical evidence suggests that some effective coping strategies may slip from awareness once a stressor is mastered. As a result, people tend to be more aware of coping strategies that have been ineffective than of coping strategies that they use successfully (Horowitz and Wilner, 1980).

Instruments are needed to assess a full range of coping strategies, including intrapsychic processes directed toward reducing emotional distress and problem-solving strategies (Folkman and Lazarus, 1980).

Environmental Factors

Interpersonal Factors. A social network consists of the people with whom one communicates and the links between relationships. Potentially important features of such a network include structural availability (how reachable others are, how many in the network know each other, and how heterogeneous the types of contacts are) and nature of the links (reciprocity in relationships, intensity, and frequency of interactions) (Mitchell, 1969). Recent research evidence suggests that those who have a supportive social network are protected in crisis from a variety of pathological states, both mental and physical. Such social supports are thought to buffer individuals from potentially negative effects of crisis and change and to facilitate coping and adaptation. Various researchers view social supports differently but usually include one or more of the following in their definitions: (1) giving emotional support (showing concern and caring, indicating that the person is valued; providing a sympathetic ear); (2) conveying a sense of belonging (participating in a reciprocal network of shared obligations); (3) providing tangible help when needed; and (4) suggesting information about how to cope (Cohen et al., 1977).

Some evidence suggests that people who have social supports or assets may live longer (Berkman and Syme, 1979), have a lower incidence of physical illness (Cassell, 1976; Gore, 1973; Kaplan et al., 1977), and have better morale and more positive mental health (Cobb, 1976). Thus, studies suggest that social support can help prevent psychological reactions in children after tonsillectomy; aid recovery from congestive heart failure, heart attacks, tuberculosis, asthma, surgery, and other illnesses; reduce the need for steroid therapy in adult asthmatics undergoing considerable life stress; protect against depression in the face of life change; reduce psychological distress and physiological symptomatology following job loss and bereavement; reduce child abuse among parents who are isolated; and reduce the number of psychiatric casualties in combat (Cobb, 1976; Kaplan et al., 1977; Dimsdale et al., 1979). Patients undergoing stressful life experiences report that seeking emotional support from others was one of the most helpful coping strategies used (Horowitz and Wilner, 1980).

Social supports are thought to modify potentially negative effects of stress either by reducing the stress itself or by facilitating the individual's efforts to cope. Several studies have reported interactions between life stress and social supports Nuckolls et al. (1972) found that neither extensive life changes nor low psychosocial assets alone was a risk factor for higher rates of complications during birth of a baby; however, the risk increased if both characteristics were present. Gore (1973) found that among men who lost their jobs, those with high levels of emotional support from their wives had fewer illness symptoms and lower levels of serum cholesterol and uric acid.

The studies of associations between disease consequences and social supports are interesting and generally consistent. However, at present, most of them are cross-sectional and confounding factors are not controlled. Many studies failed to find the expected relationships; some of the most positive findings are open to alternative interpretations, because other factors such as the person's mental and physical state may inhibit support rather than elicit it. More information is needed. What are the mechanisms by which social supports can reduce mental distress and physiological symptomatology? Is it possible to specify the types of support that are most protective in specific situations such as supervisor support in the work setting? Many individuals are socially isolated and seem unable to form strong social bonds. Can people be taught how to give and receive social support (Cohen et al., 1977)?

Social networks are not always supportive. Close relationships with other people create a potential for conflict. In addition, some cohesive relationships may inhibit independence and personal growth and thus place an individual at risk in later life situations that require independent problem-solving. Stress-increasing effects of social relationships should be evaluated. Furthermore, people who avoid personal relationships may show no apparent deleterious effects. For example, Lowenthal (1964) found that old people who have been socially isolated all their lives have better morale and are no more prone to hospitalization than are those who maintain social relationships. Some people may be hard to get along with, and as a result be less likely to have many confiding relationships. Providing such individuals

168

with supportive relationships may interfere with their
wish to remain isolated from others, so that they feel
more stressed, rather than less. Thus, the fit between
need and availability of social supports may be critical.

Presently, operational definitions of social support
vary greatly across studies. Most researchers develop
their own measurements, and few studies of the validity
of such tests have been made. In addition, there is
little comparability across tests. For example, Nuckolls
et al. (1972) used the subject's perceptions of herself,
her family, and her attitudes toward pregnancy; Gore
(1973) used husbands' ratings of the dependability and
emotional support of their wives and friends; Pinneau
(1975) included ratings of ease in talking with others
and how much concrete assistance others offered; and
Cobb (1976) suggested that the unwantedness of a baby
could be taken as an indication that the mother herself
had insufficient social supports.

The critical aspects of social networks need to be
identified and measured reliably. In fact, researchers
have yet to determine whether the formal characteristics
of social relationships have the same type of health-
protective effect as those found for social supports
(Kaplan et al., 1977). Defining which aspects of a
network are supportive will be even more difficult. In
many cases, other variables such as the person's state
of mental wellbeing may be confounded with the measures
of support. The individual's mental state must be dis-
entangled from actual or potential social supports.
Studies comparing the reliability and validity of some
of the existing scales for social supports may provide
guidelines for defining such supports more precisely.

Physical and Architectural Factors. There has been
extensive work looking for associations between health
consequences and either the geographic and meteorological
characteristics of an environment or its architectural
and physical design. Thus, Lynn (1971) found that
alcoholism and suicide rates increase with storminess,
summer heat, and increased solar radiation. Schuman
(1972) found an increase in mortality associated with
heat waves in New York and St. Louis. The increase was
greatest in people with sociodemographic and physical
characteristics such as poverty, old age, physical handi-
cap, and circulatory problems. Climate variables also
have been related to the pattern of admission to mental
hospitals; to suicide, homicide, and accident rates; and
to physical symptoms (Moos, 1976).

Organizational Factors. Organizations such as factories, schools, hospitals, and correctional facilities have been studied extensively in relation to their impact on health-related variables. Psychiatric patient discharge rates and hospital size appear to have a strong inverse correlation, with smaller hospitals having higher discharge rates (Linn, 1970). The effect of size was stronger than were the contributions either of patient background and personality characteristics or of the physical conditions of the ward facilities. Organizational size also has been related to the productivity of coal mines and aircraft factories, to indices of employee satisfaction, and to absenteeism and turnover rates in industrial organizations (Porter and Steers, 1973). Organizational factors appear to be related to indices of functional effectivenesss and health services utilization patterns (Cooper and Payne, 1978). Other aspects of research on stress in such settings are examined in Chapter 5, Stress in Organizational Settings and Chapter 6, Work Stress Related to Social Structures and Processes.

Human Aggregate Factors. A social group can be defined in part by the average characteristics of the people inhabiting a particular environment. Aggregate factors such as average age, ability level, socioeconomic background, and educational attainment are situational variables, in that they define certain relevant characteristics of the environment. Much of the work in social epidemiology utilizes such clusters of average background factors to define particular experimental groups. Thus, recent studies have grouped census tracts with similar configurations of sociodemographic factors into "social areas" that override geographic boundaries.

Using aggregate data, it has been possible to show that some average background characteristics of the members of a census tract or social area correlate with certain indices of health and crime rates. However, the interpretation of such data is subject to considerable controversy. In essence, the debate revolves around the extent to which these findings reflect the causal role of personal or environment characteristics and which specific subset of characteristics is most important (Moos, 1976). Some investigators commit the fallacy of using aggregate data to test hypotheses about individuals. Thus, a correlation in a city between suicide rates and transient rates cannot be used to test the hypothesis that transient individuals are more apt to commit suicide than are more stationary individuals. Perhaps a third factor such as socioeconomic conditions both encourages

the presence of a large transient population and creates
a setting in which suicide is unusually common. This
type of fallacy, early identified by Robinson (1950),
constitutes a major flaw in interpretations of research
findings in this area.

It is important to distinguish between aggregate
properties of individuals and suprapersonal properties of
the aggregate. Thus, aggregate characteristics such as
mean income or average level of education are conceptu-
ally distinct from factors such as community structure
that consider the entire population to be the basic
unit, rather than the individuals within that population.
Such suprapersonal properties also may be a source of
stressors for an individual. For example, a classic
study by Faris and Dunham (1939) concluded that rates of
schizophrenia were determined by social processes that
produced anomie within a city. Though certainly controversial, the findings emphasize that it is not always
necessary to interpret a result in terms of individuals.
For example, suppose a study showed that city neighbor-
hoods containing a high proportion of people born in
other countries also have a high incidence of mental
disorders. One direction for further research might be
to determine if foreign-born individuals are more likely
than native-born ones to develop mental disorders. But
it might be more fruitful to explore the effects of such
a population structure on social supports and other
factors that might be conducive to illness.

Social Climate. Efforts to evaluate how the social
climate of an environmental setting influences health
outcomes are of considerable interest. Social climate
refers to the overt and covert pressures that social
environments place on individuals. For instance, some
employees work in settings in which they are assigned
specific duties and must follow prearranged schedules
and specific directions. In such settings, emphasis
probably is on manager control and on conformity on the
part of employees. These conditions establish the
climate or atmosphere of such a setting. Moos (1976,
1979b) has conceptualized basic social climate in three
broad categories: relationship dimensions assess the
extent to which people are involved in the environment,
support each other, and express themselves freely and
openly; personal-growth or goal-orientation dimensions
assess the basic directions along which personal development and self-enhancement occur in a particular setting;
and system-maintenance and change dimensions deal with
the extent to which the environment is orderly, clear in

its expectations, maintains control, and is responsive
to change (cf. Stress in Organizational Settings, Chapter 5, and Work Stress Related to Social Structures and
Processes, Chapter 6).

Social climate variables drawn from these categories
are associated with important health variables such as
complaints of physical symptoms, absenteeism, sick-call
rates, and the outcome of psychiatric treatment (Moos,
1974a, 1975, 1979b). Thus, military basic training
companies that emphasize strict organization and officer
control and de-emphasize the enlisted person's status as
an individual tend to have high sick-call rates. Similarly, psychiatric wards with few social activities,
little emphasis on involving patients in programs, poor
planning of patient activities, and staff who discourage
criticism from patients and ignore patient suggestions
tend to have high dropout rates.

The social climate also might alter the efficacy of
available strategies for coping with stressors (Mechanic,
1974). For example, children from disadvantaged backgrounds may benefit greatly from a protective school
environment that offers a wide scope of opportunities
for personal growth and an appropriate amount of environmental structure and control (Rutter, 1979). Positive
influences of that social climate may help to protect
the children against some of the undesirable consequences
usually associated with such backgrounds.

Studying Environmental Factors as Mediators

External environmental factors also can be strong
mediators of stress. For example, the presence of
gardens and open space, light-colored rooms, or quiet
surroundings may each mitigate the stressful effects of
a high population density (Rapoport, 1975; Schiffenbauer
et al., 1977). In addition, psychological mediators such
as expectations or past experience attenuate or augment
perceptions of or reactions to environmental events
(Moos, 1979a; Stokols, 1976). Some researchers believe
that certain susceptible population groups, for example
the very young or old, those with low income or little
education, and those under stress are more likely to be
affected by environmental stressors (Cohen et al., 1979;
Hinkle, 1977; Kasl, 1977). Recent evidence suggests
that women, people with little education, and the poor
are less likely than are others to use efficacious coping
mechanisms (Pearlin and Schooler, 1978). The data are

consistent with the environmental docility hypothesis, which posits that people who are disabled, impaired, or under stress are more likely to be influenced by environmental conditions (Lawton and Nahemow, 1973). These results also suggest that it may be possible to identify groups that are particularly vulnerable to environmental stressors. Such groups might be especially fruitful targets for intervention efforts.

Better methods are needed for detecting and studying factors that increase an individual's vulnerability to adverse consequences following exposure to a stressor. Improvements in the concepts and research instruments for such measures can be utilized to identify which environmetal factors are related to particular consequences. For example, Moos and his colleagues have used such an approach in studying community care settings for older people. In their studies, they have examined the influence on health of such mediators as the physical and architectural environment, organizational policies and programs, suprapersonal structures, and social-environmental resources (Lemke and Moos, 1980; Moos and Igra, 1980; Moos and Lemke, 1980).

Major Methodological Issues

Indicators versus Mechanisms

As noted repeatedly in this chapter and throughout the report, most clinical stress research has been correlational, looking for associations between the occurrence of a stressor or groups of stressors and some disease consequence. Even a very strong association does not prove that the stressors cause the disease. A correlation between two variables may result from the influence of a third variable on both or from contamination in the measurement process (Brown, 1974). For instance, an illness might be caused by anxiety, and anxiety could foster increased reporting of stressful life events. Under such conditions, there would be a positive correlation between those life events and the disease, even though the events do not cause the disease. In retrospective studies, illness itself can create spurious correlations with stress by influencing the assessment of prior life experiences.

Correlational research can identify events or conditions that are risk factors for disease. The risk factor concept is discussed in both Stress and Life

Events and Stress and Illness. For an event to be a
risk factor, it must occur prior to the onset of the
disease and its occurrence must be associated with an
increased probability of illness. Stress researchers
have become increasingly aware of the difficulties of
proving that a life event occurred prior to disease onset. Thus, an individual may have important personality
changes that precipitate life events such as marital
difficulties or job loss months before a diagnosis of
depression can be made. Similarly, some forms of cancer
may grow undetected for years before they become clinically apparent.

Identification of a life event or condition as a
risk factor for disease may provide no insights into the
mechanisms responsible for the association (Rutter,
1980b; Rutter and Madge, 1976). For example, being male
is a risk factor of early mortality, criminal behavior,
and heart disease, among other adverse consequences. It
is unclear whether the underlying mechanisms are biological, environmental, or cultural, or some combination of
all three. It is likely that many different mechanisms
link a particular indicator to a disease. Research that
tries to specify these mechanisms offers the best hope of
developing preventive strategies and rational therapies.

Disease etiology sometimes may entail a sequence of
causal events--a causal chain. It may be necessary to
evaluate such event sequences in the context of current
and previous life experiences. A good understanding of
these chains should enable investigators to identify one
or more points at which intervention is possible. For
example, stressful life events may increase tension,
which then increases the probability that the person
will smoke heavily (Horowitz et al., 1979). Smoking, in
turn, may contribute to illness outcomes. Possible
intervention sites would include: 1) preventing exposure to the stressful event, 2) using pharmacological or
psychological techniques to reduce the tension that
typically follows such an event, 3) providing alternatives to smoking as a coping strategy, or 4) treating
the illnesses that result from the smoking. Prevention
programs may need to be conceptualized broadly enough to
address several sets of potential risk factors simultaneously. It is possible to intervene either with
individuals, for example by teaching people better coping
skills, or with entire groups, perhaps by modifying
high-risk stiuations. This latter approach is explored
in detail in Work Stress Related to Social Structures and
Processes (Chapter 6). Broad-gauged prevention programs

174

combining both types of intervention strategies may be
most effective.

The chain of mechanisms between a stressor and its
possible consequences needs to be described with greater
specificity and detail, and important mediators must be
identified. As described in Stress and Life Events
(Chapter 4), stress researchers have begun to distinguish
between stressors that may have been caused, at least in
part, by the subject and those over which he or she has
no control--so-called "fateful" events (Dohrenwend and
Dohrenwend, 1980). Such an approach should be useful
for identifying risk factors, because the occurrence of
the event cannot possibly be an early symptom of an as
yet undiagnosed disorder.

Consideration only of fateful events still does not
enable stress researchers to use correlational data to
imply that a stressor causes disease. Even stressors
that are beyond the individual's personal control may result from other internal or external processes that also
cause disease. Thus, early parental death is considered
to be a fateful event that might cause alcoholism. Yet
alcoholism also both runs in families and increases the
risk of early death (Robins, 1978). The life event, a
parent's death, clearly is a risk factor for alcholism.
Yet, there may be no direct causal link between the two.
For instance, suppose that the mechanism for developing
alcoholism involves early modeling of parental behavior
or a genetic predisposition. Then both the stressor of
losing a parent and the consequence of becoming an alcoholic occur because the individual had an alcoholic
parent. Stress researchers must participate in a broader
search for causes, both genetic and environmental.

Strength of Associations

Studies of life events and illness have consistently
demonstrated statistically significant correlations; but,
most correlations have been less that 0.3, with 1.0 being
a perfect correlation. Thus, although individuals are
at greater risk of becoming ill if they have had a life
event than if they had not, they still are more likely
to remain well than to become sick. Some researchers
suggest that this is a true measure of the role of life
events, at least as measured by the typical life-events
scale. Others believe that certain vulnerable subgroups
have much higher correlations but that these correlations
are balanced by low correlations in subgroups of people

who are relatively invulnerable to stress. More work is needed to resolve this issue and to identify the mediating variables that make some people vulnerable, if such subgroups do exist.

The concept of relative risk provides another method of describing how much the occurrence of a life event increases the chances of having a disease consequence. This approach is used, for example, in stating how much smoking adds to the risk of having lung cancer. It can be especially useful when the number of people who develop an illness is relatively small but the increase induced by the risk factor is a large percentage of that number. Thus, smoking carries a high relative risk of developing lung cancer because very few nonsmokers ever have lung cancer. Furthermore, even small absolute differences can be associated with large changes. For example, suppose that the average IQ ratings for children who have high blood concentrations of lead are only five points lower than the average for children whose lead concentrations are normal. That difference would result in a doubling of the number of mental retardates in a population exposed to lead (Rutter, 1980c). However, the increase of risk for a part of the total population may have little effect on the overall incidence of the disorder, if the risk is already high for other reasons in the remainder of the population.

As researchers establish how much a stressor increases an individual's risk for a particular disease and identify ways in which to intervene effectively, strategies for prevention or treatment undoubtedly will emerge. Already there is a large industry of "stress" seminars and self-help books. It will be important to determine whether the benefits of such programs exceed the costs. For example, if only a few people benefit, it may be inefficient to attempt to treat everyone who has been exposed to a particular stressor. Treatment might be much more feasible if a relatively small, readily identified subgroup of individuals were shown to be at particular risk and to be responsive to the intervention.

Financial, social, ethical and other costs of the proposed changes must be balanced against the importance of the disorder as a public health problem. Positive and negative effects of various life style changes must be considered carefully. Environmental stressors and coping styles are tempting targets for intervention. However, these may be difficult or expensive to change;

176

and changing them may put people at risk for other problems as a result of the alteration in life goals and
patterns. Methods are needed for predicting possible
costs as well as expected benefits to be gained from
intervention. The panel recommended, therefore, that
support be made available for both substantive and basic
research in stress and that stress research be broadened
so that causal hypotheses concerning stress must compete
with other causal hypotheses. Further, research into
the consequences of intervening to reduce stress or its
effects should be supported, so that rational application
of stress research findings will be possible.

Specific Research Needs

- The development of sensitive, valid, and reliable
  instruments for identifying and measuring psychosocial components of the stress response should
  receive high priority. Better techniques for
  assessing independent, moderating, and outcome
  variables will help investigators to explore more
  fully the processes that influence relationships
  between stress and disease.

- A conceptual framework is needed for classifying
  important psychosocial mediators of stress. At
  present, researchers use a variety of categories
  such as personal resources, personality, environmental resources, appraisal, coping, and life
  events. These may not provide an exhaustive list
  of possible mediators, and they offer no insights
  into common characteristics of important psychosocial factors. Further, many ambiguities remain
  about assigning particular causal variables to one
  of these categories. Funding for a critical review
  of the conceptual structure of research in psychosocial aspects of stress could provide a useful
  impetus for developing alternative nomenclatures
  for describing such factors.

- At least a few selected research groups should
  receive relatively stable funding for a period long
  enough to permit them to plan, conduct, and evaluate
  the longitudinal studies that are needed to answer
  some important questions about psychosocial modifiers of stress. Such projects are impractical if
  funding is uncertain and variable, as often happens
  with grants that must be renewed yearly.

- When studying associations between stressors and consequences, investigators should consider a broad range of potential outcomes, both desirable and undesirable. Studies should include measures of multiple biological, psychological, and social endpoints and should examine both short-run and long-run consequences.

- Investigators should explore the mechanisms through which psychosocial factors can influence the effects of stressors on physical and mental disorders. Stress research must go beyond a proliferation of studies that document associations between stressors and disease states. A better understanding of mediating factors will help to identify those points at which intervention is possible.

- Investigators should be encouraged to design studies that look at multiple disease consequences. The structure of federal funding encourages disease-focused research. Yet, such psychosocial variables as Type A behavior, anxiety, and coping may relate to more than one disease outcome. Innovative institutional arrangements may have to be devised to review and fund such studies.

- Studies are needed of the influence on health of situations that do not involve change or discrete events but may be stressful. Research is needed to compare psychological and physiological effects of each of the following types of stressors: (1) acute time-limited events, (2) stress-event sequences, (3) chronic intermittent stressors, and (4) chronic stress conditions. Such studies should consider not only immediate physiological and psychosocial reactions and long-term physiological, psychological, and social consequences, but also the effectiveness of different coping strategies in dealing with each type of stress situation.

References

Alexander F. _Psychosomatic Medicine_ New York: Norton, 1950.

Andrew, J. M. Recovery from surgery, with and without preparatory instruction, for three coping styles. _J. Pers. Soc. Psychol._ 15: 223-226, 1970.

Antonovsky, A. Conceptual and methodological problems in the study of resistance resources and stressful life events. IN: _Stressful Life Events: Their Nature and Effects_ (Dohrenwend, B. S., and Dohrenwend, B. P., eds.) New York: Wiley, 1974, pp. 245-258.

Antonovsky, A. _Health, Stress, and Coping_ San Francisco: Jossey-Bass, 1979.

Austin, S. H. Coping and Psychological Stress in Pregnancy, Labor, and Delivery, with "Natural Childbirth" and "Medicated" Patients Unpublished doctoral dissertation, University of California, Berkeley, 1974.

Averill, J. R., and Opton, E. M., Jr. Psychophysiological assessment: rationale and problems. _Adv. Psychol. Assess._ 1:265-288, 1968.

Beck, A. T. Cognition, affect, and psychopathology. _Arch. Gen. Psychiatry_ 24:495-500, 1971.

Beiser, M., Feldman, J. J., and Engelhoff, C. Assets and affects: a study of positive mental health. _Arch. Gen. Psychiatry_ 27:545-549, 1972.

Benner, P., Roskies, E., and Lazarus, R. S. Stress and coping under extreme conditions. IN: _Survivors, Victims, and Perpetrators: Essays on the Nazi Holocaust_ (Dimsdale, J. E., ed.) Washington, D.C.: Hemisphere, 1980, pp. 219-258.

Berkman, L. F., and Syme, S. L. Social networks, host resistance, and mortality: a nine-year follow-up study of Alameda County Residents. _Amer. J. Epidemiol._ 109:186-204, 1979.

Block, J. _Lives Through Time_ Berkeley: Bancroft, 1971.

Bourne, P. G., Rose, R. M., and Mason, J. W. Urinary 17-hydroxycorticosteroid levels. _Arch. Gen. Psychiatry_ 17:104-110, 1967.

Brim, O. G., Jr., and Kagan, J. Constancy and change: a view of the issues. IN: _Constancy and Change in Human Development_ (Brim, O. G., Jr., and Kagan, J, eds.) Cambridge: Harvard University Press, 1980.

Brown, G. W. Meaning, measurement, and stress of life events. IN: _Stressful Life Events: Their Nature and Effects_ (Dohrenwend, B. S., and Dohrenwend, B. P., eds.) New York: Wiley, 1974, pp. 217-243.

Brown, G. W, Harris, T., and Copeland, J. R. Depression and loss. _Brit. J. Psychiatry_ 130:1-18, 1977.

179

Byrne, D. The Repression-Sensitization Scale: rationale, reliability, and validity. J. Person. 29:334-
349, 1961.

Byrne, D. Repression-sensitization as a dimension of
personality. IN: Progress in Experimental Personality Research, Vol. 1 (Maher, B. A., ed.) New York:
Academic Press, 1964, pp. 169-220.

Carr, A. T. Compulsive neurosis: a review of the literature. Psychol. Bull. 81:311-318, 1974.

Cassell, J. The contribution of the social environment
to host resistance. Amer. J. Epidemiol. 104:107-123,
1976.

Chodoff, P., Friedman, S. B., and Hamburg, D. A. Stress,
defenses, and coping behavior: observations in
parents of children with malignant disease. Amer. J.
Psychiatry 120:743-749, 1964.

Cleary, P. J. Life events and disease: a review of
methodology and findings. IN: Reports from the
Laboratory for Clinical Stress Research (No. 37)
Stockholm: Karolinska Institute, 1974.

Cobb, S. Social support as a moderator of life stress.
Psychosom. Med. 38:300-314, 1976.

Cohen, F. Personality, stress, and the development of
physical illness. IN: Health Psychology--A Handbook
(Stone, G. C., Cohen, F., and Adler, N. E., ed.) San
Francisco: Jossey-Bass, 1979, pp. 77-111.

Cohen, F., Dornbusch, S., and Kaplan, B. H. Preliminary
Task Force Report on Social Support and Health.
The President's Commission on Mental Health, 1977.

Cohen, F., and Lazarus, R. S. Active coping processes,
coping dispositions, and recovery from surgery. Psychosom. Med. 35:375-389, 1973.

Cohen, F., and Lazarus, R. S. Coping with the stresses
of illness. IN: Health Psychology--A Handbook
(Stone, G. C., Cohen, F., and Adler, N. E., ed.) San
Francisco: Jossey-Bass, 1979, pp. 217-254.

Cohen, S., Glass, D., and Phillips, S. Environment and
health. IN: Handbook of Medical Sociology, 3rd Ed.
(Freeman, H., Levine, S., and Reeder, L. G., eds.)
Englewood Cliffs: Prentice-Hall, 1979, pp. 134-149.

Cooper, C. L., and Payne, R. (Eds.) Stress at Work New
York: Wiley, 1978.

Croog, S. H., Shapiro, D. S., and Levine, S. Denial
among male heart patients: an empirical study.
Psychosom. Med. 33:385-397, 1971.

Depue, R. A. (Ed.) The Psychobiology of the Depressive
Disorders: Implications for the Effects of Stress
New York: Academic Press, 1979.

Depue, R. A., Monroe, S. M., and Shackman, S. L. The
psychobiology of human disease: implications for
conceptualizing the depressive disorders. IN: The

Psychobiology of the Depressive Disorders: Implications for the Effects of Stress (Depue, R. A., ed.) New York: Academic Press, 1979, pp. 3-22.

Dimsdale, J. E., Eckenrode, J., Haggerty, R. J., Kaplan, B. H., Cohen, F., and Dornbusch, S. The role of social supports in medical care. Soc. Psychiatry 14: 175-180, 1979.

Dohrenwend, B. P., and Dohrenwend, B. S. Overview and prospects for research on stressful life events. IN: Stressful Life Events: Their Nature and Effects (Dohrenwend, B. S., and Dohrenwend, B. P., eds.) New York: Wiley, 1974, pp. 313-331.

Dohrenwend, B. P., and Dohrenwend, B. S. Psychiatric disorders and susceptibility to stress: reactions to stress of varying magnitudes and varying origins. IN: The Social Consequences of Psychiatric Illness (Robins, L. N., Clayton, P., and Wing, J., eds.) New York: Brunner-Mazel, 1980, pp. 183-197.

Dweck, C. S., and Bush, E. S. Sex differences in learned helplessness: I. Differential debilitation with peer and adult evaluators. Dev. Psychol. 12: 147-156, 1976.

Dweck, C. S., Davidson, W., Nelson, S., and Enna, B. Sex differences in learned helplessness: II. The contingencies of evaluative feedback in the classroom; and III. An experimental analysis. Dev. Psychol. 14: 268-276, 1978.

Engel, G. L. A life setting conducive to illness: the giving up/given up complex. Bull. Menninger Clin. 32: 355-365, 1968.

Engel, G. L., and Schmale, A. H., Jr. Psychoanalytic theory of somatic disorder. J. Amer. Psychoanal. Assoc. 15:344-365, 1967.

Faris, R. E. L., and Dunham, H. J. Mental Disorders in Urban Areas: an Ecological Study of Schizophrenia and Other Psychoses Chicago: University of Chicago Press, 1939

Folkman, S., and Lazarus, R. S. An analysis of coping in a middle-aged community sample. J. Health Soc. Behav. 21:219-239, 1980.

Fox, B. H. Premorbid psychological factors as related to cancer incidence. J. Behav. Med. 1:45-133, 1978.

Frankenhaeuser, M. The role of peripheral catecholamines in adaptation to understimulation and overstimulation. IN: Psychopathology of Human Adaptation (Serban, G., ed.) New York: Plenum, 1976, pp. 173-191

Frankenhaeuser, M., and Gardell, B. Underload and overload in working life: outline of a multidisciplinary approach. J. Hum. Stress 2: 35-46, 1976.

Friedman, S. B., Mason, J. W., and Hamburg, D. A. Urinary 17-hydroxycorticosteroid levels in parents of children with neoplastic disease: a study of chronic psychological stress. Psychosom. Med. 25:364-376, 1963.

Gal, R., and Lazarus, R. S. The role of activity in anticipating and confronting stressful stiuations. J. Hum. Stress 1:4-20, 1975.

Gardner, R. W., Holzman, P. S., Klein, G. S., Linton, H. B., and Spence, D. P. Cognitive control: a study of individual consistencies in cognitive behavior. Psychol. Issues 1(4):1-185 1959.

Garfield, S. R. The delivery of medical care. Sci. Amer. 222:15-23, 1970.

Gersten, J. C., Langner, T. S., Eisenberg, J. G., and Orzeck, L. Child behavior and life events: undesirable change or change per se? IN: Stressful Life Events: Their Nature and Effects (Dohrenwend, B. S., and Dohrenwend, B. P., eds.) New York: Wiley, 1974, pp. 159-170.

Gleser, G. C., and Ihilevich, D. An objective instrument for measuring defense mechanisms. J. Consult. Clin. Psychol. 33:51-60, 1969.

Goldstein, M. J. The relationship between coping and avoiding behavior and response to fear-arousing propaganda. J. Abnorm. Soc. Psychol. 58:247-252, 1959.

Gore, S. The Influence of Social Support and Related Variables in Ameliorating the Consequences of Job Loss Unpublished doctoral dissertation, University of Michigan, 1973.

Grinker, R. R. Psychosomatic Research New York: Norton, 1953.

Haan, N. Coping and Defending: Processes of Self-Environment Organization New York: Academic Press, 1977.

Hackett, T. P., Cassem, N. H., and Wishnie, H. A. The coronary-care unit: an appraisal of its psychologic hazards. New Engl. J. Med. 279:1365-1370, 1968

Hinkle, L. E., Jr. The effect of exposure to culture change, social change, and changes in interpersonal relationships on health. IN: Stressful Life Events: Their Nature and Effects (Dohrenwend, B. S., and Dohrenwend, B. P., eds.) New York: Wiley, 1974, pp. 9-44.

Hinkle, L. E., Jr. Measurement of the effects of the environment upon the health and behavior of people. IN: The Effect of the Man-Made Environment on Health and Behavior (Hinkle, L. E., Jr., and Loring, W. C., eds.) Washington, D.C.: U.S. Government Printing Office, 1977, DHEW Publ. No. (CDC) 77-8318, pp. 197-239.

Hinkle, L. E., Jr., Kane, F. D., Christenson, W. N., and Wolff, H. G. Hungarian refugees: life experiences and features influencing participation in the revolution and subsequent flight. Amer. J. Psychiatry 116: 16-19, 1959.

Holmes, D. S., and Houston, B. K. Effectiveness of situation redefinition and affective isolation in coping with stress. J. Person. Soc. Psychol. 29:212-218, 1974.

Holmes, T. H., and Masuda, M. Life change and illness susceptibility. IN: Stressful Life Events: Their Nature and Effects (Dohrenwend, B. S., and Dohrenwend, B. P., eds.) New York: Wiley, 1974, pp. 45-72.

Holmes, T. H., and Rahe, R. H. Schedule of Recent Experiences Seattle: University of Washington School of Medicine, 1967.

Horowitz, M. J. Depressive disorders in response to loss. IN: Stress Anxiety (Spielberger, C. D., and Sarason, I. G., eds.) Washington, D.C.: Hemisphere, 1979, pp. 235-255.

Horowitz, M. J. Intrusive and repetitive thoughts after experimental stress. Arch. Gen. Psychiatry 32:1457-1463, 1975.

Horowitz, M. J. Stress Response Syndromes New York: Aronson, 1976.

Horowitz, M. J., Benfari, R., Hulley, S., Blair, S., Alvarez, W., Borhani, N., Reynolds, A. M., and Simon, N. Life events, risk factors, and coronary disease. Psychosomatics 20:586-592, 1979.

Horowitz, M. J., Schaefer, C., Hiroto, D., Wilner, N., and Levin, B. Life event questionnaires for measuring presumptive stress. Psychosom. Med. 39:413-431, 1977.

Horowitz, M. J., and Wilner, N. Stress films, emotion and cognitive response. Arch. Gen. Psychiatry 33: 1339-1344, 1976.

Horowitz, M. J., and Wilner, N. Life events, stress and coping. IN: Aging in the 1980's: Selected Contemporary Issues (Poon, L., ed.) Washington, D.C.: American Psychological Association, 1980.

Horowitz, M. J., Wilner, N., and Alvarez, W. Impact of event scale: a measure of subjective stress. Psychosom. Med. 41:209-218, 1979.

Horowitz, M. J., Wilner, N., Marmar, C., and Krupnick, J. Pathological grief and the activation of latent self images. Amer. J. Psychiatry 137:1157-1162, 1980.

Hudgens, R. W. Personal catastrophe and depression: a consideration of the subject with respect to medically ill adolescents, and a requiem for retrospective life-event studies. IN: Stressful Life Events: Their Nature and Effects (Dohrenwend, B. S., and Dohrenwend, B. P., eds.) New York: Wiley, 1974, pp. 119-134.

Jenkins, C. D. Psychosocial modifiers of response to stress. J. Hum. Stress 5:3-15, 1979.

Jenkins, C. D. Recent evidence supporting psychologic and social risk factors for coronary disease. New Engl. J. Med. 294:987-994, 1033-1038, 1976.

Jenkins, C. D., Hurst, M. W., and Rose, R. M. Life changes: do people really remember? Arch. Gen. Psychiatry 36:379-384, 1979.

Johns, M. J., Dudley, H. A. F., and Masterton, J. P. Psychosocial problems in surgery. J. Royal Coll. Surg. Edinburgh 18:91-102, 1973.

Kanner, A. D., Coyne, J. C., Schaefer, C., and Lazarus, R. S. Comparison of two modes of stress measurement: daily hassles and uplifts versus major life events. J. Behav. Med. 4:1-39, 1981.

Kaplan, B. H., Cassel, J. C., and Gore, S. Social support and health. Med. Care 15 (Suppl. 5):47-58, 1977.

Kasl, S. V. The effects of the residential environment on health and behavior: a review. IN: The Effects of the Man-Made Environment on Health and Behavior (Hinkle, L., and Lorning, W., eds.) Washington, D.C.: U.S. Government Printing Office, 1977, DHEW Publ. No. (CDC) 77-8318.

Kasl, S. V. Epidemiological contributions to the study of work stress. IN: Stress at Work (Cooper, C. L., and Payne, R., eds.) New York: Wiley, 1978, pp. 3-48.

Katz, J. L., Weiner, H., Gallagher, T. F., and Hellman, L. Stress, distress, and ego defenses. Arch. Gen. Psychiatry 23:131-142, 1970.

Klausner, S. Z. (Ed.) Why Man Takes Chances: Studies in Stress-Seeking New York: Anchor Books, 1968.

Kobasa, S. C. Stressful life events, personality, and health: an inquiry into hardiness. J. Person. Soc. Psychol. 37:1-11, 1979.

Lawton, M. P., and Nahemow, L. Ecology and the aging process. IN: The Psychology of Adult Development and Aging (Eisdorfer, C., and Lawton, P., eds.) Washington, D.C.: American Psychological Association, 1973, pp. 619-674.

Lazarus, R. S. Psychological Stress and the Coping Process New York: McGraw-Hill, 1966.

Lazarus, R. S. The stress and coping paradigm. IN: Theoretical Bases for Psychopathology (Eisdorfer, C., Cohen, D., and Kleinman, A., eds.) New York: Spectrum, 1981, pp. 173-209.

Lazarus, R. S., Averill, J. R., and Opton, E. M,. Jr. Towards a cognitive theory of emotion. IN: Feelings and Emotions (Arnold, M., ed.) New York: Academic Press, 1970, pp. 207-232.

Lazarus, R. S., Deese, J., and Osler, S. F. The effects of psychological stress upon performance. Psychol. Bull. 49:293-317, 1952.

Lazarus, R. S., and Launier, R. Stress-related transactions between person and environment. IN: Perspectives in Interactional Psychology (Pervin, L. A., and Lewis, M., eds.) New York: Plenum, 1978, pp. 287-327.

Lemke, S., and Moos, R. H. Assessing the institutional policies of sheltered care settings. J. Gerontol. 35:96-107, 1980.

Levine, M., and Spivack, G. The Rorschach Index of Repressive Style Springfield: Thomas, 1964.

Linn, L. S. State hospital environment and rates of patient discharge. Arch. Gen. Psychiatry 23:346-351, 1970.

Lipowski, Z. J. Psychosomatic medicine in the seventies: an overview. Amer. J. Psychiatry 134:233-244, 1977.

Lowenthal, M. F. Social isolation and mental illness in old age. Amer. Sociol. Rev. 29:54-70, 1964.

Luborsky, L., Todd, T. C., and Katcher, A. H. A self-administered social assets scale for predicting physical and psychological illness and health. J. Psychosom. Res. 17:109-120, 1973.

Lynn, R. Personality and National Character Oxford: Oxford University Press, 1971

Mason, J. W. Over-all hormonal balance as a key to endocrine organization. Psychosom. Med. 30:791-808, 1968.

Mason, J. W. A historical view of the stress field: Part II. J. Hum. Stress 1:22-36, 1975.

Mechanic, D. The concept of illness behavior. J. Chron. Dis. 15:189-194, 1962.

Mechanic, D. Medical Sociology New York: Free Press, 1968.

Mechanic, D. Social structure and personal adaptation: some neglected dimensions. IN: Coping and Adaptation (Coelho, G. V., Hamburg, D. A., and Adams, J. E., eds.) New York: Basic Books, 1974, pp. 32-44.

Mitchell, J. C. (Ed.) Social Networks in Urban Situations: Analyses of Personal Relationships in Central African Towns Manchester: Manchester University Press, 1969.

Moos, R. H. Evaluating Treatment Environments: A Social Ecological Approach New York: Wiley, 1974a.

Moos, R. H. Psychological techniques in the assessment of adaptive behavior. IN: Coping and Adaptation (Coelho, G. V., Hamburg, D. A., and Adams, J. E., eds.) New York: Basic Books, 1974b, pp. 334-339.

Moos, R. Evaluating Correctional and Community Settings New York: Wiley, 1975.

Moos, R. H. The Human Context: Environmental Determinants of Behavior New York: Wiley, 1976.

Moos, R. H. Social-ecological perspectives on health. IN: Health Psychology--A Handbook (Stone, G. C.,

Cohen, F., and Adler, N. E., eds.) San Francisco: Jossey-Bass, 1979a, pp. 523-547.

Moos, R. H. Evaluating Educational Environments: Procedures, Measures, Findings and Policy Implications San Francisco: Jossey-Bass, 1979b.

Moos, R. H., and Igra, A. Determinants of the social environments of sheltered care settings. J. Health Soc. Behav. 21:88-98, 1980.

Moos, R., and Lemke, S. Assessing the physical and architectural features of sheltered care settings. J. Gerontol. 35:571-583, 1980.

Murphy, L. B., and Associates. The Widening World of Childhood: Paths Toward Mastery. New York: Basic Books, 1962.

Neufeld, R. W. J. The effect of experimentally altered cognitive appraisal on pain tolerance. Psychonom. Sci. 20:106-107, 1970.

Neufeld, R. W. J. Effect of cognitive appraisal on 'd' and response bias to experimental stress. J. Person. Soc. Psychol. 31:735-743, 1975.

Neugarten, B. L. Dynamics of transition of middle age to old age: adaptation and the life cycle. J. Geriatr. Psychiatry 4:71-87, 1970.

Nuckolls, K. B., Cassel, J., and Kaplan, B. H. Psychosocial assets, life crisis, and the prognosis of pregnancy. Amer. J. Epidemiol. 95:431-441, 1972.

Paykel, E. S. Life stress and psychiatric disorder: Applications of the clinical approach. IN: Stressful Life Events: Their Nature and Effects (Dohrenwend, B. S., and Dohrenwend, B. P., eds.) New York: Wiley, 1974, pp. 135-149.

Pearlin, L. I. Sex roles and depression. IN: Life-Span Developmental Psychology: Normative Life Crises (Datan, N., and Ginsberg, L. H., eds.) New York: Academic Press, 1975a, pp. 191-207.

Pearlin, L. I. Status inequality and stress in marriage. Amer. Sociol. Rev. 40:344-357, 1975b.

Pearlin, L. I., and Schooler, C. The structure of coping. J. Health Soc. Behav. 19:2-21, 1978.

Pesznecker, B. L., and McNeil, J. Relationship among health habits, social assets, psychologic well-being, life change, and alterations in health status. Nurs. Res. 24:442-447, 1975.

Phillips, L. Human Adaptation and Its Failures New York: Academic Press, 1968.

Pinneau, S. J., Jr. Effects of Social Support on Psychological and Physiological Strains Unpublished doctoral dissertaion, University of Michigan, 1975.

Porter, L., and Steers, P. Organizational, work and personal factors in employee turnover and absenteeism. Psychol. Bull. 80:151-176, 1973.

Rabkin, J. G., and Struening, E. L. Life events, stress, and illness. Science 194: 1013-1020, 1976.

Rahe, R. H., and Arthur, R. H. Life change and illness studies: past history and future directions. J. Hum. Stress 4:3-15, 1978.

Rahe, R. H., Meyer, M., Smith, M., Kjaer, G., and Holmes, T. H. Social stress and illness onset. J. Psychosom. Res. 8:35-44, 1964.

Rapoport, A. Toward a redefinition of density. Environ. Behav. 7:133-158, 1975.

Robins, L. N. Sturdy childhood predictors of adult anti-social behavior: replications from longitudinal studies. Psychol. Med. 8:611-622, 1978.

Robinson, W. S. Ecological correlations and behavior of individuals, Amer. Sociol. Rev. 15:351-357, 1950.

Rose, R. M. Endocrine responses to stressful psychological events. Psychiatr. Clin. N. Amer. 3:251-276, 1980.

Rosenman, R. H., Brand, R. J., Jenkins, C. D., Friedman, M., Straus, R., and Warm, M. Coronary heart disease in the western collaborative group study: final follow-up experience of 8.5 years. J. Amer. Med. Assoc. 233:872-877, 1975.

Ruesch, J. The infantile personality: The core problem of psychosomatic medicine. Psychosom. Med. 10:134-144, 1948.

Rutter, M. Protective factors in children's responses to stress and disadvantage. IN: Primary Prevention of Psychopathology, Vol III. Social Competence in Children (Whalen, M., and Rolfe, J. E., eds.) Hanover: University Press of New England, 1979, pp. 49-74.

Rutter, M. Emotional development. IN: Scientific Foundation of Developmental Psychiatry (Rutter, M. ed.) London: Heinemann Medical, 1980a, pp. 306-321.

Rutter, M. Changing Youth in a Changing Society: Pattern of Adolescent Development and Disorder Cambridge: Harvard University Press, 1980b.

Rutter, M. Raised lead levels and impaired cognitive/behavioural functioning: a review of the evidence. Devel. Med. Child Neurol. 22 Suppl. 42, 1980c.

Rutter, M., and Madge, N. Cycles of Disadvantage London: Heinemann Educational, 1976.

Sarason, I. G., Johnson, J. H., and Siegel, J. M. Assessing the impact of life changes: development of the life experiences survey. J. Consult. Clin. Psychol. 46:932-946, 1978.

Schiffenbauer, A. I., Brown, J. E., Perry, P. L., Shulack, L. K., and Zanzola, A. M. The relationship between density and crowding: some architectural modifiers. Environ. Behav. 9:3-14, 1977.

Schmale, A. H., Jr. Giving up as a final common pathway to changes in health. Adv. Psychosom. Med. 8:20-40, 1972.

Schuman, S. H. Patterns of urban heat-wave deaths and implications for prevention: data from New York and St. Louis during July 1966. Environ. Res. 5:59-75, 1972.

Selye, H. The Stress of Life New York: McGraw-Hill, 1956.

Shapiro, D. Neurotic Styles New York: Basic Books, 1965.

Sifneos, P. E. The prevalence of alexithymic characteristics in psychosomatic patients. Psychother. Psychosom. 22:255-262, 1973.

Singer, M. T. Engagement-involvement: a central phenomenon in psychophysiological research. Psychosom. Med. 36:1-17, 1974.

Stokols, D. The experience of crowding in primary and secondary environments. Environ. Behav. 8:49-86, 1976.

Vaillant, G. E. Adaptation to Life Boston: Little, Brown, 1977.

Vinokur, A., and Selzer, M. L. Desirable versus undesirable life events: their relationship to stress and mental distress. J. Person. Soc. Psychol. 32: 329-337, 1975.

Weiner, H. M. Psychobiology and Human Disease New York: Elsevier, 1977.

Wershow, H. J., and Reinhart, G. Life change and hospitalization--a heretical view. J. Psychosom. Res. 18: 393-401, 1974.

White, R. W. Strategies of adaptation: an attempt at systematic description. IN: Coping and Adaptation (Coelho, G. V., Hamburg, D. A., and Adams, J. E., eds.) New York: Basic Books, 1974, pp. 47-68.

Witkin, H. A. Psychological differentiation and forms of pathology. J. Abnorm. Psychol. 70:317-336, 1965.

Wolff, C. T., Friedman, S. B., Hofer, M. A., and Mason, J. W. Relationship between psychological defenses and mean urinary 17-hydroxycorticosteroid excretion rate. I. A predictive study of parents of fatally ill children. Psychosom. Med. 26:576-591, 1964.

Zuckerman, M. Sensation Seeking: Beyond the Optimal Level of Arousal Hillsdale: Erbaum, 1979.

CHAPTER 8

Panel Report on
Biological Substrates of Stress

Panel Members:
Roland Ciaranello, M.D., Co-chair
Morris Lipton, Ph.D., M.D., Co-chair

Jack Barchas, M.D.	Carlos Ferrario, M.D.
Patricia R. Barchas, Ph.D.	Seymour Levine, Ph.D.
John Bonica, M.D.	Marvin Stein, M.D.

This panel was asked to identify promising directions of research on the biological and physiological mechanisms through which stress may affect health. Panel members agreed that much of the relevant scientific investigation was not done as stress research. Many of the most promising leads have come from efforts to learn more about the biological system generally, with relatively little emphasis placed on possible relations to stress. The panel obtained background papers from its members and consultants on the fields of endocrinology, neurochemistry, pain, immunology, genetics, physiological sociology, and cardiovascular physiology (Appendix C). Each contributor was asked to identify recent advances that might be relevant to the stress field, promising directions for further research in stress, and difficulties that investigators might face.

The following synthesizes those background papers. The large amount of relevant research prohibits a comprehensive review. Rather, the group selected research efforts that are representative, focusing especially on those that seem to reflect notable trends. The panel was impressed with the tremendous potential of applying the many new developments in all aspects of basic biological research to pressing problems in the stress field.

Definitions of Stress

In considering the varied literature relating to research on biological changes that are associated with stress, the panel concluded that a continuing inability to define "stress" with any precision has contributed to substantial problems in the field. Often, stress is used interchangeably with the word "stressor" to refer to a force, burden, or pressure imposed on an organism or individual. Other times it is used to refer either to a reaction to a stressor or to the entire process of

stressor, reaction, and result. In early studies, stress
reactions were assessed primarily by behavioral criteria
such as verbal reports of subjective responses in man or
vocalization and abnormal activity in animals. Later,
investigators began to focus on anatomical, physiological, endocrinological, and biochemical changes. As
assays have become increasingly sensitive and versatile,
more and more organ systems have been noted to react to
stressors.

Most biological scientists use the term "stressor"
to refer to a dramatic or major stimulus that galvanizes
an organism into a reaction. The term usually refers to
a discrete event or series of events, but it also is
applied to such conditions as sensory deprivation or
physical restraint, in which the absence of a condition
is stressful. Many basic scientists in these fields are
interested primarily in some physiological system. They
use stressors as tools to manipulate the system and
deliberately select overwhelming stimuli to minimize the
probability that some test subjects will react and others
will not. Electric shock, food deprivation, massive
infection, loud noises, novel situations--these and many
more are used by investigators seeking to learn how the
body and brain work. In such a setting, a precise
definition of "stressor" is seldom a concern.

The challenge to stress researchers is to apply
information about the effects of severe stressors on
various biological systems to efforts to learn how stress
can affect health under more usual circumstances. Using
the model discussed in Chapter 2, Conceptual Issues in
Stress Research, such studies must consider the factors
that help to shape the transition from potential activator to reaction, including the characteristics of the
stressors themselves and the mediators that influence the
x-y step. This requires an integration of physiology
and psychology--disciplines that have traditionally been
separated. Many factors must be assessed simultaneously
or carefully controlled for so that a few variables can
be studied in isolation. Efforts in this area are vital
to any attempt to gain a better understanding of the
biological substrates through which stressors affect
health and disease consequences.

The panel concluded that basic scientists should
use definitions of stressors that are independent of
physiological or psychological reactions. Consideration
only of events or conditions that produce reactions
ignores critical questions about what mediators help to

determine if a reaction will occur. The concept of
potential stressor may be useful in this regard. It
should be possible to identify a number of stimuli that
produce reactions under some conditions. Attention then
can be directed toward defining and studying relevant
mediators. Until critical characteristics of important
stressors, mediators, and reactions are better defined,
investigators should state explicitly what they are
studying: what is being used as a stressor, what reaction or group of reactions are being measured, and what
biological or psychosocial mediators appear to affect
this stressor-to-reaction step?

Neuroregulation: Basic Concepts

There are 10 to 100 billion nerve cells in the
brain. Each cell makes many connections with other
neurons, receiving information that can help to either
facilitate or inhibit cell action. The keystone of
advances in the neurosciences over the past fifty years
has been an increasingly precise understanding of how
those cells communicate with one another and how the
brain monitors and modulates activities in the rest of
the body. For most neurons, specific compounds are involved in transmitting information between cells and for
regulating such transmissions. For many years, scientists believed that very few substances were involved in
neuronal regulation. However, the past few years have
added tremendously to the list of such compounds (Barchas
et al., 1978). Table 8.1 outlines a nomenclature that
helps to identify and distinguish among agents that act
at nerve synapses. The term "neuroregulators" emphasizes
that these compounds have in common an ability to regulate communication among nerve cells. This is only one
of a number of nomenclatures that have been proposed over
the past few years to provide a comprehensive system for
identifying such substances (Dismukes, 1979).

Neurotransmission

A brief review of an idealized synapse illustrates
the salient features of the current model of neuro-
transmission. Figure 8.1 is a representation of a
dopamine synapse. In the presynaptic terminal, the
neurotransmitter, dopamine, is synthesized in two steps
from its aminoacid precursor tyrosine. Tyrosine hydroxylase, the first step in this conversion, is present only
in neurons in which dopamine and other catecholamines

193

TABLE 8.1

CATEGORIES OF NEUROREGULATORS

Neuroregulators: substances involved in interneuronal communication.

Neurotransmitters: neuroregulators that act within a neuronal synapse to transmit a presynaptic signal to a postsynaptic neuron.

Neuromodulators: neuroregulators that act on neuronal communication through mechanisms other than synaptic transmission.

    Hormonal neuromodulators: substances that alter neuronal activity at relatively great distances from the site of release, possibly at many targets simultaneously; they exert their effects either via specific membrane receptors or by selectively interfering with some aspect of neurotransmission.

    Synaptic neuromodulators: substances that affect neuronal function locally by altering neurotransmitter activity at the synapse through a specific site which may or may not be a membrane receptor.

---

are formed; dopa decarboxylase, which completes the synthesis, is present in many neuronal and nonneuronal cells. Exactly where synthesis occurs remains to be established; it may be associated with membranes of the presynpatic vesicles, or granules, in which dopamine is stored after its synthesis.

Electrical depolarization of the presynaptic membrane starts a chain of events that results in the release of dopamine into the synaptic cleft between the two neurons, where the transmitter interacts with specific membrane receptors in a "lock-and-key" fashion. Interaction with postsynaptic receptors is thought to produce conformational changes in the receptor. These, in turn, affect membrane ion permeability to cause either depolarization or hyperpolarization, thereby altering the electrical activity of the postsynaptic neuron. For dopamine, receptor activation also initiates a complex series of intracellular events that are mediated by the synthesis of cyclic adenosine monophosphate (cyclic AMP). These

FIGURE 8.1

IDEALIZED REPRESENTATION OF A DOPAMINERGIC SYNAPSE

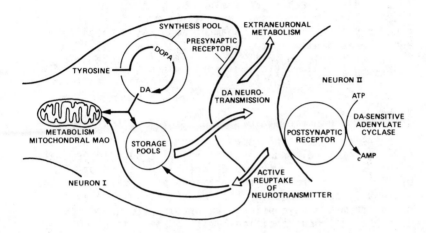

Dopamine (DA) is synthesized in two steps from the amino acid tyrosine and then stored in synaptic vesicles. An action potential depolarizes the presynaptic membrane, resulting in the release of dopamine into the synaptic cleft. The neurotransmitter then interacts with specific postsynaptic receptors, initiating a complex series of events that include changes in membrane permeability to specific ions and cyclic AMP formation; the latter, in turn, facilitates other intracellular processes. There also is some evidence for presynaptic receptors, which may alter dopamine synthesis as a function of synaptic activity. The neuronal signal is terminated when dopamine is cleared from the synaptic cleft, primarily via an active reuptake mechanism that returns it to the presynaptic terminal, where it is either metabolized by monoamine oxidase (MAO) or restored in vesicles for later use. Reproduced with permission from Barchas et al., Science 200:964-973, May 26, 1978. Copyright 1978 by the American Association for the Advancement of Science.

processes may be important in the cellular actions of the transmitter. There also appear to be presynaptic receptors for dopamine that probably are part of a feedback loop to regulate neuronal activity.

Termination of a signal requires removal of the transmitter from the synaptic cleft. This occurs partly as a result of passive diffusion out of the cleft and of extraneuronal metabolism. But, as is true for several other neurotransmitters, dopamine also has a specific reuptake mechanism in the presynaptic terminal. It then is either stored again in vesicles for later use or destroyed enzymatically.

Neuromodulation

The concept of neuromodulation arises from the discovery of several endogenous neuroactive substances that do not satisfy the criteria described for a neurotransmitter. Their presence suggests the possibility that the brain utilizes compounds which do not act by conveying a signal from a presynaptic to a postsynaptic neuron but do profoundly and specifically affect neuronal function.

The term "hormonal neuromodulators" refers to substances that regulate neuronal activity at locations that are relatively distant from their release site. Hormonal neuromodulators might be released from neurons, glia, true secretory cells, or other tissue sources to produce widespread effects throughout the brain, either at specific synaptic or nonsynaptic receptors or at specific steps in neurotransmitter regulation (Figure 8.2). In contrast to the short action of neurotransmitters, effects of hormonal neuromodulators might be prolonged, altering the baseline activity of spontaneously firing neurons or affecting responses to other neuronal input. Such a mechanism could permit precise modulation of the activity of an entire neuronal system. Hormones produced in other organs also might have a role as hormonal neuromodulators in the brain, as might substances formed in different parts of the brain.

Synaptic neuromodulators may be yet another type of neuroactive substances. Unlike hormonal neuromodulators, such compounds would not act directly on postsynaptic neurons. Instead, they might modulate the activity of a neurotransmitter by altering its synthesis, release, receptor interactions, reuptake, or metabolism (Figure 8.2). This concept is still being explored. Contrary to initial expectations, investigators have found that some

196

FIGURE 8.2

POSSIBLE SITES OF ACTION OF NEUROMODULATORS

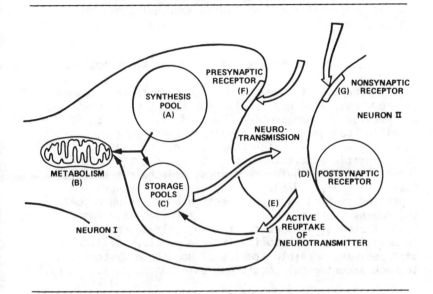

Each letter indicates a potential site for synaptic or hormonal neuromodulation of neuronal activity:

A) inhibition or stimulation of neurotransmitter synthesis;
B) blockade or induction of neurotransmitter metabolism;
C) interference with neurotransmitter storage, possibly by replacing it with a less active analogue (false transmitter);
D) inhibition at postsynaptic neurotransmitter receptor sites;
E) blockade of reuptake mechanisms;
F) competitive or noncompetive inhibition at presynaptic neurotransmitter receptor sites; and
G) interaction with specific nonsynaptic receptors that affect basal neuronal activity or alter neuronal responsiveness to other input.

From Elliott, G. R., and Barchas, J. D. IN: Hormones and the Brain (de Wied, D., and van Keep, P. A., eds.) Lancaster: MTP Press, 1980 (Figure 2). Reproduced by permission of MTP Press, Lancaster, England.

neurons contain more than one substance that may be a neuroregulator. A possible explanation for this finding is that one is a neurotransmitter and the others are synaptic neuromodulators. Such an arrangement would provide a great potential for fine-tuning neuronal activity at the synapse.

Ways to Study the Effects of Stress on Neuroregulators

In the past few years, neuroscientists have begun to study dozens of neuroactive substances whose presence was previously unsuspected. Much of this research is possible because of newly developed fluorimetric, gas-chromatographic, mass-spectometric, radioimmunologic, and enzymatic assays that can detect and quantitate these compounds, their precursors, and their metabolites (Barchas et al., 1975). In addition, researchers are beginning to find ways to investigate in living animals and humans the basic controls on neuroregulator function, including synthesis, storage, release, receptor interaction, and metabolism (Holman et al., 1977). Such advances make possible studies of how these systems react to such experimental conditions as exposure to stressors.

Most studies of the biological substrates of stress have involved measurements of changes that occur when a stressor is administered. Until recently, such studies were done mainly in animals, because the measurement techniques were too destructive or dangerous to use in humans. Animal studies continue to be vital, and investigators now can monitor and obtain samples from nearly every part of the body, including the brain, while the animal moves about freely or undergoes controlled exposure to stressors or other behavioral manipulations. For example, a tiny electrode can be placed in specific parts of the brain to record neuronal activity during a behavior. Or, a small, hollow needle can be surgically implanted into the brain. Samples of brain neuroregulators then can be removed through it for assay, or compounds that interfere with neuroregulator function can be administered to localized areas. In addition, it is becoming practical to augment these data with human studies. Thus, for decades, scientists have associated blood concentrations of the catecholamines with stress responses; but only in the past few years have they been able to take small blood samples from freely moving human subjects and measure how these substances change during exposure to a stressor. In combination, animal and human

198

studies should provide a wealth of new information about the effects of stress.

Central Neuroregulators

Norepinephrine, epinephrine, and serotonin were among the first peripheral and brain neuroregulators to be identified, and most stress-related research on brain neuroregulators involves studies of how concentrations of these substances change in reaction to a stressor.

Norepinephrine

Following the initial observation by Barchas and Freedman (1963) that forced cold-water swimming results in a significant depletion in whole-brain norepinephrine, a number of investigators demonstrated that a variety of other stressors, including footshock, produce comparable changes (Maynert and Levy, 1964; Zigmond and Harvey, 1970). Bliss and Zwaniger (1966) have suggested that, during stress, both synthesis and utilization of norepinephrine are increased and that depletion occurs when the increased rate of synthesis cannot keep pace with an even greater increase in utilization. Although such a proposal is consistent with events following acute stressors, it does not explain the effects of repeated stressors. Thus, Zigmond and Harvey (1970) found that acute and chronic inescapable shocks produced differential effects on brain norepinephrine concentrations in rats. Acute, intermittent footshock depleted brain norepinephrine; however, repetition of this stressor at 24 hour intervals for 14 successive days produced no depletion in brain norepinephrine following the last stress session. The mechanism for this adaptation to the stressor still is unclear, but the phenomenon illustrates the importance of the novelty of the stressor as a mediator for the reaction.

A comparison of acute and chronic stressors may be a valuable tool in elucidating neurochemical mechanisms. It seems reasonable to assume that the observed changes are attempts to return the norepinephrine neuronal system to equilibrium. If so, then comparisons of the neurochemical effects of acute stressors with those of chronic stressors may highlight biological processes that are responsible for the shift from the dysequilibrium state following acute stressors to one of equilibrium between synthesis and degradation of norepinephrine seen in chronically stressed animals. Such information should provide insights into the mechanism of regulation of this system.

Epinephrine

As discussed later in this chapter, peripheral epinephrine has long been recognized as an important hormone in relation to stress. More recently, scientists also have found that epinephrine is synthesized and utilized independently as a brain neuroregulator (Hokfelt et al., 1974). Methods now are available for studying this brain system. The potential role of brain epinephrine in reactions to stressors is of great interest, especially in terms of a possible regulatory function for other aspects of reactions to stress such as adrenal activation.

The distribution of epinephrine and the enzymes for its synthesis have been detailed in the central nervous system of both animals and man (Koslow and Schlumpf, 1975; Mefford et al., 1978). At present, relatively few investigators have studied potential behavioral roles of epinephrine. Saavedra et al. (1979) reported that use of restraint as an acute stressor in rats produced a larger percent decrease in brain epinephrine than in dopamine or norepinephrine. Also in rats, brain epinephrine has been implicated in motivation and in goal-directed behavior (Katz et al., 1979). Holz et al. (1977) have suggested that brain epinephrine has a role in producing the state of anxiety. The work of various investigators has begun to suggest that chronically stressed organisms may have important changes in epinephrine concentrations in the hypothalamus. This system merits much more research on its regulatory mechanisms and on the effects of acute and chronic stressors on those mechanisms.

Endorphins

A set of neuroregulator systems of immense current interest are the endogenous morphine-like peptides (endorphins), which have been found in brain. Already there is evidence that stressors affect concentrations of these substances. For example, inescapable shock in rats causes an increase in certain brain endorphins, with a parallel change in pain threshold (Madden et al., 1977). Thus, there may be a scientific basis for the common observation that individuals are not as aware of

200

pain during some stressful situations as they would be otherwise. Implications of such work for the study of stress, as well as of pain mechanisms, are enormous. For example, both adrenocorticotropic hormone (ACTH) and beta-endorphin are produced from the same precursor protein and are located in the pituitary in two types of cells (Mains et al., 1977; Watson et al., 1978), suggesting that there may be links between the endorphins and the pituitary-adrenal system, perhaps as a means of coordinating stress responses. Also, Torda (1978) observed that rats which were exposed repeatedly to pain-related stressors during early postnatal life exhibited an increased number of endorphin receptors and higher concentration of brain endorphins as adults.

Indoleamine Neuroregulators

Serotonin is found throughout the brain. It is associated with such behavioral states as sleep and pain perception (Barchas and Usdin, 1973). In response to certain stressors, the concentration of brain serotonin is elevated, and formation increases markedly. The responsible mechanisms remain to be determined; little is known about the regulation of serotonin formation and utilization. Serotonin is a particularly interesting neuroregulator, because some people with depression may have an alteration in brain serotonin utilization (Zarcone et al., 1977). Also of interest is the observation that many of the hallucinogens act, at least in part, by affecting serotonin mechanisms in the brain (Aghajanian and Haigler, 1975). Further study of this neuroregulator in relation to its biochemical regulation and changes may offer important clues into the myriad effects that stressors can have on mental disorders (cf. Chapter 9, Stress and Illness).

Melatonin, another indoleamine, is produced primarily in the pineal gland of the brain. It also may have a role in some aspects of stress reactions. For example, in humans, administration of melatonin produces mild sedation (Lerner and Case, 1960). It also has been reported to have some antianxiety effects, possibly by decreasing the excitability of the central nervous system (Anton-Tay et al., 1971). Similar effects of decreasing emotionality have been seen in animals (Datter and King, 1977). Animal studies also indicate that melatonin may decrease motivation and attention (Marczynski et al., 1964) and inhibit memory (Kovacs et al., 1974). The behavioral correlates of these effects may be an

201

increased ability to respond to stressful aspects of the environment. Sensitive and accurate assays for melatonin have become available only recently, opening the way for studies of its role in stress.

Regulatory Mechanisms

The preceding material has focused primarily on neuroregulator concentrations, but concentrations reflect only one aspect of potential reactions. Theoretically, stressors might affect such processes as formation, storage, release, and inactivation in ways that could lead to disease consequences. It also might alter the number of receptor sites or their sensitivity. Innovations in technology are making it increasingly feasible to examine changes in these biochemical mechanisms during exposure to stressors.

The catecholamine system offers a good example of potential effects of stressors on metabolic reactions. As described earlier, tyrosine hydroxylase is the enzyme involved in the first step of the synthesis. It is the rate-limiting step in the reaction, so that changes in the activity of this one enzyme can alter the amount of catecholamine available to a neuron. Recent studies have shown that tyrosine hydroxylase activity can increase markedly in reaction to a stressor. Two types of increases can occur. In response to acute stressors, the number of enzyme molecules remains the same, but a change in the enzyme conformation greatly increases the rate at which it can catalyze the formation of catecholamines (Raese et al., 1976). Enhanced activity also plays a role in reactions to chronic stressors; in addition, there is an increase in the number of enzyme molecules (Joh et al., 1978). Each of these processes affects rates of catecholamine formation and might be important determinants of how an individual responds to stress.

Peripheral Neuroregulators

Early in the history of stress research, the primary interest in biological components of stress were corticosteroids and catecholamines. In subsequent years, many other hormones have been implicated in the stress response. Among these are prolactin, growth hormone, insulin, testosterone, and luteinizing hormone. As discussed in Conceptual Issues of Stress Research (Chapter 2), Selye taught that the stress response was generalized and nonspecific. However, a growing body of literature suggests that hormonal responses to stressors are not uniform and that the reactions can be affected by a variety of biological and psychosocial mediators. Different physiological systems may respond to different intensities of the same stimuli or may be differentially sensitive to certain stressors. Unfortunately, the research on other hormonal systems is sparse in comparison with what is known about the pituitary-adrenal system.

The adrenal gland is located just above the kidney. The outer portion of the adrenal gland, the adrenal cortex, forms various steroid hormones, known collectively as corticosteroids, that are secreted in times of stress. It also plays a crucial role in maintaining salt and water balance. The adrenal cortex is distinct from the inner part of the gland, the adrenal medulla. The medulla is specially adapted to respond to stressors and secretes epinephrine. The adrenal medulla also forms other catecholamines, dopamine and norepinephrine, but less is known about their role in the stress response. Norepinephrine may be actively secreted after exposure to certain types of stressors. In addition, the adrenal forms neuroactive peptides. These have been described only recently, but they are thought to be released in times of stress. Schultzberg et al. (1978) have shown that the adrenal medulla is innervated by enkephalin-containing neurons. The capacity of the adrenal to form these materials is considerable, and there is suggestive evidence of a variety of such substances in human plasma. Their role is under active investigation, and their relevance to stress reactions must be determined.

Although both the adrenal cortex and the adrenal medulla are activated in response to stressors, the two parts work in different ways. For both, major control of reactions to stressors is through the brain; indeed, the brain controls all of the hormonal responses to stress. For the adrenal cortex, messages from the brain are sent to the pituitary gland; it secretes the polypeptide messenger ACTH, which is transported in the blood to the adrenal cortex, where it stimulates corticosteroid synthesis. In contrast, a message is sent from the brain via nerve cells directly to the adrenal medulla; those impulses provide the stimulus for the release of the adrenal medullary hormones, particularly epinephrine.

Plasma Corticosteroids

Corticosteroid response was initially considered to be a hallmark of stress, and many investigators still use elevated steroids as an indicator of stressful events or conditions. More recent investigations have begun to define the conditions under which corticosteroids are elevated and to identify factors that mediate changes in plasma levels.

Unpredictability appears to activate the pituitary-adrenal system. For example, Coover et al. (1971) studied the effects of first training animals to work for food by pressing a lever and then eliminating the food reward. This paradigm produced elevations in plasma steroids that were as high as those seen in response to noxious stimuli. However, if the behavior was prevented by removing the lever and making the food freely available, there was a significant suppression of circulating steroids (Davis et al., 1976). Levine and Coover (1976) found that animals maintained on a food or water deprivation schedule had a change in the circadian rhythm of plasma corticosteroids, so that an elevation in the levels occurred just prior to the feeding or watering time. Actual presentation of either food or water--or of stimuli associated with food or water, such as an empty drinking tube--resulted in a rapid suppression of pituitary-adrenal activity.

These studies suggest that, when a set of predictable events is altered so that expectancies are no longer met, this change leads to activation of an arousal system that subsequently results in increased pituitary-adrenal activity and, eventually, to a new set of expectancies. Changing from predictable to unpredictable events is sufficient to increase pituitary-adrenal activity. An animal that functions in a random, ambiguous situation does not appear to respond to a shift in predictability, probably because it has developed no expectancies in a given framework of stimulus contingencies (Levine et al., 1972). If expectancies are fulfilled, or even if only the cues associated with reinforcement are presented, pituitary-adrenal activity is suppressed.

The processes producing neuroendocrine activation from changes in expectancies may be explained by a model elaborated by Sokolov (1960) to account for the general process of habituation. A subject presented with an unexpected stimulus shows an alerting or orienting reaction. The physiological components of this reaction are well established: general activation of the brain, changes in the electrical resistance of the skin, cardiovascular changes, and an increase in circulating corticosteroids. If the same stimulus is repeated frequently, all of these reactions gradually diminish and eventually disappear; the subject is said to be habituated. Sokolov suggests that an individual matches immediate events to a central nervous system representation of prior events. This matching process can be defined as the development of expectancies (Pribram and Melges, 1969; Gray, 1975). When the environment contains no new contingencies, there will no longer be physiological responses related to arousal.

Plasma Catecholamines

Animal Studies. The central role of the sympathetic and adrenomedullary systems in orchestrating the complex of adjustments needed to preserve the internal environment has long been recognized. Cannon (1935) pioneered in demonstrating the importance of the sympathoadrenal system in fight-or-flight responses marshalled to meet an external stressor. He showed also that both physical and emotional disturbances can trigger such reactions and that there are limits to an animal's ability to compensate. Those limits vary under different conditions and as a function of changes that occur during the life course.

Classically, researchers have considered sympatho-adrenal activation during stress to involve mainly a relatively nonspecific release of adrenal catecholamines. This concept must be reevaluated. Several lines of evidence suggest that mechanisms exist for shaping reactions to stressors more precisely. Wurtman and Axelrod (1966) have shown that glucocorticoids released from the adrenal cortex can alter the rate at which norepinephrine is converted to epinephrine in the adrenal medulla. Thus, they may be mediators that shape the magnitude of the adrenal response and also affect the relative amounts of norepinephrine and epinephrine that are secreted.

Human Studies. Studies of peripheral catecholamines have been hindered by methodological limitations. Until a few years ago, the only way to assess them was to measure the amounts excreted in urine. The relatively long intervals required between urine sample collections make it impossible to control completely for a multitude of postural and physical changes that occur concurrently with the psychological changes and also mask any transient fluctuations in plasma catecholamine concentrations.

Despite the limitations of this approach, urinary catecholamine excretion is affected by some types of stressors. An early hypothesis was that epinephrine and norepinephrine are released selectively under different emotional experiences. Epinephrine release was thought to reflect fear and anxiety, and norepinephrine release was associated with aggressiveness and anger (Ax, 1953; Funkenstein, 1956). Direct tests of this hypothesis failed to confirm it. Thus, Levi (1965) examined urinary catecholamine excretion following exposure to films selected to evoke a feeling of amusement, anger, fright, or equanimity. Epinephrine excretion increased in response to all of the arousal films and decreased with the nonarousing one; norepinephrine excretion showed a similar pattern, but changes were less marked. Questions about the possible significance of differential changes in these two substances continue to be of interest.

New assay techniques permit accurate measurement of catecholamines in human blood under a variety of conditions. Such methods should enable many interesting and informative studies of peripheral catecholamines. Some studies have examined the effects of psychological stressors on plasma catecholamines. Thus, Dimsdale and Moss (1980) compared the effects on plasma catecholamines of public speaking and moderate exercise. Both raised plasma concentrations of norepinephrine and epinephrine. Norepinephrine increased more than twice as much during exercise as during speaking, but epinephrine increased about three times more for speaking than for exercise.

There also has been interest in catecholamine response patterns of Type A individuals as a possible factor in the increased risk of cardiovascular disease that is associated with the behavior pattern (cf. Stress and Illness, Chapter 9). Friedman et al. (1979) examined the effects of puzzle solving on plasma catecholamines and found that both resting and post-puzzle-task plasma norepinephrine was significantly higher in Type A subjects than in Type B subjects, with no differences in epinephrine concentrations. Glass et al. (1980) studied the effects of harrassing subjects during competition. Harrassed Type A subjects had much larger increases in plasma epinephrine than did nonharrassed Type A subjects or either harrassed or nonharrassed Type B subjects; plasma norepinephrine showed similar trends, but the differences did not reach statistical significance.

One of the particularly interesting aspects of catecholamine response is that, unlike other hormonal responses, it does not appear to diminish after repeated exposure to the stressor, at least when involvement is high. For example, Bloom et al. (1963) studied urinary catecholamine excretion in new and experienced parachute jumpers; both groups experienced comparable elevations in excretion during the jump. These elevations may reflect some particular aspect of the response, for example vigilance, rather than a direct reaction to the stressor. With novel acute stressors, when all systems appear to respond, it is hard to discriminate between responses to stressors that are a consequence of heightened arousal and responses that may be more closely associated with attention and vigilance. However, when arousal is reduced, attention and vigilance may still persist.

Other Hormonal Neuroregulators

Excretion of several other hormones also is known to change in response to stressors (Rose, 1980). This is particularly true for excretion of growth hormone and prolactin from the pituitary. Growth hormone usually responds in a pattern similar to that observed for corticosteroids, but it seems not to be as reactive as the pituitary-adrenal system. Subjects who display a growth hormone response also will have elevated corticosteroid concentrations; the converse need not be true, suggesting that a more intense stimulus is needed to produce a change in growth hormone excretion (Rose and Hurst, 1975). Studies of growth hormone are difficult, because it is released in episodic bursts even under normal conditions, making it hard to distinguish episodic release from reactions to stimuli. When other hormones such as steroids and testosterone cease to be responsive to stress, growth hormone also ceases to respond.

The few available studies indicate that pituitary prolactin also responds to stressful stimuli (Boyd and Reichlin, 1978). As with growth hormone, increased prolactin excretion may not be a response to a stressor, because it has other normal functions. For example, prolactin is secreted in women following childbirth, secondary to the stimulation of the nipple, and is involved in the production of milk; it also may modulate androgen metabolism and plasma osmolality (Thorner, 1977). The extent to which prolactin responds to both physiological and psychological stressors, as well as its time course and many of its dynamics have not been investigated systematically.

Unlike the other hormones, all of which are elevated during stressful conditions, testosterone and insulin concentrations usually fall following exposure to a variety of stressors. Studies of men undergoing training in the army suggest that psychological stressors can

207

produce a sustained fall in testosterone concentration, which returns to normal after the stressors cease (Kreuz et al., 1972). In monkeys, there is evidence that the testosterone response may depend on the type of stressor. Thus, when monkeys engaged in aggressive encounters, the victorious monkey shows a brief rise in testosterone, but the defeated one shows a prolonged fall (Bernstein et al., 1978). Analogous studies could be made in humans. Mason (1975) found that insulin concentrations also decreased during exposure to a chronic stressor; when the stressor was removed, it overshot control levels for a few days before returning to normal.

Cardiovascular System

The ability of stressors to affect cardiovascular function has long been recognized by both laymen and scientists, yet many have been reluctant to accept the possibility that stress might play a significant role in the pathogenesis of cardiovascular disorders. Several factors have hindered serious consideration of this possibility. As discussed in Stress and Illness (Chapter 9), two major problems in clinical research are the difficulty of quantifying and predicting the impact of stressors on autonomic nervous system function and the ambiguity about conclusions drawn from retrospective studies. Little is known about the mechanisms through which reactions of the cardiovascular system to stressors can lead to disease consequences.

During the past three decades, progress has been made in elucidating the function of the central nervous system in controlling normal cardiovascular function. This knowledge has enhanced our appreciation of the ways in which environmental or behavioral factors can contribute to disease. A wealth of information suggests that cardiovascular diseases are multifactorial in origin. Thus, the effect of acute or chronic stressors on the pathogenesis of cardiovascular disorders must be viewed in context with other metabolic or hemodynamic abnormalities that contribute to the disease process.

Acute Stressors

A large literature has accumulated on the effects of acute stressors on the cardiovascular function of animals and man. Investigators have used stressors ranging from direct stimulation of various areas of the brain to a variety of classical conditioning procedures. The influence of the autonomic nervous system in mediating the cardiovascular response has been studied in detail. It involves brain activation of the sympathetic nervous system, with a resulting increase in heart rate and facilitation of adrenomedullary secretion. Of great importance, but less well understood, is the role of other regulatory mechanisms for the circulatory system, as mediators of autonomic nervous system responses and of arterial blood pressure changes in normal and disease processes.

Powerful and complex cardiovascular responses can be obtained by activating sensory nerve fibers in the major arteries. This raises the possibility that these fibers are involved in disturbed cardiovascular function. For example, it has been shown that cardiac reflexes may participate in the pathogenesis of primary hypertension, a disease in which stress may play an important adjuvant role. Several investigators have proposed that subtle alterations in cardiac function may influence the onset of transient changes in the cardiovascular system that can lead to chronic sustained hypertension. In this context, it is interesting that the hemodynamic alterations associated with fight-or-flight reactions to severe stressors resemble those accompanying the development of experimental and human hypertension. This suggests, but does not prove, that the stimulus which elicits primary hypertension affects brain mechanisms regulating cardiovascular function.

Several studies have shown that cardiovascular reactions are specific to the stressor employed. Thus, Zanchetti and Malliani (1974) found that cats preparing to fight (agonistic behavior) had constricted peripheral blood vessels and decreased output from the heart; defense behavior involving physical movement produced an increase in cardiac output and in muscle blood flow. Hilton (1975) has suggested that the repertoire of basic response patterns may be quite limited but that the basic cardiovascular patterns can interact when behavior involves several activities such as protective movements, exercise, and escape. Perhaps the intensity of hemodynamic characteristics associated with the occurence of a specific behavior is modified simultaneously by the peripheral systems that signal the brainstem to activate the sympathetic system. Thus, parallels between defense-evoked behavior and hemodynamic changes in experimental hypertension may be more than coincidental.

The distinct pattern of biochemical and neuro-endocrine responses associated with physiological and behavioral stressors should be studied further in animals exposed to physiological manipulations that increase the risk of hypertension. These experiments may yield vital information about mechanisms by which chronic behavioral or environmental stressors may accelerate, sustain, or aggravate hypertension. Particular attention should be paid in the future to clarifying the neuroanatomy and neurochemistry of sensory neurons in the cardiovascular system and to discovering the mechanisms by which they might be involved in the origin and expression of cardiovascular disease processes.

In man, information about acute effects of stressors abounds in clinical experience, but the number of controlled laboratory studies is small. Shapiro (1960, 1961) has shown that simple stimuli such as venipuncture and mental calculations can increase blood pressure, with changes in both cardiac output and peripheral resistance. In addition, both hypertensives and pre-hypertensives appear to exhibit greater responses to environmental and behavioral stressors than do normotensive controls. It now is possible to continuously monitor arterial pressure and heart rate in man. This technique has provided insights into the degree of variability that blood pressure shows in all patients with hypertension, as well as in healthy persons during a 24-hour period (Richardson et al., 1964).

In man and animals, hemodynamic variability shows no association with blood pressure. Usually, the lability of pressure is influenced significantly by stressors. Animals whose sensory nerves from the cardiovascular system have been severed have an exaggerated response to such stimuli as eating, sleeping, grooming, or the sound of a bell. These observations suggest the possibility of an important interplay between acute or chronic stressors and cardiovascular pressure receptors in the development of hypertension. Thus, a primary or secondary dysfunction in the receptors might lead first to increased cardiovascular responsiveness, so that reactions to usual life events are amplified beyond normal limits. As suggested by Folkow and Rubinstein (1966), repeated bouts of exaggerated blood pressure and heart rate lability then might affect blood vessels and cause cardiovascular hypertrophy and hypertension.

Another aspect of cardiovascular function that must be elucidated is whether learning can substantially contribute to the production or elimination of cardiovas-

cular disease. As discussed in Stress and Illness
(Chapter 9), there is some evidence that learning does
play a role in the normal regulation of specific patterns of cardiovascular response. However, the evidence
is not conclusive. Additional work in animal models
will be required.

Chronic Stress

There have been many attempts to produce hypertension in rats, dogs, mice, and cats by exposing them to
chronic stressors. For example, audiogenic and electric
stressors can produce hypertension in rats (Weiner et
al., 1962). Henry et al. (1972) found that social
overcrowding, which forced competition for territory,
produced sustained blood pressure elevations in mice.
The conditions are severe, however; and factors other
than crowding may contribute to the observed changes.
In general, the literature suggests that a chronic
stressor is a risk factor of chronic hypertension, if
the animal is constantly exposed to a highly stressful
situation that contains elements of fear and uncertainty. Genetic states or physiological manipulations
such as increased dietary sodium intake or renal artery
ligation, both of which predispose to cardiovascular
disorders, appear to augment these effects.

Most of the chronic stressors used to produce
hypertension in animals also produce major neuroendocrine
reactions. Observed reactions include changes in plasma
renin activity, catecholamines, and steroids. Any of
these alone could result in transient changes in heart
rate, cardiac output, and arterial pressure; but it is
unclear which of them, alone or in combination, is
followed by chronic hypertension. It is important to
determine whether long-term factors accounting for the
persistence of cardiovascular disease are the same as
those associated with the triggering event or reflect
secondary adjustments of the cardiovascular system to
maintain homeostasis. Fruitful research will entail
more detailed studies of animal models in which stressors
are applied in the presence of an underlying genetic,
dietary, or organ factor that is itself a risk factor.
It seems unlikely that acute stressors, even if repeated
at frequent intervals, can be the sole cause of permanent
cardiovascular pathology. On the other hand, they may
aggravate an underlying disturbance in metabolism or
hormonal control of the circulation.

211

Neuroendocrine Relationships

Additional basic research also is needed to learn
more about associations between stress and neuroendocrine
factors. It is well known that the pituitary regulation
of endocrine responses is itself influenced by the hypothalamus, which integrates inputs from the rest of the
central nervous system. Understanding of primary hypothalamic involvement in cardiovascular disorders depends
on a precise analysis of the complex interrelationships
between peripheral hormones and the brain. Recent demon-
strations of endorphin-like substances in the adrenal
gland raises the possibility that these compounds also
are involved in the regulation of cardiovascular function
and the expression of the stress response. More attention also is needed to the role of other neuronal systems
that might affect the cardiovascular system and what
effects stress may have on them.

In approaching the question of neuroendocrine disturbances specifically associated with cardiovascular
diseases, it will be necessary to separate endocrine
abnormalities that result from the disease process from
those that alter its course. This will require better
evaluations of regulatory processes involved in the
interaction among neuroregulators in those parts of the
brain that influence cardiovascular function. Investigators should take advantage of existing techniques to
obtain profiles of substances that are involved in the
adaptive response to changes in the environment and to
study how they change during acute and chronic stress
situations. Interactions between hypothalamic and peripheral hormones in controlling cardiovascular function
and their pathology remain to be investigated fully.

Some hormones such as epinephrine are present in
both the periphery and the brain. The function of the
newly discovered brain systems remains to be determined,
but it is possible that they help modulate the output of
the autonomic nervous system. Neuroanatomical, immuno-
histofluorescent, and iontophoretic techniques are now
well established and should be applied to animal models
of cardiovascular disease that utilize acute or chronic
stressors alone or in combination with a target organ
disease (ischemic heart disease, hypertension, diet-
induced atherosclerosis). When possible, such studies
should strive for an integrative evaluation of how stress
can affect the neuroendocrine changes that result in and
accompany progressive cardiovascular disease alone or in
combination with stress factors. These data will be use-

ful in understanding not only the adaptative response but
also the basic mechanisms by which the brain regulates
homeostasis.

Pain System

Acute pain is a complex constellation of unpleasant
perceptual and emotional experiences and inextricably
interrelated physiological, psychological, and behavioral
changes or responses caused by tissue damage (Bonica and
Albe-Fessard, 1976). Seldom considered explicitly, pain
is associated closely with stress in many instances.
Tissue damage and the consequent nerve impulses constitute the stressor. These are often referred to as
"pain" impulses, but they do not produce the unpleasant
perceptual and emotional experience that we call pain
until they reach the brain. Until then they are called
"noxious" or "nociceptive," and their transmission is
called "nociception."

The association of physiological and psychological
stress reactions to disease and injury was implicit in
the pain concepts of the ancient Chinese, Hindus, and
Egyptians. Aristotle and most other ancient Greek
philosophers believed that the pain experience was a
negative emotion, felt in the heart and not the brain.
Historically, scientific research on pain has not been
commensurate with its clinical importance. Only recently
have basic and clinical scientists begun serious studies
of the mechanisms of acute and chronic pain syndromes.

Acute Stressors

A few investigators have attempted to determine in
humans whether physiological responses provoked by pain
(nociceptive stimulation) are nonspecific or are distinct
from those provoked by strong emotions such as fear and
anger. In these studies, experimental pain was induced
by a pressor test, electric shock, radiant heat, or a
tight metal headband; the effects of such a physical
stressor were compared with those that accompanied fear
and anger induced through a variety of verbal and non-
verbal communications as psychologic stressors (Bridges,
1974; Roddie, 1977). Schachter (1957) found that fear
produced a predominantly epinephrine response, and pain
produced a predominantly norepinphrine response. Anger
resulted in an epinephrine response in about 50 pecent of
the subjects, a norepinephrine response in 40 percent,

and a mixed response in about 10 percent. In contrast, a recent direct measure of plasma catecholamines showed that physical stressors produced an increase in norepinephrine and epinephrine, and a psychologic stressor increased only norepinephrine (Halter and Pflug, 1980).

Masuda and Dudley (1968) have used a headband to produce severe head pain. The nearly intolerable pain provokes in subjects a constellation of psychological changes, including frustration, anger, and anxiety. The accompanying physiological changes include an increase in respiratory rate and oxygen consumption, an increase in blood pressure with no change in heart rate, and no change in urinary excretion rates of major catecholamine metabolites. The last measure, an indirect assessment of catecholamine activity, suggests that secretion is not elevated under these conditions. Another study used hyponosis to induce anger, anxiety, exercise, depression, or pain and compared this with the effects of actual pain (Dudley et al., 1963). In this setting, actual pain and hypnotically induced pain, anger, and anxiety produced the same type of respiratory responses, providing evidence that there is no difference between the response to pain and strong emotion. Neuroendocrine responses were not assessed.

Sandman et al. (1973) studied the endogenous plasma levels of melanocyte-stimulating hormone (MSH) and ACTH before and after electric shock and before and after an acute psychological stressor. The electrical stressor elevated both MSH and ACTH, whereas the psychological stressor increased only plasma MSH levels. Morishima et al. (1978) noted that, in pregnant baboons, fear increased norepinephrine plasma and decreased uterine blood flow to the same degree as did pain provoked by intense pinching of the foot. Shnider et al. (1979) have published similar findings in pregnant ewes.

Current Concepts of the Acute Pain Process

Recent data clearly demonstrate that pain is a complex phenomenon. Acute pain is a constellation of unpleasant perceptual and emotional experiences and of inextricably interrelated physiological and psychological changes. Invariably, acute pain is provoked by a noxious or tissue damaging stimulation produced by injury or disease; it is rare that acute pain is caused primarily by psychopathology. This contrasts with chronic pain, in which psychopathology plays a primary etiological

214

role in many patients. Space limitations permit only a brief summary of current knowledge on substrates of acute pain. For more details, see Bonica et al. (1979), Cannon et al. (1978), and Mayer and Price (1976).

Tissue damage caused by injury or disease provokes noxious stimulation that is transduced into noxious impulses by "bare" nerve endings called nociceptors, which are the terminals of specific types of nerve fibers. In the spinal cord, these nerve fibers make complex synaptic connections to many other neurons in specific areas of the cord and brainstem. Some areas relate exclusively to nociception, but others make contact with neurons involved in other aspects of body function. For many years, scientists thought that the spinal cord acted only as a relay station for the pain signal. Instead, it contains a complex structure that permits not only reception and transmission but a high degree of sensory processing.

After being subjected to modulating influences, some nociceptive impulses are sent to other parts of the spinal cord at the same level of the body to produce reflexes that are familiar to anyone who has touched a hot object. Other impulses pass up the spinal cord to the brain to provoke more complicated responses and to produce the perception of pain. This pain perception has four psychological dimensions: sensory, referring to discrimination of the impulse; emotional, relating to arousal or anxiety; motivational, involving an affective response; and cognitive, reflecting an evaluation or judgment of the stimulus.

Parts of the brain, the reticular formation and the thalamus, perform an integrative function, assessing the total amount of stimulation being received and modulating the level of arousal of widespread areas of the cerebral cortex. The hypothalamus integrates and regulates autonomic nervous system activity and the neuroendocrine response to threat; it also organizes visceral and somatic reactions. The limbic system does not have primary control of behavioral processes; rather it seems to help modulate attention, mood, and motivation. The frontal cortex probably mediates between cognitive activities and motivational and affective features of pain, because it receives information from virtually all sensory areas of the brain and sends nerves to areas that strongly influence pain pathways. These modulating mechanisms make possible mobilization of all kinds of associations based on past experience, judgment, and emotion. They also are involved in the evaluation of

215

pain sensation, including the perception of pain as an undesirable motivating force. Neocortical processes subserve cognitive and psychological factors, including prior conditioning, anxiety, attention, suggestion, cultural background, and evaluation of the meaning of the pain-producing situation.

Modifiers of Nociception

In general, immediate responses to noxious stimulation consist of (1) liberation of "pain-producing substances" that, over time, produce local tenderness, altered sensation, and vasomotor responses; (2) involuntary reflex mechanisms, including reflex skeletal muscle spasm, increased sympathetic tone with consequent vasoconstriction, inhibition of gastrointestinal and genitourinary motility and function, increased ventilation, and increased cardiac output and blood pressure; and (3) cerebral and subcortical responses, including the emotional and perceptual experience of pain, psychodynamic mechanisms that produce affective reactions of anxiety and apprehension, and operant responses that are characteristic of overt pain behavior. As specific substrates of pain are identified, the nature and function of these mediators should become clearer.

Biochemical Factors. Far too little is known about neuroregulatory systems that mediate pain responses. The recent discovery of the endorphins has suggested a biochemical means by which the brain may suppress pain perception: endorphin receptors are densest in the portions of brainstem known to mediate the affective dimensions of pain. However, other neuroregulators, including substance P and several amino-acid neurotransmitters, undoubtedly are involved in regulating the pain system. New methods for studying the location and function of these substances are among the most promising advances in the neurosciences.

Psychological Factors. During the past 25 years, scientists and clinicians have established the importance of motivational, affective, cognitive, emotional, and other psychological factors on the pain experience. Any of these factors can exacerbate effects of the noxious input and be affected by it. For example, the anxiety and emotion arousal provoked by the nociceptive input activate psychophysiological mechanisms and thus increase skeletal muscle tension, which adds to the nociceptive barrage; nociceptive signals also may cause vasospasm and

216

consequent ischemia that produce biochemical changes in tissues which lower the threshold of nociceptors.

Pain in Physical Illness and Injury

It is widely appreciated that acute pain of disease and certain injuries have the important function of warning the individual that something is wrong, initially prompts him or her to seek medical counsel, and is used by the physician as a diagnostic aid. Moreover, the ensuing reactions usually help the organism cope with disease or injury and thus help to restore and maintain homeostasis. What is not generally appreciated, however, is that continued pain has no known useful function; if not adequately relieved, it can produce serious abnormal physiological and psychological reactions that cause complications which may progress to death. Similar deleterious effects result if, after it has served its biological function, the severe pain of myocardial infarction, pancreatitis, and other serious acute visceral disorders is not effectively relieved. Indeed, even severe pain associated with physiological processes such as parturition, if allowed to persist, can produce deleterious effects. Reflex responses are more likely to become abnormal and cause complications in patients who are in poor physical condition or have preexisting emotional problems. Several examples help to illustrate that such pain-induced changes could be one mechanism through which stressors can produce reactions that lead to adverse health consequences.

Postoperative Pain. Deleterious consequences of severe, unrelieved postoperative pain include pulmonary, intestinal, and urinary problems, thromboembolism, altered muscle metabolism, increased load on the heart and circulatory system, increased oxygen consumption, and postoperative emotional problems. Pulmonary complications occur primarily after upper abdominal or thoracic surgery, which can cause severe pain and abnormal reflex responses, with a consequent spasm and splinting of the respiratory muscles, producing marked impairment in ventilation (Bonica and Benedetti, 1980). Resulting changes in the lung airways, coupled with an inability or unwillingness to breathe deeply or cough because of fear of aggravating pain, predispose the individual to bacterial infection and pneumonia. This, in turn, can increase morbidity; in patients in poor physical condition or with preexisting chronic lung disease, pain related destruction of tissue may progress to death.

217

Postraumatic Pain. Severe pain following a traumatic accident may contribute to medical difficulties.
Often, pain-induced reflexes and cortical responses are
excessive. Instead of helping the system to return
toward normal, they initiate and maintain the vicious
circle of shock (Chien, 1970). In such instances, a
persistent, grossly excessive constriction of the blood
vessels produces tissue hypoxia and consequent biochemical and metabolic disturbances and toxic products
that, in turn, lead to new nociceptive stimulation and
widespread deleterious effects which further aggravate
the physiopathology. Vasoconstriction is most marked in
the splanchnic vascular bed; the resulting intestinal
ischemia causes hypoxic tissue damage and consequent release of toxic substances that depress the cardiovascular
system, particularly the heart muscle (Lefer, 1970). A
few studies have shown that blocking nociceptive and
sympathetic pathways with local anesthetics prior to or
soon after injury will prevent or promptly eliminate the
pain and the abnormal reflex responses, with improvement
in cardiovascular function (Fine, 1965). Unfortunately,
these interesting leads have not been pursued.

Parturitional Pain. In pregnant ewes, baboons, and
other animals, pain markedly increases plasma catecholamines, particularly norepinephrine, with a consequent
decrease in uterine blood flow (Morishima et al., 1978).
These effects were also noted in animals subjected to
psychological stressors. Severe pain and anxiety during
human labor increases plasma norepinephrine, epinephrine,
and corticosteroids; that increase is blocked by regional
analgesia (Morishima et al., 1980). Changes in blood
chemistry caused by the hyperventilation and increased
norepinephrine release combine to reduce uterine blood
flow, which may impair placental blood gas exchange
during uterine contractions. The effects of such a
series of intermittent impairments of placental blood
gas exchange apparently are tolerated by the normal
fetus; but, for a fetus at risk because of obstetric
complications, the pain-induced reduction in uterine
blood flow might lead to morbidity or even mortality.

Immune System

The immune response is responsible for maintaining
the integrity of the organism against foreign substances
such as bacteria, viruses, tissue grafts, and neoplasia.
Many cell types and plasma constituents are involved in
the immune process, including blood monocytes, tissue
macrophages, polymorphonuclear leukocytes, mast cells,

218

and complement. However, the major burden for immune responses by the organism resides with lymphocytes. A primitive stem cell located in the bone marrow differentiates into two major lymphocyte classes known as the T and B lymphocytes.

T lymphocytes, which mature in the thymus, are involved in cell-mediated responses; B lymphocytes, from bone marrow, are concerned with producing antibodies for humoral immune responses. Cell-mediated immune responses protect against viral, fungal, and slow bacterial infections; mediate transplantation immune reactions and other autoimmune phenomena; and provide immune surveillance against tumors. Humoral immunity provides resistance against acute bacterial infections. At times, the immune response can be pathological, resulting in anaphylaxis, asthma, and autoimmune disorders such as systemic lupus erythematosus. The classical division of the immune system into cellular and humoral components probably is oversimplified. Recent research has revealed a complex interaction between T and B lymphocytes and macrophages that serve to regulate the responses of the system. These interactions may have both protective and pathological effects.

Stress and Immune-Related Disease Processes

The concept of multiple causation of disease is well illustrated by the observation that colonization of an organism by bacteria does not necessarily result in illness. Clinically, it has been noted for many years that infectious diseases result from host-microorganism interactions. There is a growing interest in factors that modify host resistance, as reviewed in Stress and Illness (Chapter 9). Some basic scientists also have attempted to explore the nature of the association between psychosocial factors and infectious disease. Most animal studies have employed avoidance learning procedures that require mice to jump a barrier at the presentation of a signal to avoid an electric shock. Daily exposure to this stress increases susceptibility to such infectious agents as herpes simplex virus (Rasmussen et al., 1957) and polio virus (Johnsson and Rasmussen, 1965). Physical restraint (Rasmussen et al., 1957), unavoidable electric shock (Friedman et al., 1965), and loud noises (Jensen and Rasmussen, 1963) produce similar results.

Social factors such as isolation and crowding also can affect disease susceptibility. Friedman et al.

(1969) found that mice housed alone were much more susceptible to encephalomyocarditis virus and less susceptible to Plasmodium berghei than were animals housed in groups. Mice subject to conditions that led to fighting showed decreased resistance to trichinosis (Davis and Read, 1958), and those placed near a predator developed increased parasite reinfection rates (Hamilton, 1974). Tobach and Bloch (1956) studied several parameters of susceptibility to tuberculosis in mice. Male and female mice were exposed to the tubercle bacillus in doses designed to produce either an acute or a chronic infectious process. With chronic infection, crowding prior to innoculation increased mortality for males but decreased it for females. In contrast, males exposed to crowding had a lower mortality rate from acute infections, and crowding increased survival when it preceded inoculation but decreased it when it followed exposure to tuberculosis.

A few human and animal studies have measured immune parameters such as antibody titers or interferon along with disease susceptibility. An important study by Meyer and Haggerty (1962) utilized members of 16 families in a one-year prospective study with periodic throat cultures for hemolytic streptococci, measurements of antistreptolysin O antibody titers, and clinical evaluation of illness. Acute or chronic family stressors were significant factors in determining whether the individual became a host for the organism, became ill following colonization, and showed rises in the antistreptolysin O following infection. More recently, Solomon et al. (1967) found that male mice exposed to electric shock prior to the inoculation of Newcastle virus increased subsequent interferon production. In a similar study, Jensen (1973) found that avoidance learning or confinement decreased subsequent interferon levels in female mice, suggesting that sex difference may be important.

Psychosocial factors also appear to play a role in graft acceptance or rejection. Experimental studies in animals have shown that some kinds of psychosocial stressors enhance graft survival. Wistar and Hildemann (1960) found that chronic avoidance learning prolonged skin homograft survival in mice. Solomon et al. (1974) reported that the stress of limiting the feeding schedule of rats depressed the graft-versus-host reaction induced by parental lymphocytes injected into the animals. Further study in this area may be of considerable usefulness in the management of transplantation patients.

220

Psychosocial Processes and Humoral Immune Responses

A variety of psychological and social stressors have been found to affect the humoral immune response in animals. For example, exposure to light, movement, or noise decreased the primary antibody response of mice to a foreign protein (Hill et al., 1967). Overcrowding of rats reduced both the primary and secondary antibody responses to flagelin, a bacterial antigen; but low voltage repeated electric shock enhanced it (Solomon, 1969). Crowded mice had signficiantly lower titers of circulating antibody than did isolated mice (Vessey, 1964).

Available studies suggest that timing, frequency, and intensity of the stimulus can influence how the humoral immune system will react. For example, Gisler (1974) used a plaque-forming-cell (PFC) assay of humoral immunity to study the effect of restraint and crowding in mice. He found that a single session of varying lengths suppressed the immune response; but, after three days of repeated presentation of the stimulus, the response returned to control levels. Sexual differences also may play a role. Measuring the antibody response of rats sensitized to human thyroglobulin, Joasoo and McKenzie (1976) found that both isolation and crowding suppressed the antibody response to this antigen in males, but females showed an enhanced response with crowding and a decreased response with isolation.

One interesting explanation of changes in immune responses over time is the possibility that the humoral immune response is subject to learning. A few studies have examined this question directly. For example, Il'enko and Kovaleva (1960) found that an antibody response to bacterial antigens could be elicited by conditioned stimuli that were independent of the antigen. Ader and Cohen (1975) paired a conditioned stimulus with a pharmacological immunosuppressant; subsequent exposure to the conditioned stimulus alone resulted in suppression of the antibody response. Monjan and Collecctor (1977) found that mice subjected to a sound stressor for varying lengths of time had time-dependent responses; the immune response was suppressed during the first 20 days of exposure and enhanced during the next 19 days.

Psychosocial Processes and Cell-Mediated Immune Responses

Like humoral immune responses, cell-mediated immune responses are sensitive to psychological and social stressors. The major difference with these types of studies is that the end point is the stimulation of T cell lymphocytes with mitogens like Conconavalin A (ConA). Monjan and Collector (1977) used ConA in experiments in which mice were exposed to a sound stressor. As with the humoral immune response, short-term exposure to the stressor suppressed the cell-mediated immune response, but extended exposure enhanced it. Several groups are studying qualitative and quantitative aspects of stressors that might differentially influence cell-mediated immunity, and more work in this area is needed.

Mediation of Psychosocial Influences on Immune Function

The processes that may mediate psychosocial influences on immune function are complex and need further clarification. Consideration should be given to the full range of neuroregulators that might play a role. To date, most studies have focused on the effects of steroids, but studies of a few other potential modulators also are available.

Adrenal corticosteroids have long been known to affect immune function. Usually, they suppress the immune response, but occasionally they enhance it (Fauci, 1975). Studies of the effects of steroids typically involve parallel measurements of adrenocortical activity and immune function. Thus, Marsh and Rasmussen (1960) found that, in mice, both avoidance learning and confinement were accompanied by adrenal enlargement, decreased lymphocyte counts, and a slow involution of the thymus and spleen that occurred in temporal relation to increased susceptibility to viral infection. Gisler (1974) and Monjan and Collecctor (1977) studied in vitro, cell-mediated responses of mouse lymphocytes and found that increased corticosteroid concentrations correlated with suppressed immune function. The temporal relationship between a hormone such as cortisol and a possible modulating effect on the immune response also appears to be important. Hill et al. (1967) exposed monkeys to various chronic stressors and found decreased antibody responses even at six weeks; in contrast, steroid levels were initially elevated, but had returned to normal by two weeks after the initiation of stress.

Other hormones also may have a role in psychosocial influences on immune function. As discussed earlier, growth hormone is released in response to stressors, and the response often is dissociated from the steroid rise

222

(Yalow et al., 1969). The role of growth hormone is of
particular interest, because it has been shown to reverse
steroid immunosuppressive in an in vitro assay of cell-
mediated response (Gisler, 1974) and to enhance graft
rejection (Comsa et al., 1975). It also is required for
the development of the immune system (Denckla, 1978).
Denckla has emphasized the role of the thyroid hormone
in modulating immune responses, and testosterone has a
suppressive effect on immune function (Wyle and Kent,
1977). Epinephrine and norepinephrine both can decrease
immune responses, including anaphylaxis and delayed
cutaneous hypersensitivity (Schmutzler and Freundt,
1975). The role of cyclic adenosine monophosphate
(cyclic AMP) in this response remains to be assessed
fully. Schmutzler and Freundt (1975) reported that
cyclic AMP inhibited immune function, but Wang et al.
(1978) found that it enhanced response. Other well-known
changes following exposure to stressors include elevation
in free fatty acids and cholesterol, both of which may
be immunosuppressants (Dilman, 1977).

Central Nervous System and Immune Processes

    The hypothalamus is a likely place to seek mechan-
isms by which the brain might modulate immune function.
Stein et al. (1980) have reported that bilateral anterior
hypothalamic lesions protect against lethal anaphylaxis
in the guinea pig. In an attempt to determine the
reason for this effect, they studied circulating and
tissue-fixed antibodies, antibodies binding to host
tissue, the content and release of histamine and other
mediators by the tissues, and the responsiveness of the
target tissue to the pharmacological agents liberated by
the antigen-antibody reaction. None of these factors
provide a complete explanation of the observed effects,
and further studies are needed to clarify how such
lesions can alter the anaphylactic response.

    Brain mechanisms for modulating cell-mediated
immune responses also require more study. Stein and his
coworkers found that, as with humoral immune responses,
anterior hypothalamic lesions suppressed delayed cutaneous hypersensitivity reactions in the guinea pig (Macris
et al., 1970). More recently, they studied the effects
of such lesions with in vitro measures of lymphocyte
functions and correlated it with in vivo findings (Keller
et al., 1980). They found no changes in the absolute
numbers of either B or T lymphocytes. In vitro activity
was suppressed in whole blood samples, but not in iso-

223

lated lymphocyte cultures. These data suggest the
possibility of a circulating humoral inhibiting factor
that may be regulated by the hypothalamus. Much work
remains to be done to determine the nature and function
of such a substance.

Special Topics

Genetics of Stress

An understanding of stress genetics requires studies
of the genetic basis of differences in the biological
and behavioral reactions to stressors and in their
consequences. These range from differences in the perception of external and internal stimuli as stressors to
differences in the responses of body tissues and brain
functions to the hormones released during stress. The
main substances that have been studied in this context
are the corticosteriods and catecholamines produced by
the adrenal gland. Equally important, however, are the
neuroregulators in the brain and in the sympathetic
nervous system that modulate stress responses.

Animal Studies. Early papers by Wragg and Speirs
(1952) and by Levine and Treiman (1964) on strain differences in the response of mice to stress have led to an
accumulation of evidence of a considerable genetic
variation in the stress response (cf. Barchas et al.,
1974; Ciaranello, 1979; Shire, 1979). These studies
have shown that all the major components of stress responses involving catecholamines and corticosteroids are
under genetic control. Among the mechanisms that have
been studied are hormone synthesis, hormone transport and
degradation, and the responsiveness of target organs.
In vitro cultures of target cells show permanent, heritable differences in responses to the hormones that are
involved in stress reactions (Coffino et al., 1976;
Yamamoto et al., 1976). What is needed is the identification of the genes that are responsible for such
differences. In some cases this has been done for strain
differences affecting the stress-response systems of
normal rats (Rapp and Dahl, 1976) and mice (Ciaranello,
1979; Shire, 1979).

Only three pathological mutations affecting adrenal
function are known in mice (Beamer, 1979) and only one in
rabbits (Fox and Crary, 1978). Thus, nearly all genes
involved in stress responses still must be isolated and
identified. The effects on the stress response for each

224

identified gene then must be investigated to establish
which are regulatory and which structural. Genetic
mapping of these variants is necessary to identify
regulatory sites.

Particularly for studying acute stressors, dynamic
processes such as the induction of enzymes or the modulation of receptor molecules also must be investigated
(Ciaranello et al., 1974; Levine and Treiman, 1964).
The systems should be studied in both developing and
mature animals, because stress susceptibility changes
considerably during development (Salomon and Pratt,
1979; Shire, 1979). Studies on somatic cells in culture
will be important in these investigations, especially if
the gap between somatic cell genetics and whole-animal
genetics can be bridged by using genetic chimeras (Dewey
et al., 1977). Research on major pathological mutants
affecting the stress response systems of experimental
animals should be an important priority, because such
studies may provide animal models of specific human
diseases. However, a systematic search for spontaneous
mutants is not likely to be useful: the symptoms that
lead to their discovery, such as perinatal or infant
mortality, failure to thrive, or increased sensitivity
to disturbance, are nonspecific and frequently result
from nongenetic factors.

In some cases, differences in stress responses
between animal strains may result from variation at
several gene sites. Important potential interrelationships for genetic variants that merit further study
include the corticosteroid and catecholamine systems,
behavioral variation and stress-response activation, and
associations between hormone levels and the number and
affinity of receptors. Consideration should be given to
studies in which selective breeding over several genera-
tions is used to produce extreme combinations of the
genetic variants already present within laboratory
species (Shire, 1974). It would be particularly useful
to see whether it is possible to select simultaneously
for the desirable consequences that are associated with
stressors against undesirable ones by affecting the
several target systems differentially.

There is a great need for genetic studies to be
integrated with work on environmentally caused variation
in stress reactions. Different individuals can respond
quite differently to the same environmental stressor, and
patterns of immediate and delayed responses to stressors
also may differ markedly. Such genetic-environmental

interactions can help to reveal differences that were previously hidden (Shire, 1980a). Thus, a low-fat diet unmasked differences in corticosteroid breakdown between two strains of mice that did not differ on a high-fat diet (Shire, 1980b). Similarly, Kakihana et al. (1968) found that two mouse strains had similar steroid elevations in reaction to several acute stressors; but alcohol increased steroid secretion in one strain and decreased it in the other.

In social interactions, whether aggressive or cooperative, each animal is part of the environment of others. Interactions between mother and fetus are a special case that will be influenced by major genotype and environment interactions in the anatomical, nutritional, and behavioral consequences for the offspring of the mother's responses to stress (Salomon and Pratt, 1979). Such heritable but nongenetic effects also should be investigated.

Studies of genetically defined animal populations in natural environments are needed to provide a better understanding of the overall fitness of different genotypes under natural conditions. Research on genetic events that occur during the dramatic seasonal and sporadic increases in population size of wild rodents, and of the genetic consequences of ensuing population crashes, would be useful (Berry, 1980).

Human Studies. There are individual differences among people in their susceptibility to stress and in their risks of suffering stress-related disease consequences. It will be important to supplement animal research with studies in man of the form and extent of genetic variation affecting the components of the stress-response systems. Although there have been studies of rare, inborn errors of metabolism affecting corticosteroids (Degenhart, 1979; Hamburg, 1967), there has been only sporadic research on the extent of normal genetic variation (Shire, 1974). Exceptions are studies of corticosteroid-binding globulin in plasma (Lohrenz et al., 1968) and of some of catecholamine metabolic enzymes (Weinshilboum et al., 1973). There is a need for studies of twins and of multigeneration pedigreed families of biochemical and behavioral parameters of stress and of the relation of these to stress-induced disease consequences. Again, genetic-environmental interactions will be important.

Studies on cell cultures derived from genetically related individuals should reveal much about variations affecting some of the target organs. Knowledge of the position of homologous genes in experimental animals should enable marker genes to be found for genes predisposing to excessive or inappropriate stress responses. Such markers could improve counselling procedures. The recent discovery of a genetic marker for an enzyme deficiency in steroid synthesis (Levine et al., 1978) will allow the testing of the hypothesis that people who are carriers for the enzyme deficiency react abnormally when stressed (Hamburg, 1967). Assessment of the genetically determined risks of exposure to stress will require acquisition of more knowledge about the genetic sites involved in normal and overtly pathological variation.

Biological Correlates of Coping

Most clinical research on coping has sought to examine defense mechanisms involved in the individual coping styles (cf. Chapter 7, Psychosocial Assets and Modifiers of Stress). Another approach, used primarily in animal models, has been to examine the effects of psychological variables in stressful situations. The general procedure consists of exposing two or more animals to the same physical stressor while maintaining the subjects in different psychological states. Differences that result from the treatment can be attributed to the psychological factors. It appears that psychological factors are often more important in influencing certain outcomes than are the physical stimuli, even if those stimuli are intense and noxious. Psychological variables that have been studied most often are those related to uncontrollability and unpredictability of stress, the ability to perform appropriate responses during stress, and the previous experience of the organism in relation to these factors.

Weiss (1970) examined the effects of unpredictability on a variety of stress responses such as the development of stomach ulcers, changes in body weight, and increases in plasma corticosteroid concentrations. Animals receiving unpredictable shocks showed greater somatic stress reactions and more stress-induced pathology than did animals receiving the same amount of predictable shock. Gliner (1972) found that signaled or predictable shock also produced fewer somatic reactions to stressors. In this case, rats were given a choice between predictable or unpredictable shock; animals chose predictable shock and developed fewer ulcers under this condition than did animals not given a choice and receiving the same amount of shock unpredictably. Other

investigators have shown this same phenomenon: when
given a choice, both animals and people will choose
signaled rather than unsignaled shock, even when no
escape from shock is possible (Arabina and Desiderato,
1975; Averill, 1973; Badia et al., 1974; Lockard, 1963;
Seligman et al., 1971). In fact, animals will choose
signaled shock that is four to nine times longer and two
to three times more intense than unsignaled shock (Harsh
and Badia, 1975).

Two hypotheses have been proposed to account for a
preference for signaled shock. The preparatory-response
hypothesis postulates that a warning signal provides
information to subjects which permits a preparatory response, thereby reducing aversiveness of shock (Perkins,
1968). The safety-signal, or "safe/unsafe," hypothesis
proposes that the effect of the signal is primarily a
psychological one, in that it identifies shock-free
periods and thus acquires reinforcing properties (Badia
and Culbertson, 1972; Lockard, 1963; Seligman and Meyer,
1970). Predictable shock is preferred because it reliably predicts the absence of shock. During shock-free
periods subjects can relax their preparations for shock.
Without the signal, fear is chronic and more aversive.
Both behavioral and physiological indexes of fear support this hypothesis.

Escapability is another important determinant of
the effects of shock. Pretreatment of an animal with
inescapable shock severely impairs learning, compared to
pretreatment with the same amount of escapable shock--a
phenomenon known as "learned helplessness." As first described, dogs receiving inescapable shock in a Pavlovian
harness had severe performance deficits when later tested
for escape-avoidance behavior in a shuttlebox (Overmeier
and Seligman, 1967). Most of the dogs sat passively and
took the shock. Occasionally a dog would jump the
barrier and escape, but it would then revert to failing
to escape. It was proposed that animals exposed to
inescapable and unavoidable shocks learned that shock
termination was independent of their behavior. Such
learning then interfered with subsequent formation of an
association between responding and shock termination,
even if the shock became escapable.

Analogous effects have been found in rats (Looney
and Cohen, 1972; Maier et al., 1973; Seligman and Beagley, 1975), cats (Seward and Humphrey, 1967), and humans
(Seligman, 1975). Similar results have also been found
using tests other than avoidance responding. Measuring

classically conditioned fear, Osborne et al. (1975)
showed that animals exposed to inescapable shock were
more fearful than were those exposed to escapable shock.
In addition, helplessness transfers across different
aversive motivational states (Rosellini and Seligman,
1975), and an animal can be "immunized" against helplessness by exposure to escapable shock prior to exposure to
inescapable shock (Seligman et al., 1975).

Weiss and Glazer (1975) found the same effects of
inescapable shock on later avoidance learning but proposed an alternative hypothesis to explain the results.
They suggested that high-intensity, inescapable shocks
do indeed produce deficits in later performance but that
the deficits are temporary, reflecting a "motor activation deficit." In their hypothesis, the inescapable
shock produces a temporary depletion of norepinephrine
in the brain. As a result, animals can perform only a
limited amount of motor activity--an amount insufficient
for learning and performance of the correct responses in
the shuttlebox task on which they were tested. Lower
levels of inescapable shock produced a long-term escape-
avoidance deficit, and it was proposed that this was due
to learned competing motor responses; that is, the
animals learned to be inactive during shock. Under
Weiss's conditions, when such animals were tested on an
avoidance task that required very little movement, their
performance was facilitated.

Another psychological variable that has a significant influence on the response to noxious stimuli is the
ability to perform a coping response. Weiss (1968) observed that rats which could press a lever to avoid shock
showed less severe physiological disturbances (weight
loss, stomach ulcers) than did yoked controls which could
not respond, even though both groups received the same
amount of shock. According to Weiss (1971a,b,c), the
amount of stress an animal actually experiences when
exposed to noxious stimuli depends on (1) the number of
coping attempts the animal makes and (2) the amount of
relevant feedback that these coping attempts produce.
Thus, for the same amount of shock, aversive effects were
ameliorated if the animal could respond, that is, avoid
or escape rather than be yoked (helpless), or the situation was signaled by either a warning signal preceding
shock or a feedback signal to indicate that the shock
was ending.

At times, the behavioral and physiological indexes
of coping can be dissociated. This dissociation can

create definitional problems. Two studies have shown that what might be viewed as inappropriate coping behavior still leads to a reduction of the physiological response. Weinberg (1977) compared nonlearners with animals that learned in an avoidance conditioning situation. The two groups showed the same gradual reduction of plasma corticosteroid responses to the stressor over time. Thus, even though nonlearning can be considered to be inappropriate coping behavior, the physiological reaction to the stressor changed as though the animals were learning to cope. In another study, animals were permitted to escape the shock chamber but not to avoid electric shock (Davis et al., 1977). Plasma steriod reduction still occurred, but only after significantly more trials. Thus, when animals could make an appropriate response, even though they could not avoid the electric shock, a change in physiological arousal occurred.

Coover et al. (1974) found that specific brain lesions also could produce a dissociation between behavioral and physiological indexes of coping. Rats with lesions restricted to the cingulate cortex could readily learn an avoidance response; in fact the learning curves were indistinguishable from those of normal animals. However, after their performance reached criterion, these experimental animals did not exhibit the diminished pituitary-adrenal response to the avoidance situation to the same degree as did controls.

Issues relating to the potential independence of psychological and physiological reactions to stressors are of great importance to an understanding of how stress can affect health. As mentioned earlier, most clinical studies rely on verbal reports to determine if subjects are stressed or on the occurrence of events that are stressful for most people. However, it seems likely that subjects from such studies may present a wide range of concomitant physiological changes. Some may report no feelings of stress and exhibit large physiological reactions. Others may have a vigorous psychological reaction and yet show no physiological changes. Such individual differences may do much to explain the relatively low correlations that are observed in most life events studies.

Physiological Sociology and Stress

Stress is one of three rubrics--along with attention and generalized arousal--under which investigators have studied the influence of the social system on psychological and physiological factors in the individual, an area of research called physiological sociology. Often, stressed individuals experience some degree of disruption or discomfort in their social system. Coping strategies may be viewed as efforts to recreate the original condition; to replace it; to deny its alteration; or to do without it, presumably by making other adjustments (cf. Psychosocial Assets and Modifiers of Stress, Chapter 7). Studies of interactions between the biological and social systems often have assumed that biology drives behavior. Stress research emphasizes the reverse possibility, that social system and social bonding can alter biological function.

For some structural and affective relationships, informed use of social variables is needed to explain certain types of stress data. As discussed throughout this report, human studies have shown repeatedly that there is an inverse correlation between quality and stability of the social environment and the incidence of physical and mental illness. Such diverse events as tuberculosis, schizophrenia, and multiple accidents occur significantly more often among people who are not engaged in intimate social relationships, compared with those who have close friends or family (Chen and Cobb, 1960; Dunham, 1961; Mishler and Scotch, 1963). Similarly, there is a high death rate from a variety of causes for spouses following bereavement (Parkes et al., 1969).

These and other studies have shown convincingly that there are statistically significant associations between living in a disordered or disrupted social environment and suffering adverse health consequences. Still, most people who report life changes do not become ill (Rahe and Arthur, 1978). In fact, evidence suggests that certain aspects of the social environment, for example a strong social support network, may have a protective effect on health (Cobb, 1976; Dean and Lin, 1977; Kaplan et al., 1977). As discussed in Psychosocial Assets and Modifiers of Stress (Chapter 7), much more must be learned about how the timing, severity, and frequency of such events modify their effects.

Biological factors that mediate associations between changes in an individual's social milieu and changes in health have received little attention. Interactions between biological substrates and the social environment undoubtedly occur in both directions. Thus, a social event may alter the activity of a neuroregulatory system, which, in turn, may affect responses to future social events. With particular predispositions, long-term biological changes could, in effect, "lock in" certain response patterns at several levels, thereby producing vulnerability or resistance to disease. At present, the understanding of the biological reactions produced by social stressors is rudimentary. However, some interesting animal and human studies do suggest the potential value of further research.

Animal Studies. Animal studies, primarily with rodents, have verified a causal link between social environment and health. For example, rodents housed under conditions that induce continual territorial conflict, thereby inhibiting development of stable, predictable interactions, suffer reproductive failure due to high rates of maternal loss, infant mortality, and infanticide and exhibit such physiological changes as adrenal hypertrophy, hypertension, and peptic ulcers (Henry and Cassel, 1969). These effects are not due solely to population density; they are observed only when strangers are introduced to the environment and are not apparent when the same number of litter mates are similarly housed.

Most studies of biological correlates of social stressors in animals have focused on the relationship of adrenocortical function to dominance (one dimension of status). For example, if rats are maintained in a paired situation for several weeks, subordinate animals have higher adrenal weights and lower gonadal weights than do dominant ones. Barnett (1955, 1963) found that, after ten days of social interaction, high-ranking rats had lower adrenal weights than did low-ranking rats. Such findings may be relevant to physiological changes that occur under crowded conditions, where it has been found that, in rodents, increased group density results in higher adrenal weight and lower body and testicular weight (Christian, 1955; Theissen and Rodgers, 1961). However, in a single trial against a new, nonaggressive antagonist, the behavior of previously subordinate animals does not differ from that of animals who had been dominant (Brain, 1972).

Measures of plasma corticosteroids as an indicator of adrenocortical activity have confirmed the earlier impressions based upon adrenal weight. Barnett (1955), studying wild rats, found that fighting markedly depleted plasma steroids in the subordinate animal but not in the dominant animal, even though both appeared to have had

232

an equal amount of overt stress. In addition, isolated
male mice display lower resting levels of plasma corticosterone and a decreased response to stress (Davis and
Christian, 1957; Louch and Higginbotham, 1967). The
causal nature of the relationship has not been established, but a stress interpretation of the relationship
is attractive; it should be replicated in other species.

Studies of adrenomedullary reactions to behavioral
processes to social stressors have involved measurements
of plasma norepinephrine and epinephrine and of the
catecholamine-forming enzymes in the adrenal as a function of behavioral states. The rapid changes that can
occur in the adrenomedullary system and the powerful
psychological effects of epinephrine make this system a
particularly interesting one for investigation. Several
studies suggest that such social stressors as isolation
and group housing can influence the enzymatic processes
that control catecholamine formation. Thus, Welch and
Welch (1968) found decreased levels of catecholamines in
the brain and adrenal of group-housed mice, compared
with individually housed animals.

Although the results of such studies may depend on
the species used, differential housing can markedly alter
catecholamine mechanisms. Henry et al. (1971, 1972) have
studied the effects on catecholamine activity of a
variety of mutual interaction situations designed to
produce frequent confrontations and severe social stimulation. Animals exposed to this stressor exhibited
increases in plasma catecholamine concentrations and in
catecholamine synthetic enzymes in the adrenal. A
decrease in the enzymes was noted in isolated animals.
In addition, preliminary studies suggest that dominant
animals may have lower levels of the catecholamine
enzymes than do subordinate animals (Henry et al., 1971,
1972). Many of these studies involved long time periods,
often involving periods up to six months. As noted
earlier, changes in these enzymes can occur within a few
hours after exposure to certain stressors, suggesting
that it would be of interest to investigate the acute
effects of briefer social interactions.

Human Studies. Some form of status differentiation
seems to occur universally in human groups and can be
observed in both natural and experimental settings.
This differentiation often is the organizing force in
role relationships. When members of a group have a
collective task, they evolve patterns of interaction
that reflect differences in the distribution of power

233

and prestige among the members--even when they are
strangers at the onset of observation and are matched
for external status characteristics. These differentia-
tions often are transformed into divisions of labor and
determine other role relationships.

Few investigators have studied physiological effects
of status relationships as a potential social stressor.
Barchas and Barchas (1975) have measureed urinary catecholamines in some small-group situations. Individuals
of equal external status, as determined by education,
age, race, and sex, were allowed to interact for one
hour. Status differentials established between the
individuals through interaction were assessed by observers and by questionnaires to the subjects. There
was no relationship between acquired status and the
concentrations of catecholamines in urine samples taken
before the interaction; however, individuals with higher
acquired status had higher epinephrine and lower norepinephrine in samples taken at the end of the test
hour. The relevance of such results to other laboratory
settings or to normal social stressors is unknown. Perhaps interactions in an experimental group of strangers
differ in important ways from those in which individuals
already are acquainted. Adequate study of such mediating
variables will require new research designs.

Several investigators have demonstrated powerful
effects of psychosocial interaction variables on adrenomedullary secretion. The studies showed that a variety
of behavioral situations that involve tense, anxious,
but passive emotional displays elevate epinephrine excretion. This can be said of certain novel or distressing
situations as well. Levi (1975) collected a number of
pioneering studies about physiological changes that
accompany psychological states in a monograph. Urinary
catecholamines were found to increase in a wide variety
of arousing situations such as viewing films with both
"unpleasant" and "pleasant" aspects, and bland materials
reduced urinary excretion. In general, the effect of
psychosocial stimuli on catecholamine excretion depended
on the stimulus used and the initial state of the individual, with no simple relationships between anxiety and
epinephrine secretion or aggression and norepinephrine
secretion.

Frankenhaeuser (1971) has conducted a series of
investigations relating cognitive and emotional patterns
to endocrine secretion. Her studies in children suggest
that social interrelationships may affect endocrine func-

234

tion. Thus, there was a positive correlation between
the mother's epinephrine urinary excretion rates and the
frequency with which the fathers punished their children.

Plasma concentrations of free fatty acids provide
an indirect measure of adrenomedullary activity, because
they correlate highly with sympathetic activation. In
studies of conformity and leadership, Back and Bogdonoff
(1964) found that the meaning of the social situation to
the test subject influenced the relationship between
behavioral response and changes in free fatty acid.

Until very recently, technological limitations
greatly hindered clinical research in physiological
sociology. For example, urinary catecholamines were used
to estimate adrenomedullary activity because samples
could be obtained with relative ease and because accurate
measures of plasma catecholamines were not available.
The potential inaccuracies and loss of information of
this technique have already been discussed. Recent
improvements in sample collection and marked advances in
analytical chemistry should now make it possible to
assess changes in a variety of neuroregulators found in
blood. New, continuous blood sampling systems enable
precise determinations of minute-to-minute changes in
blood chemistries. Application of these and other new
technologies should foster major advances in our understanding of sociophysiology in the next few years.

Specific Research Needs

In considering the available data relating to biological substrates of stress, the panel identified some
particularly important research needs in each of the
major areas covered, as well as several general research
needs in the field.

Central and Peripheral Neuroregulators

Recent advances have suggested many ways in which
stressors might affect health and many new tools with
which to study those possibilities. How does the brain
transduce internal and external stressors into specific
physiological responses? Does a single system process
such stimuli and coordinate responses; or are several
systems involved, acting either in concert or independently? Good progress has been made in identifying
brain systems that affect pain, the cardiovascular

235

system, and endocrine function. Do analagous regulatory
mechanisms exist for the immune system? If so, what
neuroregulators are involved, and what are its interconnections with other parts of the brain?

Precise identification of specific neuroregulatory
mechanisms through which stressors exert their effects is
of great importance. One area of interest is the enzymes
and enzymatic mechanisms involved in synthesizing neuroregulators such as the catecholamines. Activation of
some enzymes clearly can occur during stress, but the
importance and function of those changes remain to be
established. Similarly, newly acquired information about
the regulation of enzyme degradation may be directly
relevant. Hormones and enzyme cofactors are known to be
essential for maintaining enzyme stability against intracellular breakdown. More information is needed both
about the basic regulatory processes and about how such
effects are altered during and after stress. Similar
questions must be asked about receptor sites, which provide yet another mechanism that may be altered by stress.

Cardiovascular System

More information is needed about the neuronal and
neuroendocrine systems that mediate circulatory and
cardiac responses to acute or chronic stressors. The
analysis should include studies of the brain sites involved, as well as evaluation of the combined influences
of peripheral and brain inputs on the activities of those
sites under normal conditions. Parallel studies should
be carried out in experimental disease stages in which
either environmental or physical stress is recognized to
play a contributory part. It also will be important to
study the effects of known biological and psychosocial
risk factors for cardiovascular disease, including
smoking, high serum cholesterol, and Type A behavior.

Pain System

Research on problems of pain and stress needs to
exploit the vast amount of scientific knowledge and
technology in all of the scientific disciplines. Much
more information is needed about basic physiological,
biochemical, pharmacological, anatomical, and psychological aspects of pain. What neuroregulatory systems
are involved in the transmission of, interpretation of,
and reaction to pain? What are the activation patterns

236

and interactions among such systems over time for acute
and for chronic pain? The search also should continue
for ways to quantify the pain experience more precisely.
What are the mediating effects of personality, past
experience, information, expectancy, and sociocultural
factors on the incidence and intensity of pain following
operations, trauma, burns, and myocardial infarction?
Comprehensive, multidisciplinary studies could begin to
identify in humans important issues relating to the time-
intensity profile; neuroregulator response; the role of
psychologic factors including cognition, emotion, and
motivation; and the role of interpersonal transactions
and other sociocultural factors in determining the degree
of pain and stress and the consequences of definitive
therapy.

Immune System

Techniques are now available for systematic studies
of immunity on a number of levels, ranging from tissue
responses at the organ level to immune function at levels
of the individual cell. A number of central and peripheral neuroregulators appear to influence immune function.
Which neuroregulators are involved, and how does stress
affect them? The ways in which these substances interact
are far from clear, but it should be possible to study
their effects with existing methodologies. Animal models
from several species are available for investigating
relationships between stress and immunity. Such models
can be used in conjuction with severe stressors to begin
to define precisely reactions of the immune system and
the potential consequences of such reactions. The
importance of changes in immune response as a precursor
to disease is a relatively neglected area of research
that requires further study.

Special Topics

Genetics of Stress. The role of genetics in the
stress response has not been well studied; it should
receive greater attention. Genetic predisposition
pervades the entire stress field. Potentially, genetic
factors can influence every biochemical step described
in this chapter. For example, the genetic regulation of
the catecholamine enzymes may be important in determining
both the magnitude and the rapidity of a reaction to an
acute or chronic stressor. Similarly, genetic mutations
altering receptor sensitivity may shape the reaction to

237

stressors and determine the consequences of that reaction. Both basic and clinical information are needed in this area. A better understanding of genetic predisposition to specific types of reactions to stressors may suggest ways in which individuals can be protected from or prepared for potentially adverse consequences to specific types of stressors.

Biological Correlates of Coping. Efforts to understand the coping mechanisms need to go beyond studies of corticosteroids and catecholamines to include a wide range of neuroregulators. Combinations of physiological and psychochological reactions probably are far more important to the success of coping than are isolated reactions. For that reason, it may be necessary to examine several neuroregulators simultaneously. Studies of stress and coping will test the limits of available neurochemical technology and often may require refinements in data acquisition and interpretation. However, the wealth of new information that should result will offer a foundation for continuing efforts to understand both functional and dysfunctional coping.

Physiological Sociology. More information about the ways in which social events interact with physiological variables is vital, if stress is ever to be understood within the social context. For example, how do developmental patterns and behavioral attitudes such as self-esteem or affiliation influence biochemical responses? Can early experience alter the response of endocrines or brain neuroregulators to stressors later in life? What changes in the various mechanisms involving neuroregulatory agents are associated with different sociological states? What are the short- and long-term biochemical effects of different types of sociological situations? To what degree does biochemical state influence social behavior? Such questions will require both animal and human studies. Animal models for overcrowding and interpersonal conflict are a promising beginning, but models also are needed for other social conditions such as changes in social status and peer pressure. Primate models may be particularly useful in this context, because their social interactions come closest to matching those for humans.

General Research Needs

It should be possible to extend past efforts to identify specific patterns of response to acute stres-

sors. The effects of stress on many of the most recently
discovered neuroregulators have yet to be studied; such
research may uncover new stress reactions. Even with
neuroregulators that are reasonably well known, few
studies have examined effects of stressors on specific
regulatory mechanisms, including synthesis, storage,
release, receptor interactions, reuptake, and metabolism.
Consideration of mediators in this type of research is
vital. What are the effects of mediators such as genetic
predisposition, past history, social setting, and psychological state? Are such effects predictable? Do they
act similarly for different kinds of stressors?

Also of special interest are chronic stressors. In
general, it has been difficult, both in the laboratory
and in natural settings, to find a chronic stressor that
can maintain high degrees of physiological responding
over long periods of time. How are the effects of stressors counteracted over time? What are the short- and
long-term costs of activating these mechanisms? Furthermore, what are the special features of situations such
as highly unstable social conditions or conditions of
complete uncontrollability, in which high responding is
maintained? Both areas of research are vital and may
provide invaluable information for prevention and treatment efforts.

As specific patterns are identified in animals, it
may be possible to look for them in humans as well.
Consideration must be given to the study of biological
changes that occur in people who experience severe
natural or manmade disasters such as earthquakes, floods,
fires, and imprisonment. With careful research designs,
it should be possible to study the biological changes
that occur under such conditions. These data would be
an invaluable addition to animal work and could greatly
enhance knowledge about the effects of disasters on subsequent health. They also might contribute to efforts
to develop effective prevention programs for individuals
who undergo such severe trauma.

The implications of the kinds of basic research
discussed here for prevention and treatment of disease
are considerable. A better understanding of underlying
mechanisms through which stress promotes changes in
health should suggest points at which effective interventions can be made. For example, an immune or other
biochemical marker might help to identify people who are
at particular risk following stressful life events.
Perhaps psychological or social techniques could be

239

developed to modify specific reactions to stress that
lead to undesirable health consequences such as heart
disease. Pharmacological interventions also might be
developed. These may block specific reactions that can
lead to disease consequences in some organ such as the
stomach or the heart. Naturally, introduction of such
agents would have to proceed cautiously; they might affect other physiological mechanisms in ways that negate
any beneficial effects they have on a single system.

                              Summary

     Although much is known about many biological sys-
tems, information about the effects of stress on them is
distributed unevenly. In its survey of the literature,
the panel found that most of the available data document
the size or magnitude of a reaction to an overwhelming
stressor. Much less attention has been given to underlying mechanisms of such reactions. Still less is known
about important characteristics of milder stressors and
about the mediators that affect the stressor-to-reaction
process. Despite the diversity of topics covered, panel
members identified several common themes:

   •   Investigators within the field must describe their
       research more precisely. Too often, generalizations
       about "stress" are made from data that may not be
       broadly applicable. Clear descriptions of stres-
       sors, reactions, and potential mediators can help
       to build a sound data base from which it may be
       possible to derive general principles in the future.

   •   Application of recent advances in the neurosciences
       to the stress field could enhance substantially
       knowledge about the effects of stress on health.
       Continued basic research also is needed to improve
       understanding of the regulatory mechanisms and
       interrelationships of relevant neuroregulators.
       That information can then be applied directly to
       studies related to stress. Key to such studies
       will be efforts to better define the systems within
       the brain that are involved in perceiving stressors
       and in translating that perception into a reaction.

   •   Many of the needed studies of biological substrates
       will require multidisciplinary approaches. Coopera-
       tion among biological, psychological, and social
       scientists could be tremendously valuable, because

each of these fields offers a different perspective
of stress. Such collaborations are especially
vital for efforts to identify and characterize
important mediators of stress. Combined approaches
undoubtedly will demand imaginative innovations in
experimental design to enable each to maximize the
amount and quality of information obtained. They
may be the only way to begin to unravel the array
of confusing and contradictory data that now char-
acterizes the field.

The charge to this panel was to determine whether
there were promising lines of research that might relate
biological mechanisms to stress. We found a wide array
of promising areas of investigation, many of which seem
not to have been pursued. There are several possible
explanations for such unfilled research opportunities.
Many of the most compelling research leads have arisen
relatively recently as byproducts of advances in other
fields. Most investigators involved in the original
work have no direct interest in stress, and few stress
researchers have mastered the necessary techniques for
application to their studies. In addition, the complexities of the stress response can pose formidable barriers
to successful application of biochemical methods. Many
basic scientists prefer to work with enzymes and brain
slices, avoiding the complications that a behaving
animal or a human subject can add. Fortunately, some
investigators have begun to demonstrate that productive
marriages between innovative biochemical investigations
and sound stress research are possible. We hope that
the successes of such people will encourage others to
enter this fascinating and vital area of study.

References

Ader, R., and Cohen, N. Behaviorally conditioned immuno-suppression. Psychosom. Med. 37:333-340, 1975.

Aghajanian, G. K., and Haigler, H. J. Hallucinogenic indoleamines: preferential action upon presynaptic serotonin receptors. Psychopharmacol. Comm. 1:619-629, 1975.

Anton-Tay, F., Diaz, J. L., and Fernandez-Guardiola, A. On the effects of melatonin upon human brain: its possible therapeutic implications. IN: The Pineal Gland (Worstenholme, G. E. W., and Knight, J., eds.) Edinburgh: Churchill Livingston, 1971, pp. 363-364.

Arabina, J. M., and Desiderato, O. Preference for signalled shock: a test of two hypotheses. Anim. Learn. Behav. 3:191-195, 1975.

Averhill, J. R. Personal control over aversive stimuli and its relationship to stress. Psychol. Bull. 80: 286-303, 1973.

Ax, A. F. The physiological differentiation of fear and anger in humans. Psychosom. Med. 15:433-442, 1953.

Back, K. W., and Bogdonoff M. D. Plasma lipid responses to leadership, conformity, and deviation. IN: Psychobiological Approaches to Social Behavior. (Leiderman, P. H., and Shapiro, D., eds.) Stanford: Stanford University Press, 1964, pp. 24-42.

Badia, P., and Culberston, S. The relative aversiveness of signalled vs. unsignalled escapable and inescapable shock. J. Exp. Analysis Behav. 17: 463-471, 1972.

Badia, P., Culberston, S. and Harsh, J. Relative aversiveness of signalled vs. unsignalled avoidance and escapable shock situations in humans. J. Compar. Physiol. Psychol. 87:338-346, 1974.

Barchas, J. D., Akil, H., Elliott, G. R., Holman, R. B., and Watson, S. J. Behavioral neurochemistry: neuroregulators in relation to behavioral states and mental disorders. Science 200:964-973, 1978.

Barchas, J. D., Ciaranello, R. D., Dominic, J. A. Deguchi, T., Orenberg, E. O., Renson, J., and Kessler, S. Genetic aspects of monoamine mechanisms. Adv. Biochem. Psychopharmacol. 12: 195-204, 1974.

Barchas, J. D., Elliott, G. R., and DoAmaral, J. R. Neurosciences applications of mass spectrometry. Finnigan Spectra 5:1-3, 1975.

Barchas, J. D., and Freedman, D. X. Brain amines: response to physiological stress. Biochem. Pharmacol. 12:1232-1235, 1963.

Barchas, J. D., and Usdin, E. (eds.) Serotonin and Behavior New York: Academic Press, 1973.

Barchas, P., and Barchas, J. D. Physiological sociology: endocrine correlation of status behavior. IN:
American Handbook of Psychiatry, Vol. 6 (Hamburg, D.,
Brodie, H. K. H., eds.) New York: Basic Books,
1975, pp. 623-640.
Barnett, S. A. Competition among wild rats. Nature
175:126-127, 1955.
Barnett, S. A. The Rat: A Study in Behavior Chicago:
Aldine, 1963.
Beamer, W. G. Mutant genes with endocrine effects:
mouse. IN: Biological Handbooks: Inbred and Gene-
tically Defined Strains of Animals, Part 1: Mouse
and Rat Bethesda: Federation of American Societies
for Experimental Biology, 1979, pp. 101-102.
Bernstein, I. S., Gordon, T. P., and Rose, R. M. Influ-
ences of sexual and social stimuli upon circulating
levels of testosterone in male pigtail macaques.
Behav. Biol. 24:400-404, 1978.
Berry, R. J. Population dynamics. IN: Biology of the
House Mouse (Berry, R. J., ed.) London: Academic
Press, 1980.
Bliss, E. L., and Zwaniger, J. Brain amines and emo-
tional stress. J. Psychiatr. Res. 4:189-198, 1966.
Bloom, G., von Euler, U. S., and Frankenhaeuser, M.
Catecholamine excretion and personality traits in
paratroop trainees. Acta Physiol. Scand. 58:77-89,
1963.
Bonica, J. J., and Albe-Fessard, D. (Eds.) Advances in
Pain Research and Therapy, Vol. 1 New York: Raven
Press, 1976.
Bonica, J. J., and Benedetti, C. Postoperative pain.
IN: Surgical Care: A Physiologic Approach to Clini-
cal Management (Condon, R. E., and DeCosse, J. J,
eds.) Philadelphia: Lea & Febiger, 1980.
Bonica, J. J., Liebeskind, J. C., and Albe-Fessard, D.
(eds.) Advances in Pain Research and Therapy, Vol. 3
New York: Raven Press, 1979.
Boyd, A. E., III, and Reichlin, S. Neural control of
prolactin secretion in man. Psychoneuroendocrinology
3:113-130, 1978.
Brain, P. F. Endocrine and behavioral differences
between dominant and subordinant male house mice
housed in pairs. Psychom. Sci. 28:260-262, 1972.
Bridges, P. K. Recent physiological studies of stress
and anxiety in man. Biol. Psychiatry 8:95-112, 1974.
Cannon, J. T., Liebeskind, J. C., and Frenk, H. Neural
and neurochemical mechanisms of pain inhibition. IN:
The Psychology of Pain (Sternbach, R. A., ed.) New
York: Raven Press, 1978.

Cannon, W. B. Stresses and strains of homeostasis. Amer. J. Med. Sci. 189:1-14, 1935.

Chen, E., and Cobb, S. Family structure in relation to health and disease. J. Chron. Dis. 12:544-567, 1960.

Chien, S. Role of the sympathetic nervous system in hemorrhage. Physiol. Rev. 47:214-288, 1970.

Christian, J. J. Effect of population size on the weights of the reproductive organs of white mice. Amer. J. Physiol. 181:477-480, 1955.

Ciaranello, R. D. Genetic regulation of the catecholamine synthesizing enzymes. IN: Genetic Variation in Hormone Systems, Vol. 2 (Shire, J. G. M., ed.) Boca Raton: CRC Press, 1979, pp. 49-61.

Ciaranello, R. D., Hoffman, H. J., Shire, J. G. M., and Axelrod, J. Genetic regulation of the catecholamine biosynthetic enzymes. II. Inheritance of tyrosine hydroxylase, dopamine-beta-hydroxylase and phenyl-ethanolamine N-methyl transferase. J. Biol. Chem. 249:4528-4536, 1974.

Cobb, S. Social support as a moderator of life stress. Psychosom. Med. 38:300-314, 1976.

Coffino, P., Bourne, H. R., Friedrich, U., Hochman, J., Insel, P. A., Lemaire, I., Melmon, K. L., and Tomkins, G. M. Molecular mechanisms of cyclic AMP action: a genetic approach. Rec. Prog. Horm. Res. 32:669-684, 1976.

Comsa, J., Leonhardt, H., and Schwarz, J. A. Influence of the thymus-corticotropin-growth hormone interaction on the rejection of skin allografts in the rat. Ann. N. Y. Acad. Sci. 249:387-401, 1975.

Coover, G. D., Goldman, L., and Levine, S. Plasma corticosterone increases produced by extinction of operant behavior in rats. Physiol. Behav. 6:261-263, 1971.

Coover, G. D., Ursin, H., and Levine, S. Corticosterone levels during avoidance learning in rats with cingulate lesions suggest an instrumental reinforcement deficit. J. Compar. Physiol. Psychol. 87:970-977, 1974.

Datter, P. C., and King, M. G. Effects of MSH and melatonin on passive avoidance and emotional response. Pharmacol. Biochem. Behav. 6:449-452, 1977.

Davis, D. E., and Christian, J. J. Relation of adrenal weight to social rank in mice. Proc. Soc. Exp. Biol. Med. 94:728-731, 1957.

Davis, D. E., and Read, C. P. Effect of behavior on development of resistance in trichinosis. Proc. Soc. Exp. Biol. Med. 99:269-272, 1958.

Davis, H., Memmott, J., Macfadden, L., and Levine, S. Pituitary-adrenal activity under different appetitive extinction procedures. Physiol. Behav. 17:687-690, 1976.

Davis, H., Porter, J. W., Livingstone, J., Herman, T., Macfadden, L., and Levine, S. Pituitary-adrenal activity and leverpress shock escape behavior. Physiol. Psychol. 5:280-284, 1977.

Dean, A. and Lin, N. The stress-buffering role of social support. J. Nerv. Ment. Dis. 165:403-417, 1977.

Degenhart, H. J. Normal and abnormal steroidogenesis in man. IN: Genetic Variation in Hormone Systems (Shire, J. G. M., ed.) Boca Raton: CRC Press, 1979, pp. 11-42.

Denckla, W. D. Interactions between age and neuroendocrine and immune systems. Fed. Proc. 37:1263, 1978.

Dewey, M. J., Martin, D. W.,Jr., Martin, G. R., and Mintz, B. Mosaic mice with teratocarcinoma-derived mutant cells deficient in hypoxanthine phosphoribosyl-transferase. Proc. Natl. Acad. Sci., USA 74:5564-5568, 1977.

Dilman, V. M. Metabolic immunodepression which increases the risk of cancer. Lancet 2:1207-1209, 1977.

Dimsdale, J. E., and Moss, J. Plasma catecholamines in stress and exercise. J. Amer. Med. Soc. 243:340-342, 1980.

Dismukes, R. K. New concepts of molecular communication among neurons. Behav. Brain Sci. 2:409-448, 1979.

Dudley, D. L., Holmes, T. H., Martin, C. J., and Ripley, H. S. Changes in respiration associated with hypnotically induced emotion, pain, and exercise. Psychosom. Med. 26:46-57, 1963.

Dunham, J. H. Social structures and mental disorders: competing hypotheses of explanation. Milbank Mem. Fund Q. 39:259-311, 1961.

Elliott, G. R., and Barchas, J. D. Changing concepts about neuroregulation: neurotransmitters and neuro-modulators. IN: Hormones and the Brain (de Wied, D., and van Keep, P. A., eds.) Lancaster: MTP Press, 1980, pp. 43-52.

Fauci, A. S. Corticosteroids and circulating lympho-cytes. Transplant. Proc. 7:37-40, 1975.

Fine, J. Current status of problem of traumatic shock. Surg. Gynecol. Obstet. 120:537-544, 1965.

Folkow, B., and Rubinstein, E. H. Cardiovascular effects of acute and chronic stimulations of the hypothalamic defense area in the rat. Acta Physiol. Scand. 68:48-57, 1966.

Fox, R. R. and Crary, D. D. Genetics and pathology of hereditary adrenal hyperplasia in the rabbit. J. Hered. 69:230-234, 1978.

Frankenhaeuser, M. Behavior and circulating catechola-mines. Brain Res. 31:241-262, 1971.

Friedman, M., Byers, S. O., Diamant, J., and Rosenman, R. H. Plasma catecholamine response of coronary-prone

245

subjects (Type A) to a specific challenge. Metabolism 4:205-210, 1979.

Friedman, S. B., Ader, R., and Glasgow, L. A. Effects of psychological stress in adult mice inoculated with Coxsackie B viruses. Psychosom. Med. 27: 361-368, 1965.

Friedman, S. B., Glasgow, L. A., and Ader, R. Psychosocial factors modifying host resistance to experimental infections. Ann. N. Y. Acad. Sci. 164:381-393, 1969.

Funkenstein, D. H. Norepinephrine-like and epinephrine-like substances in relation to human behavior. J. Ment. Dis. 124:58-68, 1956.

Gisler, R. H. Stress and the hormonal regulation of the immune response in mice. Psychother. Psychosom. 23: 197-208, 1974.

Glass, D. C., Krakoff, L. R., Contrada, R., Hilton, W. F., Kehoe, K., Mannucci, E. G., Collins, C., Snow, B., and Elting, E. Effect of harassment and competition upon cardiovascular and plasma catecholamine responses in Type A and Type B individuals. Psychophysiology 17:453-463, 1980.

Gliner, J. A. Predictable vs. unpredictable shock: Preference behavior and stomach ulceration. Physiol. Behav. 9:693-698, 1972.

Gray, J. A. Elements of a Two-Process Theory of Learning London: Academic Press, 1975.

Halter, J., and Pflug, A. Differential neuroendocrine responses to pain and psychic stress during dental surgery in man. Endocrinology 106, Suppl:191, 1980.

Hamburg, D. A. Genetics of adrenocortical hormone metabolism in relation to psychological stress. IN: Behavior-Genetic Analysis (Hirsch, J., ed.) New York: McGraw-Hill, 1967, pp. 154-175.

Hamilton, D. R. Immunosuppressive effects of predator induced stress in mice with acquired immunity to Hymenolepis nana. J. Psychosom. Res. 18:143-153, 1974.

Harsh, J. and Badia, P. Choice of signalled over unsignalled shock as a function of shock intensity. J. Exper. Analysis Behav. 23:349-355, 1975.

Henry, J. P., and Cassel, J. C. Psychosocial factors in essential hypertension: recent epidemiologic and animal experimental evidence. Amer. J. Epidemiol. 90:171-200, 1969.

Henry, J. P., Stephens, P. M., Axelrod, J., and Mueller, R. A. Effect of psychosocial stimulation on the enzymes involved in the biosynthesis and metabolism of noradrenaline and adrenaline. Psychosom. Med. 33:227-237, 1971.

Henry, J. P., Stephens, P. M., and Santisteban, G. A. A model of psychosocial hypertension showing reversibil-

246

ity and progression of cardiovascular complications. Circ. Res. 36:156-164, 1972.

Hill, C. W., Greer, W. E., and Felsenfeld, O. Psychological stress, early response to foreign protein, and blood cortisol in vervets. Psychosom. Med. 29: 279-283, 1967.

Hilton, S. M. Ways of viewing the central nervous control of the circulation--old and new. Brain Res. 87: 213-219, 1975.

Hokfelt, T., Fuxe, K., Goldstein, M., and Johansson, O. Immunohistochemical evidence for the existence of adrenaline neurons in the rat brain. Brain Res. 66: 235-251, 1974.

Holman, R. B., Elliott, G. R., and Barchas, J. D. Perspectives in behavioral neurochemistry. Essays Neurochem. Neuropharmacol. 2:1-20, 1977.

Holz, W. C., Pendleton, R. G., Fry, W. T., and Gill, C. A. Epinephrine and recovery from punishment. J. Pharmacol. Exp. Ther. 189:379-387, 1977.

Il'enko, V. I., and Kovaleva, G. A. The conditioned reflex regulation of immunological reactions. Zh. Microbiol. Epidemiol. Immunobiol. 31:108-113, 1960.

Jensen, M. M. Possible mechanisms of impaired interferon production in stressed mice. Proc. Soc. Exp. Biol. Med. 142:820-823, 1973.

Jensen, M. M., and Rasmussen, A. F., Jr. Stress and susceptibility to viral infections: II. Sound stress and susceptibility to vesicular stomatitis virus. J. Immunol. 90:21-23, 1963.

Joasoo, A., and McKenzie, J. M. Stress and the immune response in rats. Int. Arch. Allergy Appl. Immunol. 50:659-663, 1976.

Joh, T. H., Park, D. H., and Reis, D. J. Direct phosphorylation of brain tyrosine hydroxylase by cyclic AMP-dependent protein kinase: mechanism of enzyme action. Proc. Natl. Acad. Sci. USA 75:4744-4748, 1978.

Johnsson, T., and Rasmussen, A. F., Jr. Emotional stress and susceptibility to poliomyelitis infection in mice. Arch. Ges. Virusforch. 17:392-397, 1965.

Kakihana, R., Noble, E. P., and Butte, J. C. Corticosterone response to ethanol in inbred strains of mice. Nature 218:360-361, 1968.

Kaplan, B. H., Cassel, J. C., and Gore, S. Social support and health. Med. Care 15, Suppl.:47-58, 1977.

Katz, R. J., Turner, B. B., Roth, K. A., and Carroll, B. J. Central adrenergic neurons as mediators of motivation and behavior--evidence from the specific inhibition of PNMT. IN: Catecholamines: Basic and Clinical Frontiers (Usdin, E., Kopin, I. J., and

Barchas, J. D., eds.) New York: Pergamon Press, 1979, pp. 1687-1689.

Keller, S. E., Stein, M., Camerino, M. S., Schleifer, S. J., and Sherman, J. Suppression of lymphocyte stimulation by anterior hypothalamic lesions in the guinea pig. Cell. Immunol. 52:334-340, 1980.

Koslow, S. H., and Schlumpf, M. Quantitation of adrenaline in rat brain nuclei and areas by mass fragmentography. Nature 251:530-531, 1975.

Kovacs, G. L., Gajari, I., Telegdy, G., and Lissak, K. Effect of melatonin and pinealectomy on avoidance exploratory activity in the rat. Physiol. Behav. 13:349-355, 1974.

Kreuz, L. E., Rose, R. M., and Jennings, J. R. Suppression of plasma testosterone levels and psychological stress. Arch. Gen. Psychiatry 26:479-482, 1972.

Lefer, A. M. Role of a myocardial depressant factor in the pathogenesis of circulatory shock. Fed. Proc. 29: 1836-1847, 1970.

Lerner, A. B., and Case, J. D. Melatonin. Fed. Proc. 19:590-592, 1960.

Levi, L. The urinary output of adrenaline and noradrenaline during pleasant and unpleasant emotional states. Psychosom. Med. 27:80-85, 1965.

Levi, L. (Ed.) Emotions: Their Parameters and Measurement New York: Raven Press, 1975.

Levine, L. S., Zachmann, M., New, M. I., Prader, A., Pollock, M. S., O'Neill, G. J., Yang, S. Y., Oberfield, S. E., and Dupont, B. Genetic mapping of the 21-hydroxylase deficiency gene within the HLA linkage group. New Eng. J. Med. 299:911-914, 1978.

Levine, S., and Coover, G. D. Environmental control of suppression of the pituitary-adrenal system. Physiol. Behav. 17:35-37, 1976.

Levine, S., Goldman, L., and Coover, G. D. Expectancy and the pituitary-adrenal system. IN: Physiology, Emotion and Psychosomatic Illness (Porter, R., and Knight, J., eds.) Amsterdam: Elsevier, 1972, pp. 281-296.

Levine, S., and Treiman, D. M. Differential plasma corticosterone response to stress in four inbred strains of mice. Endocrinology 75:142-144, 1964.

Lockard, J. S. Choice of a warning signal or no warning signal in an unavoidable shock situation. J. Compar. Physiol. Psychol. 56:526-530, 1963.

Lohrenz, F. N., Doe, R. P., and Seal, U. S. Idiopathic or genetic elevation of corticosteroid-binding globulin? J. Clin. Endocrinol. 28:1073-1075, 1968.

Looney, T. A., and Cohen, P. S. Retardation of jump-up escape responding in rats pretreated with different

248

frequencies of noncontingent electric shock. J. Compar. Physiol. Psychol. 78:317-322, 1972.

Louch, C. D., and Higginbotham, M. The relation between social rank and plasma corticosterone levels in mice. Gen. Comp. Endocrinol. 8: 441-444, 1967.

Macris, N. T., Schiavi, R. C., Camerino, M. S., and Stein, M. Effect of hypothalamic lesions on immune processes in the guinea pig. Amer. J. Physiol. 219: 1205-1209, 1970.

Madden, J., Akil, H., Patrick, R. L., and Barchas, J. D. Stress-induced parallel changes in central opioid levels and pain responsiveness in the rat. Nature 265:358-360, 1977.

Maier, S. F., Albin, R. W., and Testa, T. J. Failure to learn to escape in rats previously exposed to inescapable shock depends on nature of escape response. J. Compar. Physiol. Psychol. 85:581-592, 1973.

Mains, R. E., Eipper, B. A., and Ling, N. Common precursor to corticotropins and endorphins. Proc. Natl. Acad. Sci. USA 74:3014-3018, 1977.

Marczynski, T. J., Yamaguchi, N., Ling, G. M., and Grodzinska, L. Sleep induced by the administration of melatonin (5-methoxy-N-acetyltryptamine) to the hypothalamus in unrestrained cats. Experientia 20: 435-437, 1964.

Marsh, J. T., and Rasmussen, Jr., A. F. Reponse of adrenal thymus, spleen and leukocytes to shuttle box and confinement stress. Proc. Soc. Exp. Biol. Med. 104:180-183, 1960.

Mason, J. Emotion as reflected in patterns of endocrine integration. IN: Emotions: Their Parameters and Measurement (Levi, L., ed.) New York: Raven Press, 1975, pp. 143-181.

Masuda, M., and Dudley, D. L. Physiologic responses to noxious head stimuli. J. Psychosom. Res. 12:205-214, 1968.

Mayer, D. J., and Price, D. D. Central nervous system mechanisms of analgesia. Pain 2:379-404, 1976.

Maynert, E. W., and Levy, R. Stress-induced release of brain norepinephrine and its inhibition by drugs. J. Pharmacol. Exp. Ther. 143:90-95, 1964.

Mefford, I., Oke, A., Keller, R., Adams, R. N., and Jonsson, G. Epinephrine distribution in human brain. Neurosci. Lett. 9:227-231, 1978.

Meyer, R. J., and Haggerty, R. J. Streptococcal infections in families: factors altering individual susceptibility. Pediatrics 29:539-549, 1962.

Mishler, E. G., and Scotch, N. A. Sociocultural factors in the epidemiology of schizophrenia: a review. Psychiatry 26:315-351, 1963.

Monjan, A. A., and Collecctor, M. I. Stress-induced modulation of the immune response. Science 196:307-308, 1977.

Morishima, H. O., Pedersen, H., and Finster, M. The influence of maternal psychological stress on the fetus. Amer. J. Obstet. Gynecol. 131:286-290, 1978.

Morishima, H. O., Pedersen, H., and Finster, M. Effects of pain on mother, labor, and fetus. IN: Obstetric Analgesia and Anesthesia (Marx, G. F., and Bassell, G. M, eds.) Amsterdam: Exerpta Medica, 1980.

Osborne, F. H., Mattingly, B. A., Redmon, W. K., and Osborne, J. S. Factors affecting the measurement of classically conditioned fear in rats following exposure to escapable versus inescapable signalled shock. J. Exper. Psychol.: Anim. Behav. Processes 1:364-373, 1975.

Overmeier, J. B., and Seligman, M. E. P. Effects of inescapable shock upon subsequent escape and avoidance responding. J. Compar. Physiol. Psychol. 63:28-33, 1967.

Parkes, C. M., Benjamin, B., and Fitzgerald, R. G. Broken heart: a statistical study of increased mortality among widowers. Brit. Med. J. 1:740-743, 1969.

Perkins, C. C., Jr. An analysis of the concept of reinforcement. Psychol. Rev. 75:155-172, 1968.

Pribram, K. H., and Melges, F. T. Psychophysiological basis of emotion. Handbook Clin. Neurol. 3:316-342, 1969.

Raese, J. D., Patrick, R. L., and Barchas, J. D. Phospholipid-induced activation of tyrosine hydroxylase from rat brain striatal synaptosomes. Biochem. Pharmacol. 25:2245-2250, 1976.

Rahe, R. H., and Arthur, R. J. Life change and illness studies: past history and future directions. J. Hum. Stress 4:3-15, 1978.

Rapp, J. P., and Dahl, L. K. Mutant forms of cytochrome P-450 controlling both 18 and 11 beta-steroid hydroxylation in the rat. Biochemistry 15:1235-1242, 1976.

Rasmussen, A. F., Jr., Marsh, J. T., and Brill, N. Q. Increased susceptibility to Herpes simplex in mice subjected to avoidance-learning stress or restraint. Proc. Soc. Exp. Biol. Med. 96:183-189, 1957.

Richardson, D. W., Honour, A. J., Fenton, G. W., Stott, F. H., Pickering, G. W. Variation in arterial pressure throughout the day and night. Clin. Sci. 26:445-460, 1964.

Roddie, I. C. Human responses to emotional stress. Irish J. Med. Sci. 146:395-417, 1977.

Rose, R. M. Endocrine responses to stressful psychological events. Psychiatr. Clin. N. Amer. 3:251-276, 1980.

Rose, R. M., and Hurst, M. W. Plasma cortisol and growth hormone responses to intravenous catheterization. J. Hum. Stress 1:22-36, 1975.

Rosellini, R. A., and Seligman, M. E. P. Frustration and learned helplessness. J. Exper. Psychol.: Anim. Behav. Processes 104:149-157, 1975.

Saavedra, J. M., Kvetnansky, R., and Kopin, I. J. Adrenaline, noradrenaline and dopamine levels in specific brainstem areas of acutely immobilized rats. Brain Res. 160:271-280, 1979.

Salomon, D. S., and Pratt, R. M. Involvement of glucocorticoids in development of the secondary palate. Differentiation 13:141-154, 1979.

Sandman, C. A., Kastin, A. J., Schally, A. V., Kendall, J. W., and Miller, L. H. Neuroendocrine responses to physical and psychological stress. J. Compar. Physiol. Psychol. 84: 386-390, 1973.

Schachter, J. Pain, fear, and anger in hypertensives and normotensives: a psychophysiological study. Psychosom. Med. 19:17-29, 1957.

Schmutzler, W., and Freundt, G. P. The effect of glucocorticoids and catecholamines on cyclic AMP and allergic histamine release in guinea pig lung. Int. Arch. Allergy Appl. Immunol. 49:209-212, 1975.

Schultzberg, M., Lundberg, J. M., Hokfelt, T., Terenius, L., Brandt, J., Elde, R. P., and Goldstein, M. Enkephalin-like immunoreactivity in gland cells and nerve terminals of the adrenal medulla. Neuroscience 3:1169-1186, 1978.

Seligman, M. E. P. Helplessness. On Depression, Development and Death San Francisco: Freeman, 1975.

Seligman, M. E. P., and Beagley, G. Learned helplessness in the rat. J. Compar. Physiol. Psychol. 88:534-541, 1975.

Seligman, M. E. P., and Meyer, B. Chronic fear and ulcers in rats as a function of the unpredictability of safety. J. Compar. Physiol. Psychol. 73:202-207, 1970.

Seligman, M. E. P., Maier, S. F., and Solomon, R. L. Unpredictable and uncontrollable aversive events. IN: Aversive Conditioning and Learning (Brush, F. R., ed.) New York: Academic Press, 1971.

Seligman, M. E. P., Rosellini, R. A., and Kozak, M. J. Learned helplessness in the rat: time course, immunization, and reversibility. J. Compar. Physiol. Psychol. 88:542-547, 1975.

Seward, J. and Humphrey, G. L. Avoidance learning as a function pretraining in the cat. J. Compar. Physiol. Psychol. 63:338-341, 1967.

Shapiro, A. P. Psychophysiologic mechanisms in hypertensive vascular disease. Ann. Int. Med. 53:64-83, 1960.

Shapiro, A. P. An experimental study of comparative responses of blood pressure to different noxious stimuli. J. Chron. Dis. 13:293-311, 1961.

Shire, J. G. M. Endocrine genetics of the adrenal gland. J. Endocrinol. 62:173-207, 1974.

Shire, J. G. M. Corticosteroids and adrenocortical function in animals. IN: Genetic Variation in Hormone Systems, Vol. 1 (Shire, J. G. M., ed.) Boca Raton: CRC Press, 1979, pp. 43-67.

Shire, J. G. M. Genes and hormones in mice. IN: Biology of the House Mouse (Berry, R.J., ed.) London: Academic Press, 1980a.

Shire, J. G. M. Corticosterone metabolism by mouse liver: interactions between genotype and diet. Horm. Metab. Res. 12:117-119, 1980b.

Shnider, S. M., Wright, R. G., Levinson, G., Roizen, M. F., Wallis, K. L., Rolbin, S. H., and Craft, J. B. Uterine blood flow and plasma norepinephrine changes during maternal stress in the pregnant ewe. Anesthesiology 50:524-527, 1979.

Sokolov, E. N. The Central Nervous System and Behavior. New York: Josiah Macy Foundation, 1960.

Solomon, G. F. Stress and antibody response in rats. Int. Arch. Allergy Applied Immunol. 35:97-109, 1969.

Solomon, G. F., Amkraut, A., and Kasper, P. Immunity, emotions and stress with special reference to the mechanisms of stress effects on the immune system. Psychother. Psychosom. 23:209-217, 1974.

Solomon, G. F., Merigan, T. C.. and Levine, S. Variation in adrenal cortical hormones within physiologic ranges: stress and interferon production in mice. Proc. Soc. Exp. Biol. Med. 126:74-79, 1967.

Stein, M., Keller, S. E. and Schleifer, S. J. The hypothalamus and the immunoresponse. Brain Behav. Bodily Dis. 59:45-64, 1980.

Thiessen, D. C., and Rodgers, D. A. Population density and endocrine function. Psychol. Bull. 58:441-451, 1961.

Thorner, M. O. Prolactin. Clin. Endocrinol. Metab. 6: 201-222, 1977.

Tobach, E., and Bloch, H. Effect of stress by crowding prior to and following tuberculous infection. Amer. J. Physiol. 187:399-402, 1956.

Torda, C. Effects of recurrent postnatal pain-related stressful events on opiate receptor-endogenous ligand system. Psychoneuroendocrinology 3:85-91, 1978.

Vessey, S. H. Effects of grouping on levels of circulating antibodies in mice. Proc. Soc. Exp. Biol. 115:252-255, 1964.

Wang, T., Sheppard, J. R., and Foker, J. E. Rise and
fall of Cyclic AMP required for onset of lymphocyte
DNA synthesis. Science 201:155-157, 1978.

Watson, S. J., Akil, H., Richard, C. S., III, and Barchas, J. D. Evidence for two separate opiate peptide
neuronal systems and the coexistence of beta-lipotro-
pin, beta-endorphin and ACTH immunoreactivities in the
same hypothalamic neurons. Nature 275:226-228, 1978.

Weinberg, J. Modulation of the deleterious effects of
preshock by shock-induced fighting in rats or fighting
is its own reward. Unpublished doctoral dissertation,
Stanford University, 1977.

Weiner, H., Singer, M. T., Reiser, M. F. Cardiovascular
responses and their psychological correlates. A study
in healthy young adults and patients with peptic ulcer
and hypertension. Psychosom. Med. 24: 477-498, 1962.

Weinshilboum, R. M., Raymond, F. A., Elveback, L. R.,
and Weidman, W. H. Serum dopamine beta-hydroxylase
activity: Sibling-sibling correlation. Science 181:
943-945, 1973.

Weiss, J. M. Effects of coping responses on stress. J.
Compar. Physiol. Psychol. 65:251-260, 1968.

Weiss, J. M. Somatic effects of predictable and unpredictable shock. Psychosom. Med. 32:397-408, 1970.

Weiss, J. M. Effects of coping behavior in different
warning signal conditions on stress pathology in rats.
J. Compar. Physiol. Psychol. 77:1-13, 1971a.

Weiss, J. M. Effects of punishing the coping response
(conflict) on stress pathology in rats. J. Compar.
Physiol. Psychol. 77:14-21, 1971b.

Weiss, J. M. Effects of coping behavior with and without
a feedback signal on stress pathology in rats. J.
Compar. Physiol. Psychol. 77:22-30, 1971c.

Weiss, J. M., and Glazer, H. I. Effects of acute exposure to stressors on subsequent avoidance-escape
behavior. Psychosom. Med. 37:499-521, 1975.

Welch, B. L., and Welch, A. S. Greater lowering of brain
and adrenal catecholamines in group-housed mice
administered DL-alpha-methyl-tyrosine. J. Pharm.
Pharmacol. 20:244-246, 1968.

Wistar, R., Jr. and Hildemann, W. H. Effect of stress on
skin transplantation immunity in mice. Science 131:
159-160, 1960.

Wragg, L. E., and Speirs, R. S. Strain and sex differences in response of inbred mice to adrenal cortical
hormones. Proc. Soc. Exp. Biol. Med. 80:680-684,
1952.

Wurtman, R. J., and Axelrod, J. Control of enzymatic
synthesis of adrenaline in the adrenal medulla by

adrenal cortical steroids. J. Biol. Chem. 241:2301-2305, 1966.

Wyle, F. A., and Kent, J. R. Immunosuppression by sex steroid hormones. Clin. Exp. Immunol. 27:407-415, 1977.

Yalow, R. S., Varsano-Aharon, N., Echemendia, E., and Berson, A. HGH and ACTH secretory responses to stress. Horm. Metab. Res. 1:3-8, 1969.

Yamamoto, K. R., Gehring, U., Stampfer, M. R., and Sibley, C. H. Genetic approaches to steroid hormone action. Recent Prog. Horm. Res. 32:3-32, 1976.

Zanchetti, A., and Malliani, A. Neural and psychological factors in coronary disease. Acta Cardiol. Suppl. 20:69-93, 1974.

Zarcone, V., Berger, P. A., Brodie, H. K. H., Sack, R., and Barchas, J. The indoleamine hypothesis of depression: a pilot study and overview. Dis. Nerv. Syst. 38:646-653, 1977.

Zigmond, M., and Harvey, J. Resistance to central norepinephrine depletion and decreased mortality in rats chronically exposed to electric foot shock. J. Neuro-Visc. Relations 31:373-381, 1970.

CHAPTER 9

Panel Report on
Stress and Illness

Panel Members:
William Bunney, Jr., M.D., Co-chair
Alvin Shapiro, M.D., Co-chair

Robert Ader, Ph.D.	Dorothy Krieger, M.D.
John Davis, M.D.	Steve Matthysse, Ph.D.
Al Herd, Ph.D.	Albert Stunkard, M.D.
Irwin J. Kopin, Jr., M.D.	Myrna Weissman, Ph.D.

Richard J. Wyatt, M.D.

The Stress and Illness panel divided its work into two sections, one concerned with physical illness and the other with mental illness. The myriad definitions of stress and the different ways in which investigators approach the concept are major problems in stress research. However, panel members agreed that illness-related stress research typically involves efforts to evaluate the role of psychological and behavioral stimuli, in contrast with physical or infectious agents, in disease development. Therefore, the group adopted a working definition of stress research as studies of the role of psychologically mediated stimuli in the development and course of disease. The panel took as its assignment a brief, critical assessment of the research evidence linking stressors, or activators, to the predisposition, precipitation, and perpetuation of disease.

The panel took an organ-systems approach to the immense and complex body of stress-related literature. Background papers were solicited from a number of scientists and clinicians in the stress field (Appendix C). Each contributor prepared a brief paper on the role of stress in a particular disorder or group of disorders, including:

• A description of how stress usually is defined in research relating to the area. Was that definition useful in organizing the relevant data? If not, what other concepts would be of greater value?

• A critical review of existing evidence about the role of stress in the predisposition, precipitation, and perpetuation of illness. Does the illness itself have an important function as a stressor?

• An evaluation of the methods used to measure stressors, reactions, and health consequences.

- Identification of particularly promising directions for research and of critical needs for basic research in other fields that eventually might be applied to stress research. Does the literature suggest appropriate directions for research into treatment or prevention strategies?

- Consideration of problems for and obstacles to research in this field, including anticipated difficulties in implementing appropriate priorities for future research.

Using these background papers, the panel looked for broad trends within the field and common themes that might suggest especially useful directions for future research. The panel did not undertake an exhaustive review of any aspect of the field. Rather, the group tried to select the most interesting and representative examples of research that relate stress to illness. Only highlights of the copious and often confusing research can be provided even for those diseases that are discussed. However, these vignettes should convey the importance of research in this field.

Definitions of Stress

As discussed in Chapter 2, Conceptual Issues of Stress Research, the hypothesis that stress can cause illness usually is attributed to Hans Selye. He popularized the concept that physiological mechanisms can counteract deleterious effects of environmental stressors and that the eventual breakdown of those mechanisms results in "diseases of adaptation." Over the past 30 years, this concept has broadened markedly. A wide range of psychosocial disturbances now are called stressors, and reactions in a variety of organ systems have been labeled as stress responses.

In the research literature, definitions of stress tend to be implicit, often having little apparent similarity across different types of studies. Sometimes the term "stress" is used interchangeably with "stressor" to refer to an environmental event, condition, or characteristic. Usually such environmental stimuli are labeled as stressors because of the reactions they produce. Some researchers concentrate on biological effects, defining a stressor as something that produces specific, objectively measurable, physiological reac-

tions. Others emphasize the perceived stressful quality
of the psychosocial stimuli, which can be assessed with
psychoanalytic or psychometric techniques. Still other
investigators believe that such approaches are inadequate, because an identical event may be a stressor for
one person and not a stressor for another, with no way to
state in advance that a particular event is a stressor
in a given circumstance. Yet, despite slow progress in
resolving the many controversies within the field, there
is widespread agreement that certain life events and
situations are associated with an altered risk for
illness.

Stress as a Risk Factor for Illness

Often, people will explain that they have a peptic
ulcer or high blood pressure "because of the kids" or
"because of pressure at work." Similarly, many depressed
patients will identify a specific event or series of
events as the "cause" of their depression. In contrast
to the many anecdotal reports of dramatic associations
between the occurrence of stressful events and the
development of disease, systematic efforts to study the
effects of stress on health have been few. In part, this
may reflect an inability of many scientists to understand
how stress, a psychological phenomemon, could cause
physiological malfunction.

In recent years, the medical profession has become
increasingly aware of the value of identifying people who
may be unusually likely to develop a particular disease.
The Framingham study of coronary heart disease has been
especially influential in demonstrating the value of
such an approach (Kannell, 1966). Using a prospective
epidemiological design with a large population, this
study investigated the influence of various behavioral,
physiological, and genetic factors on the incidence of
myocardial infarction or sudden coronary death. The
project demonstrated that specific factors such as high
blood pressure and smoking markedly increase the risk
for having coronary heart disease. One of the important
conceptual points about the results was that these risk
factors are of predictive value even without a proven
causal link between them and heart disease. Thus, a
heavy cigarette smoker is at increased risk for having a
heart attack, even though the reason for that increased
risk has yet to be established. These results also have
suggested directions for studies of underlying mechanisms
and encouraged efforts to find ways to modify the risk

factors, to see if such interventions decrease the disease incidence.

Risk factors can be defined as measurable characteristics whose presence increases the risk for future illness. This is a stricter requirement than mere association, because it means that factors must exist before the disease and increase its probability of appearing. Thus, characteristics of the illness itself are excluded; their occurrence would coincide with disease onset. However, a risk factor may not be an etiologic agent: it could reflect some unknown process that eventually produces the disease state. The test of etiology involves manipulating the risk factor or behavioral or physiological mechanisms that it affects. If the risk factor causes the disease, such interventions should decrease disease rates.

Mental disorders should be as amenable to risk-factor analyses as are physical illnesses. Depression is an excellent example. Studies suggest that family history of depression is an important risk factor for the relatively small group of depressed patients with bipolar depression but much less so for other types of depression (Nurnberger and Gershon, in press). Depression is accompanied by a number of biochemical abnormalities. To date, identified changes appear to be disease-dependent, making them inappropriate for consideration as risk factors; but, additional research may identify physiological markers that precede the disorder. Environmental stressors also may be risk factors for depression. The most important life events seem to be those involving loss and separation, although demographic variables such as sex, race, religion, marital status, social class, and profession may be important. Finally, use and abuse of alcohol and other drugs may be strong predictors of subsequent depression, as might the presence of certain personality traits such as moodiness or mood swings (Gershon et al., 1975).

A risk-factor orientation toward the effects of stress on physical and mental illness may provide new insights into disease processes. Too often, investigators become so embroiled with trying to determine how stressors cause a disease that they ignore the more basic questions of whether specific activators actually increase the risk of negative health consequences. Both types of research are vitally important, but failure to distinguish between them can lead to confusion. Risk-factor analysis also promotes consideration of multiple influences on disease precipitation. For example, stressors might be only one of several risk factors that have additive or even synergistic effects.

Stress and Physical Disorders

The following brief descriptions provide a flavor of the types of research being done to gain a better understanding of how stress contributes to disease processes. When possible, we have used an organ systems approach; but, some disorders such as obesity and some forms of cancer are not clearly associated with a particular organ system. No effort has been made to provide exhaustive reviews of any area or to cover all relevant studies. Some obviously important topics, including gastrointestinal and cardiovascular diseases, have received relatively little emphasis, compared with newer areas of investigation, for example disorders of the immune system. These inequities reflect the panel's desire to emphasize new and promising lines of inquiry, rather than to recapitulate information already available elsewhere. The brief reviews of research that refute or support a role of stress in a disease process serve mainly as backgrounds for describing additional work needed to advance the field.

Gastrointestinal Disease

Peptic Ulcer Disease

Most studies of stress and gastrointestinal disease relate to ulcers. Peptic ulcers have long been identified as having some relationship to stress. Yet, a 1977 meeting of major contributors to the field concluded that, after 30 years of investigation, scientists still do not know exactly how emotional processes are linked to pathological changes in the gastrointestinal tract (Wolf et al., 1979). In fact, the group noted that the prevalence and incidence of peptic ulcer disease has decreased in recent years--a seeming paradox if society is, as many people believe, more stressful now than in the past. There is a strong probability that factors other than stress also are important.

A major unresolved methodological problem in studies of stress and ulcers is the unequivocal identification of individuals with the disease. A variety of methods exist for detecting ulcers, including clinical presentation, biochemical measures, radiological evidence, and direct observation through either endoscopic examination or surgery. These techniques differ in specificity, sensitivity, and safety and in their ability to distinguish among several different types of ulcers, including gastric ulcers, duodenal ulcers, and stress ulcers. Presently, no agreement exists about which technique should serve as the standard for diagnosing an ulcer and what criteria should be used in large population studies to detect and distinguish among ulcers and to monitor changes in them over time.

Predisposing Factors. Several good studies suggest that certain types of chronically stressful situations may be risk factors of peptic ulcer disease. For example, many investigators have confirmed the initial finding by Dunn and Cobb (1962) that peptic ulcers are more prevalent among men in supervisory roles than among either executives or craftsmen. Cobb and Rose (1973) found that peptic ulcers occurred nearly twice as often among air traffic controllers as among civilian copilots and more frequently among air controllers working at high-stress control centers than among those at low-stress centers. Such studies cannot prove a causal relationship between the stressors and the disease, but they suggest the need for further study of the factors that mediate ulcer formation in such settings.

Little recent work has been done on the role of psychological factors in the perpetuation of peptic ulcer disease. Older studies characterized ulcer patients as having an oral-dependent character structure. Thus, Weisman (1956) proposed that vacillation between active/seeking and passive/yielding behaviors exacerbate pre-existing ulcers. In the best of this research, Weiner et al. (1957) conducted a double-blind prospective study of military inductees in which they measured serum pepsinogen concentrations and made a number of psychological tests. Psychological profiles reliably distinguished between low and high pepsinogen secretors and predicted those at risk for developing ulcers during training. Only high secretors developed ulcers, so the two measurements together were even better predictors than either alone. The important psychological feature was major, unresolved conflicts over dependency and oral gratification. Engel (1975) has postulated that frustration of dependency needs is the underlying mechanism that explains why ulcer patients become more symptomatic following such stressful life events as separation, bereavement, or job loss.

These studies need to be replicated and extended
with the more advanced psychological and physiological
techniques now available. Multivariate analyses of a
number of potential risk factors may be especially useful. For example, Sturdevant (1976) has identified more
than 20 factors that may alter the risk for peptic ulcer
disease. These range from biological markers such as
blood type, sex, and HLA antigen type through disease
states such as alcoholic cirrhosis, hypertension, and
chronic obstructive pulmonary disease to habits such as
cigarette smoking and consumption of coffee, carbonated
beverages, or milk during college. Nor have there been
adequate efforts to control for other predisposing factors such as acid secretory capacity or the mass of
parietal cells of the stomach. Even the work with serum
pepsinogen must be reexamined in light of recent evidence
that only pepsinogen I may be a risk factor for peptic
ulcer disease (Rotter et al., 1979).

    Precipitation and Perpetuation. Emotional states
can influence stomach acid secretion. Elegant studies of
patients with gastric fistulas have provided invaluable
insights into psychological factors that can alter acid
secretion (Engel et al., 1956; Wolf and Wolff, 1943).
Anger and hostility increase acidity; depression and
withdrawal decrease it. Still, there is no evidence that
usual acute life stressors produce peptic ulcer disease.

    Much of the interest in stress and ulcers stems from
clinical data on the high frequency of stress ulcers in
patients who experience severe trauma, extensive surgery,
major burns or infections, brain injury or surgery, or
other catastrophic events. Such ulcers differ distinctly
from peptic ulcers of the duodenum and stomach. They
are acute, hemorrhagic, and usually preceded by shock;
they are caused by diffusion of hydrogen ions through an
impaired gastric mucosal barrier (Skillman and Selen,
1976). Because most animal models of ulcers probably
are of this type, some misunderstandings have arisen in
attempts to extrapolate experimental findings in animal
studies to the clinical problem of chronic peptic ulcers.
In fact, the typical stress ulcer offers only limited
support to the concept that peptic ulcer has a significant behavioral component.

Other Gastrointestinal Disorders

    Engel's (1954, 1955) classic studies on ulcerative
colitis suggested that a constellation of psychosocial

influences was important in precipitating and exacerbating ulcerative colitis but could not produce the
disease; he concluded that more information about the
physiological mechanisms involved in the disease was
needed. Engel believed that ulcerative colitis was a
vascular disease and that emotional stimuli affected
this aspect of intestinal physiology and probably
influenced immunological mechanisms. More recently,
ulcerative colitis has been shown to be at least two
separate disorders, one that is mucosal and ulcerative
and a second that is granulomatous, affects all layers,
and resembles Crohn's disease (Lamont and Isselbacher,
1980). Studies of stress and ulcerative colitis should
be redone, using the improved methods of prospective
designs that now are available.

A number of other gastrointestinal problems, including esophageal spasm, various diarrheal states,
"spastic colon," and ill-defined gastrointestinal discomfort, have probable relationships to emotional stress
that remain to be studied adequately. Although seldom
life threatening, such illnesses account for much discomfort; pragmatic solutions would be most welcome as well
as providing a good deal of physiologic information.

Cardiovascular Disease

Studies of the effects of stress on cardiovascular
disease have been particularly productive, and strong
evidence exists of an association between specific
psychosocial factors and some cardiovascular diseases.
Research on stress and diseases of the cardiovascular
system falls into three broad, somewhat overlapping
areas--atherosclerosis and its sequelae, arrhythmogenesis and sudden cardiac death, and hypertension.

Methodological problems for this field resemble
those for studying peptic ulcer disease. Most cardiovascular disorders first present in such relatively
advanced stages as essential hypertension, angina, a
nonfatal heart attack, or death. A variety of sophisticated methods is available for assessing cardiovascular
function; but, except for measurements of blood pressure
and pulse rate, electrocardiograms, and blood lipid
assays, few diagnostic tests are sufficiently reliable,
safe, and inexpensive for use in widespread screening of
asymptomatic individuals. Therefore, many studies use
as their endpoints major clinical syndromes rather than
early physiological changes that produce such conse-

quences. Progress has resulted mainly from epidemiological, primarily retrospective studies. Innovations for
increasingly precise assessments of the heart and blood
vessels, including ways to continuously record blood
pressure and pulse rate, noninvasive measures of cardiac
function, and improved assays of catecholamines and
other hormones that modulate the cardiovascular system,
promise better studies in the future.

Atherosclerosis and Its Sequelae

Atherosclerosis refers to the accumulation of large
plaques of lipids in the major arteries, cutting off the
blood supply to such vital organs as the heart. The two
most common problems arising from this process are angina
and myocardial infarction. For both, some evidence
exists that acute and chronic stressors play a role.

Predisposition. Most stress-related studies of
predisposing factors for atherosclerosis relate to the
Type A behavior pattern (cf. Psychosocial Assets and
Modifiers of Stress). Friedman and Rosenman (1959)
identified as Type A those people whom they characterized as being unusually aggressive, competitive, and
work-oriented and as having a constant sense of urgency
about their activities. Studies have shown repeatedly
that people with Type A characteristics have a much
higher incidence of heart attacks than do Type B people,
who exhibit fewer of those traits (Rosenman, 1978). This
finding has stimulated much excellent research, but it
presently is only of limited clinical utility. The behavior pattern is quite common, particularly among males
in the Western culture; yet relatively few get heart disease. Also, the Type A/Type B designation artificially
dichotomizes what is undoubtedly a continuous variation
of behavioral traits. Furthermore, no data exist to
show that it is possible to change Type A behaviors in
ways that alter the risk for heart disease, although
some pilot studies have been promising (Rahe et al.,
1975; Rosenman, 1978). Moreover, potentially adverse
socioeconomic consequences of encouraging such a major
change in life style have yet to be examined adequately.

Certain biochemical, physiological, and anatomical
phenomena may be associated with fully developed Type A
behavior. Although some are in dispute, associations
include elevated blood concentrations of cholesterol,
triglycerides, and glucocorticoids; a greater insulin
response to glucose; increased severity of coronary

265

artery lesions; and greater lability and magnitude of blood pressure and catecholamine responses to time-demand tasks (cf. Rosenman, 1978). Any of these might contribute to the pathogenesis and consequences of atherosclerosis. For example, elevated plasma catechol-amines enhance platelet aggregation, lower the threshold to cardiac arrhythmias, induce vasoconstriction, and suppress insulin secretion (Buell and Eliot, 1979; Haft and Arkel, 1976). Discovering which Type A behaviors are relevant to atherosclerosis and whether identification of those factors will improve detection of people at particular risk for heart disease are important areas of research. Also crucial are studies of the interrela-tionships between specific Type A behavioral traits and concomitant physiological characteristics. Moreover, a variety of other psychosocial factors such as socioeco-nomic status, educational level and work history also may play a role.

Precipitation and Perpetuation. Clinicians have known for many years that emotional disturbances can precipitate anginal pain. The ability of acute stres-sors to aggravate heart failure through increased left ventricular work load also has been well documented (Chambers and Reiser, 1953; Lane, 1973). Except possibly for rare situations of exposure to extreme stressors (Cebelin and Hirsch, 1980), reactions to stressors must interact with preexisting cardiac pathology to produce disease. Bereavement, loss of prestige, and loss of employment have all been implicated as risk factors for myocardial infarctions (Kavanagh and Shepard, 1973). In a six-month prospective study of new widowers, Parkes et al. (1969) found that mortality from myocardial infarc-tions was 67 percent higher than expected. Affected individuals usually experienced reactions of depression and felt helpless and hopeless. Such sociocultural changes as major changes in living arrangements or occu-pation and discrepancies between the culture of origin and the current cultural milieu also significantly increase the risk of having a heart attack (Syme, 1975).

Many of the effects of stress on the cardiovascular system have been attributed to actions of the autonomic nervous system (Lown et al., 1978). However, recent discoveries of pathways for central control of cardiac function suggest that other mechanisms also may be in-volved (Cohen and Cabot, 1979). One study showed that dogs can be trained to regulate their coronary blood flow (Ernst, 1979). If analogous mechanisms exist in people, particularly if they function in diseased hearts, they might suggest a novel way to treat individuals at risk.

Arrhythmogenesis and Sudden Cardiac Death

Sudden cardiac death, one of the most dramatic medical disorders, encompasses a wide variety of phenomena
that have in common the production of rapid, unexpected
cardiac death (Buell and Eliot, in press; Cobb et al.,
1980). Interest in the role of stress in this disorder
arose from the observation that, under some conditions,
people seem to be literally scared to death (Engel,
1971). Some people who die of sudden cardiac death have
massive heart attacks, but many others die from no
obvious cause. Most are thought to die from defects in
the heart's electrical system, causing arrhythmias that
prevent normal function.

Most work on chronic life stressors has not distinguished sudden cardiac death from myocardial infarctions
more generally. Friedman et al. (1973) observed that a
disproportionately large number of Type A individuals who
have heart attacks die immediately or within a few hours.
Whether this reflects an increased risk for sudden cardiac death or some more general phenomenon such as a
tendency to have more massive infarctions is unclear.

Some research suggests that acutely stressful life
events are associated with sudden cardiac death. For
example, Rahe et al. (1974) interviewed relatives of sudden cardiac death victims, using survivors of myocardial
infarctions as controls. Both victims and survivors
experienced substantial changes in their lives during
the six months before the event, but those who died
experienced more changes than did those who survived.
No uniquely important life events were found, although
those who died had increased problems at home and work
and with interrelationships with family and friends.

The few prospective studies that are available
generally support the above conclusions, but sample
sizes are small. Theorell and Rahe (1975) studied charts
of patients who had been seen regularly as out-patients
after they had survived a myocardial infarction. Half of
the subjects had died from a second attack, and the other
half had survived at least 6 years. After information
about final outcome was removed from the charts, the
investigators divided the records into six-month blocks
and scored them for life events. Patients who died had
a marked accumulation of stressful events that peaked
during the year before death; those who survived showed
no accumulation. A major limitation of this study is
the inability to ascertain whether the observed life
events resulted from deteriorating medical status. If

so, they would be a result of the disease process, rather than a risk factor for it. Also, after suffering from a catastrophic illness, people often will be able to recall temporally related events that otherwise would not have been important to them.

In another study, Wolf (1969) made psychological assessments of patients who had recently suffered a myocardial infarction. Ten of the patients were markedly depressed, and all ten died during the four-year study-- eight from sudden cardiac death and two from suicide. A study by Parkes et al. (1969), which showed an increased incidence of death from myocardial infarction in recent widowers, was mentioned earlier; most of those were sudden cardiac deaths. The relationship of these findings to severity of myocardial infarction, the subsequent development of arrythmias, and other physiological variables that alter the risk of sudden cardiac death is an important area for further study.

Causal links between life stressors and sudden cardiac death remain to be established. Most investigators believe that cardiac arrhythmias are involved. Lown et al. (1977) found that an emotionally disturbing interview could elicit arrhythmias from patients with a recent myocardial infarction, even though no arrhythmias were present under resting conditions. Dimsdale (1977) has argued that the parasympathetic and sympathetic components of the autonomic nervous system interact with damaged cardiac tissue to produce rhythm disturbances. Verrier et al. (1975) found that aversive conditioning in dogs can lower cardiac threshold to electrical dysfunction and increase its sensitivity to catecholamine effects. Frequently, however, behavioral stressors appear to have relatively minor effects compared with changes induced by physical effort. Whether all types of challenges to the cardiovascular system have the same effects on the heart is a subject of intense interest.

Hypertension

The relationship between stress and hypertension has received so much attention that most people assume that it is well understood. In fact, much remains to be learned about the role of stress in its pathogenesis. Both systolic blood pressure, which generally reflects cardiac output, and diastolic blood pressure, which relates to the peripheral resistance, vary with the level of physical exertion and psychological excitement.

Definitions of high blood pressure are statistical, involving a deviation from the population average. In research, hypertension usually is defined as several carefully taken readings on an individual at rest that exceed a value such as 140/90 mm Hg. Measurements of blood pressure and characterization of normal and abnormal variations in it have advanced greatly in recent years. Application of those advances to gaining a better understanding of the role of stress in hypertension has gone more slowly.

Predisposition. Clinical evidence of an association between chronic stressors and hypertension is inconclusive. Hypertensives may be withdrawn, uncommunicative, and anxious to avoid confrontation even when it is appropriate. An early hypothesis was that hypertension is "anger directed inward," caused by an inability to express anger properly to others (Alexander, 1950). Kalis et al. (1957) proposed that such behaviors might be beneficial to the hypertensive, because they minimize situations in which rage reactions occur. In accord with this hypothesis, Weiner et al. (1962) demonstrated that hypertensives tend to respond in ways that avoid involvement. In addition, Sapira et al. (1971) compared responses of hypertensives and normotensives to movies of a "good" and "bad" doctor-patient relationship. Hypertensives did not perceive obvious conflicts. Prospective studies could clarify whether such a personality trait is a risk factor for hypertension or a result of it. A recent study by Shapiro et al. (1980) indicates that young, mild hypertensives have perception and performance abnormalities that are suggestive of central nervous system impairment.

Epidemiological studies have repeatedly revealed correlations between hypertension and psychosocial variables that seem to have in common a stressful quality (Henry and Stephens, 1977). Even though intervening factors, for example sodium intake, might be involved, these studies emphasize the need to explore ways in which chronic stressors can alter cardiovascular physiology.

Animal experiments have been helpful in confirming some of the effects of chronic stressors on the cardiovascular system. Some stressors such as loud noise produce hypertension during exposure to them, but blood pressure returns to normal once the stressor is removed (Farris et al., 1945). Others, including avoidance conditioning in monkeys (Benson et al., 1969) and social crowding in mice (Henry et al., 1975), can produce

sustained hypertension. These latter stressors require
animals to adjust continually to threat and uncertainty.
Only recently, investigators have begun to trace the
brain pathways involved in such changes, offering the
promise of a much more extensive understanding of
potential mechanisms (Nathan et al., 1978).

Precipitation and Perpetuation. Like most associations between stress and disease, the initial support for
a connection between hypertension and recent stressful
events came from retrospective studies. For example,
investigators found that severely traumatic events such
as natural disasters or wars increase the incidence of
hypertension (Graham, 1945; Miasnikov, 1961; Ruskin et
al., 1948). Employing a more normal setting, Reiser et
al. (1951a) compared the natural history of hypertension
with temporally related life events. Subjects were asked
not only about events that anyone would perceive as
stressful but also about seemingly minor events that had
special significance to the patient. Inclusion of such
minor events greatly enhanced the association between
stressors and hypertension. Weiner (1970) reviewed
several other studies that present similar data. Unfortunately, all of them suffer from the same limitations.
In addition to being retrospective, they used observers
who knew which subjects had hypertension. In such a
setting, observers might examine the time preceding the
onset of hypertension increasingly closely until an
event is uncovered.

Still unclear are the mechanisms through which
psychosocial stressors might produce hypertension. In
experimental settings, a variety of physical and psychological stressors can elevate blood pressure (Brod, 1963,
Shapiro, 1961). Blood-pressure responses to stressors
are exaggerated in hypertensives and in normotensives
who have a family history of hypertension (Shapiro,
1960). Continuous monitoring of blood pressure in freely
moving subjects has demonstrated a wide variability in
blood pressure over time and in different settings for
both hypertensives and normotensives. However, these
fluctuations in blood pressure are transient. It is
unclear whether such changes contribute to the etiology
of hypertension, although they are involved in perpetuation and exacerbation of the disease (Reiser et
al., 1951b). Identification of the hemodynamic and
biochemical factors that affect hypertension would
greatly assist efforts to develop better treatment and
prevention strategies. Biofeedback and relaxation
techniques for lowering blood pressure have direct

implications for research on neuropsychological and
neurophysiological mechanisms that can modulate cardiovascular responses (Schwartz et al., 1979; Shapiro et
al., 1977).

Immune Disease

The effects of stress on the immune system are a
new area of research. For many years, most scientists
and clinicians have believed that immunulogical function
was independent of psychosocial factors. Some recent
studies suggest that that assumption is no longer tena-
ble. The immune system appears to be integrated with
other physiological processes and to be subject to some
regulation or modulation by the brain (Ader, 1981).
Thus, stressors might influence immune function and
immunologically mediated disease processes. Given the
known or suspected role of the immune system in many
major physical disorders, including some forms of cancer,
exploration of influences of stress on immune function
is vital. Associations between stress and cancer are
discussed in the next section.

Clinically, psychological stressors have long been
thought to affect several immune-related disorders
(Solomon and Amkraut, 1981). Rheumatoid arthritis has
been studied most extensively. In retrospective studies,
women described as rebellious, aggressive, and highly
self-controlled were at greater risk for developing
rheumatoid arthritis than was the general population
(Bourestom and Howard, 1965). Also, separation from a
love object has been reported to precipitate an arthritic
attack in a predisposed individual (Heisel, 1972). The
reactions that such stressors produce and how those lead
to the consequence of arthritis are unknown. Research
has suffered from the fact that there still is no satis-
factory understanding of the etiology of rheumatoid
arthritis; in fact, it is even unclear whether the disease begins in connective tissue or in its vasculature.

Stressors can affect the susceptibility to and
recovery from infectious diseases. For example, both
streptococcal infections (Meyer and Haggerty, 1962) and
respiratory infections (Jacobs et al., 1970) have been
reported to occur more frequently after stressful life
events. Also, recovery from such self-limiting illnesses
as influenza (Imboden et al., 1961) or mononucleosis
(Greenfield et al., 1959) correlate with the presence of
stressors. Again, almost nothing is known about mechan-

271

isms for these effects, and most of the data derive from retrospective studies using life-event scales. It is clear that stress is neither a necessary nor a sufficient condition for the development of infectious disease. Rather, as with all of the other disorders discussed in this chapter, it can be a risk factor when combined with other pathogenic stimuli and host factors.

Basic scientists are beginning to uncover mechanisms through which psychosocial stressors might alter immune function. A few relevant human studies are available. For example, Bartrop et al. (1977) found that bereavement depressed lymphocyte function independently of other hormonal responses. Schleifer et al. (1980) confirmed this finding in a small, prospective study of spouses of women with metastatic breast cancer. They compared several variables of immune function in these men before and after death of the spouse. Other studies suggest that a combination of high life event scores with a presumed unsuccessful coping response are associated with depressed immunological defenses (Greene et al., 1978; Roessler et al., 1979).

Some current basic research holds promise for suggesting ways in which stress may affect the immune system, as discussed in more detail in Chapter 8, Biological Substrates of Stress. A considerable body of work exists on the revelance of stress to infectious disease in animals. Disease rates change if bacteria or viruses are presented in close conjunction with such stressors as fighting, avoidance conditioning, physical restraint, or social crowding. For example, Friedman et al. (1965) showed that neither exposure to a stressor nor innoculation with Coxsakie B virus was sufficient to induce disease in adult mice; only the appropriately timed combination produced symptoms. Depending on the animal studied, the infectious agent used, and the stressor chosen, a stressor may either decrease (Marsh et al., 1963) or increase (Levine et al., 1962) the risk of infection. Particularly intriguing is recent evidence that immune responses in animals can be conditioned, strongly suggesting the presence of mechanisms through which the brain can modulate immune activity (Ader and Cohen, 1975; Cohen et al., 1979).

Cancer

Most studies of causes of cancer have involved identification of physical agents such as asbestos or cigarette "tars" that are risk factors for the subse-

quent development of cancer. Among other known predisposing factors are familial susceptibility, immune
deficiency, congenital defects, and aging. A brief
survey of the growing list of known or suspected risk
factors emphasizes that their links to cancer often are
complex.

As with stress, there is no universally acceptable
definition of cancer (Terry, 1978). Neoplasms are a
group of diseases of largely unknown, probably multiple
causes that arise in all tissues composed of cells having
the potential to divide. Cancer cells have no known
ultrastructure or biochemical feature that uniformly
distinguishes them from normal cells. Most cancers are
diagnosed after a prolonged but variable latency period.
A few tumors will regress spontaneously; others can be
removed surgically, if sufficiently localized; still
others can be eradicated or arrested with chemotherapy,
radiotherapy, hormone treatments, or immunotherapy.
Most of the findings discussed relate only to a few of
the many types of cancers. Whether the results hold for
all types of cancer remains to be determined.

A major, unresolved issue in stress-related cancer
research is how to assess the effects of stressors on a
disease process that may take 20 years to become clinically apparent. Most studies share problems common to
all retrospective research (Cohen, 1979). Cancers are
identified by clinical diagnosis; yet the disease process starts long before it is diagnosed. Thus, even
prospective studies cannot define temporal relationships
between a stressor and disease onset (Fox, 1978). As a
result, most studies of cancer predisposition have
examined chronic stressors present from early childhood. For acute stressors, attention must be limited to
associations with a clinical diagnosis of cancer.

Predisposition. Several investigators have tried
to determine whether certain chronic psychosocial conditions predispose to cancer. An early review concluded
that people with cancer are more likely to have had
feelings of isolation, desertion, and loneliness as
children than are controls (LeShan and Worthington,
1956). These findings have been confirmed in retrospective studies of several types of cancer, including lung
(Kissen, 1963) and uterine cervical (Schmale and Iker,
1971). In a prospective study, Horne and Picard (1979)
also found that a reported lack of closeness to parents
during childhood was a risk factor for having lung
cancer. In a longitudinal, prospective study of Johns
Hopkins medical students, Thomas et al. (1979) examined

273

20 white males who had developed cancers of any type by
the 15 to 20 year follow-up. A review of their records
revealed that those students were more likely than their
cohorts to have reported a lack of closeness with parents, particularly with the father, when they entered the
study. This feature also was present in participants who
had been hospitalized for mental illness or committed
suicide but was absent for subjects who were healthy at
follow-up, were hypertensive, or had had a myocardial
infarction.

Other personality characteristics also have been
suggested as risk factors for cancer, but with less
consistency. Those who develop cancer have been characterized as extroverted and emotional (Hagnell, 1966),
introverted (McCoy, 1976), and depressed (Bieliauskas et
al., 1979). Thomas et al. (1979) found that all of the
Johns Hopkins students who developed major malignancies
had reported little or no nervous tension, depression,
or anger in reaction to high stress in their initial
evaluations. Still further afield, Abse et al. (1974)
studied young patients who were undergoing tests to rule
out lung cancer. Those who were found to have cancer
were more conscientious at their work and more constricted in their interpersonal relationships than were
those who did not have cancer.

High ratings of stress have been associated with
longer, rather than shorter, survival in patients who
have cancer. Early studies of breast cancer patients
(Bacon et al., 1952) and lymphoma and leukemia patients
(Blumberg, 1954) suggested that patients who had higher
levels of hostility tended to live longer. Derogatis et
al. (1979) confirmed those findings in a study of women
who had metastatic breast cancer: compared with short-
term survivors, long-term survivors reported more of
such psychological symptoms as hostility, anxiety,
alienation, depression, and guilt; they also had markedly
poorer attitudes towards their physicians. Similarly,
Rogentine et al. (1978) found that, on the average,
patients with malignant melanoma relapsed one year later
if they had relatively high psychological distress.

Precipitation and Perpetuation. Early work on
leukemia and lymphoma patients suggested that recent,
significant losses were a strong risk factor for cancer
(Greene and Miller, 1958); this has been extended to
other types of cancer (Kissen, 1963; LeShan, 1966). All
of this work emphasized helplessness as a stressor for
physical illness, but all were retrospective. Schmale
and Iker (1971) obtained similar results in interviews

274

with women about to undergo biopsy for cervical cancer. Also, Horne and Picard (1979), interviewing patients who had an undiagnosed X-ray lesion in the chest, found that the three greatest risk factors for a subsequent diagnosis of cancer were a recent significant loss, lack of job stability, and lack of plans for the future. Even with these studies, psychological state and life events could have been influenced by the occult disease process, so that they are not truly prospective. Also, given the latency period of most cancers, they almost certainly are risk factors of receiving a diagnosis of cancer, rather than of developing cancer.

At present, the evidence is suggestive but inconclusive and often conflicting. Some types of chronic stressors seem to be associated with increased risk for cancer, but the relevant features of those stressors and the magnitude of the risk remain to be determined. Acute loss with accompanying depression may be associated with an increased likelihood of receiving a diagnosis of cancer; but depression might be a consequence of the cancer, even before the latter is diagnosed. Those who have cancer may survive longer if they have relatively high levels of hostility and psychological symptoms; again, however, this might reflect some other aspect of the disease process.

Endocrine Disease

Research on the endocrine system and stress has been the most complete of all systems that have been studied (Rose, 1980). Technological advances now permit rapid, repeated measurements of many hormones, so that even relatively short-term changes in endocrine activity can be identified and quantified. Developments such as the use of antibodies to assay tiny amounts of these compounds have greatly facilitated the study of endocrine disorders, and the stress field has shared in this advance. However, in stress research, hormones typically have been of secondary interest. Investigators have used measurements of such hormones as cortisol or plasma catecholamines to assess whether an event or condition is a stressor for a particular individual. Such studies do not relate directly to stress and illness, so we will not consider them here. Major hormones relating to stress responses are discussed in Biological Substrates of Stress (Chapter 8).

Several specific endocrine diseases should be mentioned. One of these is diabetes mellitus. Clinically, it is clear that physical or psychosocial stressors can alter insulin needs in diabetics; stressors often may be responsible for episodes of loss of control, particularly in the juvenile diabetic. However, as discussed later, the aspect of stress research receiving the most recent attention involves diabetes as a stressor for the patient and for the family.

Hyperthyroidism

Hyperthyroidism has a long history in psychosomatic research, and ample anecdotal evidence documents that the disorder can develop acutely after a frightening or stressful experience (Weiner, 1978). In the 1950s and 1960s hyperthyroid patients were characterized as insecure, self-demanding, and often having a strong but unconscious dependence on one person (Ham et al., 1951). Studies also suggested that stressful life events were associated with the precipitation of hyperthyroidism. In one report, at the time their disease developed, 82 percent of the hyperthyroid females and 28 percent of the males faced an actual or threatened loss of a significant relationship or a demand to provide care of others that exceeded their capacity; 18 percent and 72 percent, respectively, had lost some self-sufficiency as a result of a job loss, an illness, or submission to another person (Bennet and Cambor, 1961). These studies were retrospective and lacked necessary controls; but, the general consistency of the findings suggest that research on possible underlying mechanisms might be useful.

Most research on hyperthyroidism was done before scientists could measure many of the hormones involved in regulating thyroid function. Initially, the development of a situation in which the patient could no longer be self-sufficient was thought to lead to excessive production of thyroid stimulating hormone (TSH), which produced hyperthyroidism. Since then, investigators have demonstrated that TSH overproduction does not play such a central role, at least in the maintenance of hyperthyroidism. Improvements in research methodologies have not been used to determine if certain personality types actually are at increased risk of having hyperthyroidism or to elucidate potential triggering mechanisms involved in excessive thyroid function. Some investigators have suggested that the triggering mechanisms for hyperthyroidism may be in the hypothalamus. Radioimmunological techniques now enable the measurement of thyrotropin releasing factor (TRF), which stimulates TSH release

276

from the pituitary. Much has been learned about genetic predisposition to hyperthyroidism and about the immune mechanisms involved in the disorder, but this knowledge has not been applied to the question of how stress affects the disorder. Also needed are more current data on prevalence, incidence, and associations with environmental stressors.

Female Reproductive Dysfunction

Stress may affect the function of the female reproductive system. Anecdotally, severe life stressors are widely credited with disrupting reproductive processes, but almost no systematic research is available. A number of reports suggest that such varied stressors as a new school or work setting, electroconvulsive therapy, and disasters can produce menstrual dysfunction, with more severe stressors causing amenorrhea in a greater proportion of the women affected (Drew, 1961). Cessation of menstrual cycles in young women without functional endocrine abnormalities is one of the most common types of amenorrhea.

A remarkably high proportion of these women report psychosexual problems and socioenvironmental trauma (Yen, 1978). Using a retrospective study design with matched controls, Fres et al. (1974) found that such patients had a higher incidence of stressful life events preceding the onset of symptoms. Regular, strenuous exercise in the form of jogging also can produce amenorrhea (Feicht et al., 1978). One of the few available prospective studies found that hospitalization alone resulted in delayed ovulation in two healthy subjects (Peyser et al., 1973). A few reports suggest that women who are chronic aborters (Grimm, 1962) or who are infertile (Fioretti et al., 1977) tend to be more anxious or emotionally unstable than are controls.

No precise data are currently available to show which stressors are associated with reproductive dysfunction and under what conditions. There also is little understanding of mechanisms that might produce such effects. One possible lead is the observation that prolactin, commonly elevated during stress, is high in a substantial number of women with secondary amenorrhea or infertility (Reichlin et al., 1979). Many of these women may have had small prolactin-secreting pituitary tumors; but some at least show no radiological evidence of such tumors, suggesting that they were secreting prolactin for other reasons.

Obesity

The stress concept seems not to have been as helpful for understanding obesity as have learning theories
and applied behavioral and sociological techniques.
Four areas of research in obesity can be viewed as
stress-related. First, laboratory studies of obese
people suggest that eating does not lower anxiety levels
and that high levels of anxiety do not produce any
consistent increase in eating (Abramson and Wunderlich,
1972; McKenna, 1972; Schacter et al., 1968). Second,
taste-test studies suggest that anxiety and depression
may decrease restraint from eating for some obese people,
at least transiently; this might lead to loss of dieting
control (Herman and Polivy, 1980). Third, some anecdotal
and retrospective studies suggest that individuals with
bulimia have more frequent episodes of binge eating
during situations that are perceived as stressful; however, the effect seems to be of practical importance
only at early stages of the disorder (Stunkard, 1976).
Several prospective studies of the use of behavioral
techniques and pharmacological agents to reduce binge
eating merit follow-up (Monti et al., 1977; Wermuth et
al., 1977). Fourth, in rats, tail pinching produces
overeating, and chronic stimulation can produce mild
degrees of obesity (Antelman and Szechtman, 1975). A
specific neuronal pathway has been identified for this
tail-pinch hyperphagia, suggesting one mechanism by which
the brain might affect obesity (Luparello et al., 1964).
The relevance of this system to human obesity is unknown.

Pulmonary Disease

Almost all stress-related research of pulmonary disorders has been on bronchial asthma. It may be useful
to broaden the research scope. Rapid breathing, or
hyperventilation, and shortness of breath, or dyspnea,
are frequent reactions to stressors. Basic studies of
the physiological mechanisms and consequences of such
reactions would provide a better understanding of some
of the effects of stress.

Bronchial Asthma

Bronchial asthma is a reversible obstruction of the
air passages that is produced by a combination of edema,
bronchospasm, and excess secretion. Several variants of
asthma differ in their etiology and in the underlying

pathology (Weiner, 1977). Precise classification of these subtypes remains to be developed, which may help to explain why the influence of stressors on the disorder is still not well understood, even after years of research. At least some forms have a genetic contribution, but studies of identical twins suggest that environmental influences also are important (Edfors-Lubs, 1971).

Predisposition. Early psychoanalytic studies concluded that asthma was a "repressed cry for mother" (French and Alexander, 1941). Subsequent work has failed to yield a consistent picture. Abramson (1954) proposed that mothers of asthmatic children were "engulfing," rather than rejecting. Jacobs et al. (1967) found that mothers could be controlling, rejecting, or both. All of these studies were retrospective. The issue should be reexamined.

Precipitation and Perpetuation. Several lines of research implicate acute stressors as precipitants of asthmatic attacks in susceptible individuals. For example, Purcell et al. (1969) confirmed a clinical observation that children who have chronic asthma often improve when away from their parents. When parents went on vacation and skilled substitutes provided care and monitored asthmatic status, about half of the children improved markedly. The changes may have resulted from removal of an interaction that produced frequent stressful situations. In a logical extension of this work, Liebman et al. (1974) successfully used family therapy to treat severe, chronic asthma in all of seven children.

Some of the clearest evidence of the importance of psychological stressors in precipitating asthmatic attacks comes from learning experiments. Luparello et al. (1968) produced severe bronchoconstriction by exposing asthmatics to a harmless substance to which they thought they were allergic. Similarly, Feldman (1976) showed that biofeedback techniques can help subjects learn to alter airway resistance. Also, biofeedback studies have had some positive results in the mangement of recurrent asthma, as has hypnosis (Knapp, 1977).

Physiological mechanisms for psychologically induced changes in lung function must be delineated. Investigators have identified both immunological and neurological mechanisms that might be involved. The former includes interactions between antigens and IgE antibodies that lead to the release of histamine and other mediating agents. The latter involves the autonomic nervous sys-

279

tem, which affects bronchial size and may mediate many acute, psychologically induced changes (Gold et al., 1972). The importance of such mechanisms in asthma and their relevance to stress reactions and consequences remain to be explored.

Chronic Obstructive Pulmonary Disease (COPD)

Although not often considered in stress research, COPD deserves careful study. The disorder has multiple causations, all of which produce changes in the lung that cause poor gas exchange, with dyspnea as the major symptom. Cigarette smoking is a leading etiologic agent. In its mild form, patients have trouble getting enough oxygen; as the disease progresses, retention of carbon dioxide increases and considerable energy must be expended to maintain oxygen levels even at rest. People with comparable amounts of lung disease may differ greatly in their subjective distress (Dudley, 1969), depending in part on the extent of imbalances between lung perfusion and ventilation.

Adjustment to severe COPD can go to one of two extremes. "Blue bloaters" expend only as much energy on breathing to get enough oxygen to survive; they are cyanotic and retain carbon monoxide. "Pink puffers" breath vigorously, maintaining more normal oxygen and carbon dioxide levels but expending considerable amounts of energy. Representing opposite ends of a continuum, these two responses to lung disease typically have been attributed to differences in the sensitivity of the brain's respiratory center to carbon dioxide (Howell, 1966). However, factors that affect that sensitivity remain to be studied, and psychosocial stressors might be influential. For example, blue bloaters might be people who are depressed and have given up in the face of their disease. More information about psychological aspects of these different types of reactions to COPD has important therapeutic implications. Techniques for measuring pulmonary function should enable prospective studies of various factors, including smoking, that may be important.

Hematological Disease

Literature on stress and hematological disease is scant. Data on leukemias was reviewed earlier, with other cancers. Also of interest are the hemophilias--

life-long, inherited bleeding disorders that afflict
mainly males and that manifest themselves primarily as
bleeding into the soft tissues and joints. Although
rare, hemophilia has a strong impact both on those who
have it and on the health-care system.

Anecdotal reports suggest that stressful situations
can lead to spontaneous bleeding in hemophiliacs (Browne
et al., 1960), but it is difficult to prove such a connection. Clinical trials typically use small sample
sizes, because the disorder is rare; yet ethical concerns
prevent controlled laboratory trials that might deliberately induce bleeding in hemophiliacs. Still, a few
studies suggest that further research in this area might
be fruitful. Garlinghouse and Sharp (1968) found that
hemophiliac subjects with a positive self-concept had
fewer bleeding episodes than did those with poorer
self-concepts. Also, some investigators have reported
that hypnosis can help to reduce the number of bleeding
episodes (LaBaw, 1975; Lucas, 1975).

Many factors other than stress could account for
the results just cited. For example, hemophiliacs with
a good self-image might have less bleeding because they
engage in fewer activities that carry a risk of injury.
Also, because the studies use self-reporting, the underlying course of the disease might be unchanged, and only
reports of bleeding decreased. Arguing against a direct
effect of stress, Mattsson et al. (1971) found no correlation between bleeding episodes and urinary steroid
excretion, which they used as a physiological indicator
of stress. But, some evidence supports an effect of
stressors. Animals exposed to severe stressors can have
increased bleeding, apparently because of changes in the
blood vessel wall (Jaques, 1964). Blood vessel changes
also have been implicated in a rare clinical syndrome
called psychogenic purpura (Agle and Ratnoff, 1962).
Furthermore, emotional stressors can alter platelet
function in normal subjects (Arkel et al., 1977). It is
possible that research on mechanisms might uncover a
system through which the brain monitors and modulates
this important aspect of cardiovascular function.

Physical Diseases as Stressors

Physical disorders, particularly chronic ones, are
themselves stressful both to the patient and to those
who provide support. A side effect of improving medical
care has been longer lives for people who have severe

281

handicaps that limit their ability to cope physically, socially, and economically. Effects both of the disease itself and of the treatments required to maintain life make many demands on patients and family. Some researchers are beginning to explore positive and negative consequences of these stressors. Aspects of coping with illness are discussed in Chapter 7, Psychosocial Assets and Modifiers of Stress.

Chronic renal dialysis and transplantation offer a laboratory for learning the processes of adjusting to chronic illness. Dialysis imposes severe stressors on patients, who not only must undergo the procedure at regular intervals but also must maintain a special diet and tolerate the side effects of being anemic and having persistent metabolic abnormalities. Depression and suicide occur frequently. Reichsman and Levy (1972), following 25 patients over four years, reported that all 25 patients were depressed when they entered the hemodialysis program. Abram et al. (1971) found that of 3500 patients studied, 37 attempted suicide--20 successfully; 22 died after voluntarily withdrawing from hemodialysis programs; and 117 died because they failed to follow treatment regimens. It is possible that depression arises purely from an assessment of the situation, but metabolic changes associated with the disease also might have some role. Many different programs, for example home dialysis, self-care hospital dialysis, in-patient hospital dialysis, and transplantation, now are available. It will be important to study which patients do best with a particular type of therapy.

Similar observations can be made about diabetes, especially about juvenile-onset diabetes. Patients must stay on an appropriate diet, monitor urine or blood sugar, and adjust daily insulin dosages. A resurgence of interest in strict glucose control and the introduction of such devices as insulin pumps will require even greater patient sophistication. Relatively little attention has been given to the effects of such demands, especially on adolescents. A recent conference highlighted the need for and importance of learning more about the stressful aspects of diabetes (Hamburg et al., 1980). Mattsson (1980) has pointed out that the stresses of the illness, combined with the expected upheavals that accompany adolescence, may have a number of outcomes, ranging from improved coping because of past successes to complete deterioration of a therapeutic program. Studies in this area may suggest ways to improve control of the disease and facilitate recognition and treatment of associated behavioral problems.

Cancer patients often feel extremely vulnerable in
the first months after the disease is diagnosed, finding
themselves preoccupied with thoughts of dying (Weisman
and Worden, 1976). Worden and Sobel (1978) reported that
patients who scored high on what they called "emotional
distress" had more disease symptoms and greater feelings
of distress and vulnerability than did those with low
emotional distress. High emotional distress could be
reduced with brief, directed therapy. Even those who are
cured of their cancer may suffer severe aftereffects.
O'Malley et al. (1979) found that, among children who had
been free of disease for at least five years, 59 percent
had some type of mental disturbance; for 23 percent of
children, impairment was moderate or severe. Given the
increasing success of cancer treatments, long-term problems of survivors need careful study.

Specific Research Needs

In examining the data about the effects of stress on
the major organ systems, the panel identified a number of
questions in need of answers. Several important research
directions for each area are discussed below.

Gastrointestinal Disease

New studies should be made of potential psychosocial
risk factors of gastrointestinal diseases such as peptic
ulcer disease and ulcerative colitis. Most available
data, particularly for disorders other than peptic ulcer
disease, are outdated. It should be possible to capitalize on recent advances in techniques both for assessing
risk factors and for studying the gastrointestinal tract.
Such studies could sort through risk factors identified
in the older literature, discarding spurious ones and
seeking commonalities among valid ones.

Investigators should look for interactions between
physiological and psychological risk factors. Data
suggesting that pepsinogen concentrations and certain
psychological traits are additive risk factors are
intriguing. It is possible to measure parietal cell
mass, acid secretion, and blockade of acid secretion
with cimetidine, a histamine receptor blocker. Do such
measures improve identification of people at risk for
peptic ulcers?

Efforts should be made to identify psychosocial
factors that predict successful treatment. The recent

trend of treating peptic ulcers with cimetidine is of
special interest, because the drug blocks the release of
hydrochloric acid in response to various stressors,
including emotional stimuli. It has greatly altered the
way physicians treat ulcers. Much more information is
needed about psychosocial factors that may modify response to the therapy. What factors influence the way
people respond? What are the short-term and long-term
effects of blocking this end-organ reaction? Do new
symptoms appear in different organ systems?

Systematic attention also should be given to the
meaning of the decline in the incidence in peptic ulcers
in recent years. If stressors are risk factors for the
disorder, this trend poses important questions. Is the
society becoming less or more stressful? Are the types
of stressors changing? If our society is becoming more
stressful, what diagnostic, psychosocial, dietary, and
other factors account for the decrease in disease?

Cardiovascular Disease

Pathways through which the brain monitors and
modulates cardiovascular activity must be identified.
Advances in the neurosciences offer powerful tools for
tracing neuronal pathways. Biofeedback techniques may
allow selective behavioral approaches. How do renin-
angiotensin, corticosteroids, and sodium transport
complement the autonomic nervous system in controlling
the heart and blood vessels? Does the brain influence
processes such as atherosclerosis, platelet formation,
and clotting that are involved in cardiovascular disease?

Studies of the principal components of personality
traits that are risk factors for disease may help to
increase diagnostic acumen and suggest possible mechanisms. Data associating the Type A behavior pattern with
myocardial infarction and coronary artery disease are
convincing, but only at the group level. Many people at
risk do not develop arteriosclerotic heart disease. Do
some Type A people have specific physiological response
patterns that further increase risk? What other behavioral and personality traits are risk factors?

It should be possible to identify mediators that
influence whether specific cardiovascular reactions to
stressors have negative health consequences. Acute
cardiovascular reactions to emotional stressors differ
from those to such physical stressors as exercise. Do

284

such differences involve changes in hemodynamic response patterns or hormonal release? What mediators help to mold such reactions? Both environmental and genetic factors appear to precipitate or perpetuate specific reactions in some individuals.

Studies are needed of the effects of trying to change psychosocial factors associated with increased risk of cardiovascular disease. Are any of the factors amenable to change? Are such interventions useful in prevention or treatment? If so, do they have negative consequences? Cardiovascular disease is one of the few areas in stress research in which some psychosocial risk factors have been identified precisely enough to permit studies of potential interventions. Experience with changing other risk factors such as smoking and hypertension should provide useful models.

Immune Disorders

Mechanisms by which the brain may influence the immune system must be identified and characterized. The following areas are among those needing study: developmental immunology; brain function and immune processes, including neurophysiological evaluations of anatomic sites of various functions; hormonal changes in immune function; pharmacological control of immune processes; and behavioral effects on immune competence.

Studies in people should examine both the specific changes in immune function that can occur with psychological stressors and the health consequences that may be associated with them. Particular care is needed in this emerging field to distinguish between stressors as risk factors and stressors as potential activators that produce reactions in the immune system. Many changes in the immune system may produce no observable health consequences. Standardized, nontraumatic, and noninvasive psychological stressors will be needed for experimental investigations of immune reactions.

The specificity of stressors as risk factors for immune-related disorders should be assessed. Are immune reactions to stressors nonspecific, with consequences determined by other factors such as the presence of an infectious agent? Or do some stressors alter only some aspects of the immune system, predisposing to a specific disease? Which stressors may have positive consequences, and why?

285

Cancer

Studies of psychosocial risk factors of cancer require innovative solutions to the problems posed by the long latency of most cancers. New strategies may help. Thus, it may be useful to study fast-growing cancers in which the latent period of the disease is relatively brief. It also may be beneficial to address directly questions about whether psychosocial stressors encourage behavior that results in detection of a preexisting cancer. Demonstration of such an association could be relevant to other types of life-event studies of illness.

Basic research is needed on the ways in which stressors could affect cancer precipitation and perpetuation. Most investigators have assumed that the primary mechanism is suppression of the immune system, but many questions remain unanswered. Do stressors promote the formation of neoplastic cells or inhibit their destruction? Are all types of cancer equally affected, or do certain stressors increase the risk of developing only some types of neoplasms? What mechanisms contribute to the process, and how do they interact with one another?

Multidisciplinary studies of populations at risk for some form of cancer may help to identify relevant psychosocial, immune, endocrine, and neuronal factors. Drawing on past retrospective work, it should be possible to design longitudinal, prospective studies that would help to refine estimates of the relative predictive power of different risk factors and to define more precisely the conditions under which they are most important.

Additional studies of the effects of specific support measures on the outcome of diagnosed cases of cancer may suggest useful psychosocial supplements to existing therapies. Information about factors that affect cancer outcomes is inconclusive, but there are enough hints about psychosocial influences to warrant continued studies of psychological reactions to cancer and their influence on detection, treatment, and outcome.

Endocrine Disorders

Studies of stress effects on endocrine disorders such as female reproductive dysfunction and hyperthyroidism should be renewed, taking advantage of recent technological advances. Major improvements in assays

286

for hormones and a greatly expanded list of known neuroregulators suggest the need to repeat many studies of the
effects of psychosocial stressors on endocrine systems.

Pulmonary Diseases

More information is needed about ways in which the
central nervous system and endocrine system can modulate
respiratory function. The availability of new technologies invites reassessments of previous findings. It now
is possible to study many aspects of immunological,
neuronal, and pulmonary function. Application of these
techniques in controlled settings should enable investigators to determine how psychosocial stressors affect
the onset and course of brochial asthma and help to
explain why some emotional stimuli can precipitate
asthmatic attacks in predisposed individuals.

Retrospective evidence that chronic stressors can
precipitate or perpetuate asthma should be tested pro-
spectively. Older research indicates that some social
settings are strong risk factors of bronchial asthma.
Rigorous confirmation of those results would be a first
step in exploring the use of family therapy, social
management, and behavioral modification to alter family
interactions that appear to be associated.

Effects of stressors on the course of other pulmonary diseases, particularly chronic obstructive pulmonary
disease (COPD), should receive greater attention. Except
for asthma, pulmonary disorders generally have been of
little interest to stress researchers. A growing understanding of mechanisms through which the brain can alter
pulmonary function suggests the value of expanding
stress-related research in this area. For example, can
psychosocial stressors affect the way in which a person
adapts to chronic obstructive lung disease?

Hematological Disorders

Research is needed on how psychosocial stressors can
alter mechanisms that regulate blood clotting. Recently,
there have been major strides in elucidating the inter-
dependent systems that control bleeding. Do stressors
modify some of these systems? The hemophilias offer one
model in which to study such associations. The resulting
information also may have implications for other disorders, including some cardiovascular diseases.

Better controlled studies of stressors as risk factors for bleeding episodes in hemophiliacs should clarify their importance. Although existing research is suggestive, too many mechanisms unrelated to stress might explain the apparent associations between stress and bleeding. Studies should utilize more objective measures for assessing bleeding status and consider other factors, for example differences in risk-taking.

Physical Disorders as Chronic Stressors

Investigators also should consider possible effects of physical disorders as stressors that may have health consequences. Chronic illnesses such as renal failure, diabetes, and hypertension offer opportunities to look for such stress-related reactions and consequences. Are there patterns for either reactions or consequences? What are the mediating factors? Do the results suggest any intervention strategies?

Stress and Mental Disorders

Definitions of Mental Disorders

Many people believe that diagnoses of mental disorders are much more idiosyncratic and unreliable than are those for physical disorders. Such beliefs represent two types of misperceptions. First, some kinds of physical diseases can be diagnosed reliably and objectively, but many others cannot, particularly in mild or early forms. For example, the diagnosis of rheumatic fever is based on a list of major and minor criteria; cases that present with unusual symptoms can be extremely difficult to classify. Second, efforts over the past decade have improved the consistency of diagnoses of mental disorders. Although there still are no objective biological or physiological measurements to supplement psychological assessments, it is possible to categorize patients by diagnostic subtypes in a highly reliable way.

In the United States, the principle classification system for mental disorders is the third edition of the Diagnostic and Statistical Manual of Mental Disorders (DSM-III) (American Psychiatric Association, 1980). DSM-III conceptualizes a mental disorder as a behavioral or psychological syndrome or pattern that is associated with a clinically significant painful symptom or functional impairment. It defines syndromes according to

288

important manifestations that can be assessed with reasonable objectivity. Except for some clearly organic brain disorders, etiologies of the mental disorders still are unknown. For that reason DSM-III names and groups them on the basis of shared clinical features. Thus, the affective disorders include syndromes in which depression is a predominant feature; they are subdivided according to other characteristics that appear to distinguish among important types of depressed patients.

In an approach that differs markedly from previous editions of this manual, DSM-III recommends a multiaxial evaluation of patients. Two axes of the diagnosis relate to descriptors of mental disorders, a third pertains to physical disorders and conditions, a fourth provides information about the severity of psychosocial stressors, and the fifth axis assesses the highest level of adaptive functioning during the past year. Thus, in its full form, the DSM-III diagnosis evaluates far more than the presence or absence of a specific mental disorder.

Schizophrenia

Environmental stressors could affect schizophrenics in several ways. Chronic life stressors might progressively limit competence and coping skills, interacting with genetically determined biological factors to enhance vulnerability to the onset of schizophrenia; they also might increase the risk for and severity of recurrence of symptoms in a schizophrenic in remission. Acute life stressors might initiate onset of symptoms or shorten periods of remission.

Chronic Life Stressors

Of many environmental factors studied, only lower socioeconomic status and sustained exposure to disordered family relationships have correlated consistently with increased vulnerability for the first episode of schizophrenia. Disordered family relationships and socioeconomic status are not independent. There are more father-absent families in low-status families, but high-status families may have less of an extended-family structure to provide support.

Schizophrenia and lower socioeconomic status are inversely correlated: a disproportionately high incidence of schizophrenia is present in the lowest classes

289

(Kohn, 1973). Investigators have made varied hypotheses about downward social drift, downward genetic drift, and negative impact of poverty in attempts to explain this association.

Evidence of a correlation between the development of schizophrenia and the presence of disordered family relationships is not as strong as that for lower socio-economic status. Still, some research suggests that individuals who later become schizophrenic are more likely than others to have gone through crucial developmental periods while in families that could not maintain appropriate communication, had deviant or atypical role structures, and had a negative affective environment (Goldstein and Rodnick, 1975). In a five-year, prospective study, Doane et al. (1981) found that deviant communication patterns within the family and parental expression of negative feelings toward an adolescent were risk factors for schizophrenia. These two risk factors were independent of one another and additive. Although interesting, this study does not prove that a stressful family environment increases the risk of being schizophrenic. For example, genes that create vulnerability to schizophrenia also might cause deviant communication patterns in the family. Only studies of adopted or cross-fostered subjects could distinguish between these alternative explanations of the data.

Several excellent studies suggest a correlation between disordered family relationships and risk that a schizophrenic will relapse after symptoms have remitted. Brown et al. (1972) used the term "high expressed emotion" for homes in which families are highly critical of and overinvolved with a schizophrenic member. They found that over 50 percent of patients returning to such a home relapsed, compared with 13 percent of patients returning to a home with low expressed emotion.

Acute Life Stressors

The influence of stressful life events on the onset of a schizophrenic episode is controversial (Dohrenwend and Egri, 1981; Rabkin, 1980). Several groups have compared the rates and types of life events recently experienced by patients having a schizophrenic episode with those experienced by controls. The two best studies (Brown and Birley, 1968; Jacobs and Myers, 1976) used appropriate controls and tried to identify and date the

290

occurrence of schizophrenic episodes. They also considered whether the stressful events were independent of
the disease course, because major life events such as
increased job loss, family disagreements, and change in
economic status might be early manifestations of the
disease (cf. Chapter 4, Stress and Life Events). In both
studies, schizophrenic patients experienced significantly
higher rates of life events during the reporting period
than did controls. However, most of the excess was in
events that could reflect the mental disorder, which
might be interpreted as meaning that schizophrenic
patients are more likely to get themselves into stressful situations (Fontana et al., 1972). Still, Brown and
Birley (1968) also found an excess of independent events
in the three-week period before the onset of a patient's
first episode, or before recurrence in subsequent episodes. Of the patients, 46 percent experienced at least
one such episode during that period, compared with 12
percent for controls. Leff et al. (1973) found a similar
build-up of independent events in the period just prior
to relapse in a sample of schizophrenics being treated
in the community with antipsychotics.

As a group, schizophrenics do not seem to experience
markedly more severe or catastrophic events just prior to
disease onset or recurrence than do controls; but, some
of them do have such events (Dohrenwend and Egri, 1981).
Furthermore, individuals at risk for schizophrenia may
react idiosyncratically to seemingly minor stressors.
In agreement with such an interpretation, Serban (1975)
found that the magnitude of stressful responses to daily
living was much higher for chronic schizophrenics than
for normal controls, with acute schizophrenics falling
between the two. It is also possible that stressful life
events do not change the symptoms that a schizophrenic
is having but do precipate a visit to the doctor, which
results in a diagnosis. Further research is needed to
determine how personal and social conditions affect the
occurrence and accumulation of events in the interval
just before the onset of a schizophrenic episode.

Depression

Most people have experienced the sadness, tearful-
ness, and disturbed sleep and appetite that can be a
part of the grief response to an unexpected loss and can
imagine that some stressors might produce a prolonged
episode of depression.

291

Chronic Life Stressors

Only two published epidemiological studies have employed DSM-III criteria for diagnosing depression. Brown
and Harris (1978) found a strong inverse association
between social class and unipolar depression; this is
consistent with reports of a similar relationship between
social class and scores on a scale of depressive symptomatology (Weissman and Klerman, 1977). Weissman and
Myers (1978) found such a relationship for prevalance but
not for life-time incidence. Debates about the meaning
of these differences continue. To date, studies have not
had enough patients among diagnostic subgroups to test
for differences in social class. Paykel and Rowan (1979)
have suggested that people with bipolar depression may
have some social advantage from the hypomanic component
of the syndrome and that lower socioeconomic status may
increase the risk of stress-related types of depressions.
This hypothesis remains to be tested adequately.

The potential contribution of chronic stressors to
the etiology of depression has received relatively
little research. Brown and Harris (1978) reported that
individuals who lived for two years in situations they
perceived as threatening had an increased risk of depression. Depressed patients who live in families of high
expressed emotion, particularly of a critical and hostile
kind, also may be more likely to relapse (Vaughan and
Leff, 1976). Several studies have shown that rates of
depression for women are two to three times higher than
are those for men; rates are particularly high for young
wives and mothers (Weissman and Klerman, 1977). There
is some evidence that women are more stressed than men
or are more sensitive to stressors that they encounter
(Dohrenwend et al., 1978), but other studies failed to
find such differences (Uhlenhuth et al., 1974). One of
the difficulties of such studies may be that many of the
stressors for women are not events but the absence of
events, including boredom and the lack of opportunity for
interesting activities. It might be useful to examine
biological, psychological, and sociological sex differences that could contribute to differential responses
to stress. Comparisons among high- and low-risk groups
for each sex would help to clarify the magnitude and
specificity of such effects.

Several groups have studied the loss of a parent
during childhood as a risk factor for adult depression.
A recent critical review of more than 20 controlled
studies found no conclusive evidence of an association

(Crook and Eliot, 1980), but some suggestive findings
about the effects of certain types of childhood bereavement need more research (Brown and Harris, 1978;
Dohrenwend and deFigueiredo, in press). Much of the
uncertainty about the effects of early bereavement arises
from the difficulty of obtaining adequate controls for
factors such as socioeconomic status and age of parents.
Also, rates of early death have declined throughout this
century, and divorce rates have risen, altering the
cause and probability that a child will lose a parent.
Furthermore, some types of early death, such as by suicide or as a result of alcoholism, may themselves be risk
factors for depression in the offspring. The rigors of
trying to control for these and other critical factors
make it unlikely that additional retrospective studies
will resolve the central issues. Long-term prospective
studies would be much more informative, because many of
the important confounding variables can be excluded.
Such studies also could explore what aspects of growing
up in a disturbed family affect the later development of
mental disorders.

Acute Life Stressors

There have been a number of retrospective, controlled studies of life events and depression (Paykel, in
press). Two large studies found that depressed patients
experienced many more life events just prior to the onset
of an episode than did the general population (Brown et
al., 1973; Paykel et al., 1969). They also have more
life events before an episode than do schizophrenics
(Rabkin, 1980), but differences between depression and
anxiety states are equivocal (Uhlenhuth and Paykel,
1973). Compared with the general population, individuals entering a depressive episode appear to experience
more events that produce loss of other persons or threats
to self esteem. Events involving marital disharmony
figure prominently. Specificity seems to be limited:
depressive episodes are preceded by a wide range of
events, although most are unwanted or produce negative
feelings.

Some depressions seem to be unrelated to life
events. In fact, the presence or absence of a clear precipitating event has been a criterion for distinguishing
among different subtypes of depression. However, several
studies have recently suggested that the number of life
events differs, at most, only slightly as a function of
the type of depression (Brown et al., 1979). Character-

istics of depressions that are not associated with major life events should be determined.

Bipolar depression, in which individuals experience both depressive and manic episodes, also is of interest. Acute events preceding mania have not received much study. One group reported that manics experienced more life events before a disease episode than did controls about to have surgery (Patrick et al., 1978). The difference was particularly evident in patients having their first manic attack, raising the possibility that stressors might be more important in precipitating the disorder than in perpetuating it. However, this study did not look at life events that were independent of the illness. Because mania may lead to many life events before diagnosis, such distinctions are crucial.

Little is known about the effect of acute and chronic stressors on relapse rates. In one early study, patients who no longer faced factors during follow-up that had been present at the onset of the episode had better outcomes than did those for whom such factors still existed (Havens, 1957). In a more recent study, the occurrence of undesirable life events during the preceding three months increased the risk of relapse (Paykel and Tanner, 1976).

Suicide is a dramatic manifestation of depression. Both the intensity and the timing of threatening life events correlate with suicide and attempted suicide (Paykel, 1976). The life events seem to have little specificity, although an event that isolates an individual from significant relationships can be particularly influential. Again, existing studies often have lacked proper controls, and there have been few efforts to establish temporal relationships between a particular stressor and suicidal behavior.

Studies of suicide suggest that stressful events interact with individual vulnerability. As a group, those who attempt suicide have a higher incidence of personality disorders, with character traits such as impulsivity and chronic anger; those who succeed are more likely to have had diagnoses of major depression, alcoholism, or schizophrenia (Barraclough et al., 1974; Hankoff, 1976). Pokorny and Kaplan (1976) tried to identify vulnerability factors that are unrelated to disease processes by comparing depressed patients who committed suicide with controls matched both for type and severity of depression and for other socioeconomic factors. On admission for the last hospitalizaton before the suicide attempt, subjects differed from controls by having a higher "defenseless score," consisting of feelings of guilt and inferiority, anxiety, depressed mood, and suicidal ideation. Unfortunately, no information is available about how the subjects felt at the time of suicide. The search for vulnerability factors that increase the risk of suicidal behavior after adverse life events merits further support, because it may help to identify those who are in particular danger.

Anxiety Disorders

Anxiety is a feeling that everyone has had at some time. It is not viewed as a problem unless it becomes so severe that it interferes with daily life. Typically, anxiety develops when individuals believe that circumstances are making or will make demands that exceed their abilities (Johnson, 1975; Sarason, 1980); in some ways, it is a prototype of stress-induced emotional disturbances. DSM-III defines anxiety disorders as conditions in which overt anxiety and accompanying symptomatology predominate or in which anxiety is experienced if the individual tries to master the symptom, as in confronting a phobia or resisting a compulsion. Also included are the post-traumatic stress disorders.

A better understanding of the physiological and psychological characteristics of anxiety might reveal ways in which stressors produce other psychological and physical changes. Some disorders might result either from inattention to early warnings because of anxious preoccupation or from overattentiveness to relatively benign stimuli. The well person is of particular interest. Given a specific adverse situation, how do reactions of anxious and unanxious people differ? What are the respective psychological and physiological consequences of those reactions? The life course also is an important consideration. Stressors and accompanying anxieties vary throughout life. There is some evidence that people use different coping mechanisms at different stages in their lives (Valliant, 1977). It is less clear what stimulates an individual to develop new coping styles and what factors determine whether they will be more or less adaptive than those they replace.

Recent research into biological aspects of anxiety has produced interesting results and promising leads. Redmond (1977) found that chemical or electrical stimula-

tion of an area in the brain called the locus coeruleus
can lead to behavior that is indistinguishable from that
seen in fear-producing situations. He has hypothesized
that the brain may have a specific "alarm system" for
which the feeling of anxiety is a psychological manifestation. The discovery in the 1960s of benzodiazepines,
which reduce anxiety, provided considerable impetus for
studies of brain systems that might be involved. They
are the most commonly prescribed drugs in the United
States (Institute of Medicine, 1979a). The benzodiazepines affect many parts of the brain and may act, in
part, by increasing the inhibitory activity of the neuroregulator gamma-aminobutyric acid (GABA) (Tallman et al.,
1978). Some nerve cells appear to have benzodiazepine
receptors, suggesting that they might enhance the action
of an as yet unidentified endogenous "antianxiety" substance (Braestrup and Squire, 1978). However, discovery
of an antianxiety system might leave unanswered questions
about what produces the physiological effects of anxiety
such as motor tension (trembling, restlessness, easy
startle) and autonomic hyperactivity (rapid pulse and
respiratory rate, sweating, dry mouth, frequent urina-
tion) (cf. Biological Substrates of Stress, Chapter 8).

Posttraumatic Stress Disorders

Posttraumatic stress disorders typically occur
after exposure to a major stressor such as an earthquake, fire, or torture; they may be more severe and
longer lasting if the stressor is of human design. In
DSM-III, these disorders are characterized by repeated,
vivid recollections of the traumatic event; decreased
responsiveness to or involvement with the external world,
and a variety of symptoms, both physiological and psychological. Often, there is marked autonomic arousal, with
hyperalertness and an exaggerated startle response, and
there may be sleep disturbance. The disorder can occur
at any stage of life. Pre-existing mental problems may
be a predisposing factor.

Psychological reactions to major stressors seem to
be paradoxical, with some phases dominated by intrusive
experiences and others by denial, ideational constriction, and emotional numbing (Horowitz, 1975, 1976). The
intrusive qualities range in intensity from appropriate
disturbances of equilibrium that include mourning and
transient periods of adjustment to pathological disturbances such as the posttraumatic stress disorders.
These manifestations are not always clear enough for
definitive diagnosis of a posttraumatic syndrome. At

times, a stressor is associated with a mental illness
such as depression; at other times, a characteristic
intensification of normal stress response tendencies
warrants a diagnosis of posttraumatic stress disorder.
But even in the latter case, symptoms and signs usually
result from a combined causality: the event is invariably appraised in relation to preexisting self concepts,
vulnerabilities, and psychological conflicts. Thus,
recent studies suggest that bereavement may reactivate
latent, unfavorable self concepts that had been controlled by the positive gains of relationship (Horowitz
et al., 1980a).

Increasingly refined techniques are being used to
study the posttraumatic stress disorders (Coelho et al.,
1974; Hamilton and Warburton, 1979; Horowitz et al.,
1980b; Parad, 1976). Of special interest are clinical
and epidemiological studies of the frequency of posttraumatic stress disorders after common stressful life
events. For example, Kaltreider et al. (1979) found that
a small subgroup of women developed such a syndrome after
hysterectomy; Malinak et al. (1979) obtained similar results with parental deaths.

Phobic Disorders

Phobic disorders refer to a cluster of syndromes
that have in common the avoidance of a specific object,
activity, or situation because of irrational fears.
Many phobics believe that they became fearful following
a stressful encounter; however, efforts to document such
encounters often fail to confirm the reports. Most
available studies of associations between life events
and the onset of phobic disorders have lacked systematic
assessments of stressors or diagnosis or both, and almost
all have lacked appropriate controls. Most studies have
been retrospective, using patients who have been ill for
many years before the study and who may be unable to
remember accurately the circumstances surrounding the
onset of the disorder. Presently, there is no compelling
evidence that phobics have experienced more stressful or
qualitatively different life events than have nonphobics.
For many studies, a large minority of the patients failed
to identify any specific stressor as an etiological factor. Those who do report life events preceding illness
onset most often describe bereavement, object loss, and
leaving a role (Barrett, 1979, Shafer, 1976).

Stressors could have an etiological role in phobias
without being especially prevalent, if some people were

297

predisposed to react to daily stressors by becoming
phobic. No specific predisposing factors have been
identified (Burglass et al., 1977; Torgersen, 1979).
However, the few available family studies of anxiety
disorders, including phobias, show familial clusters
(Crowe et al., 1980), which might suggest a genetic, or
biological component. These findings are consistent with
those of Torgersen (1979), who compared monozygotic to
dizygotic twins and found that genetic factors affected
the probability of having phobic fears for all but
separation fears. Environmental stressors also might
increase the likelihood of developing a phobia indi-
rectly by altering body function. For example, Klein
(1964) has suggested that some phobic patients first
experience panic attacks during periods of endocrine
fluctuation. Efforts to identify important interactions
between genetically determined biological predispositions
and subsequent environmental stressors will require
large-scale prospective studies of patients and their
families. Such projects should help to provide more
precise information about who is at risk for developing
phobic disorders and how great that risk may be.

Alcoholism and Drug Abuse

Both alcoholism and drug abuse are widespread health
problems. Both can be difficult to define; but most
definitions require that abuse interfere with daily life,
resulting in job loss, law violations, health problems,
interpersonal disruptions, or other objective indications
of a problem. In many ways, alcoholism closely resembles other forms of drug abuse; however, alcohol's ready
availability and widespread social use have placed it in
a separate category.

Among their many causes, alcoholism and drug abuse
both might result from an effort to cope with life stresses. Presently, the importance of stressors for the
initiation of drug use is unknown. Clayton (in press)
found that alcohol use increased during the first year
following the death of a spouse, but she did not document
an increase in problem drinking or alcoholism. Patients
applying for treatment commonly report that they began
using drugs or alcohol to combat physical or psychic
pain, but McAuliffe and Gordon (1974) found that heavy
drug abusers who were not seeking treatment typically had
started and continued to use drugs for pleasure, rather
than to relieve discomfort. This study illustrates a
problem with research on mental disorders: patients who

are anxious to find a specific reason for their discomfort, particularly if being questioned about its origins, may ascribe cause to a remembered or imagined stressor.

Studies of vulnerability are central to any evaluation of the role of stress in alcoholism and drug abuse. Given that everyone is faced at times with severe life stressors, why do only some people become abusers? Would they have begun using drugs or alcohol anyway? What are the interactive effects of the availability of a particular substance and a high level of stress? Studies by Robins et al. (1978) of Vietnam veterans suggest that stressors associated with being in combat resulted in an abnormally large number of people experimenting with opiates and marijuana, compared with what should have happened had they stayed in the United States. Use of barbiturates and amphetamines, which were not so readily available, did not differ from predicted levels. But, increased drug use may not mean that a disproportionately large number of those men became abusers or remained abusers after they came home.

Recent analyses of alcohol drinking patterns of veterans two years after they returned from Vietnam suggest that exposure to dangerous situations in Vietnam resulted in an increased incidence of alcoholism among individuals who initially reported that they were light or regular drinkers; similar but less marked trends hold for those who initially reported that they were heavy drinkers (Ted Reich, personal communication). These data are preliminary, because some differences in age and education remain to be taken into account; also, assignment to combat duty was not a random process and may not be independent of developing alcoholism. The results are consistent with the experience of the Inupiat Eskimos, a tribe that had no native alcohol and no social system for using it. Faced with tremendous social stressors associated with building the Alaskan pipeline and having alcohol readily available for the first time, that tribe now has an estimated 70 percent incidence of alcoholism (Klausner et al., 1980). In a recent review of research opportunities in alcoholism and alcohol abuse, the Institute of Medicine (1980) concluded that a better understanding of the biological and psychosocial factors which affect the adoption of drug use and interfere with its cessation could be valuable in constructing effective prevention and treatment programs.

Also of considerable interest are the stressors that result from continued alcoholism or drug abuse and from efforts to stop such abuse. McLellan et al. (1979) recently described a six-year longitudinal study of drug abusers who initially were free of depression and psychosis. They found that, with continued drug use, chronic opiate abusers showed no significant changes, sedative abusers developed severe depression, and chronic psychostimulant abusers became psychotic. It is unclear whether these results relate solely to drug use, entail an unmasking of preexisting conditions, or reflect a drug preference among individuals predisposed to certain types of psychological difficulties. Similarly, physiological and psychological stressors that accompany drug withdrawal may be central to continued drug use. The mechanisms through which those stressors act are poorly understood. Studies of them requires cross-disciplinary research incorporating biological, psychological, and sociological perspectives.

Sleep Disturbance

The commonplace experience of sleep disturbances following acute stressors has been confirmed experimentally (Goodyear, 1973; Lester et al., 1967). Also, Healey (1976) found that, compared with controls, chronic insomniacs recalled having undergone significantly more stressful life events during the year in which insomnia began, suggesting that acute stressors which alter sleep might induce long-term sleep disturbances. However, other evidence is more consistent with sleep being protective. For example, Cohen (1975) noted that subjects who underwent mildly threatening experiences before bedtime had increased amounts of rapid-eye-movement (REM) sleep and suggested that sleep might provide a psychological defense. Aakvaag et al. (1978) showed that even short periods of sleep during a five-day military exercise could reverse stress-related changes in growth hormone, prolactin, and testosterone. Perhaps altered sleep is a physiological response to stress that leads to actual sleep disturbances only under certain extreme conditions.

Sleep disorders have been associated with disease consequences. In a large prospective study, Kripke et al. (1979) found that otherwise healthy individuals who initially reported that they habitually slept substantially less or more than average were much more likely than controls to have died by the six-year follow-up. There are many potential explanations for this finding,

300

but they all imply a complex relationship between sleep
habits and general health. A topic of great importance
is the appropriate use and long-term effects of pharmacological agents for those who are unable to sleep
(Institute of Medicine, 1979a).

Sleep deprivation itself is psychologically and
physiologically stressful. At least for limited periods,
it can have activating effects. Mendelson et al. (1977)
reported that from one third to one half of severely
depressed patients showed a transitory antidepressant
response after a full night of sleep deprivation. Prolonged sleep deprivation can produce marked decrements
in performance, coordination, motivation, and concentration. An increased appreciation for the importance of
biological rhythms has encouraged a reexamination of
sleep deprivation as a stressor. For example, Taub et
al. (1976) described performance deficits in normal
subjects whose sleep was displaced forward or backwards
by three hours, even though their total sleep time was
essentially unchanged. Studies of sleep deprivation are
directly relevant to concerns about adverse health consequences of jobs that require frequent changes in
schedules (cf. Chapter 6, Work Stress Related to Social
Structures and Processes).

Biological Markers of Stress Vulnerability

A critical need in stress research is a way to
identify people who are especially vulnerable to adverse
effects of stressors. For mental disorders, a biological
marker would be particularly useful, because it is objective and relatively independent of the disease process.
Interest in this area has been low, primarily because
there have been few clues about what systems stressors
might affect in ways that would alter the onset or course
of a mental disorder. However, strides that have been
made in understanding severe mental disorders and in
elucidating mechanisms involved in stress reactions have
improved the feasibitiy of such studies.

Several good studies provide evidence of genetic
effects on schizophrenia (Kety, 1975), suggesting a
biological contribution to the disorder. A few physiological abnormalities also have been found in some
schizophrenics. Thus, platelet activity of monoamine
oxidase (MAO) is low in some chronic schizophrenics,
compared with appropriate controls (Berger et al., 1978).

301

This enzyme inactivates a number of neuroregulators and therefore might be implicated in some disorder of neuronal function. More recently, some chronic schizophrenics have been found to have ventricular enlargement, with apparent cortical and cerebellar atrophy (Weinberger et al., 1979); these changes are accompanied by measurable decreases in psychological function (Golden et al., 1980). Nothing is known about the ways in which these and other factors interact with the effects of stressors on schizophrenia.

There also have been efforts to determine if some events at birth might contribute to the subsequent development of schizophrenia. The frequency and severity of obstetrical complications is higher for subjects who subsequently develop schizophrenia than for matched controls (Kinney and Jacobsen, 1978). The most common difference between the controls and schizophrenics was that the former had prolonged labor, suggesting the possibility of perinatal brain injury through anoxia. Dalen (1975) reported that from 5-15 percent more schizophrenics are born during the winter or spring than during the rest of the year. Among other possibilities, a seasonal risk factor could result from an infectious agent such as a slow virus (Matthysse and Matthysse, 1978) or from changes in nutritional status of essential vitamins and minerals that might alter, for example, the likihood of intracranial bleeding at birth (Kinney and Jacobsen, 1978).

Investigators have identified a few biological markers of depression. Some types of depression are thought to reflect a defect in the function of the brain neuroregulators norepinephrine and serotonin. A subgroup of depressed patients with a relatively low urinary excretion of 3-methoxy-4-hydroxyphenylglycol (MHPG), a norepinephrine metabolite, seem to respond to antidepressants that are believed to enhance the activity of norepinephrine neurons in the brain (Maas, 1975). Also, some depressed patients have relatively high blood concentrations of corticosteroids, which are involved in stress responses; they fail to suppress steroid secretion appropriately, suggesting a defect in the brain regulation of adrenal secretion (Carroll, 1972). Little research has been done that would relate such biochemical abnormalities to stress vulnerability. The abnormal steroid response is of particular interest, because of its direct relevance to reactions to stressors.

Some investigators have tried to identify factors that increase the overall risk for mental illness of any

302

kind. Buchsbaum et al. (1976) measured platelet MAO
activity in college student volunteers and studied the
ten percent with lowest activities and the ten percent
with highest. The suicide or attempted suicide rate of
families of subjects with low MAO activities was eight
times higher than that for families of those with high
MAO. These researchers subsequently added other measures
of the same subjects, including cortical averaged evoked
potential (Haier et al., 1980). Some people react to
repeated presentations of evoked potentials by increasing
their responses (augmenters); others show a reduced
response (reducers). Among the subjects, augmenters
with low MAO activity and reducers with high MAO both
had a markedly increased risk of receiving a diagnosis
of major depression sometime during the 18 months after
the biological measures were made. These studies again
fail to examine whether the identified individuals are
particularly vulnerable to daily stresses.

Life Course Aspects of Stress and Mental Illness

There is increasing interest in the effects of
changes that occur during the life course on reactions
to stressors. Such considerations may be particularly
cogent to mental disorders, because developmental status
and current mental state could alter profoundly the long-
and short-term consequences of a stressor. At present,
few studies have addressed this topic directly. However,
some research on children and on the elderly suggest the
types of questions that need answers.

Werner et al. (1971) found a strong interaction
between a variety of pre- and perinatal risk factors and
adverse psychosocial factors as risk factors for childhood learning and behavioral disorders. The risk factors
were predictive only in the presence of mediators such as
poor psychological and social supports during development. Whether the apparent increase in mental illness
among these children is real remains unclear; it may
reflect diagnostic or referral biases. For example,
Rutter et al. (1970) found that children with neurological illnesses such as cerebral palsy and epilepsy were
much more likely than other children to receive a
diagnosis of a mental disorder.

Many events that occur during childhood could be
risk factors for the later development of mental illness. We discussed earlier the research on bereavement
during childhood as a possible vulnerability factor for
developing depression as an adult. Despite continued

controversy about who is affected and how seriously,
there is evidence that some, but not all, children
between the ages of six months and four years experience
adverse reactions to separations from significant figures
(Glueck and Glueck, 1968; Rutter, 1974). Investigators
are only starting to delineate the important features of
such separations. Thus, Rutter (1971) found that absence
of the father from home was not demonstrably harmful to
early child development if separation resulted from a
neutral cause such as military service but was harmful if
there was a negative cause such as divorce. The effects
of other stressful events like the birth of a sibling or
moving the household also need to be examined, in light
of the implicit loss of parental attention or of peers.
A major methodological issue in such studies will be the
determination of how stressful a specific event is for a
given child, because reactions may differ greatly depending on the circumstances under which loss occurs.
Exploration of possible interactions of the stressor
with personal predispositions also will be important.
For example, Gaines et al. (1978) compared abused and
nonabused children within the same family and found that
abused children typically were males with difficult
temperament or hyperactivity.

Physical and psychological changes that occur in
the elderly may increase their vulnerability to adverse
psychosocial consequences from environmental stressors.
Heredity, personality, and life events are all implicated
as risk factors in depression in the elderly, although
the relative contribution of each remains to be established (Epstein, 1976). Certainly, the elderly face many
adverse life events, including changes in income and
employment, loss of loved ones, and increased dependence
on others. The cognitive losses associated with even
the early stages of dementia also may greatly limit
available coping strategies, thereby exacerbating the
effects of stressors on the individual. Some chronic
conditions may be tolerated well until additional stressors or the aging process deplete resources so severely
that the individual is no longer able to cope with them.
Thus, the stress of physical illness, particularly for
the poor and isolated aged, may lead to depression and
suicide (Sainsbury, in press). Studies are needed of
the effects of events earlier in the life course on the
subsequent ability to cope with stressors. Also in need
of further research are suggestions that specific characteristics of the surrounding environment may increase or
decrease coping abilities in the elderly (Rodin, 1980).

304

Mental Illnesses as Stressors

Major mental disorders can be severe stressors for the patient and the family. Patients may hear voices or feel compelled to perform peculiar acts; or they may be overwhelmed with real or imagined guilt, wishing only to die. Their interpersonal and economic relationships can deteriorate rapidly, as the illness interferes with work, family, and friends. They may have to face hospitalization, either voluntary or forced, and to cope with being labeled as a mental patient. They also may have to take medications that can have side effects. The family may be flooded with demands as they watch a loved one change and seek ways in which they can help or face the realization that a member of their family has committed suicide.

Using mental disorders as stressors creates a conceptual tangle for studies of how stressors might contribute to illness. First, a mental disorder can alter stress reactions directly by changing the way in which stressors are perceived, as occurs, for example, with paranoid overinterpretations of events, with pathological guilt about past and present activities, or with manic reinterpretation of adverse events. Second, many new stressors occur secondarily to an illness. These stressors may range from major changes in diet and sleep patterns to anxiety-provoking psychotherapy aimed at altering self concepts. Each could have its own effects or could alter the way in which a person reacts to other stressors. Research in this area will have to start slowly. Still, important questions can and should be asked.

The mentally ill utilize a disproportionately large share of medical services (Institute of Medicine, 1979b). It still is unclear if this reflects increased illness or other factors such as low tolerance for physical discomfort, indirect search for help with mental problems, perceptual distortions, or effects of socioeconomic status. The need for increased medical care also might result from nutritional deficits, poor personal hygiene, or unhealthy habits such as drinking and smoking. Epidemiological studies are needed of the distribution of bodily diseases among people who have histories of a mental disorder and among appropriate controls. Such research must be done on samples of the population and include assessments of actual illness rather than of illness behavior. Discrete subgroups such as people who

305

have attempted suicide compared with depressed but
nonsuicidal controls could be especially useful. If
associations are found between specific types of mental
disorders and certain kinds of physical illnesses, underlying mechanisms must be sought. For example, if the
evidence suggests that a nutritional deficit is involved,
an intervention trial of supplements in that population
might be warranted.

A mental disorder might act as a stressor to increase the risk of recurrence of that disorder or the
development of another one. The natural history for most
severe mental disorders is one of repeated episodes,
making it extremely difficult to identify cause and
effect in the course of a single disorder. However, the
effect of one illness on the occurrence of another might
be amenable to research. Such studies are complicated
by the current convention of making major psychiatric
syndromes mutually exclusive. Thus, a diagnosis of
depression excludes a diagnosis of schizophrenia in the
same individual. Longitudinal, double-blind, diagnostic
studies of the sequential appearance of mental disturbances might improve insights into associations that
occur between diagnostic categories. Other aspects of
the disease and treatment process also might be open to
study. For instance, one might compare people who are
untreated or treated as outpatients with equally ill
hospitalized patients, exploring formal diagnosis and
treatment as contributors to later risk of hospitalization for a mental illness.

Animal Models of Stress Effects on Mental Disorders

Animal models enable far more precise control of
test conditions and more direct measurements of brain
activity than are possible with humans. However, use of
such models requires a balance between having a relatively simple system that can be easily studied and
having a model that closely approximates the human
condition of interest (Elliott et al., 1977). For
example, reserpine may produce depression in some people
and worsen complaints of some depressed patients; in
animals it decreases locomotor activity and body temperature. This model of depression has yielded important
information about neurochemical systems involved in
reserpine-induced decreases in activity and temperature,
but it is unclear whether these systems are involved in
human depression. Data gained from such models must
always be tempered with questions about applicability to
the human state.

Models for Specific Mental Disorders

   Animal models of schizophrenia are controversial,
because the psychotic state seems to be a peculiarly
human condition. In people, amphetamines induce a
psychosis that resembles paranoid schizophrenia in many
ways, including its partial reversibility by antipsychotic drugs; in animals, they produce bizarre, stereotypic
behaviors that also are blocked by these drugs (Borison
and Diamond, 1978). Haber et al. (1977) have shown that
it is possible to examine the effects of experimentally
induced stressors on such animals. They may provide an
invaluable tool for gaining a better understanding of
some ways in which life events contribute to or ameliorate schizophrenic symptoms.

   Several animal models of depression are available.
One model involves deliberate exposure to uncontrollable
bad events. Rats, cats, dogs, or nondepressed people
who experience such events become passive, have slowed
thinking, show less aggression and dominance, and have a
decreased appetite (Seligman, 1975). These changes
probably result from the psychological and physiological
consequences of learning that response is futile--a mechanism of possible relevance to some naturally occuring
human depressions. Many drugs that are antidepressants
in man reverse the helplessness in the animal models, and
drugs without antidepressant activity are ineffective
(Porsolt et al., 1977). Also, symptoms do not occur if
animals first are "immunized" by experiencing bad events
that they can control (Hannum et al., 1976). A second
animal model of depression is that of young rhesus and
pigtail monkeys socially separated from their mothers
(Mineka and Suomi, 1978). Separation leads to lethargy,
disoriented locomotion, passivity, social withdrawal,
lack of play, self-absorption, and sleep changes. Contact with older peers during the depression may alleviate
the symptoms, and socially enriched environments prior
to the separation can prevent them. Both models offer
rich areas for research into the specific biological and
psychological mechanisms by which stress may induce
depressive symptoms. They also should provide a basis
for experiments on early environmental risk factors for
depression and for potential prevention and treatment
strategies that later may merit clinical trials.

   Cats, rats, and people exposed repeatedly to a
signal paired with inescapable electric shock subsequently show strong fear and avoidance of such a signal,
suggesting a model of phobias. Laboratory studies have

shown that only biologically relevant signals become targets of phobic fear. In humans, pictures of snakes and spiders are effective; ones of flowers, electrical outlets, or guns are not (Eysenck, 1979). This fear reaction decreases markedly after counter conditioning in which the signal is paired with pleasant events (Wolpe, 1967). Studies of this phobia model led directly to progress in clinical treatment: many otherwise intractable phobias and obsessions now are alleviated with counter-conditioning and other extinction procedures (Wolpe, 1973).

Animals usually will not self-administer alcohol or other addicting drugs voluntarily, making it difficult to obtain animal analogues of human alcohol and drug addiction. However, the potential role of stressful environments has not been explored adequately. Do some environmental and rearing conditions put animals at risk for addiction? If so, is there any specificity to the type of addiction that occurs? How does early experience with drugs and alcohol alter the risk for addiction later? As noted earlier, little yet is known beyond anecdotes about how important life stressors really are in precipitating and maintaining alcoholism and drug addiction.

General Models of Stress Effects on Behavior

Many questions about the effects of stressors on behavior remain unanswered. Chronic, intermittent stressors are probably the most common type of events that people face; yet most animal studies use either acute stressors or chronic, continuous stressors (Burchfield, 1979). Research on models in which the same stimulus is administered repeatedly over time might provide new insights into stress effects. One such model involves repeated administration to rats of the same dose of a psychomotor stimulant such as amphetamine. Instead of producing tolerance, this dosage results in increasingly abnormal behaviors, suggesting a cumulative effect (Segal and Mandell, 1974). Similarly, people who chronically abuse stimulants can develop marked affective and schizophrenic-like changes (Kosman and Unna, 1968). Antelmann et al. (1980) recently found a partial cross-reactivity in animals between the effects of repeated stimulant administration and those of repeated tail-pinch stress, starvation stress, and electric shock. The obvious potential relevance to the effects of stress on drug addiction suggests the need to extend such studies.

308

The intervals between exposures may influence the specific effects of repeated stressors. For example, continuous electrical stimulation of the amygdala region of the brain produces tolerance; intermittent stimulation leads to increasing duration and spread of electrical activity, finally resulting in a major motor seizure (Racine, 1978). Similarly, intermittent amphetamine dosage produces behavioral sensitization; continous administration leads to tolerance (Post, 1980). Might the interval between stressors alter the direction of adaptation, so that intermittent stressors lead to tolerance in some instances and to sensitization and increasing behavioral pathology in others? Such models may be useful for studies of how environmental context can affect behavioral consequences of stressors. What aspects of psychosocial stressors cross-react with psychomotor stimulants, and through what mechanisms? Which neuroregulatory systems are involved in behavioral sensitization? A longitudinal perspective on the effects of repeated stress in producing either behavioral sensitization or adaptation and tolerance may lead not only to increased understanding of underlying mechanisms but also to new approaches to preventing or treating pathological effects of stress that can result.

Specific Research Needs

In examining what is known about how stress influences the onset, course, and prognosis of mental illnesses, the panel identified many areas of needed research. Below, we have identified several important directions for stress-related research for each of the major mental disorders and for the more general concern of how stress can affect mental health.

Schizophrenia

Environmental Life Events. The interaction of stressful life events with potential mediators should be investigated. Among such mediators are: (1) biological status, including genetic predisposition, current nutritional state, and activity of relevant neuroendocrine and neuroregulatory systems; (2) psychological status, including prior experiences, available coping mechanisms, and perceived ability to cope with the problem; and (3) social status, including cultural milieu, background social stressors, and support systems. Issues to be considered in designing such studies include differentiation of events that precede an illness, and therefore may be

309

of etiological significance, from those that may occur as early manifestations of the disease. Using optimal available methods, further research into the role of the events prior to the onset of the initial and subsequent episodes of schizophrenia could be profitable. One issue that might be amenable to this approach is the high incidence of schizophrenia in lower socioeconomic groups.

Research on disordered family relationships might suggest new preventive approaches. Reliable measures of communication deviance and negative affective style could be developed from studies of parents and families containing disturbed offspring. Clinical settings might use such measures to identify family units at high risk of having schizophrenic offspring for special intervention programs designed to modify disordered family relationships. Such measures might alter the present cycle of hospitalization, remission, relapse, and rehospitalization. Efforts to alter the affective environment of the returning schizophrenic patient might be amenable to several approaches: modification of family attitudes and expectations, development of more benign living environments as a substitute for negative home situations, or provision of more support for family units during the after-care period. Also of value would be studies of families that take in disturbed or retarded children and provide for them an environement in which they do well. How do such families help the children, and how do they handle their own frustrations?

Biological Factors. The role of endocrine factors at the peak incidence of schizophrenia in adolescence should receive intensive study. Other potential risk factors that merit more research are obstetrical complications, pre- and perinatal viral infections, prenatal nutritional deficits, low platelet MAO, and enlarged cerebral ventricles. Such factors suggest possible subtypes of schizophrenics among which environmental stressors might be more or less important as precipitators of an episode.

In a few decades, an attempt to reverse genetic defects during pregnancy might be possible. For example, if schizophrenia were found to result from a receptor abnormality, then one might consider the possibility of specifically protecting people who are at high risk for developing schizophrenia by exposing them to appropriate drugs before they are born. Much animal work is needed before consideration of human applications is possible. As a useful data base for such an admittedly distant preventive measure, infants of schizophrenics are already commonly exposed to the antipsychotic medications that their mothers receive. What effects do those drugs have on the subsequent incidence of schizophrenia among those infants and of the response to antipsychotics of those who later become schizophrenics?

Affective Illness and Stress

Environmental Life Events. Further studies are needed of the role of life events in the onset both of initial and recurrent episodes of depression or mania. Such studies must differentiate between those environmental stressors that precede the onset of the first symptoms of depression and those events that increase the severity of preexisting depressive symptomatology. Relatively little attention has been given to the longitudinal study of how life events affect the patterns of recurrence for individual depressed patients. For example, are there similarities among life events that occur immediately before the first, fifth, tenth, and fifteenth depressive episodes?

Special attention should be given to how the appearance, type, and severity of depressive symptoms correlate with characteristics of the conditions under which they occur. There may be differences between independent environmental events such as a letter from the draft board that are outside the control of the individual and events such as being fired from a job that may result from the effects of the disease. Among factors to be considered are personality characteristics and coping styles, biological vulnerabilities such as altered brain neuroregulator systems, and learned psychological vulnerabilities.

Biological Factors. No one has yet determined the sequence of biological reactions to stressors that leads to the symptoms of depression. Delineation of this sequence of events would greatly advance efforts to understand how stressors can affect health. Knowledge about acute biological reactions to severe stressors is growing rapidly; but almost nothing is known about how those changes, alone or in combination, lead to the negative health consequences called mental disorders. Why, for example, do some people react to bereavement with depression, rather than with a reversible grief reaction? What is biologically different about the depressed person that leads to the onset of a depressive

episode? Why is there a higher incidence of depression
in women than in men? Many hypotheses have been generated to explain this empirical observation. Perhaps
certain psychosocial stressors unique to women are
powerful risk factors for depression.

Suicide. More should be learned about suicide and
its impact on the family and friends, and efforts should
be made to apply such information to suicide prevention.
Suicide is preceded by stressors and is also a life
stressor for close friends and family of those who commit
suicide. Several longitudinal studies of suicide may be
timely. One project could explore the interaction
between social stressors and individual vulnerability
due to concurrent mental illness. Follow-up studies of
the surviving spouse and children of completed suicides
over a prolonged period might be undertaken. Such
research could identify factors associated with poor
outcome. For example, should a child be told of the
circumstances surrounding a parent's death by suicide?

A comprehensive attempt could be made to decrease
the rate of suicide in a defined catchment area. This
would require instruction of all physicians and para-
professionals about ways to identify people at risk for
suicide. Everyone who came to physicians could receive a
routine evaluation of suicidal potential. Those showing
suicide potential on screening would receive a more
comprehensive evaluation that might include assessment
of chronic and acute life stressors; past suicidal behavior; current family, social, and community situations;
urine corticosteroids; and psychological and social
coping resources.

Anxiety Disorders

Work on mediators of pathological or adaptive reactions to situational stressors should be continued and
expanded. Existing theory in psychology and dynamic
psychiatry point to the importance of cognitive and
emotional processes and to weaknesses of existing classification schemes for those processes. Basic research
on assessing psychological developmental levels could
provide essential tools required to study intervening
psychological variables. Analogous research is needed
to define the important elements of social networks that
provide support during times of stress.

Additional information is needed about anxiety
disorders before a thorough investigation of the effects

312

of stress is possible. It might be useful to determine
whether children of parents with anxiety reactions are
at risk of developing similar syndromes. The importance
of genetic contributions to this set of disorders is
unknown. Studies of experimentally induced anxiety-like
symptoms with compounds such as yohimbine and piperoxan
also could be useful. Development of chemically induced
models of anxiety would enable investigators to look for
mechanisms through which compounds like antidepressants
and benzodiazepines exert their effects and to assess
the contributory or protective effects of stressful
psychosocial manipulations.

Posttraumatic Stress Disorders. Studies of secondary prevention of posttraumatic stress disorders appear
to be feasible. Efforts should be made to identify
populations at high risk. Such populations could be
used to test different kinds of interventions that might
prevent posttraumatic stress disorders or other psychological and physical disorders. Research on the most
effective therapy of stress response syndromes should be
a high priority. Treatment approaches should be brief,
focused on current sources of stress, and intended to
restore prestress equilibrium.

Phobic Disorders. A prospective analysis of factors that increase the incidence of phobias, including
cultural setting, family incidence, and environmental
stressors, would be valuable. Studies should make use
of DSM-III classifications of phobia. For example, is
the importance of life events related to the diagnostic
subcategory? It may be useful to study the association
between stressors and fluctuations in the course of phobic disorders, thus avoiding the problem of identifying
the point of onset of what is often a chronic illness.
Such research should include measures of biological factors that might be predictive of individual differences
in reactions to stressors.

Alcoholism and Drug Abuse

Prospective studies are needed of the effects of
stressful life events in populations at high or low risk
for alcoholism and drug abuse. Alcoholism is strongly
familial, but little is known about cultural and biological elements of transmission. Also of interest are
high-stress situations in which alcohol or drugs might
be used as self medication. What psychological and
social factors promote such uses, and what conditions
promote the progression of use to abuse? Drug abuse

313

usually is characterized by periodic involvement with
and at times dependence on various drugs. Do stressors
affect which drugs indivuduals select for use and abuse
or the timing of changes they make to different drugs?
Also, some drug addicts become highly conditioned by
such external factors as the street corner where they
obtained drugs, the paraphenalia used in taking the
drug, or the acquaintances involved in the drug-taking
behavior, so that exposure to any of these stimuli can
initiate the desire to use drugs. It would be of great
interest to examine interactions between these variables
and stressful life events.

Animal Models of Stress in Mental Illness

There are animal models for depression, psychotic-
like behavior, phobias, anxiety, and drug and alcohol
addiction. None duplicate the human conditions exactly,
and efforts to improve the models should continue. But
the available models still provide a rich resource for
exploring the effects of stressors. Can stressors in
early life be risk factors for subsequent development of
disease? Can such effects be prevented with early
interventions? Because experimental animals like rats
and mice have relatively short life spans, investigators
can test the effects of exposure during development to
conditions such as isolation, environmental enrichment,
or nutritional changes on susceptibility to disease as
adults. For example, the controllability and predictability of events markedly affects how an animal will
react. Could a series of specific events create symptoms
that mimic depression or psychosis? If so, what are the
important determinants of such an outcome? Are there
ways to protect against it, and might these be of value
in designing prevention efforts for people?

Life Course Issues in Stress

Research on stress in children has been relatively
neglected. Long-term prospective surveys of childhood
mental illness would help. Such a survey could be
included as part of the major prospective study proposed
below. Also, prospective studies could establish whether
birth trauma and anoxia are risk factors for such disorders as minimal brain disorder, learning disorders,
and schizophrenia. Naturally occurring disasters have
been utilized on a number of occasions to study adults,
but rarely to study children. Plane crashes in which a
large group of children lose their parents might provide

314

some very important information concerning the effects
on children of the sudden loss of a parent.

Studies also are needed of health-related effects
of stressors on the eldery. Are stressors associated
nonspecifically with a wide range of disorders, or does
organ vulnerability influence the diseases that occur?
What factors in institutional settings like nursing homes
contribute to or ameliorate the effects of stressors?

General Issues on Stress and Mental Illness

Risk Factors of Mental Disorders. High priority
should be given to support for a large, prospective,
longitudinal study of risk factors for mental illness.
One of the clear items of consensus for all areas of
mental illness was the need for a Framingham-like study
in the mental health field. Improvements in diagnostic
precision and measures of outcome provide the necessary
clinical tools. Advances in the understanding of genetic, biochemical, psychological, and social factors for
such diseases as schizophrenia, depression, phobias, and
alcohol and drug abuse offer clues about risk factors.
Among such factors are life events, although their specificity for particular disorders still remains uncertain.

A longterm, longitudinal study of a reasonably sized
population in a geographically limited area could provide
data with tremendous basic science and therapeutic value.
Community sources would have to be mobilized to maximize
cooperation from the target population. Baseline studies
should provide useful cross-sectional data about the
level of exposure individuals experience for a number of
environmental factors that might affect mental health.
Follow-up studies of the same subjects would greatly
enhance the value of the project, providing information
about sequential effects. Who gets ill? What has
happened to them in the past? How does physical health
affect mental health? Furthermore, it offers an ideal
structure in which to begin to identify preventive or
treatment strategies and assess their potential utility.

Periodically Recurrent Stressors. Periodic intermittent stressors deserve special research attention.
Chronic and acute stressors are of obvious practical and
theoretical importance; however, many life events fit
neither of those two categories. Instead, they entail
repeated exposure to an acute stressor over time. The
observation in animals that repeated exposure to a
stressor can increase sensitivity to it has implications

315

for stress and disease processes in man. How do people respond to repeated exposure to stressful life events? Does the reaction change for people with a severe mental disorder? Research that attempts to delineate the significance of the time interval between exposures to a stressor, the effect of repeated stressors, and the possibility that sensitization occurs in people appears to be particularly promising. If someone becomes sensitive to an environmental stressor such as a significant loss, is the effect of the second, third, or fourth loss additive because of sensitization; or does each become relatively less traumatic? Is the result affected by the timing of such losses? Does the person who becomes increasingly sensitive to loss show any cross-sensitivity to other types of life events, or is such sensitization relatively specific?

Sleep Changes and Stress. Studies are needed of the ways in which stressors exert their profound effects on sleep. One of the most frequent disturbances associated with stress is sleep disruption. This often is the first manifestation of stress and may become an additional stressor. What are the biological pathways by which a variety of stressors produce this common effect? Are these systems involved in other effects on behavior? Is sleep a successful form of coping for some people in reaction to stress? If so, how?

Major Disasters and Changes in Health. One or more teams should be developed to respond on short notice to natural experiments for studying the effects of major stressors on health. Natural and man-made disasters are profound stressors. Usually, efforts to study such situations have been too late or too poorly designed to be of value. A standing team that already had prepared for studies in such extreme settings could collect invaluable biological, physiological, and psychosocial data. As appropriate, such a group also could incorporate research into early intervention and treatment in an effort to prevent many of the adverse sequellae that can follow such disasters.

Health-Promoting Aspects of Stress. Researchers should give more attention to the potential protective or health-promoting effects of stress. For too long, stressors have been defined as necessarily harmful. Stress research has focused almost entirely on the adverse consequences of stressors. Some evidence suggests that desirable consequences also are possible. It will be important to incorporate measures of such effects

316

into studies of stress and health and to study possible interactions between negative and positive consequences.

Summary

There is a large and diverse array of evidence of an effect of stress on the predisposition to, precipitation of, and perpetuation of a number of major physical and mental disorders. Early studies of stress and physical illness generated excitement because they suggested a framework in which to understand such varied disorders as peptic ulcers, hypertension, and bronchial asthma. Similarly, more recent studies of stress and mental illness have suggested mechanisms to account for the onset and course of psychological disorders like depression and schizophrenia.

The early studies of stress effects often could not withstand careful scrutiny by the scientific and medical community. Attempts to replicate major findings sometimes yielded conflicting or equivocal results. Factors thought to be specific for one disease reappeared in the context of other, seemingly unrelated disorders. Furthermore, answers provided by such research generated yet more questions. Why were some people affected and not others? How could stressors affect such diverse systems as endocrine glands, the gastrointestinal tract, and the lung? Why did there seem to be no consistent physiological changes? For many, the inability to answer those and related questions led to disillusionment in stress research.

Many of the difficulties in the early stress studies resulted from unavoidable technological limitations. In the past few years, the biological sciences have discovered a growing number of substances and systems through which the brain can monitor and exert control over the rest of the body (cf. Biological Substrates of Stress, Chapter 8). Most were unknown when the classical stress studies were done. Similarly, over the past decade, the psychological and social sciences have developed more sophisticated research designs that avoid many of the difficulties on which the early stress studies foundered. We believe that it is time to reassess the role of stress in health and disease, taking advantage of the rich new investigative tools that are available.

Conceptual Issues of Stress Research (Chapter 2) suggests a framework in which to identify important

317

areas of stress research--potential activators (x), reactions (y), consequences (z), and mediators. The first area relates to identification of environmental events, or stressors, themselves and to their measurement and interrelationships; the second area comprises the delineation of the physiological, biochemical, and psychosocial processes that these stressors induce in the individual; the third entails assessment of ensuing health changes or disease consequences; and the last involves discovery of specific factors that modify interactions among the other three. Most available research demonstrates either that x and z are associated or that x can produce y. There is little or no information on how y leads to z or on important x-y or y-z mediators.

Our review identified a number of examples of sequences that we know are reasonably certain. These can be contrasted with examples in the same disease of what we need to know.

- We know that Type A individuals can be identified reliably and that Type A behavior is a risk factor of coronary artery disease. We need to know why only some Type A people get coronary artery disease. In other words, we are aware of the x, and x-z, but know very little about x-y and virtually nothing about y-z. We need to know what risk factors augment the effects of the Type A behavior pattern and, more basically, by what biological mechanisms it imposes its effect in the same sense that high cholesterol, another risk factor, operates by depositing more plaques in the artery.

- We know that some stressors can elevate blood pressure, producing transient hypertension. Also, we know that these reactions are more marked in people who have a genetic susceptibility to hypertension; this appears to be a mediator for the y-z transition. We need to know if these reactions result in hypertension because of their quantitative accumulation or their qualitative nature and what the relevant pathways from the central nervous sytem to the periphery are.

- We know that a variety of laboratory stressors produce changes in acid secretion and perhaps motility of the stomach; and we have some evidence that, under certain circumstances, psychosocial changes can be associated with the development of peptic ulcer. The former is an x-y transition; the latter, an x-z transition. We need to know what mediators such as parietal cell mass, levels of pepsinogen, early life experiences, or an oral dependent character combine with this reactivity to produce peptic ulcer. Also, we need to know why the prevalence and incidence of peptic ulcer has been decreasing in recent years. This latter is a complex x-z transition.

- We know that many behavioral stressors can precipitate bronchoconstriction and asthma. This x-z transition is readily apparent clinically and experimentally. We need to know more about how such events influence the interrelationships of neurogenic and immune responses in the development of bronchoconstriction. In the acute episode, this is primarily an x-y transition. In its more repetitive and chronic state, we need to know the y-z mediators that perpetuate the disorder.

- We know from several excellent studies that immune responses can be conditioned in animals, an x-y transition. We need to know much more about the central nervous system and peripheral pathways by which the antibody-antigen release and complexing come about. The demonstration that immune responses can be conditioned is exciting, because previously it had been thought that the central nervous system could not influence the immune response.

- We know that certain types of stressful life events such as job loss or bereavement are significant risk factors for major depression, an x-z association. We need to know much more about both biochemical and psychosocial x-y transitions accompanying such stressors, about interactive effects that lead to the y-z transition to depression, and about specific mediators at both of those steps that alter the risk of becoming depressed.

- We now that schizophrenics who live with families that are highly critical and overinvolved are at greater risk of relapse than are those who live in low-emotion homes, an x-z association. Such settings may produce more stressors (x) or might be mediators that affect the schizophrenic's perception of or reaction to stressors. We need to know more about the psychological and social factors that contribute to the observed increase in risk of relapse.

319

These points illustrate the breadth of information already available and the need for further research at many levels. How do stressors, as precipitating and perpetuating stimuli, interact with predisposing factors that are peculiar to each illness? The attempt to differentiate stimulus specificity from personal predisposition has been a vibrant theme in psychosomatic and stress research, but it has largely failed to find support in studies over the last thirty years. As emphasized by the x-y-z framework, it seems likely that both factors play a major role. The impact of existing illness as a stressor on individuals and on their social networks needs to be studied. This is, in effect, a z-x transition, emphasizing that the stress response is neither unidirectional nor static. Any prospective epidemiologic studies of the impact of stressors on disease need to examine a range of health measures, not just morbidity and mortality from a few causes. In measuring the consequences associated with a stressor, they must consider not only people who become ill but also those who experience desirable consequences.

At least three areas in stress research offer special promise. First, more precise data on x-z associations might yield diagnositic tools for identifying individuals at high risk of specific diseases. Second, a better understanding of x-y-z sequences relating stressors and reactions to a disease consequence may create the knowledge base needed to design preventive interventions rationally. Interventions might be made either at the x-y step, by altering specific reactions to a stressor, or at the y-z step, by blocking their adverse health consequences. Depending on the system involved, optimal interventions may entail psychotherapy, pharmacotherapy, changes in the psychosocial environment, or some combination of these. Sometimes, the best prevention may be to decrease the likelihood of exposure to certain stressors. Finally, delineation of x-y-z sequences may suggest new therapeutic approaches and ways to enhance the efficacy of existing ones. The medical profession relies heavily on pharmacological and surgical treatments for most diseases; yet, no one believes that such treatments are uniformly effective, particularly for those diseases that seem to be most closely related to stress. New, efficacious treatments undoubtedly would be welcomed eagerly.

References

Aakvaag, A., Sand, T., Opstad, P. K., and Fonnum, F. Hormonal changes in serum in young men during prolonged physical strain. Eur. J. App. Physiol. 39: 283-291, 1978.

Abram, H. S., Moore, G. L., and Westervelt, F. B., Jr. Suicidal behavior in chronic dialysis patients. Amer. J. Psychiatry 127:1199- 1204, 1971.

Abramson, E. E., and Wunderlich, R. A. Anxiety, fear, and eating: a test of the psychosomatic concept of obesity. J. Abnorm. Psychol. 79:317-321, 1972.

Abramson, H. A. Evaluation of maternal rejection theory in allergy. Ann. Allergy 12:129-140, 1954.

Abse, D. W., Wilkins, M. M., van de Castle, R. L., Buxton, W. D., Demars, J.P., Brown, R.S., and Kirschner, L.G. Personality and behavioral characteristics of lung cancer patients. J. Psychosom. Res. 18:101-113, 1974.

Ader, R. (Ed.) Psychoneuroimmunology New York: Academic Press, 1981.

Ader, R., and Cohen, N. Behaviorally conditioned immunosuppression. Psychosom. Med. 37:333-340, 1975.

Agle, D. P., and Ratnoff, O. D. Purpura as a psychosomatic entity: a psychiatric study of autoerythrocyte sensitization. Arch. Intern. Med. 109:685-694, 1962.

Alexander, F. Psychosomatic Medicine, Its Principles and Applications New York: Norton and Co., 1950.

American Psychiatric Association. Diagnostic and Statistical Manual of Mental Disorders, 3rd Ed. Washington, D.C.: American Psychiatric Association, 1980.

Antelman, S. M., Eichler, A. J., Black C. A., and Kocan, D. Interchangeability of stress and amphetamine in sensitization. Science 207:329-331, 1980.

Antelman, S. M., and Szechtman, H. Tail pinch induces eating in sated rats which appears to depend on nigrostriatal dopamine. Science 189:731-733, 1975.

Arkel, Y. S., Haft, J. I., Kreutner, W., Sherwood, J., and Williams, R. Alteration in second phase platelet aggregation associated with an emotionally stressful activity. Thromb. Haemostas. 38:552-561, 1977.

Bacon, C. L., Renneker, R., and Cutler, M. A psychosomatic survey of cancer of the breast. Psychosom. Med. 14:453-460, 1952.

Barraclough, B., Bunch, J., Nelson, B., and Sainsbury, P. A hundred cases of suicide: clinical aspects. Br. J. Psychiatry 125:355-373, 1974.

Barrett, J. E. The relationship of life events to the onset of neurotic disorders. IN: Stress and Mental Disorder (Barrett, J. E., ed.) New York: Raven Press, 1979, pp. 87-109.

321

Bartrop, R. W., Lazarus, L., Luckhurst, E., Kiloh, L. G., and Penny, R. Depressed lymphocyte function after bereavement. Lancet 1:834-836, 1977.

Bennett, A. W., and Cambor, C. G. Clinical study of hyperthyroidism. Arch. Gen. Psychiatry 4:160-165, 1961.

Benson, H., Herd, J. A., Morse, W. H., and Kelleher, R. T. Behavioral induction of arterial hypertension and its reversal. Amer. J. Physiol. 217:30-34, 1969.

Berger, P. A., Ginsburg, R. A., Barchas, J. D., Murphy, D. L., and Wyatt, J. D. Platelet momoamine oxidase in chronic schizophrenic patients. Amer. J. Psychiatry 135:95-99, 1978.

Bielauskas, L., Shekell, R., and Garron, D. Psychological depression and cancer mortality. Paper presented at the 35th Annual Meeting of the American Psychosomatic Society, 1979.

Blumberg, E. M. Results of psychological testing of cancer patients. IN: The Psychological Variables in Human Cancer (Gingerelli, J. A. and Kirkner, F. J., eds.) Berkeley: University of California Press, 1954.

Borison, R. L. and Diamond, B. I. A new animal model for schizophrenia: interactions with adrenergic mechanisms. Biol. Psychiatry 13:217- 225, 1978.

Bourestom, N. C. and Howard, M. T. Personality characteristics of three disability groups. Arch. Phys. Med. Rehabil. 46:626-632, 1965.

Braestrup, C. and Squire, R. F. Brain specific benzodiazepine receptors. Br. J. Psychiatry 133:249-260, 1978.

Brod, J. Haemodynamic basis of acute pressor reactions and hypertension. Br. Heart J. 25:227-245, 1963.

Brown, G. W. and Birley, J. L. T. Crises and life changes and the onset of schizophrenia. J. Health Soc. Behav. 9:203-214, 1968.

Brown, G. W., Birley, J. L. T., and Wing, J. K. Influence of family life on the course of schizophrenic disorders: a replication. Br. J. Psychiatry 121: 241-258, 1972.

Brown, G. W. and Harris, T. Social Origins of Depression: A Study of Psychiatric Disorder in Women London: Tavistock, 1978.

Brown, G. W., Ni-Bhrolchain, M., and Harris, T. O. Psychotic and neurotic depression: Part 3, Aetiological and background factors. J. Affect. Disord. 1: 195-211, 1979.

Brown, G. W., Sklair, F., Harris, T. O., and Birley, J. L. T. Life events psychiatric disorders. Part I: Some methodological issues. Psychol. Med. 3:74-87, 1973.

Browne, W. J., Mally, M. A., and Kane, R. P. Psychosocial aspects of hemophilia: a study of 28 hemophilic
children and their families. Amer. J. Orthopsychiatry
30:730-740, 1960.

Buchsbaum, M. S., Coursey, R. D., and Murphy, D. L. The
biochemical- high-risk paradigm: behavioral and
familial correlates of low platelet monoamine oxidase
activity. Science 194:339-341, 1976.

Buell, J. C., and Eliot, R. S. Stress and cardiovascular
disease. Mod. Concepts Cardiovasc. Dis. 48:19-24,
1979.

Buell, J., and Eliot, R. S. Review of clinical syndromes
and pathophysiologic mechanisms in sudden cardiac
death. IN: Biobehavioral Factors in Sudden Cardiac
Death--Report of a Conference Washington, D.C.:
National Academy Press, 1981.

Burchfield, S. R. The stress response: a new perspective. Psychosom. Med. 41:661-672, 1979.

Burglass, D., Clarke, J., Henderson, A. S., Kreitman, N.,
and Presley, A. S. A study of agoraphobic housewives.
Psychol. Med. 7:73-86, 1977.

Carroll, B. J. Control of plasma cortisol levels in
depression: studies with the dexamethasone suppression test. IN: Depressive Illness: Some Research
Studies (Davies, B., Carroll, B. J., and Mowbray, R.
M., eds.) Springfield: Charles C. Thomas, 1972, pp.
87-148.

Cebelin, M. S., and Hirsch, C. S. Human stress cardio-
myopathy--myocardial lesions in victims of homicidal
assaults without internal injuries. Hum. Pathol. 11:
123-132, 1980.

Chambers, W. N., and Rieser, M. F. Emotional stress in
the precipitation of congestive heart failure. Psychosom. Med. 15:38-60, 1953.

Clayton, P. Bereavement and its management. IN: Handbook of Affective Disorders (Paykel, E. S., ed.)
Edinburgh: Churchhill Livingstone, in press.

Cobb, L. A., Werner, J. A., and Trobaugh, G. B. Sudden
cardiac death. I. A decade's experience with out-
of-hospital resuscitation. Mod. Concepts Cardiovasc.
Dis. 49:31-36, 1980.

Cobb, S., and Rose, R. M. Hypertension, peptic ulcer,
and diabetes in air traffic controllers. J. Amer.
Med. Assoc. 224:489-492, 1973.

Coelho, G., Hamburg, D., and Adams, J: Coping and Adaptation New York: Basic Books, 1974.

Cohen, D. B. Eye movements during REM sleep: the influence of personality and presleep conditions. J.
Personal. Soc. Psychol. 32:1090-1093, 1975.

Cohen, D. H., and Cabot, J. B. Toward a cardiovascular
neurobiology. Trends Neurosci. 2:273-276, 1979.

323

Cohen, F. Personality, stress and the development of physical disease. IN: Health Psychology--A Handbook (Stone, G. L., Cohen, F., and Adler, N. E., eds.) San Francisco: Jossey-Bass, 1979, pp 77-111.

Cohen, N., Ader, R., Green, N., and Borbjerg, D. Conditioned suppression of a thymus-independent antibody response. Psychosom. Med. 41:487-491, 1979.

Crook, T., and Eliot, J. Parental death during childhood and adult depression: a critical review of the literature. Psychol. Bull. 87:252-259, 1980.

Crowe, R. R., Pauls, D. L., Slymen, D. J., and Noyes, R. A family study of anxiety neurosis: morbidity risk in families of patients with and without mitral valve prolapse. Arch. Gen. Psychiatry 37: 77-79, 1980.

Dalen, P. Season of Birth: A Study of Schizophrenia and Other Mental Disorders Amsterdam: North Holland, 1975.

Derogatis, L. R., Abeloff, M. D., and Melisaratos, N. Psychological coping mechanisms and survival time in metastatic breast cancer. J. Amer. Med. Assoc. 242: 1504-1508, 1979.

Dimsdale, J. E. Emotional causes of sudden death. Amer. J. Psychiatry 134:1361-1366, 1977.

Doane, J. A., West, K. L., Goldstein, M. J., Rodnick, E. H., and Jones, J. E. Parental communication deviance and affective style as predictors of subsequent schizophrenia spectrum disorders in vulnerable adolescents. Arch. Gen. Psychiatry 38:679-698, 1981.

Dohrenwend, B. P., and deFigueiredo, J. M. Remote and recent life events and psychopathology. IN: Origins of Psychopathology: Research and Public Policy (Ricks, D. L., and Dohrenwend, B. S., eds.) New York: Cambridge University Press, in press.

Dohrenwend, B. P., and Egri, G. Recent stressful life events and episodes of schizophrenia. Schiz. Bull. 7:12-23, 1981.

Dohrenwend, B. S., Krasnoff, L., Askenasy, A. R., and Dohrenwend, B. P. Exemplification of a method for scaling life events: the PERI life events scale. J. Health Soc. Behav. 19:205-229, 1978.

Drew, F. L. The epidemiology of secondary amenorrhea. J. Chronic. Dis. 14:396-407, 1961.

Dudley, D. L. Psychophysiology of Respiration in Health and Disease New York: Appleton-Century-Crofts, 1969.

Dunn, J. P., and Cobb, S. Frequency of peptic ulcer among executives, craftsmen, and foremen. J. Occup. Med. 4:343-348, 1962.

Edfors-Lubs, M. L. Allergy in 7000 twin pairs. Acta Allergol. 26:249-285, 1971.

Elliott, G. R., Holman, R. B., and Barchas, J. D. Neuroregulators and behavior. IN: Psychopharmacology

From Theory to Practice (Barchas, J. D., Berger, P.
A., Ciaranello, R. D., and Elliott, G. R., eds.) New
York: Oxford University Press, 1977, pp. 5-15.
Engel, G. L. Studies of ulcerative colitis. II. The
nature of the somatic processes and the adequacy of
psychosomatic hypotheses. Amer. J. Med. 16:416-433,
1954.
Engel, G. L. Studies of ulcerative colitis. III. The
nature of the psychologic processes. Amer. J. Med.
19:231-256, 1955.
Engel, G. L. Sudden and rapid death during psychological
stress: folk lore or folk wisdom? Ann. Intern. Med.
74:771-782, 1971.
Engel, G. L. Psychological aspects of gastrointestinal
disorders. IN: American Handbook of Psychiatry,
Vol. 4, 2nd Ed. (Reiser, M. F., ed.) New York:
Basic Books, 1975, pp. 653-692.
Engel, G. L., Reichsman, F., and Segal, H. L. A study
of an infant with a gastric fistula. I. Behavior
and the rate of total hydrochloric acid secretion.
Psychosom. Med. 18:374-398, 1956.
Epstein, L. J. Depression in the elderly. J. Gerontol.
31:278-282, 1976.
Ernst, F. Learned control of coronary blood flow. Psy-
chosom. Med. 41:79-85, 1979.
Eysenck, H. J. The conditioning model of neurosis.
Behav. Brain Sci. 2:155-199, 1979.
Farris, E. J., Yeakel, E. H., and Medoff, H. S. Develop-
ment of hypertension in emotional gray Norway rats
after air blasting. Amer. J. Physiol. 144:331-333,
1945.
Feicht, C. B., Johnson, T. S., Martin, B. J., Sparkes, K.
E., and Wagner, W. W., Jr. Secondary amenorrhea in
athletes. Lancet 2:1145-1146, 1978.
Feldman, G. M. Effect of biofeedback training on res-
piratory resistance of asthmatic children. Psychosom.
Med. 38:27-34, 1976.
Fioretti, P., Corsini, G. U., Murru, S., Medda, F., and
Genazzani, A. R. Depression and sexual behavior in
hyperprolactinemic amenorrhea. Effect of bromoergo-
cryptine treatment. Acta Endocrinol. 85 Suppl. 212:
141, 1977.
Fontana, A. F., Marcus, J. L., Noel, B., and Rakusin, J.
M. Prehospitalization coping styles of psychiatric
patients: the goal-directedness of life events. J.
Nerv. Ment. Dis. 155:311-321, 1972.
Fox, B. H. Premorbid psychological factors as related
to cancer incidence. J. Behav. Med. 1:45-133, 1978.
French, T. M., and Alexander, F. Psychogenic factors
in bronchial asthma. Psychosom. Med. Mono. 4:2-94,
1941.

Fres, H., Nilliuss, J., and Petersson, F. Epidemiology of secondary amenorrhea. Amer. J. Obstet. Gynecol. 118:473, 1974.

Friedman, M., Manwaring, J. H., Rosenman, R. H., Donlon, G., Ortega, P., and Grube, S. M. Instantaneous and sudden deaths: clinical and pathological differentiation in coronary artery disease. J. Amer. Med. Assoc. 225: 1319-1328, 1973.

Friedman, M., and Rosenman, R. H. Association of specific overt behavior pattern with blood and cardiovascular findings. J. Amer. Med. Assoc. 169:1286-1296, 1959.

Friedman, S. B., Ader, R., and Glasgow, L. A. Effects of psychological stress in adult mice inoculated with Coxsackie B viruses. Psychosom. Med. 27: 361-368, 1965.

Gaines, R., Sandgrund, A., Green, A. H. , and Power, E. Etiological factors in child maltreatment: a multivariate study of abusing, neglecting and normal mothers. J. Abnorm. Psychol. 87:531-540, 1978.

Garlinghouse, J., and Sharp, L. J. The hemophilic child's self-concept and family stress in relation to bleeding episodes. Nurs. Res. 17:32-37, 1968.

Gershon, E. S., Mark, A., Cohen, N., Belizon, N., Baron, M., and Knobe, K. E. Transmitted factors in the morbid risk of affective disorders: a controlled study. J. Psychiatr. Res. 12:283-299, 1975.

Glueck, S., and Glueck, E. Delinquents and Nondelinquents in Perspective Cambridge: Harvard University Press, 1968.

Gold, W. M., Kessler, G. F., and Yu, D. Y. C. Role of vagus nerves in experimental asthma in allergic dogs. J. Appl. Physiol. 33:719-725, 1972.

Golden, C. J., Moses, J. A., Zelazowitz, R., Graber, B., Zatz, L. M., Horvath, T. B., and Berger, P. A. Cerebral ventricular size and neuropsychological impairment in young chronic schizophrenics. Arch. Gen. Psychiatry 37:619-623, 1980.

Goldstein, M. J., and Rodnick, E. H. The family's contribution to the etiology of schizophrenia: current status. Schiz. Bull. 14:48-63, 1975.

Goodyear, M. D. E. Stress, adrenocortical activity, and sleep habits. Ergonomics 16:679-681, 1973.

Graham, J. D. P. High blood pressure after battle. Lancet 1:239-240, 1945.

Greene, W. A., Jr., Betts, R. F., Ochitill, H. N., Iker, H. P., Douglas, R. G. Psychosocial factors and immunity: preliminary report. Psychosom. Med. 40: 87, 1978.

326

Greene, W. A., Jr., and Miller, G. Psychological factors and reticuloendothelial disease. Psychosom. Med. 20: 124-144, 1958.

Greenfield, N. S., Roessler, R., and Crosley, A. P., Jr. Ego strength and length of recovery from infectious mononucleosis. J. Nerv. Ment. Dis. 128:125-128, 1959.

Grimm, E. R. Psychological investigation of habitual abortion. Psychosom. Med. 24:369-378, 1962.

Gunderson, E. K., and Rahe, R. H. (Eds.) Life Stress and Illness Springfield: Charles C. Thomas, 1974.

Haber, S., Barchas, P. R., and Barchas, J. D. Effects of amphetamine on behaviors of rhesus macaques: an animal model of paranoia. IN: Animal Models in Psychiatry and Neurology (Hanin, I., and Usdin, E., eds.) New York: Pergamon Press, 1977, pp. 107-114.

Haft, J. I., and Arkel, Y. S. Effect of emotional stress on platelet aggregation in humans. Chest 70:501-505, 1976.

Hagnell, O. The premorbid personality of persons who develop cancer in a total population investigated in 1947 and 1957. Ann. N.Y. Acad. Sci. 125:846-855, 1966.

Haier, R. J., Buchsbaum, M. S., and Murphy, D. L. An 18-month followup of students biologically at risk for psychiatric problems. Schiz. Bull. 6:334-337, 1980.

Ham, G. C., Alexander, F., and Carmichael, H. T. A psychosomatic theory of thyrotoxicosis. Psychosom. Med. 13:18-35, 1951.

Hamburg, B. A., Lipsett, L. F., Inoff, G. E., and Drash, A. L. (Eds.) Behavioral and Psychosocial Issues in Diabetes Washington, D.C.: U. S. Government Printing Office, NIH Publ. No. 80-1993, 1980.

Hamilton, V., and Warburton, D. (Eds.) Human Stress and Cognition New York: Wiley, 1979.

Hankoff, L. D. Categories of attempted suicide: a longitudinal study. Amer. J. Public Health 66:558-563, 1976.

Hannum, R. D., Rosellini, R. A., and Seligmann, M. E. P. Learned helplessness in the rat: retention and immunization. Dev. Psychol. 12:449-454, 1976.

Havens, L. L. Losses and depression: the relationship of precipitating events to outcome. J. Nerv. Ment. Dis. 125:627-636, 1957.

Healey, E. S. The Onset of Chronic Insomnia and the Role of Life-Stress Events Unpublished doctoral dissertation, Ohio State University, 1976.

Heisel, J. S. Life changes as etiologic factors in juvenile rheumatoid arthritis. J. Psychosom. Res. 16:411-420, 1972.

Henry, J. P., and Stephens, P. M. Stress, Health, and the Social Environment New York: Springer-Verlag, 1977.

Henry, J. P., Stephens, P. M., and Santisteban, G. A. A model of psychosocial hypertension showing reversibility and progression of cardiovascular complications. Circ. Res. 36:156-164, 1975.

Herman, C. P., and Polivy, J. Experimental and clinical aspects of restrained eating. IN: Obesity (Stunkard, A. J., ed.) Philadelphia: Saunders, 1980.

Horne, R. L., and Picard, R. S. Psychosocial risk factors for lung cancer. Psychosom. Med. 41:503-514, 1979.

Horowitz, M. Intrusive and repetitive thoughts after experimental stress: a summary. Arch. Gen. Psychiatry 32:1254-1463, 1975.

Horowitz, M. Stress and Response Syndromes New York: Aronson, 1976.

Horowitz, M., Wilner, N., Krupnick, J., and Marmar, C. Pathological grief and the activation of latent self images. Amer. J. Psychiatry 137:1157-1162, 1980a.

Horowitz, M., Wilner, N., Kaltreider, N., and Alvarez, W. Signs and symptoms of post-traumatic stress disorders. Arch. Gen. Psychiatry 37:85-92, 1980b.

Howell, J. B. L. Breathlessness in pulmonary disease. IN: Breathlessness (Howell, J. B. L., and Campbell, E. J. M., eds.) Oxford: Blackwell Scientific, 1966, pp. 165-177.

Imboden, J. B., Canter, A., and Cluff, L. E. Convalescence from influenza: a study of the psychological and clinical determinants. Arch. Intern. Med. 108: 393-399, 1961.

Institute of Medicine, National Academy of Sciences. Sleeping Pills, Insomnia and Medical Practice Washington, D.C.: National Academy of Sciences, 1979a.

Institute of Medicine Mental Health Care in General Health Care Systems Washington, D.C.: National Academy of Sciences, 1979b.

Institute of Medicine Alcoholism and Related Problems: Opportunities for Research Washington, D.C.: National Academy of Sciences, 1980.

Jacobs, M. A., Anderson, L. S., Eisman, H. B., Muller, J. J., and Friedman, S. Interaction of psychologic and biologic predisposing factors in allergic disorders. Psychosom. Med. 29:572-585, 1967.

Jacobs M. H., Spelken, A. Z., Norman, M. M., and Anderson, L. S. Life stress and respiratory illness. Psychosom. Med. 32:233-242, 1970.

Jacobs, S., and Myers, J. Recent life events and acute schizophrenic psychosis: a controlled study. J. Nerv. Ment. Dis. 162:75-87, 1976.

Jaques, L. B. Stress and multiple-factor etiology of bleeding. Ann. N. Y. Acad. Sci. 115:78-96, 1964.

Johnson, J. E. Stress reduction through sensation information. Stress Anxiety 2:361-378, 1975.

Kalis, B. L., Harris, R. E., Sokolow, M., and Carpenter, L. G. Response to psychological stress in patients with essential hypertension. Amer. Heart J. 53:572-578, 1957.

Kaltreider N., Wallace A., Horowitz M. J. A field study of the stress response syndrome: young women after hysterectomies. J. Amer. Med. Assoc. 242:1499-1503, 1979.

Kannell, W. B. Habits and Coronary Heart Disease. The Framingham Heart Study Washington: U.S. Government Printing Office, DHEW PHS Publ. No. 1515, 1966.

Kavanagh, T., and Shepard, R. J. The immediate antecedents of myocardial infarction in active men. Can. Med. Assoc. J. 109:19-22, 1973.

Kety, S. S. Progress toward an understanding of the biological substrates of schizophrenia. IN: Genetic Research in Psychiatry (Fieve, R. R., Rosenthal, D., and Brill, H., eds.) Baltimore: Johns Hopkins University Press, 1975, pp. 15-26.

Kinney, D. K., and Jacobsen, B. Environmental factors in schizophrenia: new adoption study evidence and its implications for genetic and environmental research. IN: The Nature of Schizophrenia (Wynne, L. C., Cromwell, R. L., and Matthysse, S., eds.) New York: Wiley, 1978, pp. 38-51.

Kissen, D. M. Personality characteristics in males conducive to lung cancer. Br. J. Med. Psychol. 36:27-36, 1963.

Klausner, S., Foulks, E., and Moore, M. Social change and the alcohol problem on the Alaskan North slope. Paper presented at the Center for Research on the Acts of Man, Philadelphia, January 15, 1980.

Klein, D. F. Delineation of two drug-responsive anxiety syndromes. Psychopharmacologia 5:397-408, 1964.

Kohn, M. L. A social class and schizophrenia: a clinical review and a reformulation. Schiz. Bull. 7:60-79, 1973.

Kosman, M. E., and Unna, K. R. Effects of chronic administration of the amphetamines and other stimulants on behavior. Clin. Pharmacol. Ther. 9:240-254, 1968.

Knapp, P. H. Psychotherapeutic management of bronchial asthma. IN: Psychosomatic Medicine, Its Clinical Applications (Wittkower, E. D., and Warnes, H., eds.) New York: Harper and Row, 1977, pp. 210-219.

Kripke, D. F., Simons, R. N., Garfinkle, L., and Hammond, E. L. Short and long sleep and sleeping pills: is increased mortality associated? Arch. Gen. Psychiatry 36:103-116, 1979.

LaBaw, W. L. Autohypnosis in hemophilia. Haematoligia 9:103-110, 1975.

Lamont, J. T., and Isselbacher, K. J. Chronic inflammatory diseases of the colon. IN: Harrison's Principles of Internal Medicine, 9th Ed. (Isselbacher, K. J., Adams, R. D., Brownwald, E., Petersdorf, R. G., and Wilson, J. D., eds.) New York: McGraw-Hill, 1980, pp. 1424-1432.

Lane, F. M. Mental mechanisms and the pain of angina pectoris. Amer. Heart J. 85:563-568, 1973.

Leff, J. P., Hirsch, S. R., Gaind, R., Rohde, P. D., and Stevens, B. C. Life events and maintenance therapy in schizophrenic relapse. Brit. J. Psychiatry 123: 659-660, 1973.

LeShan, L. L. An emotional life-history pattern associated with neoplastic disease. Ann. N. Y. Acad. Sci. 125:780-793, 1966.

LeShan, L. L., and Worthington, R. E. Personality as a factor in the pathogenesis of cancer: a review of the literature. Brit. J. Med. Psychol. 29:49-56, 1956.

Lester, B. K., Burch, N. R., and Dossett, R. C. Nocturnal EEG-GSR profiles: the influence of pre-sleep states. Psychophysiology 3:238-248, 1967.

Levine, S., Strebel, R., Wenk, E. J., and Harman, P. J. Suppression of experimental allergic encephalomyelitis by stress. Proc. Soc. Exp. Biol. Med. 109:294-298, 1962.

Liebman, R. Minuchin, S., and Baker, L. The use of structural family therapy in the treatment of intractible asthma. Amer. J. Psychiatry 131:535-540, 1974.

Lown, B., DeSilva, R. A., and Lenson, R. Roles of psychologic stress and autonomic nervous system changes in provocation of ventricular premature complexes. Amer. J. Cardiol. 41:979-985, 1978.

Lown, B., Verrier, R. L., and Rabinowitz, S. H. Neural and psychologic mechanisms and the problem of sudden cardiac death. Amer. J. Cardiol. 39:890-902, 1977.

Lucas, O. N. The use of hypnosis in hemophilia dental care. Ann. N. Y. Acad. Sci. 240:263-266, 1975.

Luparello, T., Lyons, H. A., Bleecker, E. R., McFadden, E. R., Jr. Influence of suggestion on airway reactivity in asthmatic subjects. Psychosom. Med. 30: 819-825, 1968.

Luparello, T. J., Stein, M., and Park, C. D. Effect of hypothalamic lesions on rat anaphylaxis. Amer. J. Physiol. 207:911-914, 1964.

Maas, J. W. Biogenic amines and depression: biochemical and pharmacological separation of two types of depression. Arch. Gen. Psychiatry 32:1357-1361, 1975.

Malinak, D. P., Hoyt, M. F., Patterson, V. Adult's reactions to the death of a parent: a preliminary study. Amer. J. Psychiatry 136:1152-1156, 1979.

Marsh, J. T., Lavender, J. F., Chang, S., and Rasmussen, A. F., Jr. Poliomyelitis in monkeys: decreased susceptibility after avoidance stress. Science 140: 1415-1416, 1963.

Matthysse, A. G., and Matthysse, S. A., Bacteriophage models of neurotropic virus specificity. Birth Defects 14:111-121, 1978.

Mattsson, A. Juvenile diabetes: impacts on life stages and systems. IN: Behavioral and Psychosocial Issues in Diabetes (Hamburg, B. A., Lipsett, L. F., Inoff, G. E., and Drash, A. L., eds.) Washington, D.C.: U.S. Government Printing Office, NIH Publ. No. 80-1993, 1980, pp. 43-55.

Mattsson, A., Gross, S., and Hall, T. A. Psychoendocrine study of adaptation in young hemophiliacs. Psychosom. Med. 33:215-225, 1971.

McAuliffe, W. E., and Gordon, R. A. A test of Lindesmith's theory of addiction: the frequency of euphoria among long-term addicts. Amer. J. Sociol. 79:795-840, 1974.

McCoy, J. W. Psychological Variables and Onset of Cancer Unpublished Ph.D. dissertation, Oklahoma State University, 1976.

McKenna, R. J. Some effects of anxiety level and food cues on the eating behavior of obese and normal subjects. a comparison of the Schacterian and psychosomatic conceptions. J. Pers. Soc. Psychol. 22:311-319, 1972.

McLellan, A. T., Woody, G. E., and O'Brien, C. P. Development of psychiatric illness in drug abusers: possible role of drug preference. New Engl. J. Med. 301:1310-1314, 1979.

Mendelson, W. B., Gillin, J. C., and Wyatt, R. J. Human Sleep and Its Disorders New York: Plenum Press, 1977.

Meyer, R. J., and Haggerty, R. J. Streptococcal infections in families: factors altering individual susceptibility. Pediatrics 29:539-549, 1962.

Miasnikov, A. L. The significance of higher nervous activity in the pathogenesis of hypertensive disease. IN: The Pathogenesis of Essential Hypertension (Cort, J. H., Fencl, V., Hejl, Z., and Jirka, J., eds.) Prague: State Medical Publ. House, 1961, pp. 152-162.

Mineka, S., and Suomi, S. J. Social separation in monkeys. Psychol. Bull. 85:1376-1400, 1978.

Monti, P. M., McCrady, B. S., and Barlow, D. H. Effect of positive reinforcement, informational feedback, and contingency contracting on a bulimic anorexic female. Behav. Ther. 8:258-263, 1977.

Nathan, M. A., Tucker, L. W., Severini, W. H., and Reis, D. J. Enhancement of conditioned arterial pressure responses in cats after brainstem lesions. Science 201:71-73, 1978.

Nurnberger, J. I, Jr., and Gershon, E. S. Genetics of affective disorders. IN: Handbook of Affective Disorders (Paykel, E. S., ed.) Edinburgh: Churchill Livingston, in press.

O'Malley, J. E. Koocher, G., Foster, D., and Slavin, L. Psychiatric sequelae of surviving childhood cancer. Amer. J. Orthopsychiatry 49:608-616, 1979.

Parad, D., Resnik, H., and Parad, L. Emergency and Disaster Management Bowie: Charles Press, 1976.

Parkes, C. M., Benjamin, B., and Fitzgerald, R. G. Broken heart: a statistical study of increased mortality among widowers. Br. Med. J. 1:740-743, 1969.

Patrick, V., Dunner, D. L., and Fieve, R. R. Life events and primary affective illness. Acta Psychiatr. Scand. 58:48-55, 1978.

Paykel, E. S. Life stress, depression, and attempted suicide. J. Hum. Stress. 2:3-10, 1976.

Paykel, E. S. Life events and early environment. IN: Handbook of Affective Disorders Edinburgh: Churchill Livingston, in press.

Paykel, E. S., Myers, J. K., Dienelt, M. N. Klerman, G. L., Lindenthal, J. J., and Pepper, M. P. Life events and depression: a controlled study. Arch. Gen. Psychiatry 21:753-760, 1969.

Paykel, E. S., and Rowan, P. Affective disorders. IN: Recent Advances in Clinical Psychiatry (Granville-Grossman, K., ed.) New York: Churchill Livingston, 1979, pp. 37-90.

Paykel, E. S., and Tanner, J. Life events, depressive relapse and maintenance treatment. Psychol. Med. 6: 481-485, 1976.

Peyser, M. R., Ayalon, D., Harell, A., Toaff, R., and Cordova, R. Stress-induced delay of ovulation. Obstet. Gynecol. 42:667-671, 1973.

Pokorny, A. D., and Kaplan, H. B. Suicide following psychiatric hospitalization. J. Nerv. Ment. Dis. 162:119-125, 1976.

Porsolt, R. D., LePichon, M., and Jalfre, M. Depression: a new animal model sensitive to antidepressant treatments. Nature 266:730-732, 1977.

Post, R. M. Intermittent versus continuous stimulation: effect of time interval on the development of sensitization or tolerance. Life Sci. 26:1275-1282, 1980.

332

Purcell, K., Brady, K., Chai, H., Muser, J., Molk, L., Gordon, N., and Means, J. The effect on asthma in children of experimental separation from the family. Psychosom. Med. 31:144-164, 1969.

Rabkin, J. G. Stressful life events and schizophrenia: a review of the research literature. Psychol. Bull. 87:408-425, 1980.

Racine, R. Kindling: the first decade. Neurosurgery 3: 234-252, 1978.

Rahe, R. H., O'Neil, T. O., Hagan, A., and Arthur, R. J. Brief group therapy following myocardial infarction. Eighteen month follow-up of a controlled trial. Int. J. Psychiatr. Med. 6:349-358, 1975.

Rahe, R. H., Romo, M., Bennett, L., and Siltanen, P. Recent life changes, myocardial infarction, and abrupt coronary death. Arch. Intern. Med. 133:221-228, 1974.

Redmond, D. E., Jr. Alterations in the function of the nucleus locus coeruleus: a possible model for studies of anxiety. IN: Animal Models in Psychiatry and Neurology (Hanin, I., and Usdin, E., eds.) Oxford: Pergamon Press, 1977, pp. 293-305.

Reichlin, S., Abplanalp, J. M., Labrum, A. H., Schwartz, N., Sommer, B., and Taymor, M. The role of stress in female reproductive dysfunction. J. Hum. Stress 5: 38-45, 1979.

Reichsman, F., and Levy, N. B. Problems in adaptation to maintenance hemodialysis: a four-year study of 25 patients. Arch. Intern. Med. 130:859-865, 1972.

Reiser, M. F., Brust, A. A., Ferris, E. B., Shapiro, A. P., Baker, H. M., and Ransohoff, W. Life situations, emotions, and the course of patients with arterial hypertension. Psychosom. Med. 13:133-139, 1951a.

Reiser, M. F., Rosenbaum, M., and Ferris, E. B. Psychologic mechanisms in malignant hypertension. Psychocom. Med. 13:147-159, 1951b.

Richardson, D. W., Honour, A. J., Fenton, G. W., Stott, F. H., and Pickering, G. W. Variation in arterial blood pressure throughout the day and night. Clin. Sci. 26:445-460, 1964.

Robins, L. N. Interaction of setting and predisposition in explaining new behavior: drug initiation behavior before, in, and after Vietnam. IN: Longitudinal Research in Drug Use: Important Findings and Methodologies (Kandel, D., ed.) Washington, D.C.: Hemisphere, 1978.

Rodin, J. Managing the stress of aging: the role of control and coping. IN: Coping and Health (Levine, S., and Ursin, H., eds.) New York: Plenum Press, 1980.

Roessler, R., Cate, T. R., Lester, J. W., et al. Ego
strength, life events, and body titers. Paper
presented at the annual meeting of the American
Psychosomatic Society, March 24, 1979.
Rogentine, G. N., Fox, B. H., van Kamma, D. P., et al.
Psychological and biological pictures in the short-
term prognosis of malignant melanoma. Read before
the 35th annual meeting of the American Psychosomatic
Society, 1978.
Rose, R. M. Endocrine responses to stressful psychological events. Psychiatr. Clin. N. Amer. 3:251-276,
1980.
Rosenman, R. H. Role of Type A behavior pattern in the
pathogenesis of ischemic heart disease and modification for prevention. Adv. Cardiol. 25:35-46, 1978.
Rotter, J. I., Petersen, G., Samloff, M., McConnell, R.
B., Ellis, A., Spence, M. A., Rimoin, D. L. Genetic
heterogeneity of hyperpepsinogenemic I and normopep-
sinogenemic I duodenal ulcer disease. Ann. Intern.
Med. 91:372-377, 1979.
Ruskin, A., Beard, O. W., and Shaffer, R. L. Blast
hypertension: elevated arterial pressures in the
victims of the Texas City disaster. Amer. J. Med. 4:
228-236, 1948.
Rutter, M. Parent-child separation: psychological
effects on the children. J. Child Psychol. Psychia-
try 12:233-260, 1971.
Rutter, M. Maternal Deprivation Reassessed New York:
Jason Aronson, 1974.
Rutter, M., Tizard, J., and Whitmore, K. Education,
Health, and Behavior London: Longman, 1970.
Sainsbury, P. Psychosocial factors in developed and
developing countries with regard to age and aging.
IN: Society, Stress, and Disease--Aging and Old Age
(Levi, L., ed.) New York: Oxford University Press,
in press.
Sapira, J. D., Scheib, E. T., Moriarty, R., and Shapiro,
A. P. Differences in perception between hypertensive
and normotensive populations. Psychosom. Med. 33:
239-250, 1971.
Sarason, I. G., ed. Test Anxiety: Theory, Research, and
Applications Hillsdale: Lawrence Erlbaum Associates,
1980.
Schachter, S., Goldman, R., and Gordon, A. Effects of
fear, food deprivation, and obesity on eating. J.
Pers. Soc. Psychol. 10:91-97, 1968.
Schleifer, S. J., Keller, S. E., McKegney, F. P., and
Stein, M. Bereavement and lymphocyte function. Paper
presented at the American Psychiatric Association
Meeting, May, 1980.

Schmale, A. H., and Iker, H. Hopelessness as a predictor of cervical cancer. Soc. Sci. Med. 5:95-100, 1971.

Schwartz, G. E., Shapiro, A. P., Redmond, D. P., Ferguson, D. C., Ragland, D. R., and Weiss, S. M., Behavioral medicine approaches to hypertension: an integrative analysis of theory and research. J. Behav. Med. 2:311-363, 1979.

Segal, D. S., and Mandell, A. J. Long-term administration of d-amphetamine: progressive augmentation of motor activity and stereotypy. Pharmacol. Biochem. Behav. 2:249-255, 1974.

Seligman, M. E. P. Helplessness: On Depression, Helplessness, and Death San Francisco: Freeman, 1975.

Serban, G. Stress in schizophrenices and normals. Brit. J. Psychiatry 126:397-407, 1975.

Shafer, S. Aspects of phobic illness--a study of 90 personal cases. Brit. J. Med. Psychol. 49:221-236, 1976.

Shapiro, A. P. Psychophysiologic mechanisms in hypertensive vascular heart disease. Ann. Intern. Med. 53: 64-83, 1960.

Shapiro, A. P. An experimental study of comparative responses of blood pressure to different noxious stimuli. J. Chronic Dis. 13:293-311, 1961.

Shapiro, A. P., Miller, R. E., King, H. E., Gincherean, E., and Fitzgibbon, K. Behavioral consequences of mild hypertension. Circulation 62, Suppl III:36, 1980.

Shapiro, A. P., Schwartz, G. E., Ferguson, D. C. E., Redmond, D. P., and Weiss, S. M. Behavioral methods in the treatment of hypertension. Ann. Intern. Med. 86:626-636, 1977.

Skillman, J. J., and Selen, W. Stress ulceration in the acutely ill. Ann. Rev. Med. 27:9-22, 1976.

Solomon, G. F., and Amkraut, A. A. Psychoneuroendocrinological effects on the immune response. Ann Rev. Microbiol. 35:155-184, 1981.

Stunkard, A. J. The Pain of Obesity Palo Alto: Bull Publishing, Co., 1976.

Sturdevant, R. A. L. Epidemiology of peptic ulcer. Amer. J. Epidemiol. 104:9-14, 1976.

Syme, S. L. Social and psychological risk factors in coronary heart disease. Mod. Concepts Cardiovasc. Dis. 44:17-21, 1975.

Tallman, J. F., Thomas, J. W., and Gallager, D. W. GABAergic modulation of benzodiazepine binding site sensitivity. Nature 274:383-385, 1978.

Taub, J. M., and Berger, R. J. The effects of changing the phase and duration of sleep. J. Exper. Psychol. Hum. Percep. Perform. 2:30- 41, 1976.

Terry, R. Pathology of cancer. IN: Clinical Oncology for Medical Students and Physicians (Rubin, P., ed.) Rochester: American Cancer Society, 1978, pp. 11-20.

Theorell, T., and Rahe, R. H. Life change events, ballistocardiography and coronary death. J. Hum. Stress 1:18-24, 1975.

Thomas, C. B., Duszynski, K. R., and Shaffer, J. W. Family attitudes reported in youth as potential predictors of cancer. Psychosom. Med. 41:287-302, 1979.

Torgersen, S. The nature and origin of common phobic fears. Br. J. Psychiatry 134:343-351, 1979.

Uhlenhuth, E. H., Lipman, R. S., Balter, M. B., and Stern, M. Symptom intensity and life stress in the city. Arch. Gen. Psychiatry 31:759-764, 1974.

Uhlenhuth, E. H., and Paykel, E. S. Symptom configuration and life events. Arch. Gen. Psychiatry 28: 744-748, 1973.

Valliant, G. E. Adaptation to Life Boston: Little Brown, 1977.

Vaughn, C. E., and Leff, J. P. The influence of family and social factors on the course of psychiatric illness: a comparison of schizophrenic and depressed neurotic patients. Brit. J. Psychiatry 129: 125-137, 1976.

Verrier, R. L., Calvert, A., and Lown, B. Effect of posterior hypothalamic stimulation on ventricular fibrillation threshold. Amer. J. Physiol. 228: 923-927, 1975.

Weinberger, D. R., Torrey, E. F., Neophytides, A. N., and Wyatt, J. D. Lateral cerebral ventricular enlargement in chronic schizophrenia. Arch. Gen. Psychiatry 36:735-739, 1979.

Weiner, H. Psychosomatic research in essential hypertension: retrospect and prospect. IN: Psychosomatics in Essential Hypertension (Koster, M., Musaph, H., and Visser, P., eds.) Basel: S. Karger, 1970, pp. 58-116.

Weiner, H. Psychobiology and Human Disease New York: Elsevier, 1977.

Weiner, H. Emotional Factors. IN: The Thyroid (Werner, S. C., and Ingbar, S. H., eds.) New York: Harper and Row, 1978, pp. 627-632.

Weiner, H., Singer, M. T., and Reiser, M. F. Cardiovascular responses and their psychological correlates: I. A study in healthy young adults and patients with peptic ulcer and hypertension. Psychosom. Med. 24: 477-498, 1962.

Weiner, H., Thaler, M., Reiser, M. F., and Mirsky, I. A. Etiology of duodenal ulcer. I. Relation of specific psychological characteristics to rate of gastric

secretion (serum pepsinogen). Psychosom. Med. 19:
1-10, 1957.

Weisman, A. D. A study of the psychodynamics of duodenal
ulcer exacerbations with special reference to treatment and the problem of "specificity." Psychosom.
Med. 18:2-42, 1956.

Weisman, A. D., and Worden, J. W. The existential plight
in cancer: significance of the first 100 days. Int.
J. Psychiatr. Med. 7:1-15, 1976.

Weissman, M., and Klerman, G. L. Sex differences and the
epidemiology of depression. Arch. Gen. Psychiatry
34:98-111, 1977.

Weissman, M. M., and Myers, J. K. Affective disorders in
a U.S. urban community: the use of research diagnostic criteria in an epidemiological survery. Arch.
Gen. Psychiatry 35:1304-1311, 1978.

Wermuth, B. M., Davis, K. L. Hollister, L. E., and
Stunkard, A. J. Phenytoin treatment of the binge-
eating syndrome. Amer. J. Psychiatry 134:1249-1253,
1977.

Werner, E. E., Bierman, J. M., and French, F. E. The
Children of Kauai: A Longitudinal Study from the
Prenatal Period to Age Ten Honolulu: University of
Hawaii Press, 1971.

Wolf, S. Psychosocial forces in myocardial infarction
and sudden death. Circulation 39-40, Suppl. IV:74-
83, 1969.

Wolf, S., Almy, T. P., Bachrach, W. H., Spiro, H. M.,
Sturdevant, R. A. L., and Weiner, H. The role of
stress in peptic ulcer disease. J. Hum. Stress 5:
27-37, 1979.

Wolf, S., and Wolff, H. G. Human Gastric Function New
York: Oxford University Press, 1943.

Wolpe, J. Parallels between animal and human neurosis.
IN: Comparative Psychopathology (Zubin, J., and Hunt,
N. H., eds.) New York: Grune and Stratton, 1967.

Wolpe, J. The Practice of Behavior Therapy, 2nd Ed. New
York: Pergamon Press, 1973.

Worden, J. W., and Sobel, H. J. Ego strength and psychosocial adaptation to cancer. Psychosom. Med. 40:
585-592, 1978.

Yen, S. S. C. Chronic anovulation. IN: Reproductive
Endocrinology (Yen, S. S. C., and Jaffe, R., eds.)
Philadelphia: Saunders, 1978, pp. 341-369.

APPENDIXES

Patterns of Financial Support of Research on Stress and Health*

The task of determining current funding levels for research on the relationship of stress to health and disease is complicated by the diffuseness of the stress concept, the variety of investigations that include some aspects of stress, the diversity of sources that support such studies, and the disparate systems that monitor research funding in the United States. Analyses of data obtained from computerized retrieval systems of the Smithsonian Science Information Exchange (SSIE), the National Institutes of Health Information for Management, Planning Analysis, and Coordination (IMPAC), and the Department of Defense Technical Information Service (DODTIS) provide some estimates of expenditures for research on stress. Using the best information from these sources, total support for stress research in the United States for 1979 probably did not exceed $35 million, almost all of it federally sponsored.

Research Funding Retrieval Systems

SSIE lists current research support from both governmental and nongovernmental sources. Information in the system is provided voluntarily by individual investigators and some federal agencies. Only currently funded research is listed, rather than research funded in a particular fiscal or calendar year. Our search was made in May 1980.

IMPAC contains information primarily for the institutes of the Alcohol, Drug Abuse, and Mental Health Administration (ADAMHA) and of the National Institutes of Health (NIH). Funding levels are provided only for extramural research support; no information is available

---

*Revised from a staff resource paper prepared for the committee by Caren Carney, Staff Associate, and Glen R. Elliott, Study Director, Institute of Medicine.

341

for specific research projects in intramural programs.
Several other agencies within the U.S. Public Health Service agencies also participate in this system, including
components of the Center for Disease Control, the Health
Resources Administration, the Food and Drug Administration, and the Office of Health Research, Statistics, and
Technology. Research projects are listed by fiscal year.
We obtained a search of all records for Fiscal Year
1979. Listings indicate whether a key word such as
stress is the primary, secondary, or tertiary purpose of
the research. Only standard "R01" research grants were
considered.
     DODTIS includes information about research being
supported in all branches of the Department of Defense.
Most stress-related studies are funded by the Army and
Navy. Many of the studies were physiological research
on physical stressors, for example, bone fractures from
gravitational stress or water loss in response to heat
stress. Funding was listed by fiscal year, and we
requested a search of all relevant research for Fiscal
Year 1979. Information was provided only for nonclas-
sified projects.

     For each of these systems, we requested a listing
of all projects that had key words relating to stress
(stress, stressors, environmental stress). The resulting
records were screened manually. Funding for workshops
of conferences was excluded, as were studies that involved only research on physical effects of physical
stressors, unless it considered a specific disease consequence. The remaining studies were further subdivided
into types of research, as described later.

General Findings

     Table A.1 summarizes the estimates of research
funding. SSIE listed about $25 million of stress-
related research funded by both federal and private
sources. IMPAC reported that support of extramural
stress research by the Public Health Service, primarily
by the Alcohol, Drug Abuse, and Mental Health Administration and the National Institutes of Health, was $27
million. DODTIS identified about $4 million of support
from the Department of Defense for unclassified stress
research related to health and illness. Assuming that
systems affiliated with a funding source provide the
best estimates of expenditures by that agency, total
support for stress research in the United States was
slightly more than $34 million in 1979.

342

TABLE A.1

1979 FUNDING OF RESEARCH ON STRESS AND HEALTH:
ESTIMATES FROM DIFFERENT RETRIEVAL SYSTEMS

SOURCE OF FUNDS	RETRIEVAL SYSTEM		
	SSIE ($)	IMPAC ($)	DODTIS ($)
FEDERAL AGENCIES			
Alcohol, Drug Abuse, and Mental Health Administration	11217	12661*	N/A
National Institutes of Health	9303	14436*	N/A
Other Public Health Service	1748*	323	N/A
Department of Defense	1606	N/A	4337*
National Science Foundation	546*	N/A	N/A
Other	407*	N/A	N/A
NONFEDERAL AGENCIES	111*	N/A	N/A
SUM OF BEST ESTIMATES		$34,246	

All estimates are presented in thousands of dollars.
The * identifies estimates that appear to be the most
reliable for each category. N/A indicates that information was not available. Differences among the retrieval
systems are discussed in the text.

There are several reasons why the figures reported
in Table A.1 are not comparable among the reporting
agencies. SSIE thesaurus listings under the heading
"stress" are much more inclusive than those for IMPAC.
And, because, the SSIE provides information only on
currently funded research, projects that ended in late
1979 would not be listed. No consistent reasons were
found to explain why SSIE dollar figures for a particular NIH-funded project often did not match precisely
the figures provided by IMPAC on the same project. Some
underreporting may occur because SSIE relies on voluntary
reporting of individual investigators. In addition,
whereas IMPAC designates whether the emphasis on stress
in a particular research project is primary or secondary, SSIE does not, making it difficult to assess what

343

TABLE A.2

FUNDING FOR BASIC AND CLINICAL RESEARCH ON THE RELATIONSHIP OF STRESS AND HEALTH
(SSIE Funded Research, May 1980)

GENERAL AREA		BASIC RESEARCH						CLINICAL RESEARCH	
		BIOLOGICAL $	N	PSYCHOSOCIAL $	N	TOTAL BASIC $	N	$	N
MAJOR ORGAN SYSTEM									
Cardiovascular	Human:	545	9	1005	11	1550	20	Treat: 0	0
	Nhumn:	1459	20	677	10	136	2	Prev: 184	2
	Total:	2004	20	1683	21	3686	50	Total: 184	2
Endocrine	Human:	139	1	506	4	645	5	Treat: 156	1
	Nhumn:	341	7	561	5	902	12	Prev: 0	0
	Total:	480	8	1067	9	1547	17	Total: 156	1
Gastrointestinal	Human:	0	0	0	0	0	0	Treat: 129	1
	Nhumn:	212	4	53	1	265	5	Prev: 0	0
	Total:	212	4	53	1	265	5	Total: 129	1
Immune	Human:	0	0	0	0	0	0	Treat: 0	0
	Nhumn:	0	0	89	2	89	2	Prev: 0	0
	Total:	0	0	89	2	89	2	Total: 0	0

Category												
Neurological	Human:	184	6	Human:	165	3	Human:	349	9	Treat:	50	3
	Nhumn:	995	17	Nhumn:	645	9	Nhumn:	1640	26	Prev:	0	0
	Total:	11879	23	Total:	810	12	Total:	1989	35	Total:	50	3
Respiratory	Human:	0	0	Human:	50	2	Human:	50	2	Treat:	0	0
	Nhumn:	0	0	Nhumn:	0	0	Nhumn:	0	0	Prev:	0	0
	Total:	0	0	Total:	50	2	Total:	50	2	Total:	0	0
Reproductive	Human:	0	0	Human:	142	2	Human:	142	2	Treat:	0	0
	Nhumn:	32	1	Nhumn:	232	1	Nhumn:	264	2	Prev:	78	1
	Total:	32	1	Total:	374	3	Total:	406	4	Total:	78	1

MENTAL DISORDERS

Category												
Schizophrenia	Human:	62	1	Human:	197	2	Human:	259	3	Treat:	367	2
	Nhumn:	0	0	Nhumn:	0	0	Nhumn:	0	0	Prev:	19	1
	Total:	62	1	Total:	197	2	Total:	259	3	Total:	386	3
Depression	Human:	0	0	Human:	1126	7	Human:	1126	7	Treat:	0	0
	Nhumn:	0	0	Nhumn:	314	5	Nhumn:	314	5	Prev:	0	0
	Total:	0	0	Total:	1440	12	Total:	1440	12	Total:	0	0
Anxiety Disorders	Human:	0	0	Human:	76	2	Human:	76	2	Treat:	0	0
	Nhumn:	0	0	Nhumn:	125	2	Nhumn:	125	2	Prev:	392	6
	Total:	0	0	Total:	201	4	Total:	201	4	Total:	392	6
Alcohol and Drug Abuse	Human:	0	0	Human:	981	11	Human:	981	11	Treat:	154	3
	Nhumn:	124	2	Nhumn:	346	6	Nhumn:	470	6	Prev:	0	0
	Total:	124	2	Total:	1327	17	Total:	1451	17	Total:	154	3
Aggression	Human:	0	0	Human:	801	9	Human:	800	9	Treat:	0	0
	Nhumn:	0	0	Nhumn:	165	3	Nhumn:	165	3	Prev:	0	0
	Human:	0	0	Human:	966	12	Treat:	966	12	Human:	0	0

TABLE A.2
(continued)

GENERAL AREA	BASIC RESEARCH						CLINICAL RESEARCH	
	BIOLOGICAL		PSYCHOSOCIAL		TOTAL BASIC			
	$	N	$	N	$	N	$	N
RESEARCH ON THE WORKING ENVIRONMENT								
Human:	79	1	Human: 1402	19	Human: 1481	20	Treat: 0	0
Nhumn:	0	0	Nhumn: 0	0	Nhumn: 0	0	Prev: 0	0
Total:	79	1	Total: 1402	19	Total: 1481	20	Total: 0	0
RESEARCH NOT DISEASE-TARGETED								
Human:	415	8	Human: 5259	67	Human: 5674	75	Treat: 2194	16
Nhumn:	684	8	Nhumn: 210	2	Nhumn: 894	10	Prev: 845	11
Total:	1099	16	Total: 5469	69	Total: 6568	85	Total: 3039	27
ALL AREAS COMBINED								
Human:	1424	26	Human: 11710	139	Human: 13134	165	Treat: 3050	26
Nhumn:	3847	59	Nhumn: 3217	46	Nhumn: 7264	103	Prev: 1518	22
Total:	$5271	85	Total: $14927	185	Total: $20398	268	Total: $4568	48

346

For each category, the level of funding ($) is expressed in thousands of dollars; N indicates the number of identified projects within that category. The following conventions are used: Human, research performed using human subjects; Nhumn, all other types of basic research; Treat, treatment research; and Prev, research on prevention. Basic research may involve either human or nonhuman subjects; all clinical research used human subjects. As described in the text, estimates are based on SSIE records of stress research being funded at the time these data were collected.

347

TABLE A.3

U.S. PUBLIC HEALTH SERVICE SUPPORT FOR RESEARCH
ON STRESS AND HEALTH IN FISCAL YEAR 1979

FUNDING AGENCY	STRESS-RELATED RESEARCH					
	PRIMARY		SECONDARY		TOTAL	
	$	N	$	N	$	N
NATIONAL INSTITUTES OF HEALTH (NIH)						
National Institute on Aging (NIA)						
Human:	238	5	526	7	764	12
Nhumn:	0	0	0	0	0	0
Total:	238	5	526	7	764	12
National Institute of Allergy and Infectious Diseases (NIAID)						
Human:	0	0	0	0	0	0
Nhumn:	117	1	0	0	117	1
Total:	117	1	0	0	117	1
National Institute of Arthritis, Metabolism, and Digestive Diseases (NIAMDD)						
Human:	0	0	0	0	0	0
Nhumn:	87	2	482	7	569	9
Total:	87	2	482	7	569	9
National Cancer Institute (NCI)						
Human:	298	3	1065	1	1363	4
Nhumn:	0	0	141	2	141	2
Total:	298	3	1206	3	1504	6
National Institute of Dental Research (NIDR)						
Human:	44	1	149	2	193	3
Nhumn:	0	0	0	0	0	0
Total:	44	1	149	2	193	3

348

National Institute of Environmental Health Sciences (NIEHS)	Human:	36	1	42	1	78	2
	Nhumn:	0	0	0	0	0	0
	Total:	36	1	42	1	78	2
National Institute of General Medical Sciences (NIGMS)	Human:	241	3	86	1	327	4
	Nhumn:	158	2	0	0	158	2
	Total:	399	5	86	1	485	6
National Institute of Child Health and Human Development (NICHD)	Human:	326	3	363	7	689	10
	Nhumn:	502	8	1036	19	1538	27
	Total:	828	11	1399	26	2227	37
National Heart, Lung, and Blood Institute (NHLBI)	Human:	2591	25	3369	18	5960	43
	Nhumn:	1468	16	501	8	1969	24
	Total:	4059	41	3870	26	7929	67
National Institute of Neurological and Communicative Disorders and Stroke (NINCDS)	Human:	0	0	89	2	89	2
	Nhumn:	101	2	380	4	481	6
	Total:	101	2	469	6	570	8

ALCOHOL, DRUG ABUSE, AND MENTAL HEALTH ADMINISTRATION (ADAMHA)

National Institute on Alcohol Abuse and Alcoholism (NIAAA)	Human:	212	1	226	3	438	4
	Nhumn:	0	0	49	1	49	1
	Total:	212	1	275	4	487	5
National Institute on Drug Abuse (NIDA)	Human:	20	1	77	1	97	2
	Nhumn:	0	0	89	1	89	1
	Total:	20	1	166	2	186	3
National Institute of Mental Health (NIMH)	Human:	2409	22	7924	63	10333	85
	Nhumn:	478	7	1177	15	1655	22
	Total:	2887	29	9101	78	11988	107

TABLE A.3
(continued)

FUNDING AGENCY	STRESS-RELATED RESEARCH					
	PRIMARY		SECONDARY		TOTAL	
	$	N	$	N	$	N
NATIONAL CENTER FOR HEALTH SERVICES RESEARCH (NCHSR)						
Human:	148	1	0	0	148	1
Nhumn:	0	0	0	0	0	0
Total:	148	1	0	0	148	1
HEALTH RESOURCES ADMINISTRATION (HRA), DIVISION OF NURSING						
Human:	175	3	0	0	175	3
Nhumn:	0	0	0	0	0	0
Total:	175	3	0	0	175	3
ALL AGENCIES COMBINED						
Human:	6738	69	13916	106	20654	175
Nhumn:	2911	38	3855	57	6766	95
Total:	9649	107	17771	163	27420	270

350

For each category, the level of funding ($) is expressed in thousands of dollars; N indicates the number of identified projects within that category. The following conventions are used: Human, research performed using humans as subjects; Nhumn, all other types of basic research. Principle investigators of the individual projects indicated whether stress was of primary or secondary interest. Typically, secondary research designated work on mechanisms that stressors may affect or studies that used stressors only as a research tool with which to manipulate a physiological system. These figures do not include money spent on intramural research programs of the National Institutes of Health and the Alcohol, Drug Abuse, and Mental Health Administration. As discussed in the text, the information was gathered from IMPAC.

351

part of a large research activity with many subprojects is devoted to areas relating to stress in health and disease. Conversely, limitations of IMPAC preclude an accurate determination of the true dollar portion that a subproject constitutes of a particular grant.

Table A.2 illustrates some of the major areas of inquiry in stress research. For each major organ system or mental disorder, research was classified as primarily basic or clinical, although many projects had elements of both. Clinical research was defined as studies that had as their primary purpose the prevention or treatment of a specific disease in people. Basic research was further subdivided according to whether the studies were concerned with biological or psychosocial aspects of stress and whether they were performed on people or on animals or computer simulators. Studies of stress in the work environment were listed separately; they typically were concerned with a number of different disorders. There also was a large category of research that was not disease-targeted. In basic research, such studies involved efforts to better understand the effects of stressors on normal physiological or psychological mechanisms. In clinical research, they involved interventions intended to help people cope more effectively with life events as a way of preventing or treating potential adverse effects of exposure to stressors.

Table A.3 lists research on stress in relation to health and illness by supporting agencies of the Public Health Service. Designation of primary or secondary was provided by IMPAC. Within those categories, we further subdivided the research according to whether studies used mainly human or nonhuman subjects. Most of the Institutes are oriented to a particular organ system or disease, so rough estimates of how the types of research they are funding can be obtained from Table A.2. But, all contribute to basic and clinical research that is not disease targeted. Also, the support identified by IMPAC from the Public Health Service exceeds the entire amount of funding from all sources listed by SSIE.

Table A.4 indicates the support of stress research by the Department of Defense. Usually, studies are directly relevant to military concerns--for example, the Navy submarine as a stressful environment. Still, some research is generalizable to nonmilitary settings: effects of altered work cycles on human behavior and performance, stress reduction and stress management training as a way to reduce test anxiety and improve learning, and brain function and behavior under stress.

TABLE A.4

U.S. DEPARTMENT OF DEFENSE SUPPORT FOR
RESEARCH ON STRESS AND HEALTH IN FISCAL 1979

BRANCH OF SERVICE	$	N
Uniformed Services University of the Health Sciences	10	2
Air Force	263	6
Army	2890	15
Navy	1174	26
TOTAL	$4337	49

The level of funding ($) is expressed in thousands of dollars; N indicates the number of identified projects. Information was provided by the DODTIS and was available only for unclassified projects.

The picture that emerges from an analysis of available information about stress-research funding is one of many projects being supported by a number of agencies that work largely independently of each other. No single source or group of sources can provide internally consistent information about what type of research is being done on stress in health and disease. Such a central registry of current stress research could be of great use to members of the research community wanting to find studies that relate to their own interests.

Acknowledgments

The assistance of the following people was greatly appreciated: Dr. Sally Hayes, National Institute of Mental Health; William J. Holliman, Jr., Frederick Biggs, and Rachelle Gabriel, National Institutes of Health Division of Research Grants, Statistics and Analysis Branch; Colonel John J. Mealey, Jr., Department of Defense; and Dr. James T. Lester of the Eastern/Central Regional Office of Navy Research.

Panel Members

Stress and Environment Panel

Cochairs

Robert M. ROSE, M.D., Professor and Chairman, Department of Psychiatry and Behavioral Sciences, University of Texas Medical Branch, Galveston, TX

Robert L. KAHN, Ph.D., Professor of Psychology, Survey Research Center, University of Michigan, Ann Arbor, MI

Members

Stress and Life Events

Bruce P. DOHRENWEND, Ph.D., Professor of Social Science, Department of Psychiatry, Columbia University, New York, NY (Cochair)

Leonard PEARLIN, Ph.D., Research Sociologist, Laboratory of Socio-Environmental Study, National Institute of Mental Health, Bethesda, MD (Cochair)

Paula CLAYTON, M.D., Professor, Department of Psychiatry, Washington University School of Medicine, St. Louis, MO

Beatrix A. HAMBURG, M.D., Associate Professor of Psychiatry, Children's Hospital Medical Center, Harvard Medical School, Boston, MA

Matilda W. RILEY, D.Sc., Associate Director for Social and Behavioral Research, National Institute on Aging, Bethesda, MD

Robert M. ROSE, M.D., Professor and Chairman, Department of Psychiatry and Behavioral Sciences, University of Texas Medical Branch, Galveston, TX

Barbara S. DOHRENWEND, Ph.D., Professor and Head, Division of Sociomedical Science, School of Public Health, Columbia University, New York, NY (Advisor)

Stress in Organizational Settings

Robert L. KAHN, Ph.D., Professor of Psychology, Survey Research Center, University of Michigan, Ann Arbor, MI (Chair)

Karen HEIN, M.D., Assistant Professor of Pediatrics, Columbia Presbyterian Medical Center, New York, NY

James HOUSE, Ph.D., Associate Professor of Sociology, Survey Research Center, University of Michigan, Ann Arbor, MI

Stanislav KASL, Ph.D., Professor of Epidemiology, Yale University School of Medicine, New Haven, CT

Alan A. McLEAN, M.D., Medical Director, Eastern Region, IBM, New York, NY

Work Stress Related to Social Structures and Processes

Lennart LEVI, M.D., Ph.D., Professor and Chairman, Laboratory for Clinical Stress Research, Stockholm, Sweden (Chair)

Marianne FRANKENHAEUSER, Ph.D., Professor and Head, Department of Psychology, Karolinska Institute, Stockholm, Sweden

Bertil GARDELL, Ph.D., Professor of Work Psychology, Department of Psychology, University of Stockholm, Stockholm, Sweden

Psychosocial Assets and Modifiers Panel

Chair

Frances COHEN, Ph.D., Assistant Professor of Medical Psychology, Graduate Group in Psychology, University of California, San Francisco, CA

Members

Mardi HOROWITZ, M.D., Professor, Department of Psychiatry, School of Medicine, University of California, San Francisco, CA

Richard S. LAZARUS, Ph.D., Professor, Psycnology Department, University of California, Berkeley, CA

Rudolf H. MOOS, Ph.D., Professor, Department of Psychiatry and Behavioral Sciences, Stanford School of Medicine, Stanford, CA

Lee N. ROBINS, Ph.D., Professor of Sociology, Department of Psychiatry, Washington University School of Medicine, St. Louis, MO

Robert M. ROSE, M.D., Professor and Chairman, Department of Psychiatry and Behavioral Sciences, University of Texas Medical Branch, Galveston, TX

Michael RUTTER, M.D., Professor of Behavioral Sciences, Center for Advanced Study in the Behavioral Sciences, Stanford, CA

Biological Substrates of Stress Panel

Cochairs

Roland D. CIARANELLO, M.D., Associate Professor, Department of Psychiatry and Behavioral Sciences, Stanford School of Medicine, Stanford, CA

Morris A. LIPTON, Ph.D., M.D., Sarah Graham Kenan Distinguished Professor of Psychiatry, University of North Carolina, Chapel Hill, NC

Members

Jack D. BARCHAS, M.D., Nancy Friend Pritzker Professor, Department of Psychiatry and Behavioral Sciences, Stanford School of Medicine, Stanford, CA

Patricia R. BARCHAS, Ph.D., Assistant Professor, Departments of Sociology and (by courtesy) Psychiatry and Behavioral Sciences, Stanford University, Stanford, CA

John BONICA, M.D., Professor, Department of Anesthesiology, University of Washington School of Medicine, Seattle, WA

Carlos FERRARIO, M.D., Associate Head, Department of Hypertension, Cleveland Clinic, Cleveland, OH

Seymour LEVINE, Ph.D., Professor, Department of Psychiatry and Behavioral Sciences, Stanford School of Medicine, Stanford, CA

Marvin STEIN, M.D., Professor and Chairman, Department of Psychiatry, Mt. Sinai School of Medicine, New York, NY

Stress and Illness Panel

Cochairs

William E. BUNNEY, Jr., M.D., Deputy Director, Division of Clinical and Behavioral Research, National Institute of Mental Health, Bethesda, MD

Alvin P. SHAPIRO, M.D., Professor, Department of Internal Medicine, University of Pittsburgh School of Medicine, Pittsburgh, PA

Members

Robert ADER, Ph.D., Professor, Department of Psychiatry, University of Rochester Medical School, Rochester, NY

John DAVIS, M.D., Research Director, Illinois State Psychiatric Institute, Chicago, IL

J. Alan HERD, Ph.D., Medical Director, Richardson Institute for Preventive Medicine, Methodist Hospital, Houston, TX

Irwin J. KOPIN, M.D., Chief, Section of Medicine, Laboratory of Clinical Sciences, National Institute of Mental Health, Bethesda, MD

Dorothy KRIEGER, M.D., Professor of Medicine, Mt. Sinai School of Medicine, New York, NY

Steven W. MATTHYSSE, Ph.D., Associate Professor of Psychobiology, Mailman Research Institute, McLean Hospital, Belmont, MA

Albert J. STUNKARD, M.D., Professor, Department of Psychiatry, University of Pennsylvania, Philadelphia, PA

Myrna M. WEISSMAN, Ph.D., Associate Professor, Department of Psychiatry, Yale University, New Haven, CT

Richard J. WYATT, M.D., Director, Laboratory of Clinical
Psychopharmacology, St. Elizabeth's Hospital, Washington, DC

Martin ORNE, M.D., Professor, Institute of Pennsylvania
Hospital, Philadelphia, PA (Advisor)

Joseph SAPIRA, M.D., Professor, Department of Medicine,
University of South Alabama College of Medicine, Mobile,
AL (Advisor)

Unpublished Background Papers Prepared for the Stress Study Panels*

Stress and Environment

Research on Stressful Surroundings
   Chester M. Pierce, M.D., Professor of Education and
   Psychiatry, Nichols House, Harvard University, Cam-
   bridge, MA 02138

War-Related Stress
   Norman A. Milgram, M.D., Tel-Aviv University, Tel
   Aviv, Israel

Stress, Health, and the Life Course
   Matilda W. Riley, D.Sc., Associate Director for Social
   and Behavioral Research, National Institute on Aging,
   Bethesda, MD 20205; and Beatrix A. Hamburg, M.D.,
   Associate Professor of Psychiatry, Children's Hospital
   Medical Center, Harvard Medical School, Boston, MA
   02115

Psychosocial Assets and Modifiers of Stress

A Call for the Study of Salutogenesis
   Aaron Antonovsky, Ph.D., Chairman, Department of the
   Sociology of Health, Faculty of Health Services, Ben
   Gurion University of the Negev, Beersheba, Israel

Biological Substrates of Stress

Neuroregulators in Brain and Stress
   Jack D. Barchas, M.D., Nancy Friend Pritzker Profes-
   sor, Department of Psychiatry and Behavioral Sciences,
   Stanford School of Medicine, Stanford, CA 94305

---

*Papers were provided by contributors for the use of the
panels. Authors should be contacted directly for copies
of individual background papers or of related materials.

Stress and Central Nervous System Interactions
  Stanley Watson, Ph.D., M.D., Assistant Professor, and
  Huda Akil, Ph.D., Assistant Professor, Department of
  Psychiatry, Mental Health Research Institute, Univer-
  sity of Michigan, Ann Arbor, MI 48105

The Cardiovascular System and Stress
  Carlos Ferrario, M.D., Associate Head, Department of
  Hypertension, Cleveland Clinic, Cleveland, OH 44106

The Relation of Pain and Stress
  John Bonica, M.D., Professor, Department of Anesthesi-
  ology, University of Washington School of Medicine,
  Seattle, WA 98195

Stress and Immunity: Review of Relevant Literature
  Marvin Stein, M.D., Professor and Chairman, Department
  of Psychiatry, Mt. Sinai School of Medicine, New York,
  NY 10029

Genetics of Stress
  John G. M. Shire, Ph.D., Professor of Genetics, Department of Biology, University of Essex, Colchester CO4
  3SQ, England

A Psychobiological Approach to Stress and Coping
  Seymour Levine, Ph.D., Professor, Department of Psy-
  chiatry and Behavioral Sciences, Stanford School of
  Medicine, Stanford, CA

Physiological Sociology and Stress
  Patricia R. Barchas, Ph.D., Assistant Professor,
  Departments of Sociology and (by courtesy) Psychiatry
  and Behavioral Sciences, Stanford University, Stanford,
  CA 94305

Stress and Illness

Implications of Viewing Stress as a Risk Factor
  Ernest M. Gruenberg, M.D., Dr.P.H., Professor and
  Chairman, Department of Mental Hygiene, Johns Hopkins
  School of Public Health, Baltimore, MD 21205

Cardiovascular Disease and Stress
  James C. Buell, M.D., Assistant Professor of Medicine,
  University of Nebraska Medical Center, Omaha, NE 68105

Stress and Illness: Immune Processes
  Robert Ader, Ph.D., Professor, Department of Psychia-
  try, University of Rochester Medical School, Rochester,
  NY 14642

Stress and Cancer
  Arthur Schmale, M.D., Director, Psychosocial Medicine
  Unit, University of Rochester Cancer Center, Rochester,
  NY 14642

Stress and Female Reproductive Dysfunction
  Judith M. Abplanalp, Ph.D., Assistant Professor,
  Department of Psychiatry and Behavioral Sciences,
  University of Texas Medical Branch, Galveston, TX
  77550

Stress and Obesity
  Albert J. Stunkard, M.D., Professor, Department of Psychiatry, University of Pennsylvania, Philadelphia, PA
  19104

Pulmonary Disorders and Psychosocial Stress
  Peter H. Knapp, M.D., Professor and Associate Chairman,
  Division of Psychiatry, Boston University School of
  Medicine, Boston, MA   02118

Stress and Chronic Disease: Hemophilia
  David Agle, M.D., Associate Professor, Department of
  Psychiatry, Case Western Reserve University School of
  Medicine, Cleveland, OH   44106

Stress and Illness: Hemodialysis
  Norman B. Levy, M.D., Director, Liason Psychiatry Division, Westchester County Medical Center, Valhalla, NY
  10595

Environmental Factors as Stressors in Schizophrenia
  Michael J. Goldstein, Ph.D., Professor, Department of
  Psychology, University of California, Los Angeles, CA
  90024

Stress and Schizophrenia
  Monte S. Buchsbaum, M.D., Chief, Section on Clinical
  Psychophysiology, Biological Psychiatry Branch,
  National Institute of Mental Health, Bethesda, MD
  20205

Biological Indices of Schizophrenia
  Richard J. Wyatt, M.D., Director, Laboratory of Clini-
  cal Psychopharmacology, St. Elizabeth's Hospital,
  Washington, DC   20036

Effects of Environmental Stress Factors on Affective
Illness
  Eugene S. Paykel, M.D., F.R.C.P., F.R.C.Psych., Pro-
  fessor of Psychiatry, St. George's Hospital Medical
  School, London SW17, England

Risk Factor Strategies for Affective Illness
  John I. Nurnberger, Jr., M.D., Senior Research Fellow,
  Section on Psychogenetics, David C. Jimerson, M.D.,
  Staff Psychiatrist, Section on Psychogenetics, and
  William E. Bunney, Jr., M.D., Deputy Director, Division
  of Clinical and Behavioral Research, National Institute
  of Mental Health, Bethesda, MD 20205

Biological Indices of Affective Disorders
  John M. Davis, M.D., Director of Research, Illinois
  State Psychiatric Institute, Chicago, IL 60612

Women and Depression: Evidence and Explanation for the
Higher Rate of Depression Among Women
  Myrna M. Weissman, Ph.D., Associate Professor, Department of Psychiatry, Yale University, New Haven, CT
  06519

Life Stress as a Precursor of Suicide--and Suicide as a
Stressor
  Jan Fawcett, M.D., Professor and Chairman, and David
  C. Clark, M.A., Research Associate, Department of Psy-
  chiatry, Rush-Presbyterian-St. Luke's Medical Center,
  Chicago, IL 60612

Stress, Anxiety, and Health
  Irwin G. Sarason, Professor, Department of Psychology,
  University of Washington, Seattle, WA 98195

Stress and Phobic Disorder
  Judith Godwin Rabkin, Ph.D., M.P.H., Research Sci-
  entist, and Donald F. Klein, M.D., Director of
  Psychiatric Research, New York State Psychiatric
  Institute, New York, NY 10032

Stress and Alcohol
  Theodore Reich, M.D., Head, Department of Psychiatry,
  Jewish Hospital of St. Louis, St. Louis, MO 63110;
  John Helzer, M.D., Lee Robins, Ph.D., Professor of
  Sociology, and C. Robert Cloninger, M.D., Department of
  Psychiatry, Washington University School of Medicine,
  St. Louis, MO 63110

Stress as a Factor in Drug Abuse
  Charles P. O'Brien, M.D., Chief, Drug Dependent Treat-
  ment and Research Center, Veterans' Administration
  Medical Center, Philadelphia, PA 19104

Sleep Disorders and Stress
  Wallace Mendelson, M.D., Research Psychiatrist, and J.
  Christian Gillin, M.D., Chief, Unit on Sleep Studies,
  National Institutes of Health, Bethesda, MD 20205

Child Psychiatry: Stress and Illness
  Judith L. Rapoport, M.D., Chief, Unit on Childhood
  Mental Illness, National Institute of Mental Health,
  Bethesda, MD   20205

Stress and Illness in the Aged
  Frances L. Wilkie, M.A., Department of Psychiatry and
  Behavioral Sciences, University of Washington School
  of Medicine, Seattle, WA   98195

Animal Models of Psychopathology: Present and Future
  Martin E. P. Seligman, Ph.D., Professor, and Joseph R.
  Volpicelli, Department of Psychology, University of
  Pennsylvania, Philadelphia, PA   19104

Psychomotor Stimulant and Stress Sensitization in
Animals as a Model for the Production of Increasing
Behavioral Pathology
  Robert M. Post, M.D., Chief, Section of Psychobiology,
  National Institute of Mental Health, Bethesda, MD
  20205

Mental Disorders as Stressors
  Brendan A. Maher, Ph.D., Professor, Department of
  Psychology and Social Relations, Harvard University,
  Cambridge, MA   02138

The Relationship of Stress and Persisting Pain
  C. Richard Chapman, Ph.D., Associate Professor, Depart-
  ments of Anesthesiology, Psychiatry and Behavioral
  Sciences, and Psychology, and John A. Bokan, M.D.,
  Instructor, Department of Psychiatry and Behavioral
  Sciences, University of Washington, Seattle, Washing-
  ton   98195

INDEX

Hypothalamus, 212, 215,
223-224

Illness and stress, x-xi,
7, 17, 26, 27, 29, 37,
38, 39, 40-41, 42, 51,
55, 208, 257-258. See
also Specific dis-
orders by name
  criterion measures, 154-
  157
  definitions of stress,
  258-259
  mental disorders, 288-317
  physical disorders, 261-
  288
  stress as a risk factor
  for illness, 259-261
Immune system, xiv, 151,
218-224, 237, 271-272,
285, 319
Infectious diseases, see
Immune system
Interdisciplinary nature
of research, ix-x,
xiii-xiv, xxi, xxii,
4-10, 12, 39-40, 41,
42-43, 131
Interpersonal factors, as
mediators, 159, 167-169

Job loss, 50, 56, 58, 60-
61, 63. See also Life
events, Work stress,
Retirement
Jobs, see Organizational
settings, Work stress

Leukemia, see Cancer
Life course processes, 29,
41-42, 157-158,
303-304, 314-315
Life events, stress and,
7, 9, 26, 29, 34, 49,
50, 55-57, 84, 152,
174-177, 319
  contexts, 57-59
  hypotheses about, 57,
  69-77
  mediators of, 57, 64-69

methodological problems
in measuring, 61-64
personal dispositions
and, 61, 64-67
positive vs. negative,
151-153
social conditions, 58,
60-61, 67-69
sources of, 57, 59-64
Longitudinal studies, see
Prospective, longi-
tudinal studies
Luteinizing hormone, xv,
202

Mass-production technology,
stress and, 124-127
Mediators, xix, 8, 9, 22-
23, 27-31, 57, 64-69,
157-173
Melatonin, 201-202
Mental disorders, xix-xx,
26, 121, 260-261, 288-
317. See also Specif-
ic disorders by name
  animal models of stress
  effects on, 306-309
  definitions of, 288-289
  general issues on stress
  and, 315-317
  risk-factor analysis of
  stress effects on,
  260-261, 315
  as stressors, 301-306
Myocardial infarction, see
Cardiovascular disease

Natural experiments, need
for, 42, 55, 110-111,
131-133, 316
Neuroendocrine relation-
ships, 212-213, 215,
234-235
Neuroregulators, xiii-xiv,
33-34, 194
  basic concepts, 193-198
  central, 199-202, 234-236
  neuromodulators, 196-198
  neurotransmitters, 193-
  196

369

372